DATE DUE

MY 23 05		
DE 16 06		

DEMCO 38-296

Shirl J. Hoffman, EdD
University of North Carolina at Greensboro

Editor

Human Kinetics Books
Champaign, Illinois

;ing-in-Publication Data

Includes bibliographical references.
ISBN 0-87322-341-1
1. Sports--Religious aspects--Christianity. 2. Sports--Moral and
ethical aspects. I. Hoffman, Shirl J., 1939- .
GV706.42.S655   1992
796'.01--dc20   91-685
                                                        CIP

ISBN: 0-87322-341-1

Photo on page 1 copyright by Stephen Green, all rights reserved.
Photos on pages 63 and 127 (right) courtesy of Duke University Photo Department.
Photo on page 127 (left) courtesy of Wake Forest University.
Photo on page 213 by Ron Kuntz, courtesy of Athletes in Action chapel service.

Acquisitions Editor: Rick Frey
Developmental Editor: Robert King
Managing Editor: Julia Anderson
Assistant Editors: Kari Nelson,
    Moyra Knight, and Dawn Levy
Copyeditor: Sara Black
Proofreaders: Stefani Day
    and Laurie McGee

Production Director: Ernie Noa
Typesetter/Text Layout: Yvonne Winsor
Text Design: Keith Blomberg
Cover Design: Jack Davis
Printer: Edwards Brothers

Printed in the United States of America

10 9 8 7 6 5 4 3 2 1

Human Kinetics Books
A Division of
Human Kinetics Publishers, Inc.
Box 5076, Champaign, IL 61825-5076
1-800-747-4457

UK Office:
Human Kinetics Publishers (UK) Ltd.
P.O. Box 18
Rawdon, Leeds LS19 6TG
England (0532) 504211

Canada Office:
Human Kinetics Publishers, Inc.
P.O. Box 2503, Windsor, ON N8Y 4S2
1-800-465-7301 (in Canada only)

For Sharol and Dale

Contents

Preface

This book explores the relationship between two aspects of American life that appear to have little in common. Religion is serious and solemn and concerns things eternal. By contrast, sport is frivolous, lighthearted, and ephemeral. Yet they bear remarkable similarities. Each, for example, stirs passions deep in the human spirit, and each can have profound and enduring effects on the individual and on society. Both offer unique windows into the collective social conscience. Understanding the forms of play and the religious life of a society furthers one's understanding of the values, motivations, and character of its people. Moreover, sport and religion seem comfortable with one another. Wherever sport is played at high levels, one invariably finds traces of religion. At the same time, wherever one finds the organized church, sport is likely to lurk in the shadows. The importance of sport to the social and spiritual programs of American churches was recognized by the ecclesiastical hierarchy at least as far back as the turn of the century.

Although the fine interplay of religion with social, political, and economic forces has been a popular topic of study among sociologists and religion scholars, the relationship between religion and sport has received far less attention. This may be attributed in large part to the general neglect of sport as a topic of scholarly inquiry by those in the traditional disciplines. With the recent rise of interest in sport among scholars in the humanities (Vanderwerken, 1990) and social sciences (McPherson, Curtis, & Loy, 1989), it is not surprising that the relationship between sport and religion has begun to attract attention. Recent years have also witnessed increased interest in the study of sport from a religious perspective. Prominent periodicals in both Catholic and Protestant circles have published special issues exploring the implications of religious belief on the conduct of sport (e.g., *Christianity Today*, 1986; *New Catholic World*, 1986). Although the diffusion of interest has yet to lead to a major work on the relationship, certain points of contact have been covered in books by Novak (1976) and Guttmann (1978), and the topic has been allocated separate chapters in recent editions of some of the more popular textbooks in sport sociology (Coakley, 1986; Eitzen & Sage, 1986; Snyder & Spreitzer, 1983).

The aim of this book is to fill the void by highlighting particular elements of this relationship and, in the process, to add to readers' understanding of the importance, individually and collectively, of both sport and religion to the social landscape. I have sought to do this through a collection of readings drawn from a wide range of disciplines and subject areas with hopes of appealing to students from various disciplines: religion, literature, sociology, cultural studies, popular culture, psychology, and, of course, physical education. Those willing to examine sport and religion through multidisciplinary lenses and to supplement their visions through recollections of personal experiences in their sporting and religious lives will be rewarded with a fresh and stimulating view of a fascinating aspect of American society.

Considerable diversity in readers' backgrounds and experiences with sport and with religion has been anticipated. Consequently, lengthy introductions precede each of the four major parts of the book. These are intended to lay a general foundation and to focus readers' attention on the critical aspects of the selections that follow.

The articles included are but a sampling of the rich mine of sources on the topic. Clearly the most difficult phase of the project was deciding which articles to print and which merely to cite, leaving it to readers to track them down on their own. The articles divide themselves into four fairly neat parts, each representing a major section in the book. The first part, "Sport as Religion," provides a general introduction to the definition of religion and considers arguments for and against the proposition that sport represents a new American religion. In "Sport as Religious Experience," the claim of sport aficionados to have discovered religious meaning through sport are examined, again by presenting a range of opinion. "Religion in Sport" includes a variety of descriptions of the pervasiveness of religion and religious trappings in American sport and the special problems this creates and offers hypotheses concerning the significance of the sport-religion mix. The last part, "Sport, Religion, and Ethics," explores the implications of theological views for sport and examines a variety of religion-based ethical positions on sport issues.

The readings were drawn from a diverse pool with an eye toward including a broad spectrum of perspectives rather than developing a single position. The approach taken to religion and theology, for example, is deliberately broad. When religion is conceived within such a liberal scheme, the boundaries between theological-religious rumination and philosophical analysis can become blurred. Although some of the excellent work of modern sport philosophers would have added an important dimension to the book, space limitations and a decision to avoid coverage available elsewhere (Morgan & Meier, 1988) precluded their inclusion here.

Although an attempt was made to keep the boundaries of religion flexible, it will be obvious that Christianity receives the lion's share of attention. This is to be expected in any study of American religion, and particularly as that religion reveals itself in American sport. Prominent American athletes are numbered among those faithful to the tenets of Judaism, Islam, and other religions, but religion in American sport is by and large a derivative of American Christianity, both in its Catholic and Protestant versions.

Grateful appreciation is extended to authors and publishers who allowed their work to be included. I give a grateful nod also to colleagues in the Department of Exercise and Sport Science at University of North Carolina at Greensboro for supporting their Department Head when he found it necessary to sequester himself in order to put finishing touches on the manuscript. I was fortunate to have Rob King as my editor at Human Kinetics. Aided by an educational background in religious studies, Rob made many valuable suggestions that helped put the book into final form. Finally, a special debt of gratitude is owed to Harol Hoffman, not only for her editorial skill and knack for unraveling my tangled syntax, but for her deft and unsparing criticism graciously mixed with praise at just the right times.

Shirl J. Hoffman

References

Christianity Today. (1986, April 4). [Special issue].

Coakley, J.J. (1986). *Sport in society: Issues and controversies* (3rd ed.). St. Louis: Mosby.

Eitzen, D.S., & Sage, G.H. (1986). *Sociology of American sport*. Dubuque, IA: William C. Brown.

Guttmann, A. (1978). *From ritual to record: The nature of American sport*. New York: Columbia University Press.

McPherson, B.D., Curtis, J.E., & Loy, J.W. (1989). *The social significance of sport*. Champaign, IL: Human Kinetics.

Morgan, W.J., & Meier, K.V. (1988). *Philosophic inquiry in sport*. Champaign, IL: Human Kinetics.

New Catholic World. (1986, July/August). [Special issue].

Novak, M. (1976). *The joy of sports*. New York: Basic Books.

Snyder, E.E., & Spreitzer, E.A. (1983). *Social aspects of sports* (2nd ed.). Englewood Cliffs, NJ: Prentice-Hall.

Vanderwerken, D.L. (1990). *Sport in the classroom: Teaching sport related courses in the humanities*. Cranbury, NJ: Associated University Press.

I still maintain that, by all the canons of modern books on comparative religion, baseball is a religion, and the only one that is not sectarian but national.
  Morris R. Cohen

It need hardly be pointed out, however, that self-sufficiency is the opposite of commitment to the human community that is at the heart of the religious impulse. It is a mistake to confuse cardiovascular fitness with *caritas* . . . A sweat suit is not a surplice. Gatorade is not communion wine. The Verrazano Bridge is not a cathedral.
  James F. Fixx

Praise the name of baseball. The word will set captives free. The word will open the eyes of the blind. The word will raise the dead. Have you the living word of baseball living inside you? Has the word of baseball become a part of you? Do you live it, play it, digest it forever?
  *Kid Scissons in **Shoeless Joe***

I've tried 'em all, I really have. And the only church that truly feeds the soul day in and day out is the Church of Baseball.
  *Annie Savoy in **Bull Durham***

Part I
Sport as Religion

A ballpark at night is more like a church than a church.

Ray Kinsella

Religion is sometimes used in an analogical sense to describe a scrupulously conscientious commitment beyond what might be considered ordinary. Thus, a person might be said to adhere "religiously" to a diet, to financial principles, or to a plan for personal improvement, as a way of capturing his or her extraordinary level of commitment. So it follows that when people express an extraordinary concern and involvement with sport beyond what might be considered ordinary, we often resort to religious terms such as devotion, sacred, and transcendent in order to characterize the radical nature of the commitment.

However, there is more than an analogical connection. Sport's potential for evoking complete devotion in its disciples is like that of religion, and there is no shortage of examples demonstrating such devotion in sport. Joseph Epstein's popular article ("Obsessed with Sport") evolved out of his struggle to get to the bottom of his addiction. "What is the fascination? Why is it that, with the prospect of a game to watch in the evening or weekend, the day seems lighter and brighter? What do I get out of it?" (1976, p. 253). In the same vein, Fred Exley, who chronicled his long love affair with the New York Giants in a book (*A Fan's Notes*) asked, "Why did football bring me to life? . . . Whatever it was, I gave myself up to the Giants utterly. The recompense I gained was the feeling of being alive" (1968, p. 6). It was Michael Novak's (1976) curiosity about how, at 40 years of age, he could still care (so much) about what happened to the Dodgers, that prompted him to write *The Joy of Sports*, his book on the theology of sports. In carefully reasoned but no less passionate tones, Bart Giamatti, Renaissance scholar, former president of Yale, and, at the time of his death, commissioner of Major League Baseball, pointed to the intensity of devotion for sport as one of the sure signs of its religious character: "If there is a religious quality to our leisure—or even to our games—does not that quality show itself in the intensity with which people follow sports, professional or amateur . . . ?" (1989, p. 23).

In what surely is the most conspicuous example, a Denver Broncos fan was reported to have shot himself in the head after watching his team lose to the Chicago Bears. His suicide note read, "I have been a Broncos fan since the Broncos were first organized, and I can't stand their fumbling anymore" (Roberts, 1976, p. xi). (Fortunately, his aim turned out to be no better than the Denver quarterback and he survived.) When scholar Joachim Wach proposed his famous four formal criteria for defining religious experience, he asserted that it is the most intense experience of which humanity is capable (Wach, 1964). Forty years later, it appears that religion now must share the honor with sport.

Definitions of Religion

Thus, the intensity of attraction sport holds for people is one way in which it lends itself to a comparison with religion. The articles presented in this section, however, are devoted to an even bolder and more outrageous claim, which is that sport not only shares some of the characteristics of religion but *is* religion as that term is defined by those who use it. To suggest that religion can be found in cultural forms outside the traditional institution may strike those with a deep commitment to religious faith as heresy. But in an impersonal, objective way it remains an intriguing possibility. In fact, some have ventured that cultural religions may have more to offer than more traditional forms of religion. Sociologist Robert Coles (1975), reflecting on Berger and Luckmann's (1967) observation that religious ceremonies, while initially giving life to religious fervor, may eventually dampen it, has suggested that the soccer field may be a more promising place for discovering religion than the church.

The debate concerning sport's status as a religion hinges largely on how one defines religion, and readers are advised to keep this in mind while studying the topic. There is a virtual smorgasbord of definitions from which to choose, but two general classifications of definitions deserve mention here. Theologians and philosophers tend to define religion in substantive terms, focusing on its content and inner core and explaining how it relates to higher beings or powers. Religion is approached through a rigorous intellectual analysis of religious statements, doctrines, and beliefs. Behavioral scientists and many religion scholars attempt to define religion in more empirically verifiable terms. Whereas philosophers and theologians are most interested in the normative problem of what an ideal religion should be, social scientists are most concerned with how religion operates in societies, independent of its specific value scheme. It shouldn't be surprising that such disparate purposes and methods can lead to different definitions of religion and, ultimately, to different opinions regarding the religious significance of sport.

Religion, the Supernatural and the Ultimate

Some scholars define religion on the basis of its object or primary referent, applying the term *religious* only to beliefs and practices related to a supernatural order of existence. Sociologist Roland Robertson, for example, defines religion as "that set of beliefs and symbols (and values deriving directly therefrom) pertaining to a distinction between an empirical and superempirical, transcendent reality; the affairs of the empirical being subordinated to the nonempirical" (1970, p. 47). This type of definition provides clear and unambiguous ground rules for determining what is and is not a religion. Consequently, it has been a useful working definition for many sociologists and anthropologists. Its principal disadvantage is that it excludes from consideration various religions (i.e., early Buddhism and early Confucianism) in which empirical and nonempirical worlds are less sharply distinguished and in which the gods are experienced as immediately as are objects in the natural world. In addition, such a limited view of religion fails to account for the fact that nonsupernaturally referenced belief systems appear to fulfill the same human needs and social functions as do supernaturally referenced systems.

Among the more expansive interpretations of religion has been that offered by influential Protestant theologian Paul Tillich, who defined religion as "the state of being grasped by an ultimate concern, a concern which qualifies all other concerns as preliminary and which itself contains the answer to the question of meaning and of our life. Therefore this concern is unconditionally serious and shows a willingness to sacrifice any finite concern which is in conflict with it" (1948, p. 6). Tillich's definition intimates that whatever people consider to be ultimate—something valued in and of itself and by which other things are judged—constitutes religion (Schmidt, 1980, p. 14). Accordingly, "ultimate reality" need not be "God," nor must it necessarily transcend the empirical world. In Tillich's view, the core component of religion is "the ground of all being" (broadly interpreted to mean ultimate concern) (1948, p. 57), which he believed was manifested in all creative functions of the human spirit (1959).

The flexibility of Tillich's definition is offset by the ambiguity that surrounds the notion of ultimacy and opens the door to a host of human endeavors to which people may be strongly committed, but which on face value appear to hold no religious meaning as religion as commonly understood by society. For example, a vegetarian who abstains from eating meat in order to enhance physical health might be regarded to be just as religious as another who refuses to eat meat because of a belief that God has commanded abstention. How far this definition of religion can be extended is seen in Frederich Streng's (1969) scheme where religion is defined as "a means toward ultimate transformation." Guided by this definition Streng identified eight ways of being religious, ranging from traditional Western notions of being spiritually reborn, to contemporary humanistic ways of enjoying the full life through sensuous experiences (Streng, Lloyd, & Allen, 1973).

Not all social scientists and theologians would agree with such expansive definitions of religion. Researchers who conduct empirical investigations of religious beliefs find it essential to define religion and religious beliefs operationally in more concrete and objective terms. Rodney Stark and William Bainbridge, for example, question whether it is meaningful to consider nonsupernatural religions and supernatural religions as variations of the same order of human behavior. In their view, "the difference between supernatural and nonsupernatural (or naturalistic) systems are so profound it makes no more sense to equate them than to equate totem poles to telephone poles" (1985, p. 3). They, and others who share their position, would require as a minimum criterion postulation of an active supernatural being or force that influences events and conditions on earth, lest it become impossible to distinguish religion from virtually any personal and sociological venture in which people register strong interest and pledge deep personal commitment.

Functional and Comparative Definitions

Social scientists, following the lead of Emile Durkheim (1915), have adopted another framework for defining religion by focusing on what are presumed to be its universal functions, specifically its role in preserving and maintaining the vitality of society. (Although contemporary sociology has constructed a number of criticisms against such functional definitions [Wilson, 1982], they continue to be regarded as plausible models for those conducting comparative analyses.) Durkheim argued that every stable society holds sacred a set of shared beliefs that, when regularly celebrated in sacred rites, increase social cohesion and insure the survival of the community. He believed that all entities invested with sacred qualities were fundamentally symbols of the community itself; thus, society was identified as the actual or ultimate object of human worship (Nottingham, 1954). Because such functions tend to be implicit (latent) rather than explicit (manifest), the social scholar is faced with the task of uncovering the deep-seated, not easily observed functions of religion, unintended and unknown by religious adherents who are conscious only of their own personal, manifest reasons for ascribing to religion. Once identified, these social functions become the bases for determining the religious significance of other social features of society. If these features supply identical latent functions they can be said, by virtue of that fact, to be religions.

Over the years, a number of latent functions have been proposed. These include the ordering of values by a society into a unified system of meaning in a way that legitimizes the purposes and procedures of the society and provides supernatural sanction for social moral codes. Religion also integrates society on the basis of shared beliefs, which are reinforced through religious rituals and which in turn function to reaffirm the significance of the group and bestow on it a special identity. Finally, religious exercises and rituals offer a way of regulating, managing, and expressing emotions, thus preventing disintegration of the social order through displays of mass uncontrolled emotion. It is sport's relationship to some of these latent functions that has attracted the most attention of scholars who describe sport as a religion.

Religion scholars also have struggled to define religion relative to its impact on individual, in contrast to communal, life. Generally, religion is viewed as a means of helping individuals answer the "ultimate questions of life," but, as sociologist J. Milton Yinger (1970) has noted, not all scholars are agreed on what these ultimate questions might be. For Christians the central question might be how they will spend eternal life, while for others religion might be sought to help deal with the uncertainties and tragedies of life, to reduce anxieties of existential doubt, to assuage feelings of guilt and powerlessness, or to accept one's place in the social hierarchy. Although it is undoubtedly true that the search for answers to such questions may give rise to a wide variety of beliefs and practices that, as Tillich noted, "often blend into religion but are not identical with it" (1969, p. 10), given a sufficiently broad definitional framework, any belief system or ritualized practice that helps individuals come to grips with the pressing, or ultimate, problems of life may be classified as a religion.

Apart from functional considerations, definitions can also be anchored in the forms taken by religion. In such form-comparative methods, the distinctive characteristics of a social phenomenon are compared with what might be regarded as a universal religious form. The form may be reflected in myths, rituals, beliefs, ceremonies, and symbols. The difficulty with this approach is in determining when similarity in form is signaling an important relationship between the forms or is merely reflecting a superficial and trivial resemblance. The following similarities are most important: creeds that explain the meaning of life; codes that prescribe moral, ethical, or customary behavior; rituals that act out and reinforce the meanings expressed in the creeds and codes; and communities, groups of people who are bound together by a common set of creeds, codes, and rituals (Albanese, 1981, p. 8).

The Sacred and the Transcendent

Almost all religions, theistic and nontheistic, implicitly or explicitly designate a "sacred realm." The sacred distinguishes between the order of familiar objects and entities that one contacts and controls in everyday life (the profane) from those that are mysterious, only occasionally contacted, and beyond one's control (the sacred). Sacred things, what Eliade (1959) calls "hierophanies," mediate divine power and reveal the holy. These can include an infinite variety of mundane objects (trees, rocks, animals, etc.), an observation that prompted Ruth Benedict to surmise that there is "probably nothing that at some time and place has not been of fundamental religious importance" (1938, p. 634).

Time and space also can be hierophanies. Sacred time represents the minutes and hours bracketed off from "ordinary time" for the purpose of enacting special religious observances and celebrations in which the holy manifests itself. Sacred space includes buildings, rooms, land, and cities in which the holy has been revealed. Like sacred time, sacred space represents aspects of reality set off from profane and ordinary space. Generally, notions of the sacred, like notions of the supernatural, refer to entities regarded as unquestionable or unchallengeable. This does not mean that they are identical. In his penetrating analysis of modern religion (*The Heretical Imperative*), Peter Berger described them as "two overlapping, but not coinciding, circles of human experience"; he denotes the supernatural as the more fundamental of the two (1979, p. 41). Although it often appears that there is little room for a supernatural consciousness in a modern secularized society, mundane entities such as the nation-state, revolutionary movements, the flag, or even science may come to be regarded as sacred even though disconnected from the supernatural, a curiosity that led Berger to suggest that even when the sacred is detached from any supernatural referent, "a more than faint echo of the latter seems to remain" (p. 42).

The concept of transcendence is closely related to the notion of the sacred. Used in a substantive sense, transcendence refers to the supernatural, which is of an order beyond the ordinary or natural world. God, for example, is a transcendent being. Used in an operational way, however, transcendence can refer to nonsupernatural powers, ideals, and symbols regarded as being of ultimate significance. Although these powers may be accessed through vehicles of ordinary culture, they are described as transcendent because they are afforded top priority in a scheme of values. For example, where Americanism is elevated to a religion, the flag may be regarded as sacred, and the ideals for which the flag stands (i.e., liberty, justice, and the pursuit of happiness) may be regarded as transcendent values. In reading the selections in this section, therefore, it is important to consider whether an author is using the terms *transcendent* or *sacred* in the traditional religious sense to refer to the supernatural or divine order or in a functional sense to refer to powers or symbols that people accept as being greater than the individual.

Sports as a Form of Religion

Even the most rudimentary study of sport in American society will disclose some key social functions it shares with religion. For example, sport has long been regarded as a shaper and reinforcer of values deemed critical to the maintenance of American society. Development of character, habits of hard work, perseverance, competitive spirit, and teamwork, presumed by-products of sport participation, have obvious social benefits. Because these presumed values lie so close to the core values of society, it is easy to understand why those who criticize sport often are suspected of harboring unpatriotic attitudes. Sports events take on properties of rituals and, like the rituals of religion, may reinforce the community's commitment to society's core values. Sports also provide a controlled environment in which to express emotion, a social function normally attributed to religion.

Some have suggested that sport, specifically American football, may represent the worship of American society in a way that mimics the social function of religions as outlined by Durkheim (Stein, 1983). Recall that Durkheim believed that the ultimate object of human worship was the society itself. Given the fact that football incorporates and celebrates the metaphor of the modern business world—specialization, division of labor, and efficiency—along with many other values deemed crucial to the "American way of life," a case might be made that in glorifying sport through elaborate collective rituals, Americans are in fact worshiping American society.

The aspect of sport that so invites a comparison with religion is the intense excitement and the spirit of community it generates. Emile Durkheim believed that the collective excitement (what he called effervescence) generated through religious ceremonies was the basis for the collective notion of the sacred. With this in mind, Elias and Dunning (1986) have suggested that it is not unreasonable to believe that the same generation of collective effervescence in sport lies at the heart of the tendency to refer to football and cricket pitches in Britain as "sacred" or "hallowed" or that for some people sport has become "a quasi-religious activity."

A comparison of forms also reveals some interesting similarities: Sociologist Harry Edwards identified the following:

Sport has a body of formally stated beliefs, accepted on faith by great masses of people . . . sport also has its "saints"—those departed souls who in their lives exemplified and made manifest the prescriptions of the dogma of sport. . . . Sport also has its ruling patriarchs, a prestigious group of coaches, managers, and sportsmen who exercise controlling influence over national sports organizations. . . . Sport has its "gods"—star and superstar athletes who, though powerless to alter their own situations, wield great influence and charisma over the masses of fans. . . . Sport has its shrines—the national halls of fame and thousands of trophy rooms and cases. . . . Sport also has its "houses of worship" spread across the land where millions congregate to bear witness to the manifestations of their faith. (1973, pp. 261-262)

To this, religious studies scholar Catherine Albanese added the following:

Both mark out a separate area for their activities—a "playground" or sacred space. Both also divide the time of their performance from the ordinary passage of minutes and hours. Furthermore, both are examples of dramatic actions in which people take on assigned roles, often wearing special symbolic clothing to distinguish them from nonparticipants. Sports and deliberate religious rituals, through their performances, create an "other" world of meaning, complete with its own rules, boundaries, dangers and successes. Finally, in sports and deliberate religious rituals, the goal of the activity is the activity. While there may be good results from the game or rite, there is a reason implicit in the action for performing it. Play or ritual is satisfying for its own sake, for each is an activity in which people may engage because of the pleasure it gives in itself. (1981, pp. 321-322)

Interestingly, Edwards and Albanese arrive at different conclusions regarding the religious significance of sport. Edwards contends that when the sports creed is justified by adherents in terms of ultimate values it can attain the status of a "secular, quasi-religious institution," although he does not consider it an alternative to formal sacred religious involvement (1973, p. 90). Albanese, on the other hand, grants sport status as a "cultural religion" on grounds that it offers symbolic vehicles, which provide windows into a transcendent world and gives people a means by which to order their lives and search for meaning in the everyday world (1981, p. 312).

Finally, an abundance of literature points to similarities in the effects of sport and religion on individual lives. Whether this is an inevitable tendency for humans, who feel uncomfortable without a supernatural referent, to transfer sacred dimensions to ordinary features of everyday life (Berger, 1979), or whether sport contains an existential element that can function as a substitute religion is a weighty question to ponder. Whatever position one takes, it is difficult to ignore the many thoughtful testimonies claiming sport as a source of deep personal meaning (e.g., Morgan & Meier, 1988; Slusher, 1967; Thomas, 1983), dramatic illustrations of the plausibility of finding in sport a means for dealing with the ultimate questions of human existence. Bart Giamatti spoke eloquently to this point, noting that "the gods are brought back when people gather" (Giamatti, 1989, p. 33). "I believe," said Giamatti, "we have played games, and watched games, to imitate the gods, to become godlike in our worship of each other and, through those moments of transmutation, to know for an instant what the gods know." Even a devoted disciple such as Giamatti, however, cautioned against stretching the comparison too far, "while [sport] mimics religion's ritual and induces its fanaticism and sensation, sport cares not at all for religion's moral strictures or political power or endless promises. Sport cares not for religion's *consequences*" (1989, pp. 36-37).

Nevertheless, readers should be mindful that scholars who study sport are far from reaching agreement on its religious significance. Snyder and Spreitzer's optimistic characterization of sport as having "intimations of the sacred, ultimacy and a quest for perfection," and instilling "quasi-religious qualities of heart and soul" (1983, p. 277) must be balanced against more pessimistic views contending that sport focuses on the secular, material, and profane world while religion deals with the sacred and supernatural (Coakley, 1986). Philosopher George Santayana's (1979) religious insights into sport as a soul-stirring spectacle that represents the basis of life must share the stage with Professor Jack Higgs's assertion that sports "belong to the realm of the beautiful and play to the world of nature, but neither to the holy" (1983, p. 65). Ultimately, resolution of the conflict will follow directly from one's conception of religion, the supernatural, and the sacred. For this reason, when reading the articles in this section it is important to attend to the author's implicit or explicit definition of religion before evaluating his or her comments about its relationship to sport.

Articles in Review

The first two articles examine sport within the context of a civil religion, a concept first described in a seminal article published by Robert Bellah in 1967. Bellah's "Civil Religion in America" (1967) ushered in an era of spirited discourse among scholars of religion and stimulated a litany of studies on the relationship between national and religious life. Bellah illustrated how common elements of religious orientation shared by the vast majority of Americans have undergirded the development and maintenance of American institutions. This civil religion is distinct from denominational religions like Methodism or Catholicism and expresses itself in patriotic rituals and ceremonies that invest national ideals with sacred qualities.

Joseph Price's article, "The Super Bowl as Religious Festival," was published in *The Christian Century* 14 years after Bellah's observations. Price digs beneath the familiar trappings of the Super Bowl to uncover two myths central to a civil religion and critical to the American identity: One recalls the founding of the nation; the other projects the hopes of the nation.

Although the relation of sport to American civil religion has been accorded passing mention in sport sociology textbooks (Coakley, 1986; Eitzen & Sage, 1986) as well as in introductory textbooks for religious studies (Albanese, 1981), it has been the subject of few in-depth analyses. Sociologist James Mathisen's original contribution to this volume fills the void; it is an especially valuable primer on the topic and will inspire further study. Noting that civil religion is not the vital force it once was, Mathisen marks the beginning of its decline with the emergence of a variation called folk religion. Folk religion is an enduring cultural religion, less institutionalized than Bellah's conception of civil religion, but no less important. It includes the ideals and elements of what Herberg (1955) called "The American Way of Life." Sport is a folk religion because it incorporates a unique set of myths, values and beliefs (creeds), and cultic observances (rituals) and evokes a sense of historical continuity and tradition, all of which function in ways similar to traditional religion.

In an article excerpted from his best-selling book, *The Joy of Sports* (1976), Michael Novak outlines the case for sport as a natural religion. Novak argues that sport can perform public functions that mediate our experience of a higher order—functions that private, sectarian religions presumably no longer are able to perform. As such, sport is a human response to a natural, godly impulse. Although sport is different from Catholicism or Presbyterianism (in fact, Novak ranks sport below such religions in a scheme of ultimacy), it attracts us in the same way and is remarkably similar in form. What interests Novak most is not similarity in form but the effect of watching and playing sports on the human spirit and the way sports articulate our experience of the structure of being. "Giving your heart to the rituals of sport," says Novak, "is very much like giving your heart to Baptism or the Eucharist."

Novak's treatise on sport has been criticized not only for overstating the significance of sport (Core, 1979; Newlin, 1977), but for threatening to bring into the orbit of religion the entire secular order, including banks, airports, drive-in theaters, even Howard Johnson's restaurants (Leonard, 1976). Nevertheless, as radical arguments go, Novak's places a distant second to Charles Prebish's unabashed claim that sport is not merely the functional equivalent of religion (i.e., it not only incorporates religiouslike rituals or inspires religious feelings or performs the functions of a cultural or civil religion), but it constitutes, in fact, a genuinely new American religion (Prebish, 1984).

Prebish develops his argument entirely on the basis of Frederich Streng's broad definition of religion as "a means toward ultimate transformation" (Streng, Lloyd, & Allen, 1973, p. 9). Recall that in Streng's scheme "ultimate" refers to a power or force (natural or supernatural) that people hold to be real and of such significance that they define their lives on its terms (Streng, Lloyd, & Allen, 1973, p. 6). This "ultimate" undergirds, conditions, and encompasses human life such that without it, in the face of death, unfilled hopes and personal alienation, life would be meaningless and dead (p. 6). Whether or not one agrees with Prebish's position, it should be noted that his argument is entirely consistent with the definition he employs. According to Streng's definition, any human activity one undertakes with hopes of moving toward the ultimate has the potential to be religious. On the basis of Streng's definition, combined with the extraordinary powers of attraction sport possesses, it is not unreasonable to admit it to the realm of the religious.

Joan Chandler's short but insightful paper concludes this section by serving as a kind of antidote to overimbibing on the religious significance and glories of sport. Chandler returns the discussion to earth by examining sport from the inside out. Sport's status as a religion, says Chandler, is not to be determined by analyzing its observable characteristics but by taking into account the reasons people give for participating in sport and for participating in religion. It is on this basis that Chandler proclaims sport to lie far outside the realm of the religious.

References

Albanese, C.L. (1981). *America, religions and religion.* Belmont, CA: Wadsworth.

Bellah, R.N. (1967). Civil religion in America. In W.G. McLoughlin and R.N. Bellah (Eds.), *Religion in America* (pp. 3-23). Boston: Houghton Mifflin.

Benedict, R. (1938). Religion. In F. Boas (Ed.), *General anthropology* (p. 634). London: Heath.

Berger, P. (1979). *The heretical imperative.* Garden City, NY: Anchor Press.

Berger, P., & Luckmann, T. (1967). *The social construction of reality.* New York: Penguin Books.

Coakley, J.J. (1986). *Sport and society: Issues and controversies* (3rd ed.). St. Louis: Times Mirror/Mosby.

Coles, R.W. (1975). Football as a "surrogate" religion? In M. Hill (Ed.), *A sociological yearbook of religion in Britain*, Vol. 8, (pp. 61-77). London: SCM Press.

Core, G. (1979). The lower mythology and the higher cliches. *The American Scholar*, **48**, 281-286.

Durkheim, E. (1915). *The elementary forms of religious life*. London: Allen and Unwin.

Edwards, H. (1973). *Sociology of sport*. Homewood, IL: Dorsey Press.

Eitzen, S., & Sage, G. (1986). *Sociology of American sport*. Dubuque, IA: Brown.

Eliade, M. (1959). *The sacred and the profane*. New York: Harcourt, Brace & World, Harvest Books.

Elias, N., & Dunning, E. (1986). *The quest for excitement*. New York: Basil Blackwell.

Epstein, J. (1976, July). Obsessed with sport. *Harper's Magazine*, p. 253.

Exley, F. (1968). *A fan's notes*. New York: Random House.

Giamatti, A.B. (1989). *Take time for paradise: Americans and their games*. New York: Summit Books.

Herberg, W. (1955). *Protestant, Catholic, Jew*. Garden City, NY: Doubleday.

Higgs, R.J. (1983). Muscular Christianity, holy play and spiritual exercises: Confusion about Christ in sport and religion. *Arete*, 1(1), 59-85.

Leonard, J. (1976, June 13). The joy of sports. *New York Times Book Review*, p. 6.

Morgan, W.J., & Meier, K.V. (1988). *Philosophic inquiry in sport*. Champaign, IL: Human Kinetics.

Newlin, P. (1977). Joyless sport. *Cross Currents*, **26**(4), 456-459.

Nottingham, E.K. (1954). *Religion and society*. New York: Random House.

Novak, M. (1976). *The joy of sports*. New York: Basic Books.

Prebish, C.S. (1984). Heavenly father, divine goalie: Sport and religion. *The Antioch Review*, **42**, 306-318.

Roberts, M.R. (1976). *Fans*. Washington, DC: New Republic Book.

Robertson, R. (1970). *The sociological interpretation of religion*. London: Oxford.

Santayana, G. (1979). Philosophy on the bleachers. In E.W. Gerber & W.J. Morgan (Eds.), *Sport and the body: A philosophical symposium* (pp. 222-226). Philadelphia: Lea & Febiger.

Schmidt, R. (1980). *Exploring religion*. Belmont, CA: Wadsworth.

Slusher, H. (1967). *Man, sport and existence*. Philadelphia: Lea & Febiger.

Snyder, E.E., & Spreitzer, E.A. (1983). *Social aspects of sport* (2nd ed.). Englewood Cliffs, NJ: Prentice-Hall.

Stark, S., & Bainbridge, W.S. (1985). *The future of religion*. Berkeley: University of California Press.

Stein, M. (1983). Cult and sport: The case of Big Red. In J.C. Harris & R.J. Parks (Eds.), *Play games and sports in cultural context* (pp. 299-309). Champaign, IL: Human Kinetics.

Streng, F.J. (1969). *Understanding religious man*. Belmont, CA: Dickenson.

Streng, F.J., Lloyd, C.L., & Allen, J.T. (1973). *Ways of being religious*. Englewood Cliffs, NJ: Prentice-Hall.

Thomas, C.E. (1983). *Sport in a philosophic context*. Philadelphia: Lea & Febiger.

Tillich, P. (1948). *The shaking of the foundations*. New York: Scribner's.

Tillich, P. (1959). *Theology of culture*. New York: Oxford University Press.

Tillich, P. (1969). *What is religion?* New York: Harper & Row.

Wach, J. (1964). Universals in religion. In L. Schneider (Ed.), *Religion, culture and society* (pp. 38-52). New York: Wiley.

Wilson, B. (1982). *Religion in sociological perspective.* New York: Oxford University Press.

Yinger, J.M. (1970). *The scientific study of religion.* New York: Macmillan.

The Super Bowl as Religious Festival

Joseph L. Price

When the Dallas Cowboys are at the top of their game, winning routinely and decisively, one of the favorite quips which circulates in north Texas concerns Texas Stadium, where the Cowboys play their home games. The stadium has a partial roof which covers much of the stands but none of the playing field. Cowboy fans say that God wants to be able to see his favorite football team more clearly.

This is the attitude which ancient societies brought to their games. In ancient Greece, for example, the Olympics were only one set of athletic contests which were performed in honor of the gods. Among the Mayans in Central America, the stadium was attached to an important temple, and the stands were adorned with images of the gods and reliefs of sacred animals. The ball game started when the high priest threw the ball onto a circular stone in the center of the field: the sacred rock, the *omphalos*, considered the sacred center and associated with creation mythology. Thus the game was connected to the Mayan story of the world's origins.

Professional football games are not quite so obviously religious in character. Yet there is a remarkable sense in which the Super Bowl functions as a major religious festival for American culture, for the event signals a convergence of sports, politics and myth. Like festivals in ancient societies, which made no distinctions regarding the religious, political and sporting character of certain events, the Super Bowl succeeds in reuniting these now disparate dimensions of social life.

The pageantry of the Super Bowl is not confined to the game itself, nor to the culture heroes who attend it—e.g., Bob Hope, John Denver, Dan Rather and other celebrities—for the largest audience watches the game via television. And the political appeal of the festival is not restricted to its endorsement by political figures such as President Reagan, who pronounced the 1984 Super Bowl's benediction. The invocation is a series of political rituals: the singing of the national anthem and the unfurling of a 50-yard-long American flag, followed by an Air Force flight tactics squadron air show.

The innate religious orientation of the Super Bowl was indicated first by the ritual of remembrance of "heroes of the faith who have gone before." In the pregame show, personalities from each team were portrayed as superheroes, as demigods who possess not only the talent necessary for perfecting the game as an art but also the skills for succeeding in business ventures and family life.

For instance, one of the most effective segments was about Joe Delaney, the former running back for the Kansas City Chiefs who died while trying to save two children from drowning. In a functional sense, Delaney was being honored as a saint. The pregame moment of silence in honor of the life and contributions of George Halas, the late owner of the Chicago Bears and one of the creators of the National Football League, was even more significant: I am not sure whether the fans were silent in memory of "Papa Bear" or whether they were offering a moment of silence to him. Nevertheless, the pause was reminiscent of an act of prayer.

Bronco Nagurski, a hall of famer (which stands for official canonization), had the honor of tossing the coin at the center of the playing field to signify the start of the game. The naming of a Most Valuable Player at the end of the game was a sign of the continuing possibility for canonization.

But the Super Bowl and its hype could not dominate the consciousness of many Americans without the existence of a mythos to support the game. Myths, we know, are stories which establish and recall a group's identity: its origin, its values, its world view, its *raison d'être*.

Two dominant myths support the festivity and are perpetuated by it. One recalls the founding of the nation and the other projects the fantasies or hopes of the nation. Both myths indicate the American identity.

The first concerns the ritual action of the game itself. The object of the game is the conquest of territory. The football team invades foreign land, traverses it completely, and completes the conquest by settling in the end zone. The goal is to carry the ritual object, the football, into the most hallowed area belonging to the opponent, his inmost sanctuary. There, and only there, can the ritual object touch the earth without incurring some sort of penalty, such as the stoppage of play or the loss of yardage.

This act of possession is itself reflective of cosmogonic myths, for, as Mircea Eliade has noted, "to organize a space is to repeat the paradigmatic work of the gods" (*The Sacred and the Profane: The Nature of Religion* [Harcourt, Brace, 1959], p. 32). Conquering a territory and bringing order to it is an act equivalent to consecration, making the space itself sacred by means of recalling and rehearsing the primordial act of creation.

The specifically American character of the mythology has to do with the violent nature of the game. Not only does it dramatize the myth of creation, it also plays out the myth of American origins with its violent invasion of regions and their settlement. To a certain extent, football is a contemporary enactment of the American frontier spirit.

Amidst the ritual of the forceful quest, there is the extended "time out" of half time, a time of turning from the aggressions of the game to the fantasies of the spirit. During the half-time show, the second dominant American cultural myth is manifest. It revolves around the theme of innocence. The peculiarly American quality about this myth is that even in our nation's history of subjugation, a sense of manifest destiny was often associated with extending the nation's boundaries. Indeed, the idea that a divine mandate had authorized the people to move into a place to which they had no claim, other than getting there and staying there, indicates that the people did not think they bore final responsibility for the displacement of natives or infringement on their hunting space. In other words, the assignment to God of the responsibility for territorial expansion was an attempt to maintain the illusion of blamelessness among those who forcibly took alien lands.

In this year's Super Bowl, the theme of righteousness was acted out in a three-ring circus which featured 2,100 performers from Walt Disney Productions. Although acts took place in the outer rings, which were colored blue, attention was focused on the largest center ring, which was white. In this area, most of the performers wore white or pastel shades of yellow. The visual effect was an overwhelming sensation of cleanliness and purity. And the extravaganza's music reinforced the impressions of the "whiteness" of it all; the harmonies sung by the Disney troupe were simple and syrupy, a kind of white sound with less harmonic complexity than that of most Muzak renditions.

The overall effect was one of feigned innocence and the naive hope often exemplified for Americans by Walt Disney's vision. Finally, the transition from this scenario was accomplished by the explosion of fireworks along the perimeter of the field. The fantasy and violence of exploding Roman candles shifted the scene back to the play of the American frontier, simultaneously reviving intimations of the festival's patriotic character. Fireworks are the hallmark of the Fourth of July, and evoke the national anthem lyrics' imagery—"the rockets' red glare, the bombs bursting in air."

As a sporting event, the Super Bowl represents the season's culmination of a major American game. As a popular spectacle, it encourages endorsement by politicians and incorporates elements of nationalism. And as a cultural festival, it commands vast allegiance while dramatizing and reinforcing the religious myths of national innocence and apotheosis.

From Civil Religion to Folk Religion:
The Case of American Sport

James A. Mathisen

Twenty-four years ago, Phillip Hammond contributed to a "Commentary" on Robert Bellah's then recently published *Daedalus* article "Civil Religion in America" (1967). Hammond liked Bellah's article, but he was concerned that Bellah had not given adequate attention to "*structural* analysis" (Hammond, 1968, p. 382). In describing how civil religion is celebrated in America's nonreligious organizations such as schools, Hammond noted that schools "supply major structural support for America's civil religion" in forms often "much broader than formal instruction." He believed the most important example was "competitive athletics" (Hammond, 1968, p. 383).

Hammond was careful to suggest that sports serve to *transmit* civil religion; he did not say that sports *are* civil religion. Since then, however, others have ascribed a functionally religious significance to sport. Loy and associates suggested that sport can function as "a civil religion or quasi-religious institution, which replaces sectarian religion for the purpose of fostering social integration" (Loy, McPherson, & Kenyon, 1978, p. 301). Similarly, Edwards has argued that sport constitutes a quasi religion, especially in a fan's quest for "confirmation." He suggested this phenomenon may be associated with decreased stability in the secular spheres of societal life (Edwards, 1973, p. 260).

Two disclaimers are necessary before proceeding. First, what follows is not an argument for sport as a religion per se. That simply is too grandiose and too simplistic a claim, and Prebish's notion of a "complete identity" between religion and sport is misguided (1984, p. 312; cf. Vance, 1984). Although obvious similarities exist between sport and religion (Coles, 1975), and their relationship is often symbiotic, Higgs's observation that "sports are like religion in many ways just as they are like war in some ways, but they are not equatable with either" (1983, p. 63) makes a great deal of sense.

Second, this is not an argument that sports are a civil religion qua civil religion (cf. Novak, 1976, p. 31), especially given the plurality of civilly religious forms. Bellah set the agenda for discussion when he operationalized civil religion as "a collection of beliefs, symbols, and rituals with respect to sacred things and institutionalized in a collectivity" that serves Americans "as a genuine vehicle of national religious self-understanding" (1967, pp. 8, 12). Admittedly, civil religion is not an exact concept, and although sport may share certain beliefs, symbols, and rituals with civil religion, sport has not sought to provide the religious self-understanding nationally that Bellah claimed for civil religion. On Bellah's terms, then, sport cannot be a civil religion. If anything, the recent histories of institutional sport and of civil religion in America suggest that since Bellah penned his article, one has waxed and the other waned. If so, it is hard to imagine their identity.

It will be argued, however, that for many Americans, particularly males, sport resembles a form of civil religion; specifically, it is a "folk religion." This position is based on three assumptions. First, if one grants the reality of civil religion, one should focus on the uses of civil religious language and symbols. Then sport can be examined to determine whether it is one of the "specific groups and sub-cultures [which] use versions of the civil religion" (Demerath & Williams, 1985, p. 166).

A second assumption is that one can distinguish in several ways between the categories of folk religion and civil religion as described by Bellah. Civil religion is larger, more inclusive than folk religion. As many as five versions or manifestations of civil religion are possible, with folk religion being the common religious version emerging out of the life of the folk (Jones & Richey, 1974, p. 15). Civil religion is more distinctive and institutionalized, whereas folk religion is more diffuse but less obvious to its practitioners. Furthermore, civil religion is for elites, "chiefly the product of the scholars' world" (Marty, 1974, p. 141), whereas folk religion is for commoners, the people on the street, a kind of "religion-in-general" (Marty, 1959).

Marty's distinctions here are helpful, as he too suggested several subtypes of civil religion; it can have either a priestly or a prophetic style, and it can emphasize either national self-transcendence or a transcendent deity (Marty, 1974). Combinations of the types of style and transcendence result in four possible forms. For example, Marty classifies both Bellah's version of civil religion and the notion of folk religion presented here as emphasizing national self-transcendence. They differ, however, in their style. Bellah's idea of civil religion was more prophetic, whereas folk religion is priestly, meaning that it reaffirms the status quo and encourages people to accept popular explanations of American life as having cultural importance along with religious significance.

A third assumption is that folk religion is persistently present, but civil religion comes and goes, especially in its nationalistic forms. "Civil religion is episodic, . . . a kind of cluster of episodes which come and go, recede back to invisibility after making their appearance" (Marty, 1974, pp. 143, 141). Civil religious expressions often have a short life span (Markoff & Regan, 1981, p. 348), whereas folk religion endures beneath the surface as an implicit part of how people assume the world works.

Based on these assumptions, two lines of argument can be advanced in support of the emergence of sport as an American folk religion—sport definitionally satisfies the requisite characteristics of a folk religion; and sport historically emerged as a folk religion about the same time as the apparent decline in strength of a recent episode of American civil religion in the 1960s. Given the functional similarities between the two, sport as folk religion in effect filled a void resulting from the waning of American civil religion. These two arguments issue from a brief description of American folk religion.

The Character of American Folk Religion

A folk religion is a combination of shared moral principles and behavioral customs that "emphasize[s] the common religion of a people as it emerged out of the life of 'the folk' . . . [plus] those religious ideas, values, symbols, ceremonies, and loyalties which the overwhelming majority of the people of any state or nation hold in common" (Linder, 1975, p. 401). For Americans, folk religion arises from their daily life experiences in order to provide social integration and the legitimation of American values (Gehrig, 1981b, p. 52). Williams believed that all societies profess a "common religion. The possession of a common set of ideas, rituals, and symbols can supply an overarching sense of unity in a society riddled with conflicts" (1951, p. 312).

In comparing the religious cult institutions (i.e., rituals and associated beliefs) of his American hometown with those of an Iroquois community, anthropologist Anthony F.C. Wallace found religion in both societies to be "a loosely organized federation of beliefs" represented in denominational congregations, superstition, the children's cult, and the religio-political cult. This latter cult he described as the "nondenominational, theistic faith used to rationalize and sanction political, military, and other secular institutions, such as schools" (1966, p. 77). Wallace also found that most people have difficulty separating religious belief from the secular aspects of their world views. "While for analytical purposes they [religion and the secular] can be distinguished, . . . in daily life the individual is apt to employ sacred beliefs and values to rationalize all aspects of his behavior" (Wallace, 1966, pp. 74-75).

This peculiarly utilitarian character of the rituals and beliefs of the American folk religion of the 1950s and 1960s was noted by Eckardt (1958).

> It fosters individual security. It aids brotherhood. It contributes to social solidarity. In a word, religion is good because it is good for people. . . . Religion bears the stamp of social approval and the social interest bears the stamp of religious approval. (Eckardt, 1958, pp. 43-44)

Marty (1959) was puzzled over what this religion should be called. Was it a "religion-in-general," which "swirls around the churches and sometimes flourishes in them" (1959, p. 32)? Was it a "religion of democracy," formed by "taking aspects of a consensus which the 'three great faiths' support and elevating them to ultimacy . . . but something quite different from the Christian faith'' (1959, pp. 84-85)? Perhaps it was an ''American Shinto'' or a ''sort of state Shinto'' (Marty, 1976, p. 185; 1959, p. 87).

It was left to Will Herberg to identify Williams's ''common religion'' and Marty's ''religion-in-general'' as the *folk religion* (italics mine) of the ''American way of life'' (1955; 1960).

> The American Way of Life is, at bottom, a spiritual structure, a structure of ideas and ideals, of aspirations and values, of beliefs and standards; it synthesizes all that commends itself to the American as the right, the good, and the true in social life. . . . The very expression ''way of life'' points to its religious essence, for one's ultimate, over-all way of life is one's religion. (1960, p. 75)

> It is an organic structure of ideals, values, and beliefs that constitutes a faith common to Americans and genuinely operative in their lives, a faith that markedly influences, and is influenced by, the ''official'' religions of American society. (1960, p. 77)

Herberg viewed democracy, free enterprise, and egalitarianism as specific manifestations of this folk religion. It is individualistic and pragmatic with an ethic combining self-reliance, merit, and achievement. It tends toward self-righteousness and is an essentially middle-class view of social reality.

Other analysts shared Herberg's vision but described America's folk religion in still different ways. Warner (1961) interpreted Memorial Day and Mother's Day observances as symbolic depictions (p. 3), suggesting the pervasiveness and diversity of American folk religion. To Bock, Christmas best illustrates these ideas, although Easter, Halloween, and pre-lenten festivals are similar symbolic manifestations (Bock, 1966, p. 206). Mensching stressed the ''salvific'' power of folk religion, which ''consists in the condition of positive relationships of the folk community'' and ''whose maintenance is the duty of the members of the folk society [as] a mystic 'life' which binds all together'' (1964, p. 254). Although the absence of a consensus on a single term for this common religion of the people is perplexing, that such a religion exists seems beyond question.

In summary, then, what is being argued here is that America has had a persisting folk religion akin to Herberg's (1960) religion of the ''American way of life.'' This folk religion is a ''structure of ideals, values, and beliefs that constitute a faith common to Americans'' (Herberg, 1960, p. 75), so that at times it may share some of the qualities of what Marty and others have termed civil religion. But folk religion is also less elitist, less transcendent, and less institutionalized than Bellah's narrower vision of a ''genuine vehicle of national religious self-understanding'' (1967, p. 12), which he also called civil religion. Although Bellah provided the stimulus for careful reflection on civil religion and although much of the ensuing discussion was on his terms, in fact he limited its scope too narrowly and so indirectly confused the issue. Instead, what Williams (1951), Herberg (1960), and Bock (1966) described in more common, folk religious terms is the subject of the discussion that follows.

Sport as Folk Religion

The common religion emerging from the life of the folk can take different forms for different groups and subcultures. One example is the subculture of sport, which journalist Robert Lipsyte labeled "SportsWorld."

> [SportsWorld] has surpassed patriotism and piety as a currency of communica-tion, while exploiting them both. By the end of the 1960s, SportsWorld wisdom had it that religion was a spectator sport while professional and college athletic contests were the only events Americans held sacred. (1975, pp. xiv-xv)

About that same time, theologian Michael Novak described how the folk religion of sport operates for Americans.

> For quite sophisticated and agnostic persons, the rituals of sport really work . . . [to] provide an experience of at least a pagan sense of godliness. Among the godward signs in contemporary life, sports may be the single most powerful manifestation. . . . Sports constitute the primary lived world of the vast majority of Americans. (1976, pp. 20, 34)

Religionist John F. Wilson then pointed out that

> the world of sports has become central to American popular culture. . . . The emphasis upon success, closely identified with money, derived from brute power melded with technical expertise, is perhaps the most direct and telling dramatization of the content of the American culture. . . . This culture created and sustained through the modern means is linked to public religion in America. (1979, p. 135)

What is important here is the diversity of perspectives and viewpoints these au-thors represent, even as they approach a consensus that sport exists as a dominant, religiouslike part of many Americans' lives. Unlike traditional religion in which charismatic leaders may lead a group of believers for a time and then pass from the scene, the folk religion of sport does not depend on each new group to keep a leader's vision alive. Instead, new generations of Americans come to experience sport as part of the American way of life, without having to justify its legitimacy or *raison d'être*. This folk religious certainty resembles Max Weber's classical sociological notion of religious authority being legitimized by traditional means and the power of "that's the way we've always understood things and done things here." A better sense of this "taken-for-granted reality" of sport as folk religion can be seen by examining three of its key component features.

First, American sport consists of a distinctive set of myths, values, and beliefs. In his book *Man, Sport, and Existence*, Howard Slusher described how sport "evolves into a symbolically developed *ideology*. Sport becomes both what it is and a declaration of the culture. . . . One need look no further than the Americanization of sport in keeping with the technological and materialistic values of our society"

(Slusher, 1967, p. 134). Similarly, Edwards identified both the "American sports creed" and its accompanying ideological system of values, attitudes, and perspectives (1973, p. 72). For Lipsyte "SportsWorld" is that "dangerous and grotesque web of ethics and attitudes, an amorphous infrastructure that acts to contain our energies, divert our passions, and socialize us for work or war or depression. . . . The melting pot may be a myth, but we will all come together in the ballpark" (1975, p. ix).

At this level of values and ideology, sport encapsulates, magnifies, and reflects back to us the primary beliefs and norms of the surrounding American culture. Sport's beliefs are "accepted on faith by great masses of people . . . from the president of the United States down to the most humble bootblack. These beliefs are stated primarily in the form of perceived attributes of sports and are widely disseminated" (Edwards, 1973, p. 261). At the same time, sport raises up particular values and myths of its own and projects them onto the culture with a normative certitude. It is this authority that emphatically characterizes sport as a folk religion.

For example, when people believe the myth that "sport builds character," they are likely to guide their children toward youthful athletic participation with a virtually untestable certainty that, without experiences as a shortstop or as a left wing, their children's lives will be less than they might have been. Likewise, people assume that the "character" of successful adult Americans who happen to have participated in sport at some point in their lives is causally related to that participation. Selective perception guarantees that we interpret biographies in terms of the ideology and mythology of sport. Not to do so would be a demonstration of lack of faith and of irreligion.

Such a commitment to the ideology of sport is not limited to an individual level. Institutionally, it works when relatively small colleges commit themselves to compete as an NCAA Division I basketball power. Institutions of 2,000 or 3,000 undergraduates accept as a legitimate educational policy that the recognition (and the potential revenue) gained by playing such a schedule justifies such a commitment. For many, Oral Roberts University became a *real* school the day it declared Division I status, regardless of other criteria by which academic institutions are evaluated (cf. Boyle, 1970, p. 64). But now that Rev. Roberts has given up Division I membership for financial reasons, his decision also calls into question whether his institution can be taken seriously academically.

Even more dramatic, however, is the internalization of this folk religious ideology by entire communities. For example, when the Chicago Bears mutter about leaving Chicago if they are not supplied a new stadium (as they have recently), then one way for community leaders to guarantee Chicago's continuing status in the eyes of fellow believers in the American sport ideology is to muster every available resource to retain a National Football League franchise for Chicago. What sets Green Bay, Wisconsin, apart from any other American small town is that it is "big league" in what really matters—its community allegiance to the significance of the presence of real, major league sport. By contrast, for Baltimore to have allowed the Colts to leave for Indianapolis under cover of night consigns Baltimore to a permanent, illegitimate status in the eyes of the true believers in sport.

The second way American sport manifests itself as a folk religion is in its collective, cultic observances. Dunning has argued that "whereas top-level representative sporting events in the modern world may not be centrally theological in character in the sense that they are connected with the worship of a divinity or divinities, they are essentially religious in the Durkheimian sense of the term" (1986, pp. 42-43). For Durkheim, inherent in religion was the presence of a "moral community" in which adherents affirmed their beliefs and practiced their rituals; this moral community unites believers by means of their "collective conscience" (Durkheim, 1915). According to Lipsky, sport is the "magic elixer" that "nourishes the bonds of communal solidarity" (1981, p. 5). For Novak, "going to a stadium is half like going to a political rally, half like going to a church" (1976, p. 19).

Folk religion depends on ritual, cultic practices to reinforce the efficacy of its shared myths and beliefs. Small towns in Indiana or Kentucky build high school gymnasiums with capacities as large as, or larger than, the towns' populations for the Friday and Saturday evening gatherings of the clans during the winter and early spring. Attending high school basketball games provides opportunities for the townspeople (as a moral community) to affirm anew their faith in the myths of sport for their youngsters—and for themselves. Not only is sport developing the "character" of the athletes, vicariously it works for spectators, also.

In her stimulating work on the role of soccer in Brazilian society, Lever cited the effects of such shared observances upon the participants. "By accepting that a particular team represents them symbolically, people enjoy ritual kinship based on that common bond" (1983, p. 15). She went on to suggest that

> sport spectacles belong to the world of the sacred rather than the profane; fans who say sport provides an escape from "real life" in effect sustain this religious distinction. . . . Like the effect of a religious celebration, sport fosters a sense of identification with the others who shared the experience. (1983, p. 15)

There is a sense in which specific sports such as baseball, football, and basketball have become sectlike versions of the common, folk religion. Although all Americans are expected to be "generic" sports fans and thus share in what Novak (1976) called the "pagan sense of godliness," each fan is also expected to have a further allegiance to one sport. This is not unlike a denominational religious affiliation displayed by Protestants responding to a pluralistic set of options. Just as social class, regional location, and level of education intervene to influence their denominational preferences, similar sociological variables affect which specific sectlike sport an American may favor as his or her own. Beneath these individual preferences, however, the fundamental requisite is that one believe in and have a commitment to sport.

The third way sport operates as folk religion is in evoking senses of historical continuity and tradition. Mandell has noted how sports' halls of fame illustrate "the steady trend for sport to become ritually integrated and earnestly or even quasi-sacrally regarded in modern life" (1984, p. 230). These halls preserve the sacred symbols, totems, and memorabilia that encourage us to rehearse the contributions of the saints who have gone before us. Golf tournaments such as the Masters and the British Open also provide annual opportunities for the faithful to return to commemorate the heroic deeds of the past and to pass on accounts of the miraculous accomplishments of past heroes with an appropriate aura of mystique and reverence.

Records and standards established by past heroes become the measures by which modern mortals are judged. "Like religion, professional sports use past generations as referents for the present and confer conditional immortality for their elect, through statistics and halls of fame" (Kearl, 1986, p. 292). Will anyone break Joe DiMaggio's consecutive-game hitting record? Will Wilt's 100 points in a single professional basketball game ever be duplicated? Is any of today's running backs the equal of Red Grange? In our desire to fix in time the achievements of those we look back upon as our representatives for time immemorial, we attribute a sense of sanctity to them and their accomplishments. Thus for Weiss, records "have a definiteness and a finality which a casteless society might need in order to make evident who is superior and who is inferior in native gifts and promise" (1969, p. 165).

Records function not unlike the sacred writings and the historical accounts of any religious group, providing a timeless, normative guide by which later disciples' accomplishments are measured. For traditional Christians, the New Testament writer of the Epistle to the Hebrews invoked the memory of those who had "shut the mouths of lions, quenched the fury of flames, and escaped the edge of the sword" (Hebrews 11:33-34). In the modern secularized world, accounts of sport accomplishments are more likely to be records in the form of quantitative distinctions, rather than qualitative ones (cf. Guttman, 1978). When a record is broken in sport, we are both happy and sad. Not only has immortality been achieved, but previous immortality proves to have been conditional and so has been stolen from our midst. Maybe we should place an asterisk next to the new record, just to ensure that we do not lose sight of the former one and of the hero who established it.

Similarly, "old timers' games" are something of an enigma. On the one hand, fans need them as a renewed opportunity to pay homage to, and to rehearse the past accomplishments of, their heroes. So the clan gathers to commemorate the past and to reassert its lineage by recounting for itself and for the next generation the worthiness of its past heroes. On the other hand, great risk is involved, as many "old timers" are only that. By coming back, they not-so-voluntarily are "made lower than the angels," and so they take back the forms of mere mortals in our eyes when we compare their aging bodies with the godlike images we had stored in our memories.

Sport thus manifests itself as an American folk religion in various forms, and these three versions—as value, myth, and ideology; as collective cultic practice; and as history and tradition—have aided sport as an American way of life to bestow meaning and cohesive solidarity upon the lives of many Americans.

The Emergence of Sport as Folk Religion

The emergence of sport as a folk religion is inextricably linked to the rise and fall of civil religion in America. Ironically, forms of civil religion that Williams (1951) called "common religion" and Herberg (1955; 1960) more fully described as the "American way of life" already were past their peaks of influence and pervasiveness in 1967—at least as far as historians were concerned—when Bellah captured the attention of academic elites with his provocative *Daedalus* (1967) article.

According to Ahlstrom, the Eisenhower era had seen the high points of civil religion, with "under God" added to the Pledge of Allegiance in 1954 and "In God We Trust" elevated to "become the country's official motto" in 1956 (1972, p. 954). President Eisenhower's role as a national spokesperson for the American common religion has been amply demonstrated (cf. Herberg, 1960; Wilson, 1979). One of Eisenhower's best-known proclamations was the Freedoms Foundation:

> Our form of government has no sense unless it is founded in a deeply felt religious faith, and I don't care what it is. . . . Have I done my duty unless, in all my conduct, in all my examples, with my fellow citizens, I am living this democracy, indeed this religion, the tenets of this religion. (1952)

As Miller observed, President Eisenhower, apparently "like many Americans, [was] a fervent believer in a very vague religion" (Hutchinson, 1954, p. 367, citing Miller).

By the early 1960s, at least on some fronts, civil religion "as the basic faith of most Americans was subjected to severe criticism. The old nationalistic rhetoric was widely repudiated as hollow and deceitful" (Ahlstrom, 1972, p. 1085). Later, even Bellah acknowledged that "civil religion came into consciousness just when it was ceasing to exist" (1976, p. 72). That this most recent "episode" of civil religion had receded (cf. Marty, 1974) was clear by 1976 when the Bicentennial celebration occurred with little of the nationalistic fanfare anticipated in a fully blown civil religious event. Marty has portrayed in capsule form (and I have supplied the identities of those involved) that brief history of an episode of American civil religion.

> A sociologist [Herberg] in 1955 writes a book critical of civic faith in an era in which intellectuals do not favor the current expressions of such faith. Between 1955 and 1967 a historian [Mead] writes articles that are increasingly positive about the idea of a religion of the Republic. In 1965 a sociologist [Bellah] reads a paper favoring Civil Religion and in 1967 prints that paper. The time for the idea had come, and other people in academic life responded positively. But by 1972 a historian [Ahlstrom] raised questions about whether Civil Religion had survived the 1960s, and a year later the sociologist himself [Bellah] . . . express[ed] some second thoughts. (1976, p. 190)

The reasons for this rise and fall of American civil religion are too complex to delineate here (cf. Mathisen, 1989). Suffice it to point out, as have Demerath and Williams (1985), civil religion's demise in the 1960s was associated with the increasing fragmentation of American political and social life.

> Broad coalitions dissolved; interest-group and issue politics emerged; many centers replaced the center. . . . While the civil-religious discourse continued

to use the culturally resonant language of cohesion, it seemed increasingly a rhetoric without a reality. (Demerath & Williams, 1985, p. 164)

"In the atmosphere of the late twentieth century, the civil millenial dream had been interrupted, if not ended" (Albanese, 1981, p. 306).

This decline in civil religion for a time paralleled, and then was succeeded by, the emergence of sport in its American folk religious manifestation. What is argued here is that this transition was not mere happenstance. Another "cultural binding force" (Gehrig, 1981a, p. 88) was necessary to provide the widespread meaning and cohesiveness previously communicated through civil religion. That force was the folk religion of American sport.

This emergence of sport as folk religion can be encapsulated with brief vignettes from the lives of two dominant American personalities in the 1960s plus a brief summary of the place of television. Because of their roles in the cultural, political, and sporting arenas of American life in the 1960s, John F. Kennedy and Vince Lombardi stood as dominant personifications of the broader significance Americans attributed generally to sport. Well-known and respected, Kennedy and Lombardi thus helped to redefine the meanings of sport as the operant folk religion for many.

John F. Kennedy

When President John F. Kennedy was killed on a Friday afternoon, November 22, 1963, many intercollegiate football games and other sporting events scheduled for the weekend were postponed or canceled, including four American Football League games on Sunday afternoon. But the National Football League announced that it would play its seven games as scheduled. "It has been traditional in sports for athletes to perform in times of great personal tragedy," declared NFL Commissioner Pete Rozelle (Sheehan, 1963, p. 1).

Rozelle attended the Sunday game in New York, and he was quoted on Monday as observing, "I went to church this morning and paid my respects, and I'm sure so did most of the people who came to Yankee Stadium" (Koppett, 1963, p. 24). Although Rozelle's decision not to cancel Sunday's games sparked criticism in some circles, by and large, Americans responded positively to playing football within 48 hours of the death of the President. Not canceling the games was justified on the basis of sport's integrative presence during a time of intense national crisis and mourning. Besides, "That's the way President Kennedy would have wanted it."

Less than 3 years before his death, President-elect Kennedy wrote an article for *Sports Illustrated* indicting "The Soft American." He wrote with passion of the physically impoverished Americans who represented a "menace to our security" as a nation, imploring us to "restore the physical soundness of our nation. . . . We must also be willing to work for the physical toughness on which the courage and intelligence and skill of man [*sic*] so largely depend. All of us must consider our own responsibilities" (1960, p. 17). Lasch has observed how this "official view" of the benefits of sport "replaced the various utilitarian ideologies of the past" by stressing sport's contribution "to the national well-being" (1979, p. 101). The role

Kennedy played in articulating and modeling the folk religion of sport was not unlike that which President Eisenhower had played a decade earlier when he proclaimed a nationalistic democracy as our common religion.

Indeed, in his life and at his death, Kennedy was revered as "The President Who Loved Sport" ("President," 1963, pp. 20-21). His youthfulness and vigor, the family touch-football games, and his reorganization of the President's Council on Youth Fitness all announced new symbolic presence, emerging roles, and folk-religious meanings for sport in American life. Ironically, it was Kennedy and his vision of the meaning of sport that were responsible for the affirmative, national reaction of playing football on the weekend following his untimely death.

Vince Lombardi

A second figure who personified the emergence of sport as folk religion was Vince Lombardi, coach of the National Football League's Green Bay Packers. Lombardi had been a successful NFL assistant coach, but his reputation on the national scene grew when he became Green Bay's head coach and general manager in 1959. (On Lombardi as a cultural symbol, cf. Lipsyte, 1975, pp. 52-59; Guttman, 1978, pp. 120-122; and Rader, 1984, pp. 96-97, 176.)

Lombardi's appointment as the Green Bay coach was an instance of historical and cultural serendipity—the right person going to the right place at the right time. Lombardi was "old world," an Italian Catholic immigrant's son committed to traditional values and goals. He also was personally committed to sport as a means of upward mobility and of achieving the American dream. "The man was a presence" (Guttman, 1978, p. 122). Green Bay also was the right place. It was small town, traditional, and a symbolic underdog nipping at the heels of the centers of national, secular power—New York, Washington, Los Angeles, and Chicago. Green Bay reminded us of our national past; it was a snapshot of what life must have been like in more tranquil days when all Americans knew who they were and where they were going. Lombardi's appointment also came at the right time. Football had fallen onto hard times in Green Bay, and losing was too easily tolerated in the late 1950s, even though the team appeared to have some skilled players. More importantly, it was the right time because professional football was surfacing as "The Game" among a more highly educated, increasingly affluent, middle-aged consuming audience. According to Lipsyte,

> addiction to [football], as much as the contest itself became a currency of communication on every level of American life; ritual manchat at water coolers and in car pools, interclass howdy-do, a way for fathers and sons to discuss loyalty, love, sacrifice, dedication, discipline, success, failure, pain, in detached and nonthreatening symbols. (1975, p. 51)

Lombardi took over the Packers and immediately produced a winning season. Within 3 years, Green Bay won the NFL championship, then again and again. With the advent of the Super Bowl as the new culmination of the professional football season, the winners of Super Bowls I and II were the Packers. Lombardi was a folk hero, larger than life, a legend in his own time—he embodied all the familiar sporting myths and clichés. "It was Lombardi's prophetic, even messianic streak that stirred that vast band of football believers and gave the taste of spiritual satisfaction to a Packer victory" (Dowling, 1970, p. 18). Not only did he coach the winning team, Lombardi said all the correct, American-way-of-life things and said them with authority and certainty. He "was always celebrated in the extreme. His saintly dedication to winning was hailed as a beacon on the path toward America's renewal" (Lipsyte, 1975, p. 52).

Lombardi moved on to coach the Washington Redskins before dying of cancer prior to the 1970 season. What Lombardi contributed to the emergence of sport as a folk religion was not unlike President Kennedy's contribution. If sport as a folk religion is priestly, these were two of its early clergy. As with Kennedy, Lombardi was proof that the traditional American values of hard work and discipline and teamwork could still produce success, an ideology that helped mollify the cultural malaise and uncertainty of the post-Kennedy and then the post-Lombardi eras.

British journalist James Lawton juxtaposed Kennedy and Lombardi in another way. While "Kennedy was preaching to Americans about the value of self-sacrifice, directing them toward heroism," Lombardi "expressed the mood on the football field. Win, said Lombardi. Win for your school, your college, your pro team, your country, yourself" (1984, p. 95). Further, Lombardi himself juxtaposed the increasingly secular themes of commitment, excellence, and winning with a modicum of the Lord's Prayer after games and of St. Paul in his interviews: "Know ye not that they which run in a race run all, but one receiveth the prize? So run, that ye may obtain" (cf. Smith, 1973, p. 6).

Sport meant clarity and certainty and traditional values in the lives of John F. Kennedy and Vince Lombardi. When the ferment of the 1960s eroded the conditions for civil religion's existence, so that it became increasingly a rhetoric without a reality (Demerath & Williams, 1985, p. 164), sport already had been anointed politically and culturally as its folk religious successor.

The Role of Television

Arguably, John F. Kennedy and Vince Lombardi would not have exerted the influence they did in redefining sport as a folk religion were it not for the prior readiness of television to ensure the mass acceptance of sport by the folk. "The significance the viewing public attaches to [sport], its cultural symbolism, [and] the core values its viewers share" (Chandler, 1988, p. 23)—all were ready for an expanded role in American life after the influence of leaders such as Kennedy and Lombardi, and television helped transmit that new role during the 1960s and early 1970s. Television in and of itself did not create sport as a folk religion, although television reflected changes occurring over two to three decades. Clearly, sport epitomized those changes, but as Chandler has noted, sports would have changed fundamentally, with or without television (Chandler, 1985, p. 86). At the same time, television's role in people's lives expanded as it brought "sport to millions of more people" and "deepened and broadened the viewers' experience of sports" (Rader, 1984, p. 5).

Following Rader, one can divide sport into two principal eras—the 1940s to the mid-1960s and the mid-1960s to the present (Rader, 1984, p. 4). It is more than mere coincidence that by the 1960s, as civil religion had declined, strong personalities were modeling sport as a folk religion; at the same time, televised sport was moving into a new era on several fronts. It was a new era technologically, which could convey sport more dramatically to affluent consumers (Klatell & Marcus, 1988, pp. 105-109). It was a new era in network policies, originally launched about 1960 with a series of ABC network decisions to emphasize sport (Rader, 1984, pp. 101ff). The proliferation of sport programming led to a new era economically, with millions and then billions of dollars at stake. It was also a new era legally, with Congressional enactment of the Sports Broadcasting Act in 1961. That act's immediate purpose allowed professional sport franchises to negotiate as a joint entity with the major networks when selling the telecast rights to events. But the far-reaching, and probably unintended, results of the act both secured the economic future of sport and guaranteed its enhanced role in American life.

Although several sports—professional baseball, collegiate basketball, the professional golf tour—eventually benefitted from the symbiotic relationship that sport developed with television, it was football, especially professional football, that emerged as the most prominent "denominational form" of this folk religion.

> Football exemplified the way many Americans lived: their "strategies" and "tactics"; their crushing disappointments and joyful triumphs. Yet football suggested that committees, systems, bureaucracies, and technologies were still only the tools of men, not their masters. . . . The popularity of the sport reflected a wideranging quest among the "successful" in the 1960s and 1970s for individual power and fulfillment apart from their jobs. (Rader, 1984, p. 94)

What television has been able to ensure in its treatment of sport since the mid-1960s is a highly selective, but ambiguous, view of American culture. In one sense, televised sport is also a manifestation of "cultural lag," but not in the term's usually deleterious sense. Television has presented a magnified, but partial, image of sport. It is a curious mixture of modern technologies that creates a sense of sport quite unlike that gained either by first-hand participation or by spectating at a live event (cf. Mandell, 1984, p. 228), plus a combination of modern symbols used to redefine traditional values. Winning now counts more than ever; that's why we have overtime to eliminate tie games. Time is of great significance, so at television's behest, we speed up tennis matches with a tie-breaker, and we add the 45-second clock to college basketball and the 2-minute warning to professional football.

By contrast, television ignores soccer—the world sport—because the outdoor game does not televise easily, nor is soccer highly compatible with the American myth, cult, and tradition. Instead, television encourages us to substitute our own indoor version of soccer, which resembles pinball on a hockey rink minus ice but televises nicely. Somehow, it all seems more American, and only American sport could be an American folk religion.

Further, television aids our selective perception to ignore, or to minimize, any of the antisocial aspects of sport not consonant with the American way of life. On television, drug and alcohol abuse among athletes is ameliorated; steroids are nonexistent; labor unrest is blamed on the players' agents' selfishness; and racism must no longer exist, now that we have a black coach and a couple of black quarterbacks. Women, meanwhile, are overwhelmingly absent as televised-sport role models, while male sport commentators prefer to dwell on female athletes' physical appearances and on their own biased assumptions of traditional femininity.

So in its power and selectivity, television guarantees that we adhere to a version of the traditional American ways of believing and behaving. Televised sport may not be real sport, just as folk religion may not be real religion. But televised sport helps us maintain a view of America, its values, and the meanings of its games, all of which continue to bond us as a people. Thus, sport is linked to both television and folk religion, and as John F. Wilson perceptively explained, modern sport "was invented to fill a new pattern of cultural space and time created by the communications industry. Through newspaper, radio, and television, the world of sports has become central to American popular culture" (Wilson, 1979, pp. 134-135). Besides, "all of this commitment to athletic performance can be seen at one level as a fundamental dramatization of the basic values and goals of the society," with the result that "this culture created and sustained through the modern means is linked to public religion in America" (Wilson, 1979, p. 135).

Conclusion

In a period of less than a generation, American sport was infused with a pervasive folk religious significance for American life. As the strength of a recent episode of civil religion faded, sport emerged to fill the void and to embody and reinforce the American way of life for increasing numbers of us. With its reordering of our myths and values, our cultic observances, and our sense of history and tradition, sport now occupies a dominant place in our shared American experience. Important cultural figures such as John F. Kennedy and Vince Lombardi proclaimed and modeled this new relationship. Television in turn has made that relationship and meaning readily available to masses of the American folk, thus becoming the medium of this latest vision of our taken-for-granted social reality. The future of sport as folk religion is impossible to predict, but experiences of the recent past suggest that the relationships described here will continue to give meaning and a basis of solidarity to large numbers of Americans' lives.

References

Ahlstrom, S. (1972). *A religious history of the American people*. New Haven: Yale University Press.

Albanese, C.L. (1981). *America, religious and religion*. Belmont, CA: Wadsworth.

Bellah, R.N. (1967). Civil religion in America. *Daedalus*, **96**, 1-21.

Bellah, R.N. (1976). The revolution and the civil religion. In J.C. Brauer (Ed.), *Religion and the American Revolution* (pp. 55-73). Philadelphia: Fortress.

Bock, E.W. (1966). Symbols in conflict: Official versus folk religion. *Journal for the Scientific Study of Religion*, **5**, 204-212.

Boyle, R.H. (1970, November 30). Oral Roberts: Small but oh, my. *Sports Illustrated*, **33**(22), 64-65.

Chandler, J. (1985). American televised sport: Business as usual. In W.L. Umphlett (Ed.), *American sport culture* (pp. 83-97). Lewisburg, PA: Bucknell University Press.

Chandler, J. (1988). *Television and national sport*. Urbana: University of Illinois Press.

Coles, R.W. (1975). Football as a "surrogate" religion? In M. Hill (Ed.), *A sociological yearbook of religion in Britain*, #8 (pp. 61-77). London: SCM Press.

Demerath, N.J., III, & Williams, R.H. (1985). Civil religion in an uncivil society. *Annals of the American Academy of Political and Social Science*, **480**, 154-166.

Dowling, T. (1970). *Coach: A season with Lombardi*. New York: Popular Library.

Dunning, E. (1986). The sociology of sport in Europe and the United States. In C.R. Rees and A.W. Miracle (Eds.), *Sport and social theory* (pp. 29-56). Champaign, IL: Human Kinetics.

Durkheim, E. (1965). *The elementary forms of religious life* (J.W. Swain, Trans.) New York: Free Press. (Original work published 1915)

Eckardt, A.R. (1958). *The surge of piety in America*. New York: Association Press.

Edwards, H. (1973). *Sociology of sport*. Homewood, IL: Dorsey Press.

Eisenhower, D.D. (1952, December 23). Text of Eisenhower speech. *New York Times*, p. 16. (Delivered to the Freedoms Foundation, December 22, 1952.)

Gehrig, G. (1981a). *American civil religion: An assessment*. Storrs, CT: Society for the Scientific Study of Religion.

Gehrig, G. (1981b). The American civil religion debate: A source for theory construction. *Journal for the Scientific Study of Religion*, **20**, 51-63.

Guttman, A. (1978). *From ritual to record*. New York: Columbia University Press.

Hammond, P.E. (1968). Commentary. In D.R. Cutler (Ed.), *The religious situation: 1968* (pp. 381-388). Boston: Beacon.

Herberg, W. (1955). *Protestant-Catholic-Jew*. Garden City, NY: Doubleday.

Herberg, W. (1960). *Protestant-Catholic-Jew* (2nd ed.). Garden City, NY: Doubleday.

Higgs, R.J. (1983). Muscular Christianity, holy play, and spiritual exercises: Confusion about Christ in sports and religion. *Arete*, **1**(1), 59-85.

Hutchinson, P. (1954, March 24). The President's religious faith. *The Christian Century*, **71**(12), 362-367.

Jones, D.G., & Richey, R.E. (1974). The civil religion debate. In R.E. Richey and D.G. Jones (Eds.), *American civil religion* (pp. 3-18). New York: Harper and Row.

Kearl, M.C. (1986). Knowing how to quit: On the finitudes of everyday life. *Sociological inquiry*, **56**(3), 282-303.

Kennedy, J.F. (1960, December 26). The soft American. *Sports Illustrated*, **13**(26), 14-17.

Klatell, D.A., & Marcus, N. (1988). *Sports for sale: Television, money, and the fans*. New York: Oxford University Press.

Koppett, L. (1963, November 25). Pro football attendance unaffected. *New York Times*, p. 24.

Lasch, C. (1979). *The culture of narcissism*. New York: Norton.

Lawton, J. (1984). *The all American war game*. London: Blackwell.

Lever, J. (1983). *Soccer madness*. Chicago: University of Chicago Press.

Linder, R. (1975). Civil religion in historical perspective. *Journal of Church and State*, **17**(3), 399-421.

Lipsky, R. (1981). *How we play the game*. Boston: Beacon.

Lipsyte, R. (1975). *SportsWorld: An American dreamland*. New York: Quadrangle.

Loy, J.W., McPherson, B.D., & Kenyon, G. (1978). *Sport and social systems*. Reading, MA: Addison-Wesley.

Mandell, R.D. (1984). *Sport: A cultural history*. New York: Columbia University Press.

Markoff, J., & Regan, D. (1981). The rise and fall of civil religion: Comparative perspectives. *Sociological Analysis*, **42**(4), 333-352.

Marty, M. (1959). *The new shape of American religion*. New York: Harper and Row.

Marty, M. (1974). Two kinds of two kinds of civil religion. In R.E. Richey & D.G. Jones (Eds.), *American civil religion* (pp. 139-157). New York: Harper and Row.

Marty, M. (1976). *A nation of behavers*. Chicago: University of Chicago Press.

Mathisen, J.A. (1989). Twenty years after Bellah: Whatever happened to American civil religion? *Sociological Analysis*, **50**(2), 129-146.

Mensching, G. (1964). Folk and universal religion. In L. Schneider (Ed. and Trans.), *Religion, culture and society* (pp. 254-261). New York: Wiley.

Novak, M. (1976). *The joy of sports*. New York: Basic.

Prebish, C.S. (1984). "Heavenly Father, divine goalie": Sport and religion. *The Antioch Review*, **42**(3), 306-318.

The president who loved sport. (1963, December 2). *Sports Illustrated*, **19**(23), 20-21.

Rader, B.G. (1984). *In its own image: How television has transformed sports*. New York: Free Press.

Sheehan, J.M. (1963, November 24). Giants face Cards today, and some angry fans will stay home. *New York Times*, (Section 5), 1.

Slusher, H.S. (1967). *Man, sport, and existence*. Philadelphia: Lea and Febiger.

Smith, R. (1973). Introduction. In G.L. Flynn (Ed.), *Vince Lombardi on football* (pp. 6-7). New York: New York Graphic Society.

Vance, N.S. (1984, May 16). Sport is a religion in America, controversial professor argues. *The Chronicle of Higher Education*, **28**(12), 25-27.

Wallace, A.F.C. (1966). *Religion: An anthropological view*. New York: Random House.

Warner, W.L. (1961). *The family of God*. New Haven: Yale University Press.

Weiss, P. (1969). *Sport: A philosophic inquiry.* Carbondale, IL: Southern Illinois University Press.

Williams, R.M. (1951). *American society: A sociological interpretation.* New York: Knopf.

Wilson, J.F. (1979). *Public religion in American culture.* Philadelphia: Temple University Press.

The Natural Religion

Michael Novak

A sport is not a religion in the same way that Methodism, Presbyterianism, or Catholicism is a religion. But these are not the only kinds of religion. There are secular religions, civil religions. The United States of America has sacred documents to guide and to inspire it: The Constitution, the Declaration of Independence, Washington's Farewell Address, Lincoln's Gettysburg Address, and other solemn presidential documents. The President of the United States is spoken to with respect, is expected to exert "moral leadership"; and when he walks among crowds, hands reach out to touch his garments. Citizens are expected to die for the nation, and our flag symbolizes vivid memories, from Fort Sumter to Iwo Jima, from the Indian Wars to Normandy: memories that moved hard-hats in New York to break up a march that was "desecrating" the flag. Citizens regard the American way of life as though it were somehow chosen by God, special, uniquely important to the history of the human race. "Love it or leave it," the guardians of orthodoxy say. Those on the left, who do not like the old-time patriotism, have a new kind: they evince unusual outrage when this nation is less than fully just, free, compassionate, or good—in short, when it is like all the other nations of human history. America should be *better*. Why?

The institutions of the state generate a civil religion; so do the institutions of sport. The ancient Olympic games used to be both festivals in honor of the gods and festivals in honor of the state—and that has been the classical position of sports ever since. The ceremonies of sports overlap those of the state on one side, and those of the churches on the other. At the Super Bowl in 1970, clouds of military jets flew in formation, American flags and patriotic bunting flapped in the wind, ceremonies honored prisoners of war, clergymen solemnly prayed, thousands sang the national anthem. Going to a stadium is half like going to a political rally, half like going to church. Even today, the Olympics are constructed around high ceremonies, rituals, and symbols. The Olympics are not barebones athletic events, but religion and politics as well.

Sports flow outward into action from a deep natural impulse that is radically religious: an impulse of freedom, respect for ritual limits, a zest for symbolic meaning, and a longing for perfection. The athlete may of course be pagan, but sports are, as it were, natual religions. There are many ways to express this radical impulse: by the asceticism and dedication of preparation; by a sense of respect for the mysteries of one's own body and soul, and for powers not in one's own control; by a sense of awe for the place and time of competition; by a sense of fate; by a felt sense of comradeship and destiny; by a sense of participation in the rhythms and tides of nature itself.

Sports, in the second place, are organized and dramatized in a religious way. Not only do the origins of sports, like the origins of drama, lie in religious celebrations; not only are the rituals, vestments, and tremor of anticipation involved in sports events like those of religions. Even in our own secular age and for quite sophisticated and agnostic persons, the rituals of sports really work. They do serve a religious function: they feed a deep human hunger, place humans in touch with certain dimly perceived features of human life within this cosmos, and provide an experience of at least a pagan sense of godliness.

Among the godward signs in contemporary life, sports may be the single most powerful manifestation. I don't mean that participation in sports, as athlete or fan, makes one a believer in "God," under whatever concept, image, experience, or drive to which one attaches the name. Rather, sports drive one in some dark and generic sense "godward." In the language of Paul Tillich, sports are manifestations of concern, of will and intellect and passion. In fidelity to that concern, one submits oneself to great bodily dangers, even to the danger of death. Symbolically, too, to lose is a kind of death.

Sports are not the highest form of religion. They do not exclude other forms. Jews, Christians, and others will want to put sports in second place, within a scheme of greater ultimacy.

For some, it may require a kind of conversion to grasp the religiousness at the heart of sports. Our society has become secular, and personal advancement obliges us to become pragmatic, glib, superficial, and cynical. Our spirits often wither. Eyes cannot see; ears cannot hear. The soil of our culture is not always fertile for religious life. Americans must read religious messages in foreign languages. And so many will, at first, be tempted to read what I am saying as mere familiar metaphor. A change of perspective, and of heart, may be necessary.

Sports are religious in the sense that they are organized institutions, disciplines, and liturgies; and also in the sense that they teach religious qualities of heart and soul. In particular, they recreate symbols of cosmic struggle, in which human survival and moral courage are not assured. To this extent, they are not mere games, diversions, pastimes. Their power to exhilarate or depress is far greater than that. To say "It was only a game" is the psyche's best defense against the cosmic symbolic meaning of sports events. And it is partly true. For a game is a symbol; it is not precisely identified with what it symbolizes. To lose symbolizes death, and it certianly feels like dying; but it is not death. The same is true of religious symbols like Baptism or the Eucharist; in both, the communicants experience death, symbolically, and are reborn, sybolically. If you give your heart to the ritual, its effects upon your inner life can be far-reaching. Of course, in all religions many merely go through the motions. Yet even they, unaware, are surprised by grace. A Hunter pursues us everywhere, in churches and stadia alike, in the pews and bleachers, and occasionally in the pulpit and the press box.

Something has gone wrong in sports today. It went wrong in medieval Christendom, too. A proverb in Chaucer expresses it: *Radix malorum cupiditas* (The root of all evils is greed). True in the fourteenth century, it is as modern as television: Money corrupts. Nothing much changes down the centuries, only the props and the circumstances. With every day that passes, the "new" world recreates the "old." The ancient sources of corruption in Athens, Constantinople, Alexandria, and Rome are as vigorous in New York, Boston, and Washington as the preparations for Olympic games. Then as now, the hunger for excellence, for perfection-in-act, for form and beauty, is expressed in the straining muscles and fiercely determined wills of heroes of the spirit: of athletes, artists, and even, sometimes, political giants like a Pericles or Cicero. In the corruption of a slave state, a fleshpot, Homer wrote of deeds of beauty. Through his writing, pieces from the flames were salvaged. So it is in every age. Rise and fall are as steady as the seasons of our sports.

But Homer seems to be nodding nowadays. Larry Merchant of the New York *Post*, no Homer he, called his column "Fun and Games" and has been called the pioneer "of modern skepticism and irreverence toward sports." Merchant modestly replies to praise: "I must state for posterity that I was merely part of a broad-based movement. . . . We were irreverent, debunking heroes and myths that didn't stand up to scrutiny." Shucks, folks. Sportswriting "has changed conceptually." His own self-image isn't bad: "We were humanistic. . . . We saw ballparks as fun-houses, not temples. We . . . [dug] for the hows and whys and whos." The intellectually fearless skeptics. Sports isn't religion. It's entertainment. "A baseball game," writes Robert Lipsyte, formerly a New York *Times* sportswriter and the author of *SportsWorld*, "is a staged entertainment, and baseball players are paid performers."

Jewish and Protestant writers draw on different intellectual traditions from mine, of course, but from my point of view, Catholic that I was born, any religion worthy of the name thrives on irreverence, skepticism, and high anticlericalism. A religion without skeptics is like a bosom never noticed (which isn't entirely farfetched, since at least one writer has said that covering sports for the New York *Times* is like being Raquel Welch's elbow). When Catholicism goes sour, as periodically down the centuries it does, almost always the reason is a dearth of critics or, worse, the death of heretics. A nonprophet church decays. When things go well, it is because critics condemn what is going ill. A decent religion needs irreverence as meat needs salt.

Temples do not require whispering. Jesus knocked temple tables over, jangling metal coins on the stones. The root of the religious sense is not the stifling of questions. It lies in asking so many questions that the true dimensions of reality begin to work their own mysterious awe. No one is less religious than the pleasantly contented pragmatist after lunch. Nothing is more religious than fidelity to the drive to understand. For that drive is endless, and satisfied by nothing on earth. It is the clearest sign in our natures that our home is not here; that we are out of place; and that to be restless, and seeking, is to be what we most are.

Sports are not merely fun and games, not merely diversions, not merely entertainment. A ballpark is not a temple, but it isn't a fun house either. A baseball game is not an entertainment, and a ballplayer is considerably more than a paid performer. No one can explain the passion, commitment, discipline, and dedication involved in sports by evasions like these.

Those who think sports are merely entertainment have been bemused by an entertainment culture. Television did not make sports possible—not even great, highly organized sports. College football and major league baseball thrived for decades without benefit of television. Sports made television commercially successful. No other motive is so frequently cited as a reason for shelling out money for a set. (Non-sports fans, it appears, are the least likely Americans to have sets.)

In order to be entertained, I watch television: prime-time shows. They slide effortlessly by. I am amused, or distracted, or engrossed. Good or bad, they help to pass the time pleasantly enough. Watching football on television is totally different. I don't watch football to pass the time. The outcome of the games affects me. I care. Afterward, the emotion I have lived through continues to affect me. Football is not entertainment. It is far more important than that. If you observe the passivity of television viewers being entertained, and the animation of fans watching a game on television, the difference between entertainment and involvement of spirit becomes transparent. Sports are more like religion than like entertainment. Indeed, at a contest in the stadium, the "entertainment"—the bands, singers, comedians, balloons, floats, fireworks, jets screaming overhead—pales before the impact of the contest itself, like lemonade served to ladies while the men are drinking whiskey.

At a sports event, there may be spectators, just as some people come to church to hear the music. But a participant is not a spectator merely, even if he does not walk among the clergy. At a liturgy, elected representatives perform the formal acts, but all believers put their hearts into the ritual. It is considered inadequate, almost blasphemous, to be a mere spectator. Fans are not mere specators. If they wanted no more than to pass the time, to find diversion, there are cheaper and less internally exhausting ways. Believers in sport do not go to sports to be entertained; to plays and dramas, maybe, but not to sports. Sports are far more serious than the dramatic arts, much closer to primal symbols, metaphors, and acts, much more ancient and more frightening. Sports are mysteries of youth and aging, perfect action and decay, fortune and misfortune, strategy and contingency. Sports are rituals concerning human survival on this planet: liturgical enactments of animal perfection and the struggles of the human spirit to prevail.

We have no truly popular operas, or suitably complex literature, or plays in which our entire population shares. The streets of America, unlike the streets of Europe, do not involve us in stories and anecdotes rich with a thousand years of human struggle. Sports are our chief civilizing agent. Sports are our most universal art form. Sports tutor us in the basic lived experiences of the humanist tradition.

The hunger for perfection in sports cleaves closely to the driving core of the human spirit. It is the experience of this driving force that has perennially led human beings to break forth in religious language. This force is in us, it is ours. Yet we did not will its existence, nor do we command it, nor is it under our power. It is there unbidden. It is greater than we, driving us beyond our present selves. "Be ye perfect," Jesus said, "as your heavenly Father is perfect." The root of human dissatisfaction and restlessness goes as deep into the spirit as any human drive—deeper than any other drive. It *is* the human spirit. Nothing stills it. Nothing fulfills it. It is not a need like a hunger, a thirst, or an itch, for such needs are easily satisified. It is a need even greater than sex; orgasmic satisfaction does not quiet it. "Desire" is the word by which coaches call it. A drivenness. Distorted, the drive for perfection can propel an ugly and considerably less than perfect human development. True, straight, and well-targeted, it soars like an arrow toward the proper beauty of humanity. Sports nourish this drive as well as any other institution in our society. If this drive is often distorted, as it is, even its distortions testify to its power, as liars mark out the boundaries of truth.

Sports, in a word, are a form of godliness. That is why the corruptions of sports in our day, by corporations and television and glib journalism and cheap public relations, are so hateful. If sports were entertainment, why should we care? They are far more than that. So when we see them abused, our natural response is the rise of vomit in the throat.

It may be useful to list some of the elements of religions, to see how they are imitated in the world of sports.

Suppose you are an anthropologist from Mars. You come suddenly upon some wild, adolescent tribes living in territories called the "United States of America." You try to understand their way of life, but their society does not make sense to you. Flying over the land in a rocket, you notice great ovals near every city. You descend and observe. You learn that an oval is called a "stadium." It is used, roughly, once a week in certain seasons. Weekly, regularly, millions of citizens stream into these concrete doughnuts, pay handsomely, are alternately hushed and awed and outraged and screaming mad. (They demand from time to time that certain sacrificial personages be "killed.") You see that the figures in the rituals have trained themselves superbly for their performances. The combatants are dedicated. So are the dancers and musicians in tribal dress who occupy the arena before, during, and after the combat. You note that, in millions of homes, at corner shrines in every household's sacred room, other citizens are bound by invisible attraction to the same events. At critical moments, the most intense worshipers demand of the less attentive silence. Virtually an entire nation is united in a central public rite. Afterward, you note exultation or depression among hundreds of thousands, and animation almost everywhere.

Some of the elements of a religion may be enumerated. A religion, first of all, is organized and structured. Culture is built on cult. Accordingly, a religion begins with ceremonies. At these ceremonies, a few surrogates perform for all. They need not even believe what they are doing. As professionals, they may perform so often that they have lost all religious instinct; they may have less faith than any of the participants. In the official ceremonies, sacred vestments are employed and rituals are prescribed. Customs develop. Actions are highly formalized. Right ways and wrong ways are plainly marked out; illicit behaviors are distinguished from licit ones. Professional watchdogs supervise formal correctness. Moments of silence are observed. Concentration and intensity are indispensable. To attain them, drugs or special disciplines of spirit might be employed; ordinary humans, in the ordinary ups and downs of daily experience, cannot be expected to perform routinely at the highest levels of awareness.

Religions are built upon *ascesis*, a word that derives from the disciplines Greek athletes imposed upon themselves to give their wills and instincts command of their bodies; the word was borrowed by Christian monks and hermits. It signifies the development of character, through patterns of self-denial, repetition, and experiment. The type of character celebrated in the central rituals, more likely than not, reveals the unconscious needs of the civilization—extols the very qualities that more highly conscious formulations are likely to deny. Thus, the cults have a revelatory quality; they dramatize what otherwise goes unspoken.

Religions also channel the feeling most humans have of danger, contingency, and chance—in a word, Fate. Human plans involve ironies. Our choices are made with so little insight into their eventual effects that what we desire is often not the path we want. The decisions we make with little attention turn out to be major turning points. What we prepare for with exquisite detail never happens. Religions place us in the presence of powers greater than ourselves, and seek to reconcile us to them. The rituals of religion give these powers almost human shape, forms that give these powers visibility and tangible effect. Sports events in baseball, basketball, and football are structured so that "the breaks" may intervene and become central components in the action.

Religions make explicit the almost nameless dreads of daily human life: aging, dying, failure under pressure, cowardice, betrayal, guilt. Competitive sports embody these in every combat.

Religions, howsoever universal in imperative, do not treat rootedness, particularity, and local belonging as unworthy. On the contrary, they normally begin by blessing the local turf, the local tribe, and the local instinct of belonging—and use these as paradigms for the development of larger loyalties. "Charity begins at home." "Whoever says that he loves God, whom he does not see, but hates his neighbor, whom he does see, is a liar and the truth is not in him."

Religions consecrate certain days and hours. Sacred time is a block of time lifted out of everyday normal routines, a time that is different, in which different laws apply, a time within which one forgets ordinary time. Sacred time is intended to suggest an "eternal return," a fundamental repetition like the circulation of the human blood, or the eternal turning of the seasons, or the wheeling of the stars and planets in their cycles: the sense that things repeat themselves, over and over, and yet are always a little different. Sacred time is more like eternity than like history, more like cycles of recurrence than like progress, more like a celebration of repetition than like a celebration of novelty. Yet sacred time is full of exhilaration, excitement, and peace, as though it were more real and more joyous than the activities of everyday life—as though it were *really living* to be in sacred time (wrapped up in a close game during the last two minutes), and comparatively boring to suffer the daily jading of work, progress, history.

To have a religion, you need to have heroic forms to try to live up to: patterns of excellence so high that human beings live up to them only rarely, even when they strive to do so; and images of perfection so beautiful that, living up to them or seeing someone else live up to them, produces a kind of *"ah!"*

You need to have a pattern of symbols and myths that a person can grow old with, with a kind of resignation, wisdom, and illumination. Do what we will, the human body ages. Moves we once could make our minds will but our bodies cannot implement; disciplines we once endured with suppressed animal desire are no longer worth the effort; heroes that once seemed to us immortal now age, become enfeebled, die, just as we do. The "boys of summer" become the aging men of winter. A religion celebrates the passing of all things: youth, skill, grace, heroic deeds.

To have a religion, you need to have a way to exhilarate the human body, and desire, and will, and the sense of beauty, and a sense of oneness with the universe and other humans. You need chants and songs, the rhythm of bodies in unison, the indescribable feeling of many who together "will one thing" as if they were each members of a single body.

All these things you have in sports.

Sports are not Christianity, or Judaism, or Islam, or Buddhism, or any other of the world religions. Sports are not the civil religion of the United States of America, or Great Britain, or Germany, or the Union of the Soviet Socialist Republics, or Ghana, or any other nation.

But sports are a form of religion. This aspect of sports has seldom been discussed. Consequently, we find it hard to express just what it is that gives sports their spirit and their power.

Athletes are not merely entertainers. Their role is far more powerful than that. People identify with them in a much more priestly way. Athletes exemplify something of deep meaning—frightening meaning, even. Once they become superstars, they do not quite belong to themselves. Great passions are invested in them. They are no longer treated as ordinary humans or even as mere celebrities. Their exploits and their failures have great power to exult—or to depress. When people talk about athletes' performances, it is almost as though they are talking about a secret part of themselves. As if the stars had some secret bonding, some Siamese intertwining with their own psyches.

The tales of *Gawain and the Green Knight*, the *Song of Roland*, the exploits of Ivanho—these are the ancient games in which human beings have for centuries found refreshment. The crowds who watched the jousts of old are still cheering, still quenching the dust in their throats with cold drinks between the acts, and still seeing enacted before their naked eyes myths of courage, brains, and skill.

We are so close to sports, so enmeshed in them, that we do not truly *see* them, we do not marvel. We overlook the wonder even the existence of sports should cause, let alone their persistence and their power. Long after the Democratic Party has passed into history, long after the United States has disappeared, human beings will still be making play fundamental to their lives.

Play is the most human activity. It is the first act of freedom. It is the first origin of law. (Watch even an infant at play, whose first act is marking out the limits, the rules, the roles: "This is the road. . . ." The first free act of the human is to assign limits within which freedom can be at play.) Play is not tied to necessity, except to the necessity of the human spirit to exercise its freedom, to enjoy something that is not practical, or productive, or required for gaining food or shelter. Play is human intelligence, and intuition, and love of challenge and contest and struggle; it is respect for limits and laws and rules, and high animal spirits, and a lust to develop the art of doing things perfectly. Play is what only humans truly develop. Humans could live as animals (and often we do, governed by instinct), envying what seems to be the freedom of the wild, the soaring aloft of birds, the unfettered wanderings of jungle felines "born free." But animals are not free, not as humans are. Animals do not multiply cultures and languages, and forms of play, and organizational patterns. Animals play as they have for centuries, while humans ceaselessly invent, produce the multiple varieties of religion and play that establish on the soil of nature the realm of culture, the field of liberty. The religions we have, like the games we have, have issued forth from the historical response of humans to their own liberty.

In all these ways, religions and sports have much in common. Sports belong in the category of religion.

"Heavenly Father, Divine Goalie":
Sport and Religion

Charles S. Prebish

Arnold Beisser begins his book *The Madness in Sports* with a reference to a famous Japanese World War II battle cry that was meant to demoralize American soldiers: "To hell with Babe Ruth!" Clearly, the attacking Japanese thought they knew what Americans valued most. In his landmark work on religion in sport, *Sports Illustrated* writer Frank Deford picked up on this same theme when he wrote, "The claim that sport has developed into a national faith may be linked to the nagging awareness that something has happened to Sunday." Deford knew just what it was that had happened, too. He correlated the decline in church attendance with the rise of professional football as the new darling of the American sportsman. For 1976, the year in which Deford's articles were published, he was quite correct: "Now, the trip out of the house on Sunday is not to visit a church, but to see a game or to play one. . . . So the churches have ceded Sunday to sports, to games." Later we shall see that, by 1982, sport had not only won the battle for Sunday, but for all other days as well. In sport religion, the sabbath is Everyday.

The response of the churches to the continually increasing American appetite for sport was to be as obliging as possible. On the one hand, the times of traditional worship services were adjusted so as to free the celebrant for his or her immersion in a Sunday of sport. Catholic churches offered Saturday afternoon services while Protestant denominations scheduled their services in harmony with *TV Guide* announcements of the sport specials of the week. For Jewish families it was somewhat easier. All that had to be sacrificed was the Friday Night Fight; Bar Mitzvah services were over on Saturdays long before the sport scene began to heat up for the day. Of course cable TV and ESPN have changed all that. On the other hand, religious groups, regardless of their specific affiliation, sought to cultivate sport as a means of keeping their clientele firmly in the fold. The holy alliance between religion and sport is not without precedent, however. By 1800, America had cast off the Puritan opposition to sport, and collectively began to realize that a life of physical inactivity was a liability rather than an asset. The American YMCA was founded in Boston in 1851, followed in 1858 by a YWCA chapter in New York. Needless to say, in the middle decades of the twentieth century, it was acknowledged by the various religious groups that participation in sport was healthy for their congregants and unifying for the congregations, and this was evidenced by the large number of church- or synagogue-sponsored athletic leagues, usually carrying the title YMCA, YWCA, CYO, JCC, or some similar identifying designation. Yet it was not until quite recently that churches and synagogues went into the sport business with a fury and passion that advertised *big-time* investments.

By the 1970s, religion was learning a valuable lesson from its secular counterpart. If lucrative television contracts were making club owners and athletes into fiscal wizards while providing ample exposure to an adoring public, then perhaps it was time for professional religion to imitate professional sport. In so doing, television evangelism was to become a hot franchise. The point here is twofold. First, religion was seeking new avenues of reaching the public that rivaled its successful sport adversary. Just like the NFL, NHL, or NBA, religion sought to catch John Q. Public's attention while he sat in his easy chair, newspaper or coffee in hand, and *before* he took his usual dose of O.J. Simpson or Walter Payton. Second, it sought to affirm sport, even champion its fundamental emphases, in order to align itself with a proven winner.

Perhaps the most visible and well-known evangelist to utilize sport in his ministry is the Reverend Billy Graham. Following his appearance as grand marshal of the Rose Bowl parade in 1971, *Newsweek* ran an often-cited article entitled "Are Sports Good for the Soul?" In citing Graham's use of sport as a basic metaphor in his preaching, the article quotes Graham's understanding of the role of sport in (at least his) religion: "The Bible says leisure and lying around are morally dangerous for us. Sports keeps us busy; athletes, you notice, don't take drugs. There are probably more really committed Christians in sports, both collegiate and professional, than in any other occupation in America." Although less well-known generally than Billy Graham, on the sporting scene, the most conspicuous religious figure is the Reverend Billy Zeoli. A flashy dresser, he is flamboyant in appearance and speech. A sample from Deford's "Reaching for the Stars" demonstrates:

> By his own proud admission, the Zeoli theology is brutally simple. "I am a total liberal when it comes to methods, but very conservative in theology," he says. As he tells the Bills, as he will tell the Jets, as he always says, Jesus was either the Son of God or a cuckoo—take it or leave it. God and man are separated by sin, which is labelled "The Problem." "The Answer" is to employ Jesus as the intermediary. So there is "The Decision," and to avoid confusion Zeoli lays out the choices: "yes," "no," and "maybe." Taken as a whole, that is what Zeoli calls "God's Game Plan."

Perhaps Billy Zeoli is the extreme case in religion's attempt to use sport, but there are others like him in the arena. These so-called jock evangelists are rapidly becoming a fixture in the locker rooms throughout our land, and organizations are emerging through which athletes are able to take their religious message to the people, playing as much on their role as American heroes as on their ministerial acumen.

The attempt on the part of clergymen to deal with the spiritual needs of athletes is not nearly so altruistic as it might seem. By playing on the widespread appeal of well-known amateur and professional athletes, the ministers are able to expand their operations, numerically and financially, many times over. Frank Deford called this new movement "Sportianity," and to aid in this endeavor the athletes are utilized as amateur evangelists or, as *The Wittenberg Door* calls them, "Jocks for Jesus." There are primarily three organizations through which athletes are used to bring new members into the fold. The first of these is the Fellowship of Christian Athletes (FCA), founded in 1954. It intends "to confront athletes and coaches and through them the youth of the nation, with the challenge and adventure of following Christ and serving him through the fellowship of the church. . . ." In order to carry out its goals, the Fellowship of Christian Athletes uses older athletes (and coaches) to recruit younger ones to Christ.

The second group in athletic religion, Athletes in Action (AIA), is a division of the Billy Graham–inspired Campus Crusade for Christ. With special permission from the NCAA, Athletes in Action fields teams of former college athletes that are allowed to compete against current college squads in basketball, wrestling, gymnastics, track, and weight lifting. During their various competitions against amateur teams, AIA members give religious speeches, often at half-time or after the match, and distribute materials for the parent organization. Although the organization claims that it relies on the "soft-sell," anyone who has ever attended an AIA event knows that the pitch is several steps up from gentle, with "feverish" a somewhat more accurate description.

As the FCA and AIA came into increasing competition for the "choice" athletes to serve in a missionary capacity, a third organization was founded to act as a buffer or intermediary between the two: Pro Athletes Outreach (PAO). An outgrowth of Sports World Chaplaincy, Inc., it is a prospering group that sends its professional athletes on what it calls "speaking blitzes" across the country. Like the other organizations, its members offer testimony sprinkled with group publicity.

What all of these groups have in common is that they are completely nondenominational, conservative in their theology, and fundamentalist in approach and lifestyle. They take no stands on questionable moral issues, exclude individuals of doubtful temperament, and insist on absolute fidelity. Everything is done for the glory of Christ, and in so doing, Deford claimed, "Jesus has been transformed, emerging anew as a holler guy, a give-it-100-percenter." Michael Novak, scholar-in-residence at the American Enterprise Institute and a noted Catholic theologian, argues against the religious defensiveness of fundamentalism by boldly stating, "Sports is, somehow, a religion." And while he does not see sport as equal or identical to any of the world's religions, he does concede, ". . . sports flow outward into action from a deep natural impulse that is radically religious: an impulse of freedom, respect for ritual limits, a zest for symbolic meaning, and a longing for perfection. The athlete may of course be pagan, but sports are, as it were, natural religions.'' Further, despite the fact that each religious group boasts big numbers of fans and converts, all may not be so rosy as claimed. Young Christian athletes often seem to be interested in religion primarily as a means to get an edge, so to speak, to get God on their side. Although such an attitude is not sanctioned religiously, it prevails nonetheless, and though some athletes do indeed stop short of asking God for victory, many do not, thus prostituting the real basis for personal and religious growth. What emerges, then, is an unclear picture with the athletes trying to improve their religious and competitive field position.

On the college campuses today, the relationship between religion and sport is equally cloudy. Although college-level sport competition was originally intended to provide recreation for those who were hard at work cultivating the best that education had to offer, these programs of intercollegiate sport rapidly changed in nature and function in the early years of this century. A plethora of church-supported institutions of higher learning began to exploit the growing American interest in sport, first as a means of publicizing the university and later as a means of attracting funding and students. In many cases, sport as a growth industry within the university was a driving force in upgrading the academic reputation of the school as well. Father James Riehle of Notre Dame was unceremoniously blunt when he said: ''Of course Catholic schools used athletics for prestige. Notre Dame would not be the great school it is today, the great academic institution, were it not for football. But the emphases have changed here. I think that now we realize the value of sport in more ways than just the financial, whereas I'm afraid once we didn't.'' Occasionally, the message does not filter down to the athlete on the field, for one recent Brigham Young quarterback remarked that classes were about the only thing he didn't like at BYU. Most recently, Oral Roberts University, founded in 1965, has utilized both sport and the gospel as a means of calling attention to itself. In fact, Roberts himself proclaims, ''Athletics is a part of our Christian witness. . . . Nearly every man in America reads the sports pages, and a Christian school cannot ignore these people.''

What effect does all this emphasis on winning, in the name of the Lord, have on individuals who are entrenched in the sports establishment? In the first place, if winning is the result of hard work, discipline, and dedication, as most coaches and athletes suppose, then such an emphasis is certainly consistent with the traditional Protestant work ethic that is such a shaping force in our culture. Some sport sociologists even argue that sport values mirror the core values of Protestantism. Over against this, however, is the growing protest of a rapidly expanding group of vocal clergy. Episcopal priest Malcolm Boyd, for example:

This sort of slick, stage-directed prayer alienates people from religion because anybody can see that it is as shoddy as anything else in the world. The gimmick use of prayer before a game for the purpose of getting psyched up, this use of prayer as *deus ex machina*—I find it simply immoral. To use God in this way—it isn't holy. Hell isn't a bunch of fires. I think that hell is when you're using anybody, even when you're trying to use God, as in this case.

The last remark suggests that sport has used religion too, just as the reverse was true. Now we need to explore this other side of the coin.

Today, almost every team in professional sport holds chapel services on Sundays, both at home and away. Many college teams do the same. And the pregame prayer is customary even in the youth leagues of America. Why? Religion provides the athlete with a basis for reinforcement, both physical and spiritual. It allays his psychological anxieties. It enables him to face the competition at hand confident and peaceful, fully concentrated. In addition, an overwhelming number of athletes claim that religious conviction has been a profound factor in enhancing the development of their sport skills. Hardly an American boy of the 1950s or 1960s could escape watching the Reverend Bob Richards pole-vault his way out of a Wheaties box. Nor will we forget Sandy Koufax's refusal to pitch on a Jewish High Holy Day.

One researcher actually did a master's thesis at the University of California, Santa Barbara, (in 1967) on *The Incidence of Prayer in Athletics by Selected California Collegiate Athletes and Coaches*. It is clearly the case that when prayer is not private, or team sponsored, then it is institutionalized as part of the sporting event. Very often now, sport events, particularly if they are significant, employ *both* the playing of the National Anthem *and a religious invocation*. Perhaps the most dramatic of these invocations was delivered by Father Edward Rupp before the 1976 World Hockey Association All-Star game:

Heavenly Father, Divine Goalie, we come before You this evening to seek Your blessing. . . . We are, thanks to You, All-Stars. We pray tonight for Your guidance. Keep us free from actions that would put us in the Sin Bin of Hell. Inspire us to avoid the pitfalls of our profession. Help us to stay within the blue line of Your commandments and the red line of Your grace. Protect us from being injured by the puck of pride. May we be ever delivered from the high stick of dishonesty. May the wings of Your angels play at the right and left of our teammates. May You always be the Divine Center of our team, and when our summons comes for eternal retirement to the heavenly grandstand, may we find You ready to give us the everlasting bonus of a permanent seat in Your coliseum. Finally, grant us the courage to skate without tripping, to run without icing, and to score the goal that really counts—the one that makes each of us a winner, a champion, an All-Star in the hectic Hockey Game of Life. Amen.

From the above, we can see that sport and religion have been more than extensively related during the last generation of American history. The relationship has been so complete, in fact, that numerous critics, from each side of the fence, have responded to the phenomenon in a variety of ways.

By 1971, though, *Newsweek* was asking, "Are Sports Good for the Soul?" Its conclusion highlights the alarm apparently felt by more than a few Americans at the time: "It may be impossible to separate sports and religion in America. Nonetheless, more and more players and viewers are now asking themselves whether treating

God as some kind of supercoach does not demean both faith and football.'' What this writer and others seemed to be saying, albeit in round-about fashion, is what sport sociologist Harry Edwards said directly in 1973: "If there is a universal popular religion in America it is to be found within the institution of sport.'' And, unlike his colleagues, Edwards included even the fan, noting that for the spectator, sport is a "quasi-religion.'' In addition, what makes Edward's treatment so important is that he demonstrated just where the parallels between religion and sport emerge and interpenetrate.

What I find overwhelmingly hard to understand is why Professor Edwards says, "In sum, sport is essentially a secular, quasi-religious institution. It does not, however, constitute an alternative to or substitute for formal sacred religious involvement.'' It is apparent that Edwards saw, or at least presented, far more material on the subject than his colleagues in any of the sub-disciplines of sport study. Yet he, too, like all other writers, insisted on stopping short of what is becoming notably obvious.

For me, it is not just a parallel that is emerging between sport and religion, but rather a *complete identity*. *Sport is religion* for growing numbers of Americans, and this is no product of simply facile reasoning or wishful thinking. Further, for many, sport religion has become a more appropriate expression of personal religiosity than Christianity, Judaism, or any of the traditional religions.

Many of the authors cited to this point made reference to the similarity of vocabulary in sport and religion. They suggested that sport has appropriated significant religious terminology as a means of expressing the sincerity, fervor, and seriousness of sport. All mentioned at least a few well-chosen examples of parallel nomenclature, resulting in a profusion of references to words like *sacred, faith, ritual*, and so forth. There are two problems obvious in such an approach. In the first place, it is only the surface of mutually shared terminology that is proverbially scratched. Even a cursory continuance of the procedure reveals that other, equally applicable expressions must be mentioned: *ultimate, dedicated, sacrifice, peace, commitment, spirit, suffering, worship, prayer, festival*, and *holiday*. With a little investigation, it would not be unreasonable to suppose that a list of fifty or more terms and phrases could be compiled. Yet it is the second problem that is critical, for we are not simply playing the numbers game here. Most authors presume a shared vocabulary with a *slightly altered meaning* for each enterprise. For Novak and others, words like *sacred, dedicated*, and *sacrifice* mean one thing for religion and another for sport. This bifurcation results from the axiom that religion is sacred while sport is secular. I would maintain, however, that in many cases there is absolutely no difference in the meaning that each term carries for the two traditions in question. Equally, the yearly Super Bowl is no less a religious holiday than Easter. The child's worship of Ted Williams is no less real than his reverential adoration of Christ, and to some, Williams's accomplishments and capabilities in baseball were unquestionably godly. And, judging from the sentiments it evoked, the Gold Medal victory of the U.S. hockey team in the 1980 Winter Olympics was quite as ultimate as anything that occurs in a traditional house of worship.

The point of ritual is to approach purity through our actions in order that our attained purity brings us closer to the fulfillment of specific goals. Regarding practicality, these rituals are enacted both publicly and privately. Public expression requires attendance at formal, sanctioned, institutional services. In traditional religion, one attends church or synagogue, whereas in sport religion, one attends the gymnasium or arena. There are numerous examples of identity between religious and sport rituals in the public sphere. It would not be going far, I think, to suggest that in Christian services, communion may well be the most significant ritual activity. For sport religion, the ritual act of the game, its religious service, would also not be complete without its respective act of communion. Richard Lipsky points out in straightforward fashion: "During the game, the social euphoria generates a festive communion and sense of solidarity between the players and fans." Finally, the post-game events explicitly replicate the rituals of traditional religion, replete with trying to catch a word with the religious professional, be he priest, rabbi, minister, *or player*. No religious service would be complete without ritual chants and hymns. These vary from tradition to tradition, but are utilized to some degree by all religions. We find the same ritual practice in sport as well, with each denomination in sport religion presenting its own specific assortment. Football, for example, might offer as its hymn, "You've Got to Be a Football Hero"; baseball counters with "Take Me Out to the Ball Game." Chants range from the traditional "We want a touchdown" to the hopeless "Let's Go Cubs." Even the stadium organist is modeled on his counterpart in traditional religion. And the result is identical in each case: individuals go beyond their own ego bonds. In so doing, they open to the possibility of experiencing a different, nonordinary reality.

No less analogous to public ritual expression is the private search for religious meaning through rites, whether the specific activity is the Muslim's daily domestic practices or the runner's solitary ten-miler at dawn. It is important to note that this is the point at which personal prayer, as a ritual activity, converges in sport and religion. The point is this: all of these ritual acts, both traditional and nontraditional, prepare the participant for what is to follow. Without proper ritual preparation, the game would be lost, a close call would be missed, the fan would feel just plain lousy, or religious catastrophe might occur. In other words, these singular, curious-looking acts bring forth the sacred; they are part of the sacraments of religion, the sport variety and otherwise.

Taken together, rituals are welded into festivals, and in sport religion, just as in its traditional counterpart, the festivals are obvious and seasonal. In each of the world's major religious traditions, it is possible to isolate and identify a series of important seasonal rituals that occur periodically throughout the calendar year, binding the devotees on a seasonal, continuing basis. Each major sport functions in quite the same way, culminating in the pinnacle of the tradition, the crowning of its national champion. The result is clear: from a combination of seasonal and personal ritual processes, sport activity provides a continual stream of resacralization and meaning for our everyday world, just as traditional religion offers.

No religious tradition would be complete or functional without a strong legendary basis to underline and accompany the historical data of the faith. It is the legends that reveal an individual in his or her depth and fullness. It is the legends that provide a three-dimensional glimpse of the person in question, generally manifesting all the characteristics considered exemplary in the particular tradition in question. It is the legends that give us a perspective rarely captured by the historical accounts. Thus, the legends offer the faithful what the history books cannot: a leader to emulate, to model themselves after, and, in some cases, to worship. Sport legends are no less imposing and function in just the same way. To be sure, even in modern times, where media gadgets, journalistic morgues, and computer banks offer instant access to accurate historical data, this is not the stuff of which sport legends are made. Sport legend captures the essence of the sporting figure, reporting little-known bits and pieces of the individual that often defy publication or widespread dissemination. It really doesn't matter whether the specific legendary figure is Babe Ruth, Mickey Mantle, Red Grange, Wilt Chamberlain, Roger Bannister, Babe Didrikson Zaharias, or numerous others. What does matter is that each provides for his or her respective sport an archetypal model that holds true and grows for future generations. As for some of the rather unsavory characteristics, one need only be reminded of similar religious circumstances in the papal line or in the lineage of the Dalai Lama in Tibetan Buddhism.

In *How We Play the Game*, Richard Lipsky tells us (of baseball), "The game takes place in an atmosphere of piety. In many ways the ballplayers themselves can be seen as priests who represent us in a liturgy (game) that is part of a sacred tradition." Lipsky's comment reveals that far too little has been said about the role of the player in sport religion. In other words, we need to reflect on the actors in sport religion. It would be incorrect, though, to suggest that it is only the actual players who fulfill the role of religious participants in sport. We must include the coaches and officials as well, in their role as functionaries in the religious process. They are not untrained, either. Sport, no doubt, has its own seminaries and divinity schools in the various minor leagues and training camps that school the participants in all aspects of the tradition, from theology to ritual. The spectators, as video viewers, radio listeners, or game-going die-hards, form the congregation of sport religion. Their attendance is not required for all religious observances, but they do attend at specified times to share in religious rites. And they bear the religious symbols of their faith: the pennants, emblems, hats, coats, gloves, and whatever other objects the media geniuses can promote to signify the glory of sport in general and the home team in particular. The sport symbol may not be the cross, rosary, or mezuzah, but it is no less valuable to the owner, and likely considered to be just as powerful as its traditional counterpart, or more so.

It is necessary to note here that one would be *incorrect in assuming that all sport is religion*. In fact, quite the opposite is true. Utilizing a definition of religion as "a means of ultimate transformation," the whole issue of sport as religion turns on the premise that sport is a religion only insofar as it brings its adherents to an experience of ultimate reality, radically alters their lives as a result of the experience of ultimacy, and then channels their positive gains back into society in a generally viable and useful fashion. This is not so simple as it sounds. In traditional religion, not everyone gets religious experience. That is to say, not everyone experiences God (or some other symbol for the ultimate), irrespective of how pious or devout in worship. Nor is the experience of the ultimate an occasion that repeats itself each time the worshiper attends church or synagogue. For the athlete, religious experience is not simply having a good time, an important win, or being "turned inward" on a run or in a workout. No less than in traditional religion, sport religion is actualized only when an aspirant genuinely experiences that which is considered to be ultimate. And it is no less awe-inspiring. Yet there is no so-called sport religion for the athlete who attains ultimate reality through sport as a means of worship or religious practice in traditional religion. For sport to be considered a religion, it must quite self-consciously attempt to be just that. It must present all the rituals, practices, holidays, myths, legends, shrines, and so forth that all traditional religions provide. The results of ultimate transformation through sport must be socially functional in a way that is consistent with sport and the ethical imperative that derives from its practice.

If the potential for experiencing ultimate reality is so readily available in sport, why is it that athletes have so far been relatively silent in affirming their personal religious encounters? There are two likely answers here. First, I think that athletes, for the most part, simply do not have the equipment to speak comfortably and intelligently about religion *or* sport. One hopes, however, that as people actively involved in sport gain some real measure of intellectual facility in these areas, they will be able to recount numerous occasions in which the case for religious experience in sport is made thoroughly and believably. In other words, we are trying to provide those engaged in all aspects of sport with a new way of looking at themselves and their religious world. The second reason for the relative silence in the sporting world is that athletes are simply afraid of being held up to public ridicule. Many in our culture will find the suggestion that sport has become a genuine and sacred religious tradition to be utterly blasphemous. For the average citizen, the person professing sport religion becomes the object of scorn and derision, but for the professional athlete, the repercussions are worse still. There are endorsements and public appearances to be lost, all of which quickly translates into loss of revenue, and we should not overlook the fact that professional sport is big business. It is both sad and unfortunate that when dollars are at stake, integrity all too often becomes an unprofitable luxury.

There are other problems in sport religion. Just who is it that gets religious experience in sport? Curiously, these experiences seem not to be specific to the athlete-participant, the specialist. Similar responses can be evoked from coaches, officials, and, not so surprisingly, spectators (present or otherwise). After all, each of the above advocates does participate in his or her own way. This latter point is particularly important, I think, because it indicates that *no special athletic talent is required in the quest for salvation in sport.* What is self-evident here, then, is that *religious experience in sport is open to anyone, at any time, anywhere*—just as it is in traditional religion. Consequently, religious experience in sport is no more confined to the participants on the playing field than is traditional experience confined to the priest, minister, or rabbi. Also problematic is the theology of sport religion. A most obvious concern is who this god of sport might be. Is it the God of ancient Israel? Is it consistent with the Trinitarian notion of Christianity? Does sport present us with a primitive polytheism in which we find a god of running, one of tennis, and still another of swimming? Is there some arena in which the pantheon of sport deities might gather? What is the gender of the sport god(s)? How much power and might is wielded? What is important in this rather lighthearted approach is the understanding that sport theology must face the same questions as traditional religious theology, and this is no simple dilemma. Conversations I have had with athletes indicate support for *each* of the above positions, including god as female with little, medium, or great powers. Still another complicating factor is that for some participants, ultimacy is defined in nontheistic terms, usually as a oneness with nature, union with an impersonal absolute.

Earlier, I suggested that if sport is to be considered a religion in the proper sense of that word, it must, in addition to bringing its followers to an experience of ultimacy, radically alter their lives and channel that positive change back into society in a useful way. Does the sport experience change lives? One need only look at the manner in which athletes persevere in increasing their training, sometimes at the expense of all else, and their religious zeal after experiencing the supremacy of union with the Absolute. Is the smile and fulfillment of the Monday-morning quarterback to be doubted when some inordinately significant ''Eureka'' occurred to him while watching Walter Payton's uncanny ability to succeed despite the ineptitude of the Bears' offensive line? The changes are far too diverse and numerous to document here, but they do occur—and with startling regularity. And as a result, everything changes: attitudes, values, frames of reference, interpersonal relationships, and social involvements. We have tacitly avoided any mention of social ethics to this point. There is no question that some sport figures today have been less than exemplary in their conduct. To be sure, sport religion faces the same series of ethical difficulties as traditional religion. The presumption is that as one's religious faith matures, so does one's ethical behavior. It is no wonder, then, that so many religious groups of all denominations emphasize charitable acts and social involvement in good works for their members. In addition, the leaders of the congregation are expected to be especially consummate in their behavior. Sport religion is no less responsive to social needs in requiring devout participation by its advocates. Well, it's no wonder. Social concern, charitable acts, and personal conduct are all founded on discipline, and it is precisely here that the follower of sport religion excels. It doesn't matter whether this discipline is expressed by a daily twelve-mile run or three hours glued to ESPN. It can be corralled and marshaled for good causes, both personal and collective.

A final problem must be noted. Is it possible to maintain multilateral religious affiliations? Can the proponent of sport religion also retain standing within his or her traditional religious affiliation? Ostensibly not! When one declares that one adheres to sport as a formal religious tradition, this implies a *constant pursuit* that is also the *most important pursuit* and a *religious pursuit*. If such individuals were to then state that they are also Jews or Protestants (or Catholics or whatever), they would be referring to their *cultural heritage only*, to the complex series of factors that are essentially ethnic and locational rather than religious.

What it all boils down to is this: if sport can bring its advocates to an experience of the ultimate, and this (pursuit and) experience is expressed through a formal series of public and private rituals requiring a symbolic language and space deemed sacred by its worshipers, then it is both proper and necessary to call sport itself a religion. It is also reasonable to consider sport the newest and fastest-growing religion, far outdistancing whatever is in second place.

Sport Is Not a Religion

Joan M. Chandler

Precisely when sport, carried on as an end in itself rather than being part of a religious ritual, was first described as "religion," I do not know. Nevertheless, I believe this topic to be of vital importance, because although we contrive to make loose connections between sport and religion, we cannot understand either, much less examine the nature of the economic and social power both institutions wield in 20th-century America.

First, let us be clear why sport has been confused with religion. Sport uses what Novak has called "sacred space" and "sacred time"[1]; like the public rituals of many religions, sports rituals are often cyclic, culminating in specific ceremonies tied to calendrical rhythms. Its initiates, its priests, endure long and arduous training, often at great physical cost, before participating in major public rituals. Sport's laypersons, the fans, organize their leisure around these festivals, often giving more psychic energy to their devotions than to their work and donating a considerable portion of their income to sport coffers.[2] Charles Prebish even believes that "for many, sport religion has become a more appropriate expression of personal religiosity than Christianity, Judaism, or any of the traditional religions."[3] This kind of thinking, however, does a disservice to both sport and religion.

The fundamental error I want to address resides in assuming that one can understand the nature of any complex phenomenon by examining its observable characteristics. Although it is true that there are outward and visible signs of inward and spiritual grace, it is also true that the grace has a separate existence from its outward manifestations. What we have to decide is not whether sport shares many of the typical, even transcendent attributes of religion, but whether people who would consider themselves religious and people who are sports fans expect the object of their devotions to meet the same needs. We have to look not from the outside *in*, but from the inside *out*; and, when we do that, I suggest that we discover sport and religion to be fundamentally different phenomena.

Let me add one parenthetical note. The parallels that have been drawn between sport and religion can equally well be drawn between opera and religion, theatre and religion, and indeed between any institutionalized activity and a devoted audience watching and/or interacting with trained participants. Sport is not unique in this regard. And if some philosophers want to stretch the term "religion" to cover all such activities, they must recognize that by so doing they have robbed the word "religion" of the actual meaning it possesses for its practitioners.

What do religious people believe their religion is for? Answers to this question, put to a random sample of participants in any religious ritual, would doubtless produce an interesting array of possibilities. If, however, we examine the precepts and practice of two particular religions, chosen because they are very different from each other, we shall find that both provide detailed explanations of the origin and purpose of the world, clear statements about questions of ultimate concern (what many would call "the supernatural"), and continuing attempts to explain and cope with the existence of pain. Let us then examine in more detail these functions of the Christian and Navajo religions.

The Christian religion is based on written sources, is institutionalized, and is interwoven with the political power structure in the United States.[4] The Navajo religion is oral, is individual, and is not a factor in whatever political activity Navajos engage in, except insofar as it tempers every Navajo's perception of the world.[5] The Christian religion is monotheistic and is based on man's need of redemption; Navajo religion is polytheistic and based on the conception of a harmonious universe. Much of Christian ceremonial is concerned with worship; much of Navajo ceremonial is concerned with seeking health. In short, these two manifestations of man's concern with the "numinous"[6] could scarcely be more apparently different; yet they both deal with the same fundamental questions.

Both the Christian and Navajo religions provide an account of man's origin. Although chanters differ in the details of their version of the origin myth,[7] as Reichard puts it, "A well-grounded Navajo chanter feels an obligation to show his knowledge of the emergence as impelling as knowledge of the Bible is to a minister. . . ."[8] For Christians and Navajos, the creation of the world and of its inhabitants was no accident. Navajos are much less certain than Christians about what happens to them after they die, but orthodox Navajos fear the dead precisely because life does not end when the body ceases to function. Both religions, then, grapple with the questions every human being has asked: "Where did I come from?" and "Where am I going to?"

For the purposes of this paper, it does not matter whether any of us finds the Christian or Navajo answers to those questions convincing. The point is that sport per se neither raises such questions nor answers them. It has been argued that all professional players suffer a "little death" when they lose a game or even lose their identity as persons when they retire.[9] Adjustment to loss of fame, prowess, and perhaps fortune must obviously be extremely painful, especially when it happens while one is, by other than sporting standards, still young. But the title of Darryl Stingley's autobiography is *Happy to be Alive*.[10] Indeed, he credits his religion with having helped him come to terms with a situation that most of us could not bear to contemplate. Sport, like so many other human activities, may give us some hints, some paradigms of the unique events of birth and death; it cannot attempt to explain them. That is the function of religion.

Similarly, Christians and Navajos relate their earthly life to questions of ultimate concern. We did not invent the world in which we have to live. For Christians, people inhabit a fallen universe, which must be redeemed by its creator; each human being is a sinner. For the Navajo, humankind was designed to live as part of a harmonious universe; when they fail, wittingly or unwittingly, appropriate ceremonies must be performed to restore that harmony. For both Christians and Navajos, actions have consequences; and no human agency can so manipulate the laws of the universe that those consequences do not occur. We are not talking here about the threadbare analogy of the player who must adhere to the rules of the game; for in religion not only are rule violations always noticed, but the very rules themselves are constructed by entities other than human beings. These rules may of course be ignored, added to, or reinterpreted by humans. If, in so doing, humans stretch the rules to breaking point, other-than-human retribution is regarded as inevitable.

Christians and Navajos specifically address the problems of pain and disease. C.S. Lewis notwithstanding,[11] Christians have traditionally relied on Job's affirmation of faith, "Though he slay me, yet will I trust in him."[12] Navajos take the view that the holy ones are obligated to bring their powers to bear if the correct ceremonies are correctly performed. Both Christians and Navajos, however, regard human suffering on an individual or larger scale as an apparent or real anomaly. For both Christians and Navajos, physical or psychological "dis-ease" may be the individual's fault, but it may equally result from someone else's machinations or from a cause that cannot presently be determined. But both the Christian and Navajo religions single out a sick or dying person for special attention. The resources of the community are brought to bear, if not to cure, then to console, and to set the illness or death in the context of the ultimate worth and destiny of each individual.

Pain figures prominently in sport. Serious players are urged to push themselves beyond the pain threshold in training and to play on regardless of pain. To have played so hard that one aches from head to foot after a game is a sign of having done the job well.[13] Injury is anticipated; sports such as boxing may even be so constructed to make pain inevitable. But the last thing any player wants to do is to think about the nature of the pain; it is there, it is a fact of life, it is to be dealt with if possible and ignored if not. This is because pain comes from the real world; that is, the world not constructed by human beings. Pain in sport may therefore be investigated, treated, or ignored, but the fact of its existence is not questioned. Further, when pain becomes intolerable and the player is removed from the game, that player ceases to exist. There are no rituals to protect a player from pain, ease the symptoms, or soften the anguish of removal from the contest. The reason for this is clear; once a player ceases to contribute, his *raison d'être* is gone. Rituals for nonpersons do not exist.

These three functions of religion, then, illuminate the fundamental difference between sport and religion. Whether we personally view religion as resulting from divine revelation or from human aspirations and anxieties does not matter; what is important is that religions seek to explain the relationship between human beings and their circumstances. This explanation may be explicit, or it may be implicit, as in the Bead Chant of the Navajo.[14] In contrast, whatever emotions may be elicited by a sporting event, that event does not seek to explain anything. While sport may epitomize or even reinforce a set of values peculiar to a class, a culture, or both, those values are not grounded in sport itself but derive from the sociocultural context within which sport is played.

The primary concerns of religion and sport are clearly illustrated by their rituals.[15] Neither Christians nor Navajos are spectators, even when the rituals they attend provide them with little overt participation. As Firth puts it, "sacramental rites have as their essential feature some change in the persons performing or attending the ritual."[16] Grace is conferred on Christians; Navajos are brought back into harmony with the universe. In both cases, powers external to the practitioners themselves are invoked.

In sporting rituals, no such change in players or spectators is required or expected. Many rituals in sport are designed simply to assert superiority. Regular-season team games are played at home or away; one team is thus impinging on another's territory. In American college football games, from which the present professional game derived, the marching band, the pregame show, the cheerleading, the mascot, are all designed to intimidate. As a graduate from the University of Houston noted bitterly of a University of Texas game, after enduring the band, the cannon, Bevo, and "The Eyes of Texas," "I'm a Texan as much as anybody in this place—why do they make me feel like I'm from New Jersey?"[17]

These rituals of superiority are worldwide. Trobriand Island cricketers have a carefully choreographed and executed series of entry and exit dances that count as much as the actual play to establish a village's reputation. During a single season, Morris collected more than 60 insulting chants, many of them obscene, sung spontaneously by the fans at one British club's professional games. Roared from the stands, such chants are aimed at undermining the opposing team's poise, while asserting the home team's pride of place and dominance.[18]

These rituals of dominance simply underscore the sporting competitor's objective: to win. The amateur may pay some attention to process; the professional is concerned with result and, therefore, with the letter rather than the spirit of the law. Winners are those who outscore their opponents according to whatever arbitrary scoring system their particular event uses; the scoring system, and the rules governing play that leads to scores, can be changed by human beings at will.

For Christians and Navajos, their opponents are unseen, malevolent, powerful beings. The strength to fight such opponents does not derive wholly from the human individuals involved, although they may be expected to "put on the whole armour of God"[19] or take part in a ceremony such as the Enemy Way. The extent to which changes can be made in the public and private rituals Christians and Navajos use to battle their unseen enemies is determined by conformity both to doctrine and tradition; changes cannot be made arbitrarily, if the rituals are to retain their purported power.

It is one thing, then, to use the word "religion" metaphorically, to illuminate certain facets of the sporting experience; it is quite another to take the metaphor literally. And to insist on the distinction between sport and religion goes beyond the desire for mere logical tidiness. If, for instance, we regard sport as a commercial enterprise, it can properly be regulated by the state. If sport is to be regarded in some sense as a religion, the state is on much shakier ground, for "Congress shall make no law respecting an establishment of religion, or prohibiting the free exercise thereof" (First Amendment to the U.S. Constitution). Fortunately, lawmakers have not yet decided to grant sports franchises tax-exempt status. Secondly, if sport is to be regarded as a "natural religion" it cannot also be regarded as entertainment. Rader's disgust with the television industry's handling of sport[20] clearly springs from his belief that sport has a significance that goes beyond the canons of entertainment. Yet the introduction of a designated hitter divided baseball fans no more than the trend toward singing opera in translation has outraged some opera aficionados. One does not have to be religious to dislike change.

More importantly, if sport is to be regarded as a religion, attacks upon its practices must be regarded as attacks upon faith, not simply as attacks upon entrenched power bases. Ross Perot, chairman of a committee organized by Texas Governor Mark White, to reform Texas public schools, stamped on the toes of the state's most powerful lobbies when he observed that school sports activities were taking too much time from academic pursuits. School boards, superintendents, coaches, and alumni united to tell Perot that sport formed character, kept students in school, cemented communities, instilled values, and generally was the state's salvation. The supporters of athletic programs could produce no evidence for their assertions; their views were indeed based on faith. Undeterred, Perot continued to attack what he perceived to be not a religious institution, but a power base.

As I have pointed out, the Christian and Navajo religions could scarcely be more different. Yet both fulfill a religion's unique function, which is that of dealing with questions of ultimate meaning. Sport has nothing whatever to do with such questions. While sport may provide us with examples of belief, ritual, sacrifice, and transcendence, all of them take place in a context designed wittingly and specifically by human beings, for the delight of human beings. Within that context, "chance," "luck," or "the fates" may be influential; players or fans may attempt to use magic to propitiate their gods. But sport per se cannot tell us where we came from, where we are going, nor how we are to behave while here; sport exists to entertain and engage us, not to disturb us with questions about our destiny. That is the uncomfortable prerogative of religion.

Notes

1. Novak, Michael, *The Joy of Sports* (New York: Basic Books, 1976). Novak's argument breaks down when it is examined; only in recent times have churches been set aside exclusively for worship services, and the Amish still worship at home. Indeed, McAllester argues that the Navajo hogan itself is a sacred place, its everyday attributes caught up in and dignified by its symbolic purpose.

[McAllester, David, *Hogans: Navajo Houses and House Songs* (Middletown, CT: Wesleyan University Press, 1980].

2. Sport and religion may also both provoke bloodshed, although neither "ought" to do so. Religious wars are among those most bitterly fought; sport fans the world over cause rioting and destruction, whether their teams win or lose, while many players have injured opponents on the field by means that would have earned them jail terms off it.

3. Prebish, Charles, " 'Heavenly Father, Divine Goalie': Sport and Religion," *The Antioch Review*, Summer 1984, Vol. 42, No. 3, pp. 306-318.

4. In what follows, I have made no attempt specifically to footnote every statement made about the Christian religion, because most represent a distillation rather than being derived from one specific source. Apart from the Bible, all the points I have made can be confirmed by reading such authors as Augustine, *City of God* (begun in 413, many editions); Karl Barth, *Dogmatics in Outline* (New York: Harper and Row, 1959); John H. Hick, *Philosophy of Religion* (Englewood Cliffs, NJ: Prentice Hall, 2nd ed., 1973), p. 3; C.S. Lewis, *Mere Christianity* (New York: Macmillan, rev. ed., 1960).

5. Statements about the Navajo religion are based chiefly but not exclusively on Father Berard Hailey, *Origin Legend of the Navajo Enemy Way* (Yale University *Publications in Anthropology* No. 17, New Haven, CT: Yale University Press, 1928); Aileen O'Bryan, *The Diné: Origin Myths of the Navaho Indians* (Washington, DC: Government Printing Office, 1956); Gladys Reichard, *Navajo Religion*, 2 vols. (New York: Pantheon Books, 1950); Katherine Spencer, *Navaho Chantway Myths* (Memoirs of the American Folklore Society, XLVIII, Philadelphia: American Folklore Society, 1957); Ruth Underhill, *Red Man's Religion* (Chicago: University of Chicago Press, 1965).

6. Otto, Rudolf, *The Idea of the Holy* (Oxford: Oxford University Press, 1923).

7. Chandler, Joan, "Navajo Mythmakers," *University of Texas Folklore Annual*, 1969, No. 1, pp. 2-27.

8. Reichard, Gladys, "Individualism and Mythological Style," *Journal of American Folklore*, 1944, Vol. XVII, p. 20.

9. The same could be said of anyone who is fired, or retires from any job.

10. Stingley, Darryl, and Mark Mulvoy, *Happy to be Alive* (New York: Beaufort Books, 1983).

11. Lewis, C.S., *The Problem of Pain* (New York: Macmillan Paperback, 1962).

12. Job 12:15.

13. *Vide* the scene in the film "North Dallas Forty" when battered players are sitting in the tub after the game, and one says to another of their agony, "Doesn't it feel great!"

14. Reichard, Gladys, *Navajo Medicine Man Sandpaintings* (New York: Dover, 1977, 1st ed., 1939).

15. There is no satisfactory definition of the word "ritual." As Skorupski puts it, "What use does a term have which brings together a man shaking hands, a man praying to his god, a man refusing to walk under a ladder, a man clapping at the end of a concert, a man placing medicine on his crops? None at all. These actions have no interesting characteristics in common." [Skorupski, John, *Symbol and Theory: A Philosophical Study of Theories of Religion in Social Anthropology* (Cambridge: Cambridge University Press, 1976), p. 171]. For the purposes of this paper, I am using Bocock's definition: "Ritual is the symbolic use of bodily movement and gesture in a social situation to express and articulate meaning" [Bocock, Robert, *Ritual in Industrial Society: A Sociological Analysis of Ritualism in Modern England* (London: Allen and Unwin, 1974), p. 37].

16. Firth, Raymond W., *Elements of Social Organization* (London: Greenwood, 1971), p. 223.

17. Inserra, Tony, "More Than A Game" (unpublished paper). See also Winningham, Geoff, et al., *Rites of Fall: High School Football in Texas* (Austin: University of Texas Press, 1979), p. 9.

18. Trobriand Cricket: An Ingenious Response to Colonialism (film); Morris, Desmond, *The Soccer Tribe* (London: Jonathan Cape, 1981), p. 311.

19. Ephesians 6:11. Paul's reference to running "the race that is set before us" (Hebrews 12:2), sporting metaphor that it is, refers to a life course chosen by human beings but not organized by them.

20. Rader, Benjamin, *In Its Own Image: How Television Has Transformed Sports* (New York: Free Press, 1984).

Needless to say, thrilled as I was to go to Boston with the team, I wasn't prepared to open myself up to football as a semi-religious experience. But, hate me for saying it if you will, the B.C. game turned out to be something like a semi-religious experience. Afterwards I felt like an agnostic who has attended Mass: and after the service finds himself reciting the Creed.

The Reverend Robert Griffin

Today, twenty-one years later, I am married, graduated from seminary, and the pastor of a small church. But although I have many other "responsible" concerns, I still get emotionally involved in professional athletic contests. Clammy palms, a racing heart, and feelings ranging from anger to euphoric elation accompany a close game between Philadelphia and an arch rival.

The Reverend Dave Greiser

In searching for the 'sounds' of sport one quickly hears the roar of the crowd, the crack of the bat and the thundering of racing feet. But if one listens a little harder and a little longer, one comes to hear silence. There is a silence within the performer, in the tenseness of the crowd, in the fear of the hunter and in the beauty of the ski slopes.

Howard Slusher

I do not believe human beings have played games or sports from the beginning merely to summon or to please or to appease the gods . . . I believe we have played games, and watched games, to imitate the gods, to become godlike in our worship of each other and, through those moments of transmutation, to know for an instant what the gods know.

A. Bartlett Giamatti

Part II
Sport as Religious Experience

Religious experience is a response to what is perceived as ultimate reality.

Joachim Wach

In a perceptive little book on the relationship between sports and the spiritual life, Paulist priest Thomas Ryan reflects on a special experience that came to him while traversing a ski slope in the Canadian Rockies:

On one occasion, I took a lift up to the very peak and crossed over the top, gliding down into a back bowl. Within seconds I discovered myself completely

63

alone in a vast expanse of space, with the jagged peaks towering above me, no other skier in sight and not a sound to be heard. I stood transfixed for a long while. The Scriptures use the word "theophany" for such moments when the divine is experienced breaking through and transfiguring natural events with a sense of the sacred. When I finally pushed off with my poles, I did so slowly and deliberately, with a sense of one touched by the Holy and visited with awe. Even now, months later, I can recall that experience and those feelings with astonishing clarity. I have no other word for it than mystical—a level of experience to which I am convinced we all are called. It is primarily a question of refining our inner and outer senses to the presence of the Holy, daily in our midst. (1986, p. 168)

Ryan's account describes a form of religious experience, an intense, personal feeling of being in the presence of the supernatural or holy. Religious experiences constitute what sociologist Peter Berger (1979) calls ruptures in the "paramount reality" of everyday life: alien zones, enclaves, or holes within it that produce "a never-to-be-denied-again sense of reality" for those who experience them (p. 32). They can range from vague mystical encounters quickly forgotten to severe jolts like that described by Ryan, where the memory of the event remains long after the individual has returned to the world of ordinary, everyday life.

Though unique, religious experiences are not uncommon. A national poll conducted in 1988 disclosed that one American in three has had " a particularly powerful religious insight or awakening" (Gallup & Castelli, 1989). Although those who attend church regularly or say that "religion is very important in their lives" are most likely to report having them (40 percent), religious experiences also occur among 25 percent of those who do not attend church and do not consider religion very important (Gallup & Castelli, 1989). Similar findings have been reported by Thomas and Cooper (1980) (34 percent) and Greeley (1974) (35 percent) when respondents were asked, "Have you ever felt as though you were close to a powerful, spiritual force that seemed to lift you out of yourself?"

We most commonly associate religious experiences with formal liturgies and religious rituals (e.g., singing, listening to religious music, reciting creeds, praying, meditating), or with deliberate meditation exercises designed deliberately to evoke subjective religious states. But as Ryan's account demonstrates, religious experiences sometimes occur spontaneously, and are not always confined to the cathedral or the altar. When such experiences are reported in connection with activities that have no apparent intrinsic religious status, questions invariably surface about their validity as religious (as opposed to merely psychological or physiological) phenomena. Implicitly or explicitly all of the articles in this section revolve around the general question of the validity of religious experiences individuals have reported during sport activities.

At the outset it should be recognized that because religious experiences are very private events, not open to social confirmation, absolute validation of their occurrence is impossible. The absolute conviction of their authenticity by subjects who report them may be the most forceful piece of evidence to support their reality. Of course, philosophers can mount convincing arguments as to their unreliability as a source of knowledge (O'Hear, 1984), but it is important to recognize that ultimately the nonempirical nature of these events precludes any resolution that will satisfy both the skeptic and the individual who claims to have experienced them.

Although they tend to be associated with the emotional or expressive side of religion, religious experiences have a reciprocal relationship with religion's more rational dimensions. On one hand they inform, confirm, and shape religious beliefs and traditions that, though vitally important, are reflections about original religious experiences, usually those reported by ancient authorities. Religious traditions sustain and mediate these experiences of another reality to those who never before had it, as well as to those who once had it but are in danger of forgetting it. As Berger so cogently put it "every [religious] tradition is a 'collective memory' in which the reality of another world broke into the paramount reality of everyday life" (1979, p. 45).

On the other hand religious traditions may affect interpretations of these paranormal experiences. One's religious or nonreligious background forms part of a sociohistorical context through which these experiences are filtered and inevitably shaped. In fact, whether or not an encounter is regarded as a *religious* experience or some other type of mysticism often is determined wholly by the subject's attribution (Proudfoot, 1985). For example, Ryan's expressly Catholic orientation (not to mention his obvious fondness for skiing) may have flavored his interpretation of his experience on the slopes. Would a Buddhist or a Baptist or an atheist have attached the same interpretation? Probably not, but in the final analysis one can't really know.

Personal perspectives on religion may also affect how one interprets the religious experiences reported by others. Atheists, for example, may consider Ryan's account to be nothing more than random biological activity. Adherents of a nonsupernatural religion may relate it to their own immanent conceptions of the cosmic order. Those within the Judeo-Christian tradition probably would be more willing to accept Ryan's account, but even here some would view it as too impersonal an encounter to have authentic spiritual significance. These observations are not intended to diminish the importance or validity of Ryan's experience, nor to suggest that a divine being is powerless to make itself known to humans. It is only to underscore the impossibility of going much beyond the primary data of such experiences, namely the descriptions of the experiences provided by the subjects themselves.

The Variety of Religious Experiences

As was seen in Part I, religion has various definitions, ranging from Streng's (1969) liberal formulation ("a means of ultimate transformation") to Stark and Bainbridge's (1985) more narrow definition ("some conception of a supernatural being, world, or force, and the notion that the supernatural is active, [and] that events and conditions here on earth are influenced by the supernatural," p. 5). Between these two poles lies an expansive territory for defining religious experience, from what subjects might describe as "an encounter between themselves and some supernatural consciousness" (Stark, 1965, p. 98) at one end, to the vague experience of having sensed "ultimate reality" at the other. If ultimate reality is broadly construed to mean "words, actions, social relations, and states of consciousness," then religious experience can be taken to mean virtually any aspect of human life that involves direct apprehension of quasi-sensible realities (Streng, Lloyd, & Allen, 1973, p. 7). This opens the door to a broad array of altered states of consciousness that proponents of a narrow (supernatural) definition would hesitate to acknowledge as authentic religious experience.

For example, Abraham Maslow (1968), the central figure in the humanistic psychology movement, popularized the term *peak experiences* to designate moments of "highest happiness and fulfillment" when individuals entertain feelings of unity, inner peace, wholeness of being, and loss of fears and inhibitions. Although they seem to be qualitatively different from Ryan's peak experiences, they share the same sense of rupturing in the ordinary reality, and, like traditional religious experiences, are relatively short in duration and are evoked spontaneously rather than deliberately. Sport psychologist Kenneth Ravizza (1977, 1984) catalogued the peak experiences reported by athletes into three types: those in which perceptions of time, space, and the quality of the task are altered; those where the subject senses "the perfect moment" and is freed from fear of injury or error; and a "transcendence of self," involving a surrender to the experience and a blending of self with movements, one's own as well as those of one's teammates.

A similar form of altered consciousness is what psychologist Mihaly Csikszentmihalyi (1975) calls flow experience, a subjective state that frequently accompanies activities humans find intrinsically rewarding. Csikszentmihalyi's concept of flow comes very close to Maslow's peak experience: Subjects report a merging of actions and awareness, a centering of attention, and a heightened sense of control of their own actions and the external environment. Flow experiences have been reported in many kinds of human activities but seem especially common in play, which Csikszentmihalyi (1975) calls "the flow experience par excellence." Certain types of sport activities seem to be especially fertile contexts for engendering these types of mental events. Csikszentmihalyi acknowledged that feelings very similar to flow have been reported in connection with ritual (Turner, 1969), meditation (Eliade, 1969), and other forms of religious experience (Laski, 1962).

In *The Psychic Side of Sports*, Murphy and White (1978) classified the altered states of consciousness reported by athletes into 11 categories: acute well-being; peace, calm, stillness; detachment; freedom, floating, flying, weightlessness; ecstasy; power and control; being in the present; instinctive action and surrender; mystery and awe; feelings of immortality; and unity. Their analysis convinced them that "sport has enormous power to sweep us beyond the ordinary sense of self, to evoke capacities that generally have been regarded as mystical, occult, or religious" (p. 5). Not all sports, however, were found to offer the same potential for these experiences. High-risk sports such as mountain climbing and long voyages at sea or sports involving extended periods of discomfort such as long-distance running were much more likely to be associated with vivid types of spiritual experiences than were low-risk games such as racquetball or tennis. The euphoric sensation that often accompanies extended periods of running, commonly referred to as *runner's high*, has been observed and reported by a large number of runners. Psychologist Michael Sachs has described it as "a heightened sense of well being, enhanced appreciation of nature, and transcendence of barriers of time and space," and "a distinct sense of affect such as increased strength, power and gracefulness" (1984, p. 438). In a moving personal testimony to the power of such moments, runner Mike Spino talks of being overwhelmed to the point where he sat on the edge of the road crying tears of joy "for a vague feeling of temporalness, and a knowledge of the impossibility of giving this experience to anyone" (Scott, 1971, p. 225).

Can these altered states of consciousness legitimately be described as examples of religious experience or are they some other phenomena? While not all would describe them as religious, most would consider them examples of mystical experiences, a broad category that includes but is not limited to authentic religious experience. In his classic, *The Varieties of Religious Experience*, William James (1961) called mystical experiences "the root and center of personal religious experience" and ascribed four characteristics to them: ineffability—the feeling that the experience is inexpressible and incapable of verbal description; noesis—a feeling that the event imparts a state of knowledge or restructures an individual's outlook; transiency—the feelings are not maintained indefinitely; and passivity—a feeling of being acted upon by an outside force. These characteristics were expanded by W.T. Stace (1960) to include loss of sense of self, perception of unity of all things, subjective experience of the objective environment, transcendence of time and space, feelings of bliss, and " a religious quality," although Stace's criteria have not been corroborated in large scale surveys of people who report having had mystical encounters (Thomas & Cooper, 1980).

Mysticism has a rich tradition in many mainline supernaturally referenced religions, including Christianity (Merton, 1970) but mystical events do not always focus on an objective or transcendent deity, nor are they always interpreted by the individuals who experience them as being in any sense religious (Hood, 1975). Thus, it has not always been easy to draw lines separating natural mysticism from spiritual mysticism. James noted that mystical experiences can be "more or less divine," "more or less religious," and that "the boundaries are always misty, and it is everywhere a question of amount and degree" (1961, p. 39).

Contrast, for example, Mike Spino's (Scott, 1971) account of runner's high with remarks by the late Flo Hyman, generally regarded as the best woman volleyball player to have played the game: "When it all works well it feels like heaven. You feel like you're playing a song" ("Scorecard," 1986, p. 21). And contrast both of these with basketball player Patsy Neal's (1972) description of a dream she had the night before she won the AAU Free Throw Championship. In the dream she was shooting free throws and "each time the ball fell through the goal, the net would change to the image of Christ" (p. 168). In this period of freedom, calmness, and peace "the sensation was that of transcending *everything*. It seems almost profane to try to describe the feeling because words are so very inadequate" (p. 168). Although she won the event, Neal claims not to have cared nearly as much about winning as she cared about what she had experienced. But she was never able to duplicate the feeling no matter how hard she tried. Her experience led her to assert, "I know there are things beyond our power to understand. I know God exists, regardless of the name we give Him, or the way we describe the way He works" (1972, pp. 168-169).

Whereas Spino's account seems unrelated to any specific religious context, and Hyman's only hints at an encounter than might be described as religious, Neal's is an explicitly religious interpretation. All three are truly mystical in character, but not all seem to be religious experiences. It appears then that, as Berger notes, mysticism "intersects with but is not to be equated with the experience of the sacred" (1979, p. 42).

Ways of Classifying Religious Experiences

There is a need, then, to try to distinguish the broader class of mystical experiences from religious experiences and, as will be seen, this is not easily done. Two of the most renowned researchers on religion, Charles Glock and Rodney Stark (1965, p. 10), define religious experience as an encounter between an individual and "some supernatural consciousness." The definition deliberately excludes parapsychological phenomena and mystical experiences that lack a supernatural referent. Using this definition, they classified religious experiences according to the frequency with which they are reported in the general population. The most frequently occurring experience is what they referred to as the *confirming experience*, an awareness that one is confronted with another mysterious, often holy entity. William James (1961) called it "the something there" experience. The confirming experience usually evokes a sense of awe and reverence, not unlike those attitudes stimulated during formal worship.

The next most commonly occurring religious experience is what Glock and Stark (1965) called the *responsive experience* in which individuals not only sense the presence of a transcendent power or being but also claim to be acknowledged by it. Generally, such acknowledgment takes the form of some salvational or miraculous action. The third type of experience is the *ecstatic experience* (from *ekstasis*, "standing outside of"), an effervescent and intoxicating experience in which individuals sense that they are standing outside the ordinary world. The least common form of religious experience is what Glock and Stark labeled the *revelational experience*, in which individuals claim to share the mind of the divine and may seek to confirm or alter religious practice. Such experiences, when encountered by particularly charismatic personalities, may lead to the revision of existing or establishment of new religious movements.

Another way of classifying religious experiences is to order them according to the object or referent of the experience, the emotional response of the subject, and the type of effects produced after the religious experience has ended.

Object of the Experience

Usually the object of religious experience is regarded as some conception of "the holy" or "the sacred." In the traditions of Judaism, Christianity, or other transcendental religions, the holy or sacred is viewed as being set apart from ordinary life. In broader religious schemes it may be an impersonal power accessible in ordinary life. In polytheistic religions it may assume many forms. In struggling to narrow the concept of the divine, which he took to be the object of religious experiences, James ultimately settled for defining it in terms of the emotional responses it evokes in the individual: "only such reality as the individual feels impelled to respond to solemnly and gravely, and neither by curse or jest" (1961, p. 48). In his pivotal work on religious experience, *The Idea of the Holy*, German theologian Rudolf Otto described the holy as the *mysterium tremendum et fascinans* (the awe-inspiring and fascinating mystery), the "wholly other," the ultimate reality, the "ground of man's existence, the context in which he is able to be aware of himself, . . . a reality that is not knowable in any other way" (Streng, 1969, p. 49). Whereas Western religions conceive of these as confrontational experiences in which God, a being distinct from the cosmos and natural order, confronts the subject from the outside, Eastern religions are more likely to describe them as interior experiences in which the divine is sought within the seeker and the cosmos.

Emotional Response of the Subject

Religious experiences are uniformly described as being extraordinary and not fitting easily within categories of human experience learned within the culture (Hargrove, 1979). In most instances subjects feel themselves to have been transported to a reality outside the existing world (paramount reality), which now appears "flawed, absurd or even illusory" (Berger, 1979, p. 32). Often there is a sense of being confronted or of having made contact with what James described as an "objective presence, a perception of what we may call 'something there' more deep and more general than any of the special and particular 'senses' by which . . . psychology supposes existent realities to be originally revealed" (1961, p. 62). This sense of objective presence usually is accompanied by a sense of mystery and of acceptance. Theologian Paul Tillich (1948) described them as a sense of "being accepted by that which is greater than you, and the name of which you do not know" (p. 162). Feelings of awe, urgency, wonder, astonishment, helplessness, and dependency on the "wholly other" are commonly a part of religious experiences, as is a feeling of being "submerged and overwhelmed by [one's own] nothingness in contrast to that which is supreme above all creatures" (Otto, 1958, p. 10).

In immanent religions where the holy is believed to be an ever-present but ordinarily unperceived level of reality, religious experiences tend to be less gratuitous and more controlled by the believer. Such experiences may involve a rigorous quest or enactment of religious exercises intended to remove barriers that prevent an assent to the sacred. In such cases feelings may range from a warm sense of security and peace to an apprehension of having grasped important insights from the depth of human existence or even having been absorbed into the cosmos.

Effects of the Experience

The significance of religious experiences usually are gauged by their practical effects on subjects' lives (James, 1961). Momentary flashes of insight that leave no indelible memory or have little impact on everyday life and conduct tend not to be taken seriously, especially when compared to truly life-transforming experiences. The most common type of life-transforming religious experience is that which leads to conversion or religious calling, and which may result in subjects forsaking jobs, reorienting their moral and social lives, or instituting some new pattern of behavior on a regular basis.

The array of experiences that have been labeled as religious seems endless, so that criteria are needed to narrow the scope of the definition, yet not so narrowly that legitimate religious experiences are excluded. The following represents what may be considered a moderate standard that may be used as a point of departure for discussing the relationship between sports and religious experience: Mystical experiences may be considered religious experiences to the extent that they are extraordinary, rare, and unlike normal sensory events; defined by subjects as being religious experiences and as having specific religious value; increase the subjects' awareness of some extraordinary power that they consider to be the ultimate or the ground of being; and produce profound and lasting emotional or behavioral effects on subjects, at least to the extent that specific experiences are capable of being recalled.

Notes on Athletic Performances and Religious Experiences

If one grants the possibility that religious experiences can indeed occur, that the above criteria for evaluating these experiences are reasonable, and that reports of these occurrences during sport activity are valid, there remains the task of determining if there really is something inherent in sporting activities capable of evoking religious experiences. Put another way, does the human experience of sport per se induce subjective states that meet the criteria for religious experience or is the experience of sport merely incidental to their occurrence?

One way to approach the problem is to examine rival explanations. For example, might it be possible that some individuals are predisposed by heredity, psychological make-up, or spiritual maturity to apprehend these experiences, and as a result, might logically be expected to report having had them while in virtually any social context, including sports? Could some athletes, quite apart from their athletic capacities, be what Max Weber (1963) called "religious virtuosos" or what Radin (1957) labeled "religious formulators," people especially prone to such experiences? There are some intimations that this might be the case. In his study of rock climbers Csikszentmihalyi (1975) discovered that only slightly more than one-third of his subjects reported having experiences they characterized as "transcendent, religious, visionary or ecstatic" while climbing. Interestingly, this approximates the proportion of Americans in the population at large who report having had religious experiences, irrespective of venues (Gallup & Castelli, 1989). Thus, the possibility that these human experiences of sport are less of a factor in the onset of these occurrences than are personal capacities for sensing or interpreting them, or even a willingness to talk about them to researchers, have to be considered legitimate alternative explanations for their occurrence in sport.

If one chooses to believe that athletic performances induce religious experiences, or that they condition in the athlete a certain receptiveness to supernatural signals, do these experiences arise out of some inherent properties of sport such as expansive movement or physical exertion, or are they more likely to stem from the social and existential environments in which sports are embedded? Although the focused concentration so vital to contemplative religious experiences may come most easily in moments of solitude and meditation, vigorous physical activity of the kind required in sports needn't prevent their occurrence. The long tradition of incorporating dance, with its elaborate movements and physiological demands, in the enactment of religious rituals suggests that sport might also be an effective human experience for mediating religious feelings.

Thus, the indispensable ingredient in most forms of religious experience is not physical inactivity as much as a "leisurely disposition," a form of consciousness commonly associated with intense aesthetic experiences. Such a disposition is a basic feature of play. (Although technical distinctions may be drawn between play and sport, such distinctions do not depreciate the existential similarities these two forms of human experiences share [Kretchmar, 1973; Loy, 1979].) Because of this, play—specifically the attitude and disposition that give rise to it—has often been appropriated by theologians as a metaphor for the religious life (Moltmann, 1972), even for the Christian liturgy (Guardini, 1935). Geardus van der Leeuw in *Sacred and Profane Beauty: The Holy in Art* used the metaphor of play to describe the meeting of man with God.

The meeting of God with man, of man with God, is holy play, *sacer ludens*. . . . For this reason, the game points beyond itself, downward, to the simple, ordinary rhythm of life; upward, to the highest forms of existence which strive toward a communion with the other, and finally for a meeting with God. (1963, p. 86)

The metaphor works for theologians only because the mental and spiritual correlates of leisure and play bear a remarkable similarity, if not identity, to those associated with religious experience. Both, for example, represent ruptures in the paramount reality. Philosopher Kenneth Schmitz (1979) claimed that play, art, and religion "are rightfully spoken of as ways of transcending the strictly natural world" (p. 32). Eugene Fink (1979), in a widely cited article, called play "a fundamentally existential phenomenon" (p. 75). Swiss theologian Josef Pieper (1965) described leisure (the existential context for play) as fundamentally a religious entity, and referred to the contemplative disposition that leisure makes possible, "expectant alertness." Although Pieper used the religious feast as a point of reference, he might as easily have used a sports event. "One must be able to look through and, as it were, beyond the immediate matter of the festival, including the festal gifts; one must engage in a listening, and therefore necessarily silent meditation upon the fundament of existence'' (Pieper, 1965, p. 13).

Although all forms of sport may lend themselves to the inducement of religious moments, not all seem to offer the same potential for the type of contemplative, religious experience Pieper had in mind. Some seem to provide a much richer context than others. As has been noted there is a greater tendency for these experiences to occur during high-risk activities, such as rock climbing, or those that require extended periods of discomfort, such as running. In retrospect, could it be that the isolated, noninteractive character of these sports, more than their high-risk properties or extended periods of discomfort, fosters religious experiences by providing an especially supportive spiritual ecology for contemplation?

These alternative explanations aside, there remains the distinct possibility that sport, like art and music, does indeed contain a unique existential ingredient that opens one up to special religious experiences. Father Ryan's (1986) personal testimony to the spiritual power of sport should not be dismissed, nor should his contention that running can be a triggering technique for opening the door to mind-spinning experiences and, ultimately, to communion. "What one has in those moments of spinning free, is an experience of *awareness*. What one experiences first of all is one's own consciousness, one's own being. From there it is only a step to realize the Infinite, Incomprehensible, Ineffable One, at the center of one's being" (1986, p. 132). It is an intriguing possibility.

Articles in Review

The articles in Part II provide broad coverage of the occurrence of religious experiences in sport. When William James (1961) undertook his famous study of religious experiences, he elected to study them in situations where they were at the extreme of their development, where there could be no question as to whether or not they were religious. Applying James' approach to this study would have limited consideration to an analysis of running and other solitary sports such as mountain climbing, surfing, and skiing. These most often are described in religious terms. But because a broader view was sought, only the first two articles focus specifically on running. Hal Higdon's article "Is Running a Religious Experience?" describes his conversations with runners about the religious meaning found on running paths. The runners' comments reflect a sense of what Jachim Wach (1970) considered a hallmark of religious experience, a response of the total being. Personal testimonies refer not only to transformations in mental states, but in total lifestyles.

This is followed by George Sheehan's article, excerpted from his best selling *Running and Being* (1978), one of the most eloquent personal testimonies to the religious element in sports and play, especially running. Although Sheehan's own religious experiences came during running, clearly he sees a much more comprehensive connection between sport, play, and religion. Sheehan's is no objective, scholarly treatise; it is written from the heart as much as from the head, and for understandable reasons. The author credits a religious experience during a long run with proving to him the existence of God.

In "Muscular Christianity, Holy Play, and Spiritual Exercises: Confusion About Christ in Sports and Religion" Robert Higgs considers the question of whether the extraordinary experiences reported in athletic contexts can be considered authentic religious experiences. Higgs's is a comprehensive analysis, perhaps the most thorough and informed study of sport and religious experiences published to date. He argues the case against sport as being inherently religious from a straightforward theistic position and, through detailed descriptions of the emotional states of athletes, the objects of their religious experiences, and the effects of those experiences on their lives, shows how sports fall far short of the ideal. In the broad sweep of his arguments, Higgs also takes issue with play theologians who see play, both metaphorically and literally, as new ground for religion and religious experience. He also draws a sharp distinction between those embarked on a serious religious quest and muscular Christians, the popular athletes who rationalize their athletic participation on religious grounds.

The last two articles deal with religious experience in a slightly different context; Denise Carmody's deals with sport as lived religious experience, and Shirl Hoffman's approaches it as a religious experience conterminous with religious ritual. Carmody presents the view of a scholar of religious studies reflecting on the meaning of sport in her own life. She suggests that an athletic spirituality in which athletes lose and then find themselves in a larger entity, an experience that fully embodies the self and the Christian faith and is a foretaste of the Church triumphant, is a possibility. However, she carefully conditions her optimism by noting the potential of sport's idolatrous strains, gender stereotyping, and overcompetitiveness to prevent it from being the true religious experience that it can be.

Hoffman's attention is focused on the increasing tendency of athletes from evangelical traditions to describe their athletic performances as rites of religious expression and acts of worship. It is an extension of an article included in Part III, "Recovering a Sense of the Sacred in Sport," that goes beyond considering the mere possibility that sport performances can be religious rituals to an examination of the underlying feelings and motivations of athletes who perform them.

It is fitting to examine this trend toward "athletic forms of worship" within the context of religious experience, because acts done to achieve some religious aim can be fully understood as religious events only by reflecting on the experience associated with them (van der Leeuw, 1963). As Wach (1970) has noted, all religious experience tends toward outward expression, either intellectually, practically, or socially. As a form of worship, the athletic experiences described in Hoffman's account would fall into what liturgists traditionally have labeled *objective* worship in which rituals are performed without deep feeling, their intent being to make some kind of effect on or to communicate with the supernatural. These have been distinguished from *subjective* forms that seek primarily to induce some desired mood or attitude. Yet the distinction may not be as clear-cut as is commonly thought (Pratt, 1964). Even the most objective forms of religious worship may induce religious sentiment as a by-product, because of the beliefs that lie behind the objective rituals. Thus, Hoffman's Christian athletes and Higgs's "muscular Christians" who appropriate athletics as rituals to express praise, to give thanks, or to otherwise "bring glory to God" may be viewed as being directly associated with religious experience that reveals itself in a special resolve and an exceptional urgency to perform well. This elevated zeal along with the personal and shared reflections on its meaning owes directly to its characterization as a medium of worship.

References

Berger, P. (1979). *The heretical imperative: Contemporary possibilities of religious affirmation*. Garden City, NY: Anchor Press.

Csikszentmihalyi, M. (1975). *Beyond boredom and anxiety*. San Francisco: Jossey Bass.

Eliade, M. (1969). *Yoga: Immortality and freedom*. Princeton, NJ: Princeton University Press.

Fink, E. (1979). The ontology of play. In E.W. Gerber & W.J. Morgan (Eds.), *Sport and the body* (2nd ed.) (pp. 73-93). Philadelphia: Lea & Febiger.

Gallup, G., & Castelli, J. (1989). *The people's religion: American faith in the 90's*. New York: Macmillan.

Glock, C.Y., & Stark, R. (1965). *Religion and society in tension*. Chicago: Rand MacNally.

Greeley, A. (1974). *Ecstasy: A way of knowing*. Englewood Cliffs, NJ: Prentice-Hall.

Guardini, R. (1935). *The church and the Catholic and the spirit of the liturgy*. New York: Sheed and Ward.

Hargrove, B. (1979). *The sociology of religion*. Arlington Heights, IL: Harlan Davidson.

Hood, R.W. (1975). The construction and preliminary validation of a measure of reported mystical experience. *Journal for the Scientific Study of Religion*, **14**, 29-41.

James, W. (1961). *The varieties of religious experience*. New York: Macmillan.

Kretchmar, R.S. (1973). Ontological possibilities: Sport as play. In R.G. Osterhoudt (Ed.), *The philosophy of sport* (pp. 64-78). Springfield, IL: Charles C Thomas.

Laski, M. (1962). *Ecstasy: A study of some secular religious experiences*. Bloomington, IN: University of Indiana Press.

Loy, J., Jr. (1979). The nature of sport: A definitional effort. *Quest*, **10**, 1-15.

Maslow, A. (1968). *Toward a psychology of being* (2nd ed.). New York: Van Nostrand Reinhold.

Merton, T. (1970). *The wisdom of the desert*. New York: New Directions.

Moltmann, J. (1972). *Theology of play*. New York: Harper.

Murphy, M., & White, R. (1978). *The psychic side of sports*. Reading, MA: Addison-Wesley.

Neal, P. (1972). *Sport and identity*. Philadelphia: Dorrance.

O'Hear, A. (1984). *Experience, explanation and faith*. London: Routledge & Kegan Paul.

Otto, R. (1958). *The idea of the holy* (John W. Harvey, Trans.). New York: Oxford University Press.

Pieper, J. (1965). *In tune with the world: A theory of festivity*. New York: Harcourt, Brace & World.

Pratt, J.B. (1964). Worship and manifest and latent functions. In L. Schneider (Ed.), *Religion, culture and society* (pp. 143-146). New York: Wiley.

Proudfoot, W. (1985). *Religious experience*. Berkeley, CA: University of California Press.

Radin, P. (1957). *Primitive religion: Its nature and origin*. New York: Dover.

Ravizza, K. (1977). Peak experiences in sport. *Journal of Humanistic Psychology*, **17**, 35-40.

Ravizza, K. (1984). Qualities of the peak experience in sport. In J.M. Silva & R.S. Weinberg (Eds.), *Psychological foundations of sport* (pp. 452-461). Champaign, IL: Human Kinetics.

Ryan, T. (1986). *Wellness, spirituality and sports*. Mahwah, NJ: Paulist Press.

Sachs, M.L. (1984). Psychological well being and vigorous physical activity. In J.M. Silva & R.S. Weinberg (Eds.), *Psychological foundations of sport* (pp. 535-544). Champaign, IL: Human Kinetics.

Schmitz, K. (1979). Sport and play: The suspension of the ordinary. In E.W. Gerber & W.J. Morgan (Eds.), *Sport and the body* (2nd ed.) (pp. 22-29). Philadelphia: Lea & Febiger.

Scott, J. (1971). *The athletic revolution*. New York: The Free Press.

Scorecard. (1986, February 3). *Sports Illustrated*, p. 21.

Sheehan, G. (1978). *Running and being*. New York: Warner Books.

Stace, W.T. (1960). *Mysticism and philosophy*. Philadelphia: Lippincott.

Stark, R. (1965). A taxonomy of religious experience. *Journal for the Scientific Study of Religion*, **5**, 97-116.

Stark, R., & Bainbridge, W.S. (1985). *The future of religion: Secularization, revival and cult formation*. Berkeley, CA: University of California Press.

Steere, D. (1957). *Work and contemplation*. New York: Harper.

Streng, F.J. (1969). *Understanding religious man*. Belmont, CA: Dickenson Publishing.

Streng, F.J., Lloyd, C.L., & Allen, J.T. (1973). *Ways of being religious*. Englewood Cliffs, NJ: Prentice-Hall.

Thomas, L., & Cooper, P. (1980). Incidence and psychological correlates of intense spiritual experiences. *Journal of Transpersonal Psychology*, **12**(1), 75-85.

Tillich, P. (1948). *The shaking of the foundations*. New York: Scribner's.

Turner, V. (1969). *The ritual process*. Chicago: Aldin.

Wach, J. (1970). *Types of religious experience: Christian and non-Christian*. Chicago: University of Chicago Press.

Weber, M. (1963). *The sociology of religion*. Boston: Beacon.

Van der Leeuw, G. (1963). *Sacred and profane beauty: The holy in art* (D.F. Green, Trans.). New York: Holt, Rinehart and Winston.

Is Running a Religious Experience?

Hal Higdon

Is running a new religion? Even to consider the question might be considered by some as sacrilegious, a form of heresy. But for an increasing number of people today, running has become if not an organized religion, at least *the* most important activity of their life. In fact, it has become a *way* of life and all hope. Running is something that now consumes their previously idle hours, or previously wasted hours: a purifying activity that often dominates their weekends with races and preparations for future races, becoming their Sabbath, taking over their Sunday mornings, the traditional time when at least the Christian majority in the United States attends church. Even the stretching that runners do before starting their activity might be considered a form of genuflection.

There is also the phenomenon of the born-again runner, akin to the born-again Christian, the individual, often middle-aged, who might have been active athletically in youth, but then lapsed into sinful ways: eating too much, drinking too much, cavorting with wicked women (or scandalous men), allowing the body, described by the scriptures as the "temple of the spirit" to degenerate to the point where the temple appeared threatened by destruction (i.e., occluded coronary arteries).

In fact, a large percentage of those swelling the fields of long-distance races throughout the country, if not a majority, are born-again runners; people who have had no (or little) base as competitive track athletes, but who have taken up running after years of wicked living.

Like born-again Christians, these individuals are often the most active proselytizers of others, attempting to convert the non-believers into practitioners of their new-found sport/faith under the theory that if it feels this good to me, everybody else should be doing it too. "Now I know what it feels like to be a born-again Baptist," comments one 35-year-old female runner of the Jewish faith. "I try to convert my non-running friends."

New-born runners often dramatically change their lifestyles, shedding cigarette-smoking friends, sometimes divorcing their wives (or in the case of running wives, divorcing their husbands), because their new evangelism no longer is compatible with their old selves. "I have abandoned the non-running world," states a Masters runner from Noblesville, Ind., whose entire family runs. "Runners are my reference now."

A 29-year-old runner adds: "Friends, or should I say acquaintances, I had before running, are sort of turned off by my enthusiasm and I don't see many of them as often as I used to. My new running friends seem more important to me." He adds wistfully, "My wife tolerates my running—sometimes barely."

Running, while having a positive effect on a person's physical well-being, thus may have a negative effect on the spiritual being if it causes weakening of the family structure, whose strength often is at the core of many religions, particularly Roman Catholicism for which divorce is a no-no punishable by excommunication.

One female runner, who was baptized a Catholic, turned off to organized religion because of what she describes as "the structuralized institution of the church. Money becomes the issue rather than true improvement of oneself." A finisher in the Boston and New York City Marathons, she recently has also turned away from racing though she continues to run noncompetitively eight miles a day. She said she abandoned competition because of being repelled by the commercialization of many races. She speculates: "Your everyday jogger and runners are the ones who are more spiritually enlightened and closer to God. The personal accomplishment is stronger than the publicity. Joggers are less concerned with victory over their fellow runners and more involved with peace among their fellow man."

When that person decides to run, it is in the form of a spiritual as well as physical reawakening, a conversion to a new discipline which will result in a rebirth of the spirit. "And for many people," states one new runner, born-again, after nearly a decade away from the sport, "running is spoken of in very religious terms: 'I saw God when running up the side of Pike's Peak,' or something like that. Maybe running is one of the religions of tomorrow. It certainly isn't any worse a religion than a few of the others making the rounds."

In considering the question of whether or not running has become a new religion, we first need to consider a definition for religion. Strictly speaking, religion means a belief in a divine or superhuman power, or powers, to be worshipped as the creator and ruler (or creators and rulers) of the universe. In other words, there is "something out there," and more than the space creatures we saw in the final reel of *Close Encounters of the Third Kind.*

Central to most religions is a belief in God. Whether or not God exists, a significant percentage of Americans believe that He (or She) does exist. Religion might further be defined as an expression of this Godly belief in conduct and ritual.

Religion, in this respect, takes on a further meaning beyond its most basic belief in God, since it also serves as a specific *system* of worship and conduct, often involving a code of ethics and a philosophy, for instance, the Christian "religion," the Jewish "religion," or the Moslem "religion." But in its broadest sense, religion might be considered *any* system of beliefs, practices, or ethical values likened to such a system. To some people, work becomes a religion. Or collecting stamps. Or sports, as in: "He follows the New York Giants religiously." Atheists deny the existence of God and reject all religious belief, but semantically speaking, you can practice atheism religiously—although some people probably would prefer substitution of the term "zealously."

Thus, in the *broadest* sense of religion being a system of beliefs and practices, running might be considered a form of religion.

Running also might provide a form by which certain individuals practice their religion. "I exhort you therefore brethren," writes St. Paul in his "Letter to the Romans" (12:1), "by the mercy of God to present your bodies as a sacrifice, living, holy, pleasing to God—your spiritual service." A body capable of carrying its owner through the 26 miles, 385 yards of a marathon might be considered more "pleasing" to God than a body which, through its owner's indolence, has been allowed to deteriorate into a blob of flesh that quivers from the strain of moving from couch to kitchen for another beer. Running is one way of serving God's will.

Some people speak in religious terms even if they do not consider themselves religious. For example, one female runner says she attends synagogue only once a year. Having started running two years ago, she runs from 3-11 miles daily. "One of the reasons I most love running is that it is the first time in my life I have ever believed in something unambivalently. The satisfaction that I get, the 'highs,' the time to think and problem-solve, the energy, are all proofs that running works. Therefore 'devotion' to running makes me happier, makes life better. This is what religion does for many people. It gives meaning to their lives. I don't completely understand why, but running has given my life a certain sense of purpose that I never had before.

"There is a difference between a traditional religion and running," she continues to explain. "When one believes in a religion and in God, it is a belief in something outside oneself, in a way an abandoning of power to something outside. On the contrary, a belief in running, 'the new religion,' is a belief in oneself, in one's power, in one's ability to improve discipline and take charge of one's own life. In the past, I've often been a little envious of people who had faith, which got them through difficult times. Now I have a faith of my own. In this sense, running has strengthened my own religious, or maybe irreligious, beliefs."

As to whether running brings people closer to God, causing them on certain occasions to have, while running, what they might consider a spiritual experience, that may more often be in the eye of the beholder. It is possible to see God in any activity, or even lack of activity.

Many people say that getting out into nature allows them to contemplate the creativity of God, in effect, confront his works. The New Testament describes Jesus Christ going up into the mountains to fast for 40 days to achieve an awareness of his own being. Physiologists likewise suggest 40 days as about the length of time it takes an untrained runner to revitalize his body, that being the period of time required for capillarization, the improvement of the oxygen transport system that causes running to suddenly become easier after earlier days of strain. Once a runner achieves this first level of training and perhaps also achieves a level of fitness that permits jogging for an hour, it is possible to experience what might be called "the 40-minute effect," the point at which certain psychologists (Thaddeus Kostrubala, for example) believe that runners experience the so-called runner's high, that sense of euphoria, the breaking free of the mind from the body which allows persons to reach a meditative state similar to that attained by Eastern mystics who place themselves into a trance by saying, over and over: "Ommmmmm."

But is this runner's high a spiritual experience? It probably is if you want to so identify it.

"Running has promoted religious thought," says Donald Higdon (no relation to the author) of Ridgewood, N.J., an Episcopalian who attends church only a few times a year but considers himself religious. "I see the world less in terms of *me* and more as a marvel in which I am fortunate to fit."

Donald Higdon, who began jogging at the age of 36, feels that he is a better person because of his running. "I am healthier, rarely ill. I feel good. In spite of old habits, I find myself desiring things that are 'good for me.' I am less tense. I accept things more willingly. I am more patient. I've discovered abilities I did not know I had. Feeling better about myself, I think better of others. I am more tolerant of the weaknesses of others, if they are beyond the person's control. However, I am less tolerant of sloth, obesity, excessive drinking, smoking and habits which are clearly controllable. I have had occasional surges of wonderment or good feeling about the world. However, the same thing has happened when I was alone in a sailboat or preparing to launch a hang glider." As to whether running had become a substitute for religion, Donald Higdon feels that it merely offers another perspective toward life and the world.

A female runner in her late 20's, who began running eight months ago and now runs five miles each morning, answers the question about whether running is becoming a substitute for religion by saying, "It probably isn't if one defines religion in terms of God and spiritual experiences. However, using a broader definition of 'religion,' running does give one a sense of order in life, a 'plan,' a chance to belong to a group and share the values and beliefs of that group and a whole new world view. Even the beginning runner like myself has to make major changes in my life to find the time to run and to put up with minor discomfort. So I'm forcing myself to develop a *commitment* to the endeavor—or else to quit. I prefer *not* to call this a substitute for religion as defined in the traditional sense of belonging to a church and believing in God."

One of the individuals we spoke with was Dan Cloeter, a minister as well as two-time winner of the Chicago Marathon. Dan said, "I've heard people say that they don't need 'church' anymore, now that they've found running. It's my opinion that those people probably only had 'church' and not a faith and trust relationship with God."

Cloeter feels that running and his faith and trust in God complement each other. "I enjoy running and experiencing things in my surroundings which reflect God's glory."

Father Kevin O'Rourke, a priest who works with the Catholic Hospital Association in St. Louis, says he often prays when he runs his regular four or six miles early in the morning: "If one knows how to pray, then running will dispose for prayer, but running is not prayer, nor does it cause prayer. While I run, I feel that I can put the coming events of the day in spiritual perspective. Getting out of the daily sedentary routine helps me appreciate more simple things in life, thus freeing me to pursue values and objectives that have spiritual meaning. Personality integration should be stressed as an important potential for running. Thus, all aspects of person—spiritual, psychological and physical—benefit and are able to work more cooperatively together.''

The 29-year-old previously quoted stated: ''Running does make me more aware of the world around me and the beauty that truly exists. It's made me feel a very common bond with hundreds and thousands of people who aren't phony and maybe this isn't a religious experience as such, but if all mankind would start running maybe the world would be a better place.''

As for whether one can meet God while running, the answer is both yes and no. He can be met in this manner, as He can be met almost anywhere, but there is no guarantee.

Playing

George A. Sheehan

Shakespeare was wrong. To play or not to play: that is the real question. Anyone with a sense of humor can see that life is a joke, not a tragedy. It is also a riddle and, like all riddles, has an obvious answer: play, not suicide.

Think about it for a minute. Is there a better way than play to handle "the slings and arrows of outrageous fortune," or take up arms against a "sea of troubles"? You take these things seriously and you end up with Hamlet—or the Nixon Gang, who came back from World War II, wrote Wilfred Sheed, "talking about dollars the way others talked about God and sex."

Neither of these ways works. Neither will bring us what we are supposed to be looking for, "the peace the world cannot give." That is also part of the riddle. You can have peace without the world, if you opt for death. Or the world without peace if you decide for doing and having and achieving. Only in play can you have both. In play, you realize simultaneously the supreme importance and utter insignificance of what you are doing. And accept the paradox of pursuing what at once is essential and inconsequential.

Play, then, is the answer to the puzzle of our existence. The stage for our excesses and exuberances. Violence and dissent are part of its joy. Territory is defended with every ounce of our strength and determination, and moments later we are embracing our opponents and delighting in the game that took place.

Play is where life lives. Where the game is the game. At its borders, we slip into heresy. Become serious. Lose our sense of humor. Fail to see the incongruities of everything we hold to be important. Right and wrong become problematical. Money, power, position become ends. The game becomes winning. And we lose the good life and the good things that play provides.

Some of those good things are physical grace, psychological ease and personal integrity. Some of the best are the peak experiences, when you have a sense of oneness with yourself and nature. These are truly times of peace the world cannot give. It may be that the hereafter will have them in constant supply. I hope so. But while we are in the here and now, play is the place to find them. The place where we are constantly being and becoming ourselves.

Philosophers have hinted at this over the centuries. Now the theologians are taking a hard look at the thought that we must become as little children to enter the Kingdom. If so, there is nothing more characteristic about children than their love of play. No one comes into this world a Puritan. If there is anything children care less about, it is work and money and power and what we call achievement.

We watch and envy as they answer the call "Come and play."

What happens to our play on our way to becoming adults? Downgraded by the intellectuals, dismissed by the economists, put aside by the psychologists, it was left to the teachers to deliver the *coup de grâce*. "Physical education" was born and turned what was joy into boredom, fun into drudgery, pleasure into work. What might have led us into Eden led us into a blind alley instead. And simply changed our view of the universe.

A universe where we are to play and enjoy ourselves and our God is one thing; a universe that is a large, forbidding place where we have to fight for everything we get is quite another. A universe where it is either "us" or "them" will certainly make us seek peace in another world. Life under those circumstances is just as Samuel Beckett described it: "A terminal illness."

Play, of course, says otherwise. You may already have found that out. If you are doing something you would do for nothing, then you are on your way to salvation. And if you could drop it in a minute and forget the outcome, you are even further along. And if, while you are doing it, you are transported into another existence, there is no need for you to worry about the future.

What our instincts (and athletes and sports psychologists) tell us is that sports and athletics will show us how to satisfy the main urges of this generation: to possess one's experience rather than be possessed by it, to live one's own life rather than be lived by it—is fine, to become all you are. Up until now that has always meant your brain. No more.

"As Prometheus (sometimes called the Greek Christ) sought to stretch the capacity of mankind," writes West Coast psychologist Wilfred Mitchell, "so do athletics."

One who has found sport stretching his capacity is Joe Henderson, the running editor of *Runners' World*. Henderson feels he can't answer the why-I-run question any better than others. But he tries. "I write," he says, "because the thoughts inside have to be put in more visible form. I run because it's inside pushing to get out."

Running is a total experience. That which some of us do best just as others find their satisfactions and fulfillment in skiing, mountain climbing, bicycling, snorkeling, pitching or what have you.

The experience is one that proceeds from one level to another. It can be merely physical fitness (which is like taking up painting to improve the strength of your arm). Or distraction: "I think" said Tug McGraw, "the reason I like baseball so much is because when I come into a game in the bottom of the ninth, bases loaded, none out, and a one-run lead, it takes my mind off all us screwed-up people." Or religious: "Surfing is a spiritual experience," says Michael Hynson, one of the world's top surfers. "When you become united with a wave, you lose your identity on one level and make contact with it again on a higher plane."

At one end of the spectrum you find a former college cross-country runner stating that the "opportunity to encounter and deal with pain is one of the aspects that makes the running experience ultimately so satisfactory." At the other, you hear Dick Cavett, a dedicated snorkeler, report, "Snorkeling is a rebirth. You just hang there in liquid space like an irresponsible fetus. For me it combines the best features of sport, sleep and religion."

This quiet revolution is spreading over the land. The rarity of the true dropouts should not fool us. For each ski-bum who belongs to the mountains there are thousands who already know that's where they come alive. For every runner who tours the world running marathons, there are thousands who run to hear leaves and listen to rain and look to the day when it all is suddenly as easy as a bird in flight.

For them, sport is not a test but a therapy; not a trial but a reward; not a question but an answer.

The first and basic commandment for health and longevity is the following: Pursue your own perfection. No one will have difficulty with this dogma. But as usual with dogma, we begin to have dissensions when the theologians start interpreting it. Then we become schismatics and heretics and start religions of our own. In health, the main problems with orthodoxy are with the word "exercise."

I am ready to start a new religion, the first law of which is, "Play regularly." An hour's play a day makes a man whole and healthy and long-lived. A man's exercise must be play, or it will do him little good. It may even, as we see regularly in the press, kill him.

I have scientific support for my position. Recent studies in both England and Ireland have shown that hard physical work did not change the coronary-risk factors or heart disease in more than thirty thousand men. However, in the same group, hard physical activity during leisure time was accompanied by a significant reduction in risk factors and heart attacks. Not by hard work, but by swimming and running and heavy gardening, and by tennis and squash and handball, and other forms of play, these men achieved health and a long life.

So it is not effort that reduces heart attacks and degenerative disease. If it were only effort, then effort on the job would do the trick. So it is not running, but running that is play, that is necessary. Exercise that is work is worthless. But exercise that is play will give you health and long life.

Exercise that is not play accentuates rather than heals the split between body and spirit. Exercise that is drudgery, labor, something done only for the final result is a waste of time. If I hated to run and ran only for longevity and was killed by a truck after five years at the sport, I would have a right to shake my fist at Providence, or at the doctor who advised it.

It is not the runner, but those impersonating the runner, who is at hazard. Those with the "hurry sickness." Those aggressively involved with achieving more and more with less and less time. Those who are always competing with or challenging other people. "Only the sick man and the ambitious," wrote Ortega, "are in a hurry.'' It is these people who use jogging to escape from death who find it taking them to their appointment in Samarra.

What, then, should you do? Run only if you must. If running is an imperative that comes from inside you and not from your doctor. Otherwise, heed the inner calling to your own play. Listen if you can to the person you were and are and can be. Then do what you do best and feel best at. Something you would do for nothing. Something that gives you security and self-acceptance and a feeling of completion; even moments when you are fused with your universe and your Creator. When you find it, build your life around it.

''Therein lies perfection,'' said Marcus Aurelius, ''to live out each day as one's last.'' That is why I run and will always run. I have built my day and my life around it.

There is no better test for play than the desire to be doing it when you die.

as yes is to if, love is to yes

e.e. cummings

The intellectuals who look at sport start with the assumption that it must serve something that is not sport. They see its useful functions of discharging surplus energy and providing relaxation, training for fitness and compensation for other deficiencies. What they don't see is that play is a primary category of life which resists all analysis.

Play, then, is a nonrational activity. A supralogical nonrational activity in which the beauty of the human body in motion can reach its zenith. Just as the supralogical feast of Christmas confirms man's unique value and destiny. So the intellectuals are probably as upset with play as the theologians are with Christmas. Men having fun is as mystical and supralogical as the Word made flesh.

Fortunately, mysticism doesn't come hard for the common man. ''History unanimously attests,'' wrote G.K. Chesterton, the master of paradox and therefore the master of Christmas, ''that it is only mysticism which stands the smallest chance of being understood by the people.''

Philosopher Jean Houston has observed, ''We tend to think of the Faustian man, the one who fabricates, manipulates, seduces and ends up destroying. But the new image will be man the creator, the artist, the player.''

The first Christians told us all that. The game plan had been changed. When the angel said, ''Rejoice, be not afraid. I bring you good news of great joy,'' we knew that everything was going to be different. The world, which had moved from ''if'' to ''yes,'' was now moving on to love.

The game would be for everyone. And the arena would be the world. And the good news is that man will eventually triumph. All of us for this once are going to be on the winning team. And not only that. All of us can be great players.

The first Christmas says with Shakespeare, ''What a piece of work is man. How noble in reason! How finite in faculties! In form and moving, how express and admirable!''

The sports fan knows all this and suspects that there is nothing more spiritual than the human body. Knows that nowhere is every man given his dignity as he is on the playing field. And instinctively feels that somewhere here is the news of the first Christmas.

Those of us weary and discouraged by the front-page tragedies caused by *Homo sapiens* and the ecological disasters of *Homo faber* can turn for uplift to the sports pages and know that there every day is Christmas. A Christmas foretold in the Book of Proverbs:

"I was with Him forming all things, and was delighted every day, playing before Him at all times; playing in the world. And my delights were to be with the children of men."

Who speaks for play? These days, almost everyone. The physiologists and the physicians, the psychologists and the psychiatrists, the economists and the sociologists all champion play.

Play and sports and the use of the body are becoming respectable. Play is good for losing weight and reducing our risk factors. For relieving stress and returning us to work relaxed. Play maintains our health and promotes our longevity. Compensates for needs not met at work, and provides a harmless way to vent antisocial emotions. Play, the experts say, is a necessity in a leisure society.

But these acceptable and respectable reasons for play are not the real reason we must play. The reason for play is much more radical than the scientists and thinkers presume. The reason for play is to be found in our reason for being. And, therefore, with the problem of God.

The problem of God has moved from the ancient question "Does God exist?" past the medieval inquiry, "What are his attributes?" to our present dilemma, "Why did He create the world?" Our difficulty now is the inability to explain the existence of the world and therefore ourselves. We are unable to define our purpose, to show how we serve, to demonstrate our usefulness.

The best answer, it seems to me, is to consider Calvin's thought that the world is "*theatrum gloria Dei.*" We are here, therefore, to glorify God. And that we do this by glorifying the God who is Himself a player. Who created in joy, in play, in sport.

Calvin, the Sunday bocce player, may not have thought of it this way, but it does answer today's question. We are in this world to give glory to God and rejoice in our own and God's existence. And we do this in play.

Muscular Christianity, Holy Play, and Spiritual Exercises:
Confusion About Christ in Sports and Religion

Robert J. Higgs

This essay is a dissent against the sanctification of both sports and play and the secularization of religion. I am certainly not the first in recent years to do so, though I suspect that the pendulum has swung so far to the other side, toward the mystification of sports, that any skeptic trying to reverse the trend will remain in a minority. Among those who have cast doubt upon current practices is Malcolm Boyd, himself a popularizer of sorts ("Are You Running With Me, Jesus?"): "Billy Graham said we should be selling Christ like soap. I don't think so. I think we should be trying to *act* like Christ. He never was a celebrity. Jesus Christ was the exact opposite of a superstar" (Deford, "Endorsing Jesus," 1976, p. 69).

Another skeptic is Harry Edwards. "All evidence indicates that U.S. sports do *not* develop Christian morals. . . . In fact, they tend to undermine them. Take brotherly love. There is a sordid history of racism, discrimination and the development of dual systems in organized American athletics" ("Are Sports Good for the Soul?", 1971, p. 52). Though he questions the character-building claims of sports, Edwards (1973, pp. 261-262) has nevertheless noted, ironically, the parallels between sports and religion.

His observations appear in a fine survey on the topic, "The Religious Dimensions of Sport" in *Social Aspects of Sports* by Eldon E. Snyder and Elmer A. Spreitzer [1978], which outlines various approaches to the study of sports and religion, sociological, theological, phenomenological, and the radical humanistic, as well as consideration of magic and superstition as they relate to both. They and the authors surveyed have served well the goal of scholarship, to find similarities amid apparent differences. What I hope to do here is to serve scholarship by moving in the opposite direction, by pointing out the *differences* between sports and religion. Emphasis, therefore, will be upon analysis instead of synthesis. All metaphor breaks down somewhere as Robert Frost shows in "Education by Poetry," and here I want to show where and how the sports-religion metaphor breaks down. Sports are like religion in many ways just as they are like war in some ways, but they are not equatable with either.

In concentrating on the differences between sports and religion, I hope to distinguish between three forms in which symbiosis has occurred: Muscular Christianity, holy play, and spiritual exercises. Though there are exceptions and variations, the first has tended to be Protestant, the second, pagan, gnostic and oriental, and the third both oriental and Catholic. Muscular Christianity tends to be a public affair while spiritual exercises are conducted in private. In Muscular Christianity emphasis is placed upon the body as a means of bringing others to Christ, while in spiritual exercises the body is an instrument in the attainment of divine knowledge. The Muscular Christian qualifies as a witness because of his success in worldly competition whereas the spiritual exercitant fortifies himself for work in the world by private ascesis. For the Muscular Christian, emotion becomes a significant factor in salvational work, while for the spiritual exercitant emotion must be drained away before the encounter with the holy that prepares one for service in the world. Hence, in literature, the Muscular Christian has become in his emotional excesses a comic figure as seen in works ranging from Sinclair Lewis's *Elmer Gantry* to Brother Buck in Lisa Alther's *Kinflicks*. The spiritual exercitant in the Christian tradition has perhaps not been common enough among us to reach any significant representation in literature, though the figure, the guru, from a kindred tradition, the Hindu discipline of Yoga, has become a familiar target of satire on television in such shows as Johnny Carson and Saturday Night Live.

Both Muscular Christianity and spiritual exercises differ significantly from the idea of holy play in which God is seen as immanent rather than transcendent, the divine order itself manifested in dance. Here the blessed state is reached not through works (Muscular Christianity) or through denial (spiritual exercises) but through a playful attitude and the aligning of individual rhythms with the absolute rhythms of the universe so that performer and form are one. In holy play the essence of mysticism is experience while in spiritual exercises the mystical state is both experience *and* vision.

There are many other differences between the three forms of religious practice, but all three make significant use of the body. It can be argued of course that spiritual exercises are not sports at all, but even here there is evident a physical asceticism strikingly similar in many ways to that associated with sports. "Helen Waddell writes in *The Desert Fathers* that asceticism had not traveled far from the ascesis, the training of the athlete, and the Fathers themselves to their contemporary biographers are the *Athletae Dei*, 'the athletes of God.'" Austerity was not an end in itself, however it was cultivated. Waddell quotes Dorotheus the Theban's ancient formula. "I kill my body, for it kills me." To the Fathers the killing of the body meant the liberation of the spirit for holy living and holy dying: to the Greek athlete, it meant a triumphant return home and possibly a celebration by Pindar; to the Green Bay packers, Vince Lombardi's ascetics, it meant two Super Bowls (Sisk, 1973, pp. 46-47).

While there is a great difference in the forms of ascesis practiced by the desert fathers and modern athletes, there is even greater difference in prizes sought. Indeed, there is a gulf between the ancient *Athletae Dei* and the modern Muscular Christian, the one living off cabbage leaves in a hole in the desert and the other prospering economically, always both well dressed and well fed as he witnesses for Christ. Still, both are "athletes," though of two quite different orders. The position taken here is that spiritual exercises are closer to the idea of holiness, the essence of religion as traditionally defined, than are Muscular Christianity and holy play, with the implication being that both *ludus* (effort, patience, skill, ingenuity) and *paidia* (gaiety, capriciousness, spontaneity) (Caillois, 1961, p. 13) are entirely profane.

Sports belong to the realm of the beautiful and play to the world of nature, but neither to the holy. In their purest form, sports are expressions of art and beauty, and play an immersion in nature for pleasure and rest of the mind and soul. Religion, by contrast, partakes of the spiritual sublime. It is a quest not so much of the beautiful as of the good and true by means of faith, hope, and charity (at least in Christendom) and exercise of the intellect and spirit as opposed to competition for worldly prizes or indulgence in dance or play. Loyola's *Spiritual Exercises*, for example, suggests a crucial contrast between the way of the spirit and the way of the world, as does Loyola's own story. God's work is to be done in the world but God himself must be approached in reverence, silence, and stillness. God begins, as it were, at least in Hebrew/Christian tradition (and I believe in Oriental as well) where play ends. "Sit still and know that I am God," says the psalmist. Such a verse, we know, would never serve as a pre-game prayer or even as an opening for an invocation by a pastor for a sports banquet. This is not to imply that the athlete cannot be a Christian or even a saint but only that athleticism works against him in his quest for the holy as the military and courtier tradition worked against St. Ignatius.

It is not surprising that so many connections have been noted between sports and religion, since both from time immemorial have had a common goal, to propitiate the gods (Rogers, 1972, p. 393).

Although Paul may have used religious metaphors in his letters, early Christianity was set squarely against the pagan activity of sport. We may offer Christian invocations at sporting events, but, as John Pearson (1973, p. 155) has noted, the cross and colosseum are entirely at cross purposes:

> Much has been done across the years to emphasize this symbolism—the stark wooden cross erected on the spot of the emperors' podium, the Christian congregations that now take the place of the packed Roman audiences: and in his Easter pilgrimage and annual service at the Colosseum, the Pope becomes as nowhere else the visible successor of the Caesars.
>
> It is an impressive scene—this pagan building, the enthusiastic Romans, and, at the centre, one small figure whose authority still rivals the power of the ancient emperors. It would be hard to pick a more telling demonstration of Rome's continuity and of the way the Church became both victor and successor to the power of the Empire. And yet the truth behind this symbolism is elusive.

The symbolism is elusive indeed but one "elusive idea"—"elusive" is the exact term used—is that of Jacob Needleman: "What student of civilization has not pondered the consequences for the world of the victory of Constantine in the year 312 and his ultimate assumption of complete power as Emperor of the faltering Roman Empire? With Constantine, Christianity as a world religion takes form and decisively breaks away from what might be called Christianity as an inner path. From that point on, there are two main histories of Christianity, a distinction, to my mind, far more fundamental than the various other aspects of Christian culture through the ages. . . ." (Needleman, 1980, p. 18). In Needleman's view, it is the inner branch of Christianity that has been lost, and his remarkable book is an attempt to find survivals of the silent stream.

The distinction between the inner and outer branches of Christianity was felt keenly by St. Ignatius Loyola, who read Erasmus's *Christian Knight*, was initially impressed by it, but eventually settled on *Imitation of Jesus Christ* by Thomas à Kempis as his spiritual guide, deciding that Erasmus's manual was "calculated to quench little by little the fervor of piety in the souls of his readers" (Joly, 1976, p. 70). In this decision, St. Ignatius reflected his devotion to the inner stream, retaining only soldierly metaphors for those who would follow him in the strenuous path. It is the mystical tradition that Loyola turns to and in so doing, in the view of Amaury de Riencourt, gave it new shape and meaning. "Here, for the first time in the West, mysticism is treated almost as a science and technique rather than art. For the first time it is handled almost in Yoga fashion, brought under control of human will, disciplined" (de Riencourt, 1981, p. 114).

Loyola's *Exercises*, "a terrifying programme to flesh and blood" (Joly, 1976, p. 22), was a means toward a dual end, to know and love Christ as much as possible and to enrich and fortify the soul for conversion of others. This is also the aim of Muscular Christianity, but one should note the differences in methods as seen in Loyola's emphasis on poverty, an attitude exactly opposite to that of adherents of Muscular Christianity who today testify in sartorial splendor and who, like most of us, have never missed a meal or even known any real anguish of spirit. There is no doubt about it: *Spiritual Exercises* are incompatible with the ways of the world, including wealth or success in sports. The schools in their names may have had great athletic teams at various times, but it was not so desired by the Jesuit Fathers. Just as Loyola rejected "Courtly Exercises" of his youth, so his most famous student, St. Francis Xavier, who had won distinction in university sports, would atone, after taking the spiritual exercises for the first time, "for the vanity of his athleticism" (Brodrick, 1971, p. 43).

It is, then, in the tradition of spiritual exercises as opposed to Muscular Christianity, that the distinction between sports and religion becomes most apparent, but as different as these two responses are to the teaching of Christ, they do not differ from each other as much as both do from the idea of divine or holy play. There are many variations on the theme of the religious nature of play, but I will list what I believe to be the essential points:

1. The cosmos is "dancing" and God Himself is dancer and dance.

2. If God is at play and the universe is dancing, then God is immanent instead of transcendent: that is, He is in the world rather than above it. Hence, he can be "known" through experience, just as the playing child does or the dancing primi-

tive. The primitive man "dances with weighty seriousness, dancing for his gods, indeed dancing in pantomime of the deeds of his gods. This brings us by a new path to the *other*, the holy: the depersonification lies in the playing of a role, the turning away from everyday life that is involved in putting on a mask. The mask unites the dancer with the being that is represented by him, whether animal, god, or spirit of the dead" (Van der Leeuw, 1963, p. 19).

3. An original unity of primitive rituals has broken down completely. Today "we dress up wonderfully in the evening for the masked ball, and the next morning, with expressions, put on our lieutenant's uniform in order to perform our 'service' in it. For the primitive man, 'entertainment' and court session, ball and 'service' coincide" (Van der Leeuw, 1963, p. 19). The original unity of seriousness and non-seriousness David Miller refers to as *spoudogeloios*, which translates "grave-Merry," but which differs considerably, Miller says, from the ideal of *eutrapelia* that Aquinas adopted from Aristotle as a Christian virtue, meaning, as Hugo Rahner points out, "well-turning," a "well-turning" person being one who can avoid extremes of buffoonery and boorishness.

4. In contrast to the old Protestant belief in the sacredness of work, the new play theologians see work as a "necessary evil," a detriment both to play and the sacred life. Says Michael Novak in *The Joy of Sports:* "*Being, beauty, truth, excellence, transcendence*—these words, grown in the soil of play, wither in the sand of work. Art, prayer, worship, love, civilization: these thrive in the field of play" (Novak, 1976, p. xii).

5. Play theology is romantic with emphasis being placed upon the way of the primitive, the child, upon, as David Miller says, "celebrated, not cerebrated sensation: the con-fusing of all senses." Meaning thus comes through the "interplay of senses" (Miller, 1970, p. 140).

Theologians, philosophers, and critics such as David Miller, Michael Novak, and Gerardus Van der Leeuw have done a great service in pointing out the possibilities of play. They have shown astounding connections between play and religion, play and art, and the serious and non-serious. For these achievements and others, we owe them a debt of gratitude. These questions, however, must be asked: Have they not in elevating play to the divine and holy levels, devalued, somehow, the old transcendent theology? In widening the possibilities of play, are they not also actually reducing the varieties of religious experience? In focusing upon parallels between the beautiful and the holy instead of distinctions, in suggesting the complementary nature of the profane and sacred, in celebrating the holy senses and the harmony of motion, have they not made religion seem as facile, accessible and anti-intellectual as Muscular Christians ever did?

The answer, I believe, to these questions is a qualified yes. Play may indeed be a route to the sacred—for who can speak with certainty on these matters?—but I wish "to play" the skeptic here just as I do in regard to the belief that muscularity is an acceptable form of witnessing for Christ. There is something just as troublesome about the new play theology as there is about "Karate for Christ."

The crux of the problem lies in the attitude toward the holy, that which has traditionally distinguished religion from all other human endeavors. It will become clear when we remind ourselves what the holy is, or has been, that sports, as different as they are from work and labor, scarcely qualify for the category of sacred. In fact, when one evaluates sports and play in terms of the holy, the temptation is to regard them as a means of satisfying the narcissistic emotions of childhood. What, then, is the holy?

Perhaps the most distinguished book on this subject is Rudolf Otto's *The Idea of the Holy* which both Van der Leeuw and Robert Neale draw upon and discuss, Neale quite extensively in the distinction he makes between magic and religion (Neale, 1970, pp. 98-125). For both, play is not at all incompatible with the holy but a means of attaining thereto. These arguments are impressive, but not entirely convincing, for reasons that I will presently outline.

Let me first, however, cite a few characteristics of the holy, as defined by Otto (1958, p. 5):

> 'Holiness'—'the holy'—is a category of interpretation and valuation peculiar to the sphere of religion. It is, indeed, applied by transference to another sphere—that of ethics—but it is not itself derived from this. While it is complex, it contains a quite specific element or 'moment,' which sets it apart from 'the rational' in the meaning we gave to that word above, and which remains inexpressible . . . —or *ineffable*—in the sense that it completely eludes apprehension in terms of concepts. The same thing is true (to take a quite different region of experience) of the category of the beautiful.

This distinction between holy and the beautiful is crucial. Sports belong to the realm of the beautiful, play the natural, and religion to the sublime. Hence, they do not mix easily, if at all. It is true that Otto says the holy may "be developed into something beautiful and pure and glorious," but this is not the holy thing itself, which is "wholly other" by Otto's definition, that which causes "blank wonder, an astonishment that strikes us dumb, amazement absolute" (Otto, 1958, p. 26).

The holy, then, is supernatural, transcendent, mysterious, aweful, wholly other, and as overpowering in wrath and energy as in love and joy.

Here then, are the characteristics of the holy, the numinous and overpowering aspect of the experience, the transcendent and supernatural quality, and the weeping of the beholder of the vision. Such an instance is not, I contend, apt to occur either in sports or play, since both serve different ends than those of the spiritual quest engaged in by mystics. Thus, here are non-holy as well as holy aspects of sports (ludus) and play (paidia).

1. *Public Performance.* Though practice may be performed in private, all athletics are invariably public since the athlete is by definition "one who contends for a prize in the public games" (*Webster's Unabridged*). The holy by contrast is sought in solitude usually with the seeker sitting still, very still.

2. *Crowds.* While Michael Novak in *The Joy of Sports* uses the filled stadium to suggest parallels between sports and a religion (the natural religion), the truth of the

matter is that crowds work against the idea of the holy, insure almost its exclusion. "Sports," Novak acknowledges, "are not the highest form of religion . . . Jews, Christians, and others will want to put sports in second place, within a scheme of greater ultimacy" (Novak, 1976, p. 20). I do not choose to see sports as religion at all, one reason being the crowd. The terrifying aspect of crowds is dealt with by Elias Canetti in *Crowds and Power*, a book that all promoters of spectator sports should read though none will. It is true that the crowd takes on aspects of the sublime as can be glimpsed in the crowd symbols Canetti employs—fire, sea, rain, rivers, wind, etc.—but this is natural sublimity, raw, unconscious energy as opposed to the religious sublime described by mystics. Howard Slusher in *Man, Sport and Existence* [1967] builds a case for the silence in the sound of sports even in the stadium, a paradox that many have experienced, but crowds certainly are not prerequisite to a sense of the silent.

Canetti sees all crowds as packs, including religious groups, which would tend to support Novak's easy comparison and also strengthen links between sports, especially hunting, and religion. The connection, though, is ironic. At the outset, there is the hunting pack which, with death of a member, changes into the lamenting pack which in turn changes into a war pack to avenge the death of "the foremost hunter." In the primitivism of its rituals, the cheering and chanting of crowds, in the totemism evident in team names and mascots, in the belief in luck and superstition of both players and fans, sports provide a key to understanding our animistic past but little or no help in pointing toward spiritual directions. We watch sports both for the pleasure they provide, both aesthetic and primitive, and to prevent their reversion to savagery which always threatens. For possibilities of what might lie ahead spiritually, we look not to athletes but to seers, Chardin, for example, who was, incidentally, a Jesuit.

3. *Sports and Order*. Whereas the purpose of religion is to lead man to the holy and then to holy action, to truth and goodness, the goal of sports is beauty, from the Greek word *cosmos* meaning order. As an aesthetic endeavor sport is eternally satisfying, reflecting perhaps more than any other human activity what Lin Yutang calls the "swing":

All good form has a swing, and it is the swing that is beautiful to look at, whether it is the swing of a Champion golf-player's club, or of a man rocketing to success, or of a football player carrying the ball down the field. There must be a flow of expression, and the power of expression must not be hampered by the technique, but must be able to move freely and happily in it. There is that swing—so beautiful to look at—in a train going round a curve, or a yacht going at full speed with straight sails (Lin Yutang, 1937, p. 375).

In this swing, there is balance, harmony, predictability. Beauty pleases, reassures, composes; the holy, by contrast disturbs, unsettles, strikes down, lifts up, and transforms, belonging entirely to the "sphere of wonder," "before which words recoil, and to which no understanding has ever attained" (Otto, 1962, p. 45). The holy is analogous to the sublime which Edmund Burke also contrasts with beauty in *A Philosophical Inquiry into the Origin of Our Ideas of the Sublime and the Beautiful* [1958].

4. *The Prize*. Perhaps no distinction is more crucial in sports and religion than that of the prize. In sports, the prize is always worldly—money, trophy, fame, personal glory—even if God, as is often the case, is given the credit for victory. In the quest for the holy, the "prize" is of a different order altogether. "The most beautiful thing which man can say of God is that, knowing his inner reaches [the prize] he becomes silent. Therefore, 'prate not of God,' say Eckhart and Sānkara" (Otto, 1962, p. 49). Put another way, "woudst thou be perfect, do not yelp about God," says Eckhart. Compare this attitude, by the way, with the vocal witnessing of Muscular Christians.

5. *Athletic Excellence*. Much has been made about the athlete's concern for excellence, and coaches such as Vince Lombardi have been called perfectionists. The athlete's desire for excellence as athlete is, however, a limited type of excellence. One engaged in spiritual exercises or a holy quest desires a higher form of excellence, higher even than the *Arete* of the Greeks. The quality that Robert Pirsig in *Zen and the Art of Motorcycle Maintenance* [1974] equates with *Dharma* and *Arete* is not the holy which would be more analogous to what Pirsig calls *terra incognita*, unknown land. Quality which is energized by the holy is a middle way between the on-going myths and the *terra incognita*: it is the cutting edge between cosmos and chaos. Quality, like love, is "quenched wrath." The "spiritual athlete" wants to go to the realm of pure being, perhaps best described by Walt Whitman [1959], the "teacher of athletes," in the immortal section 5 of "Song of Myself" in his address to the soul: "Not words, not music or rhyme I want, not custom or lecture, not even the best, only the lull I like, the hum of your valved voice."

6. *Joy and Pleasure*. Much has been written in recent years on the joy of sports and the joy of sex, both terms being titles of books. Joy, traditionally a religious term, has been appropriated by writers in the secular realm in order to elevate, if not to sanctify, activities that in themselves were always considered worldly and pleasurable. Sex, however, has been used as a means of nature mysticism as much as sports, and religious claims have been made for both, beginning with Whitman, I believe, that would have astonished the most liberal of saints. For Whitman, however, sex was not recreational but procreational; and sports was, with poetry and song, a means of celebration.

Today we have a situation in which sex, a means of continuing life, and sports and play, a means of celebrating it, have become ends in themselves with reigning goddesses and heroes, the athlete heroes, as Lewis Mumford has observed in "Sport and the Bitch Goddess," representing Mars and the beauty queen Venus (Mumford, 1963, p. 306).

Pleasure and joy have often been used indiscriminately, but the difference between them, until recently, has been clear. Pleasure derives from expansion or indulgence of the self in sports, play, sex, fantasy, eating, drinking, etc.; joy, by contrast, comes from worship of the Other, from giving due homage and praise, and on rare occasion from encounter with the Holy. Pleasure, if carried to excess, is sinful, hence invariably predictable, which is why the church has always made provisions for pleasure. Joy, too, is predictable, joy of a certain kind, but utter joy is always a surprise and only comes, so the mystics tell us, after great effort, spiritual effort that is, as opposed to the physical, though asceticism is usually a factor in both. Perhaps we might think on St. Ignatius as he too battled with this eternal problem while he conceived the idea for *Spiritual Exercises*, the instructions on discernment coming from Christ via St. Catherine of Siena. Says Christ to the saint, "If you ask me how you are to recognize what comes from the devil and what comes from me, I answer that this is the sign for your guidance: —if the idea comes from the ideal, the soul receives all at once a feeling of lively joy; but the longer the state lasts, the more the joy diminishes, and leaves you in weariness, confusion and darkness—But if the soul is visited by me, the Eternal Truth, it is, at the outset, seized with holy fear and subsequently receives gladness, sweet prudence, and the desire for virtue" (Joly, 1976, p. 16).

As yet there have not been too many instances of seizures of holy fear on the playing field. Until there are more reports of some, the mysticism of sports and play will need to be regarded with a skeptical eye as well as all shouts of "joy" coming from the stadium or playground. And joy claimed from sports should be compared (or contrasted) with that mentioned by the scientist Pascal in describing his famous "night of fire" (as quoted by de Riencourt, 1981, p. 157), "In the year of the Lord, 1654, Monday, November 23, from 10:30 p.m. until half past twelve, fire." This two-hour long mystical experience must have been staggering, for he consigned it breathlessly in terse words and pithy sentences, obviously overwhelmed by the joy that swept over him: "God of Abraham, God of Isaac, God of Jacob; not of the philosophers and the scholars. Certainty. Certainty. Certainty. Feeling. Joy. Peace." And so it goes on, "Joy! Joy! Tears of Joy!"

The distinction between joy and pleasure could not be more clear, even by implication, than in Aquinas's commentary on Aristotle's *Nicomachean Ethics*: "As man needs from time to time to rest and leave off bodily labors, so also his mind from time to time must relax from its intense concentration on serious pursuits: This comes about through play . . . Those who go to excess in merrymaking . . . are not softened by the pleasure of play" (Rahner, 1972, p. 99). Once again, as the church fathers have taught: rest relaxes the body; play (in moderation) the mind and soul. Hence play is a pleasure, but hardly a joy which belongs to another order.

7. *Play and Mysticism*. There is no doubt that play is closer to the idea of the holy than is sports competition. One cannot imagine God competing, at least as men do, while play seems a fitting activity as David Miller (1970, p. 158) argues in quoting Meister Eckart:

This play was played eternally before all natures. As it is written in the Book of Wisdom, "Prior to creatures, in the eternal now, I have played before the Father in an eternal stillness." The Son has eternally been playing before the Father as the Father has before the Son. The playing of the twain is the Holy Ghost in whom they both disport themselves and he disports himself in both.

Sport and players are the same. Their nature proceeding in itself. "God is a fountain flowing into itself," as St. Dionysius says.

Eckhart, Miller says, has achieved the view of God as a player, which is what man and the church both need to do, he argues. This is a compelling argument but there are crucial qualifications which I would like to register. It should be noted that while Eckhart sees trinity at play, he himself is *still*. True, the experience he has is not "a work" as Otto says, but it is something other than "experience," the term most often used in description and which is loaded in favor of the idea of play. Mysticism, especially that of the high order of Eckhart and Sānkara, however, is as much a matter of vision as experience:

The way may be prepared by the words of the Vedas and by meditation (pratyaya) on them, but in the end it must be our own vision. It dawns like an aperçu (Goethe) and as soon as it is perceived, the Vedas becomes superfluous. Study and reflection then cease. . . . (Otto, 1962, p. 51).

Just as study and reflection cease, so too does play, both of the mind and the body. "When the confusing play of ideas (Chittam) has come to rest and he, thus, through himself, through the purified 'inward organ' apprehends the Highest, which is wholly spirit, essentially light, then he wins through to joy" (Otto, 1962, p. 52). Jacob Boehme makes the same point when he says: "Blessed art though therefore if thou canst stand still from self-thinking and self-willing, and canst stop the wheel of thy imagination and senses" (de Riencourt, 1981, p. 113).

The message is clear: God may be at play, but play may not necessarily be the way to know him. Worship, meditation, and study may still be the safest ways, all of which imply a certain seriousness that is even on the somber side of the much praised ideal of *eutrapelia*. To know God, God the player, if play theorists prefer, it is necessary to sit still as the psalmist advised. Indeed one could almost, in the light of recent books on theology of play, amend the psalmist's verse to read, in the flip language of some play theorists themselves, "Sit still long enough and with the really right attitude, and I will put on a show the likes of which you cannot imagine!"

If we are to sit still in wonder before the play of the Lord, play being only *one* characteristic, when is there justification for play among ourselves? When the mind and soul need rest and pleasure.

Play refreshed Henry David Thoreau, the refreshment being evident in his own tale of his own fox chase.

Suddenly looking down the river, I saw a fox some sixty rods off making across the hills on my left. As the snow lay five inches deep, he made but slow progress, but it was no impediment to me. So yielding to the instinct of the chase, I tossed my head aloft, and bounded away, snuffing the air like a foxhound, and spurning the world and human society at each bound. It seemed the woods rang with the hunter's horn, and Diana and all the satyrs joined in the chase and cheered me on. Olympian and Elean youths were waving palms on the hills (Thoreau, 1965, p. 424).

In spite of Thoreau's references to cheering of the gods and goddesses, all pagan, he did not intend this experience to be regarded as divine. Divinity he sought in his hours of contemplation walking or sitting perfectly still in his doorway. Thoreau is an example of the forgotten virtue of *eutrapelia* as described by Hugo Rahner. He could "turn" from play to seriousness with relative ease, but would have been bewildered by the call for a "theology of play." To him religion meant worship or meditation, the reward of which was joy.

The problem with the theses of Miller, Neale, Van der Leeuw, and others lies in their praise of celebration of the "original unity" of religion and dance and their lament over the essential break-up of unity. Dissolution of primitive or pagan unity is simply an evolutionary law of life, a prerequisite for deeper unities in which the encounter with the Other is based not upon physical experiences alone but consciousness as well, an "intellectual" vision. The problem of our times is not so much that we have lost touch with the rhythms of our bodies, but that we have lost faith in intellectual or spiritual possibilities such as, for example, those pointed out by Chardin. One has only to teach one class of athletes or non-athletes to realize the truth of what I am saying. To lament the original unity of functions is to reduce God to immanence where He can be anything or to reduce Him altogether as did Henry Adams, the most famous lamenter of all time on the death of unity. It is also to diminish or ignore the rich and powerful accounts of the many mystics who have not only felt the presence of God, but "seen" Him with their "inward organ."

Another who clearly achieved *eutrapelia* is Loren Eiseley, a spiritual descendent of Thoreau who also had an encounter with a fox, one that was, I believe, truly holy, but which also needs to be put in perspective lest it be assumed that the encounter was experience only, devoid of vision, and hence a justification for belief in immanence.

On one of his many excursions in the natural world, Eiseley came upon a young fox under the timbers of a foundered boat who "innocently" placed a chicken bone in his mouth and shook it at the author invitingly while placing his forepaws appealingly together. "Gravely" Eiseley did likewise with a whiter bone, facing the fox and arranging his own forepaws appropriately. "Round and round," he says, "we tumbled for one ecstatic moment." For Eiseley, it was the gravest, most meaningful act he would ever accomplish, leading him to a view of the Universe "as it begins for all things. It was, in reality, a child's universe, a tiny and laughing universe" (Eiseley, 1969, p. 210).

Here on the surface appears justification for the play theology of Miller, Neale and others, but again modification is required. Certainly the incident could never have happened without a playful attitude on the part of the author. Neither could it have happened without the intellectual curiosity of a great scientist. It is this intellectual content that the play theologists overlook in their talk of psychic harmony and "seeing" with the whole body. Mysticism, in spite of the new emphasis on body knowledge, is a mental phenomenon. Eiseley did indeed experience something, shuffling round on all fours with a bone in his mouth with the innocent fox, but he also *beheld* something. God may be in the universe in other words, but he is also above it—a belief called panentheism or immanence (Wolf, 1974, p. 173).

Perhaps this explains why so many mystics, though not all, have been individuals of soaring passion and intellect: St. Paul, St. Augustine, St. Ignatius, Pascal, Jonathan Edwards, Walt Whitman, and perhaps most notably, Sānkara and Eckhart.

The Psychic Side of Sports by Michael Murphy and Lea White contains compelling testimony of several athletes which at first glance would lead one to think that both sports and play have been underrated throughout history as far as otherwordly experiences are concerned. Perhaps they have, and perhaps George Leonard, author of *The Ultimate Athlete*, from which they quote on the psychic possibilities of sports, is also right when he says:

> Pressing us up against the limits of physical exertion and mental acuity, leading us up to the edge of the precipice separating life from death, sports may open the door to infinite realms of perception and being. Having no tradition of mystical experience, no adequate mode of discourse on the subject, no preparatory rites, the athlete might refuse to enter. But the athletic experience is a powerful one, and it may thrust the athlete, in spite of fear and resistance, past the point of no return, into a place of awe and terror (Quoted in Murphy and White, 1978, p. 32).

Sports may indeed lead us into "infinite realms of perception and being," but the track record on spiritual exercises and meditation is already well established in both East and West. I would be the last to shut the door on spiritual possibilities of sports and play, but here I will play devil's advocate to the end by arguing that the psychic experiences recorded by the authors are really not spiritual at all, not even the most mystical among them.

What are the implications of the difference between nature mysticism and spiritual mysticism? Simply, the difference between expansion of self and the contraction of self before the immensity of the Other. It is the difference between power and reverential awe. The mysticism of the Nazis was of course a nature mysticism in which adherents sought more and more power in the name of their *power form* (Hitler) but knew nothing of the simple humility asked for by Christ. "Whoever truly serves beauty serves God," says Van der Leeuw. While the word "truly" can help defend the statement against several charges, it should be remarked that beauty comes in many strange packages, fascism being one; the march, the play, the dance—all are forms of beauty and action and all the opposite to meditation. Van der Leeuw convincingly cites several sources, not just gnostic, where dance is taken as "the movement of God," but how easy it is for most of us to confuse movement with the mover. One should, in arriving at a complete picture, consider not merely the spirit that "moves" us physically in dance or play or emotionally in response to art (either holy or profane) but also that spirit which has "spoken" directly to the "chosen" among us over the ages. The confusion of nature with the Divine has been one of the crucial problems of our times, and sports theorists have not shed a great deal of light upon that all-important distinction, though they have rushed in to show similarities in such numbers as to make play theology a new cult if not a new heresy.

I believe that though sports and play may provide aesthetic pleasure, natural delight, and rest for the mind and soul, they are not inherently divine and should be watched over very carefully lest they shows signs of corruption, one of which signs *is* an encroachment upon the domain of religion in ways far more subtle than Sunday baseball and on the other hand far less obvious than "Karate for Christ," the signs in all cases being indications of paganism or nature worship.

To be sure the old dissentients were not altogether right, at least in their censorious attitudes, but would anyone now argue that with our accommodating theologies, we are any more enlightened on this topic than the previous generation? (Wide World of Sports and All Sports Channels are as relentless as reality itself.) Indeed, it has occurred to me that cable television with its Christian, political science, news, and sports channels has brought right into our living rooms daily coverage of what Thorstein Veblen in *Theory of the Leisure Class* called the four occupations of a predatory culture—sports, government, warfare, and religion.

Veblen's thesis, in fact, has never been successfully refuted, and it is a troubling thesis indeed—that is, as a society moves from a peaceful, primitive state into an industrialized state of barbarism, which would now be most societies in the world, leisure-class activities, sports, religion, government, and the military become mutually supportive and interdependent to form conservative habits of thought and behavior. Play becomes institutionalized (and sanctified) while religion, especially Muscular Christianity, smiles on the status quo (MX missile and all). Thankfully, this is not altogether true—as seen, for instance, in the stand taken by the U.S. Catholic Bishops against the nuclear arms race, thus exhibiting the moral power and dissent that has traditionally been the church's prerogative.

In its passion for visibility and for influence in high places, Muscular Christianity in America has lost knowledge of the invisible, that is, the holy. The old ideal of quietude has yielded to emotion and incessant "yelping" about God. The believers in holy play, on the other hand, have also cheapened the idea of the holy by associating it with the cosmic dance without seeking a vision of the One who, like fire, is still and in motion at once. Both have misinterpreted the role of the body in Christianity, the one by witnessing through muscle, the other by implying that play or experience is the route to the holy. Though there are exceptions, one is essentially a Protestant, almost Southern, movement in the United States, while the other has turned for its lessons not so much to traditional Christianity as to primitive cultures, pagan philosophy, and Oriental thought stressing the dance of Shiva. Ironically, though, it is the quiet tradition of spiritual exercises that promises the strongest union with the East, with its emphasis upon prayer and meditation and belief in the Wholly Other which has many sides, a playful side, an awful side of unspeakable terror and wonder, and a still rapt side of silence that is worth a lifetime of effort to experience and behold, so the church fathers and Eastern mystics aver. Spiritual exercises are also the promising mode for the achievement of peace, for only "quenched wrath" can save the world, not lecture, sermon, sport, play, humor or knowledge. The most that play can do is to make the world bearable; the most that sports can do is to make it beautiful. When claims are made for them beyond these roles, they too become part of the problem.

Bibliography

"Are Sports Good for the Soul?" *Newsweek*, January 11, 1971.

Brodrick, James, S.J. *The Origin of the Jesuits*. 1940. Reprint: Westport, Ct.: Greenwood Press, 1971.

Burke, Edmund. *A Philosophical Inquiry Into the Origin of Our Ideas of the Sublime and the Beautiful*. Ed. James T. Bolton. London: Routledge and Kegan Paul, 1958.

Caillois, Roger. *Man, Play, and Games*. Trans. Meyer Barash. New York: Free Press, 1961.

Caretti, E. *Crowds in Power*. Trans. Carol Stewart. New York: Continuum, 1973.

Deford, Frank. "Religion in Sport." *Sports Illustrated*, 19 April 1976, pp. 88-102.

—"Endorsing Jesus." *Sports Illustrated*, 26 April 1976, pp. 54-69.

—"Reaching for the Stars." *Sports Illustrated*, 3 May 1976, pp. 42-60.

de Riencourt, Amaury. *The Eye of Shiva: Eastern Mysticism and Science*. New York: William Morrow, 1981.

Edwards, Harry. *Sociology of Sport*. Homewood, Ill.: Dorsey Press, 1973.

Eiseley, Loren. *The Unexpected Universe*. New York: Harcourt Brace Jovanovich, 1969.

Joly, Henri. *St. Ignatius of Loyola*. Trans. Mildred Partridge. 1899. Reprint. New York: AMS Press, 1976.

Koestler, Arthur. *The Act of Creation*. New York: The Macmillan Company, 1969.

Kuntz, Paul Grimley. "Serious Play: An Absurdity or a Paradox that Integrates Life?" *Listening: Journal of Religion and Culture*, 16:1 (Winter 1981), pp. 68-85.

Lin Yutang. *The Importance of Living*. New York: Teynal and Hitchcock, 1937.

Miller, David. *Gods and Games: Toward a Theology of Play*. New York: World, 1970.

Mumford, Lewis. *Technics and Civilization*. New York: Harcourt Brace and World, 1963.

Murphy, Michael and Lea White. *The Psychic Side of Sports*. Reading, Mass: Addison Wesley Publishing Co., 1978.

Neale, Robert E. *In Praise of Play: Toward a Psychology of Religion*. New York: Harper and Row, 1970.

Needleman, Jacob. *Lost Christianity*. New York: Doubleday and Co., 1980.

Novak, Michael. *The Joy of Sports: End Zones, Bases, Baskets, Balls, and the Consecration of the American Spirit*. New York: Basic Books, 1976.

Otto, Rudolf. *The Idea of the Holy*. Trans. John W. Harvey. New York: Oxford University Press, 1958.

—*Mysticism East and West: A Comparative Analysis of the Nature of Mysticism*. Trans. Bertha L. Bracy and Richenda C. Payne. New York: Collier Books, 1962.

Pearson, John. *Arena: The Story of the Colosseum*. New York: McGraw-Hill, 1973.

Pirsig, Robert. *Zen and the Art of Motorcycle Maintenance: An Inquiry Into Values.*
New York: Morrow, 1974.

Rahner, Hugo. *Man at Play.* New York: Herder and Herder, 1972.

Rogers, Cornish. "Sports, Religion, and Politics: The Renewal of an Alliance."
Christian Century, 89 (April 1972), pp. 392-394.

Sisk, John P. "Hot Sporting Blood." *Intellectual Digest,* 4 (November 1973), pp.
46-47.

Slusher, Howard. *Man, Sport, and Existence: A Critical Analysis.* Philadelphia:
Lea and Febiger, 1967.

Snyder, Eldon E. and Elmer A. Spreitzer. *Social Aspects of Sports.* Englewood
Cliffs, N.J.: Prentice-Hall, 1978.

Thoreau, Henry David. *Walden and Other Writings.* Ed. Joseph W. Krutch. New
York: Bantam, 1965.

Van der Leeuw, Gerardus. *Sacred and Profane Beauty: The Holy in Art.* Trans.
David E. Green. New York: Holt Rinehart and Winston, 1963.

Veblen, Thorstein. *The Theory of the Leisure Class.* New York: Macmillan, 1899.

Waddell, Helen. *The Desert Fathers.* Ann Arbor: The University of Michigan
Press, 1960.

Whitman, Walt. *Complete Poetry and Selected Prose by Walt Whitman.* Ed. James
H. Miller. Boston: Houghton Mifflin, 1959.

Wolf, William J. *Thoreau: Mystic, Prophet, Ecologist.* Philadelphia: United Church
Press, 1974.

Big-Time Spectator Sports:
A Feminist Christian Perspective

Denise Lardner Carmody

I write just after the 1985 World Series, when the State of Missouri couldn't lose and football, about halfway through its season, now has most of the prime-time sports slots to itself. (Basketball and hockey have begun, but they aren't serious competition.) My first image is of George Brett puffing his cheeks out like a chipmunk and spitting out the dark juice of his chew. It is not pleasant. Later some cameraman (I'm pretty sure of the gender) will catch one of the boys in a moment of scratching that should be private. The spitting and the scratching, like the hitting of the three-hundred-pound lineman (or the two-hundred pound boxer), remind me again that big-time sports are still largely a male preserve. Mary Lou Retton and Chris Evert Lloyd offer counter-images of feminine power and grace (no spitting yet, thank the Goddess), but most Sunday afternoons it's male rites of sublimation, where violence is as American as bible-thumping and making money. What is a good Irish Catholic featherweight (115 lbs.), with no power in either fist, to make of it all? In what way should the Christian sisterhood think about sports and salvation? Let me muse under three headings: Idolatry, Competition, and Ecstasy.

Idolatry

It is the "Protestant Principle," as enunciated by such theologians as Paul Tillich, that in recent American Christianity has spoken most forcefully about the sovereignty of God and the constant danger of idolatry. Almost as powerfully as the Muslims, for whom idolatry (*shirk*) is the greatest sin, the Christians most impressed with the priority of God (as both Creator and Redeemer) have thundered against our tendency to set things other than God in the sanctuary. These other things—various species of mammon—are distinguished from sacraments (material presences or

105

conduits of God) by their opacity. A sacrament, as Catholic theology especially has taught, flows from the incarnational nature of Christian religion and gives flesh to God's desire to fill our lives with grace. Idols, by contrast, attempt to block out the sovereign mystery of God. They would seduce us to think that our buying and selling, our poking and stroking, form something complete unto itself. The prime danger of big-time sports, I submit, is their congruence with mammon, forgetfulness, and a tiny or superficial soul. They form some of the most influential holding companies in the conglomerate industries of distraction, and as such any Christian must view them quite critically.

A properly feminist criticism certainly will confess early on that the distraction industries catering to women are no less virulent than big-time sports can be. The afternoon soaps, for example, have always been sentimental and escapist, but now they push sleaze and approach soft-core pornography. The romance series of escapist novels are little better, and sometimes I'm inclined to throw in the ladies' luncheon. The latter, combined with addictive shopping, keeps more American women distracted or chained to mammon than I can comfortably contemplate. Every time I see the bumper sticker on my neighbor's car ("When the going gets tough, the tough go shopping"), I get slightly sick to my stomach. There comes to mind Dorothy Dinnerstein's all too apt title for the sexual malaise afflicting our culture: *The Mermaid and the Minotaur*.

Apart from the quadrennial occurrence of the Olympics, I seldom associate the mermaid with big-time sports. The minotaur, pawing the ground and slavering for blood, drifts into my study many Sundays, when my husband takes "a little football break." He favors the Raiders and the Cowboys, by some Manichean formula of Evil and Good, and he claims to take it all very lightly. This probably is true, but I have watched a few of the college coaches howling on the sidelines, and I have seen fathers howling on the sidelines at Peewee games, so I'm not willing to grant such detachment to the American male at large. The football and basketball coaches at many schools, I know, earn considerably more than the full professors. The figures on the percentage of athletes who graduate, and on the racial composition of the sports teams, and on the illegal contributions of the boosters (to say nothing of the scandals of point-shaving), suggest that big-time sports are a very dubious portion of American higher (and lower) education. We have in many places a monster out of control, and I don't see the will to corral it. Even worse, in many regions of the country it would be considered as un-American and unchristian to knock football as it would be to knock the weapons industry.

What may be specifically feminist in a critical approach to these phenomena is pointing out the dimension of gender. Just as the budgets of big-time college sports are far from equally divided between male and female athletes, so the identification that goes on is less than androgynous. The biggest spectacles, with the possible exception of the Olympics, nearly exclusively deal with men. Worse, at big-time football [games] women play the role of courtesans, jiggling and grinding on the sidelines. In the perspective of worldwide evil, this play of fluff and tease of course ranks very low, but as another bit of the sexism defacing our cultural mosaic, it should not be passed by. Billie Jean King and Chris Evert Lloyd have gotten parity for women in tennis, but too many little girls still aspire to be Los Angeles Raider-ettes or Dallas Cowboy Cheerleaders (Lord forbid one should call them cowgirls: Mary Kay would be horrified). My point, then, is rather basic: a feminist Christian critique of big-time spectator sports finds more than a few ways in which the current goings-on serve not God but mammon and sexism.

Competition

If idolatry was a lens through which to study the disorders of big-time spectator sports, ecstasy (my concluding topic) will be a lens through which to study the uplifting possibilities. Competition strikes me as a mid-zone, where women and men may differ interestingly in their instinctive orientations, and where serious sports invite a serious analysis.

The stereotype is that the men in our culture have been raised to compete, while the women have been raised to cooperate. Like all stereotypes this one begs qualifi-cations and distinctions, but it does bear its quotient of truth. For example, my experience is that business is done differently in departments of Women's Studies, where women usually preside and men are rare, than it is done in departments where men preside, or even in departments where the sexual ratios are about equal. To simplify, the difference is that when women run a meeting they tend to build on one another's contributions, try to draw all participants into the discussion, and appor-tion fairly democratically the tasks that emerge. Symbolically, and frequently actu-ally, the seating arrangement is a circle. My perception of the standard meeting dominated by men (in at least half of the meetings that my job as an academic administrator entails and in which I am still the only woman) is that the dynamics are significantly different. The layout of the agenda may be a little clearer, but the clashes and disagreements are markedly more numerous. The spatial symbolism is of people sitting across from one another (at a rectangular conference table), while the flow of the discussion often is like the thrust and parry of the fencer.

This relates to graduate-school training, in which to date the style has been to hone critical skills. "Critical" has meant "finding the flaws" even more than it has meant "coming to a careful judgment," and creativity, constructive addition, complementarity, and other more positive possibilities have gotten very short shrift. Thus the typical academic (and professional) training, dominated rather unreflec-tively by stereotypically male modes of thought (linear, critical), has done little to build community or equip people to minister reconciliation or transcend the painful dichotomy between winners and losers.

What has all this to do with big-time spectator sports? Only the slow will not be raising their hands to answer. The paradigm of competition probably is masculine sports, just as the acme is outright war. The dialectic in which concepts clash, ideally to generate light but just as often to push people apart, gains manipulable form in chess. In boxing or football it clears the field of the complications of reality and lets two champions just have a go at one another. There are rules, to be sure, and older men in funny striped uniforms to enforce them. There are moments of grace, exhilaration, and reconciling handshakes. Coaches and athletes alike can be intelligent, creative, and emotionally moving. Why else would Presidents call them after the big game or business executives fawn over them at luncheons? The fall spectacle of college football, when the air is crisp and the plaid sweaters are vivid and the hormones take a trip down memory lane, is both bracing and on the whole rather innocent. When competition serves mainly to get people up to this *qui vive*, to bring out their best and focus their energies, even theologians and cultural critics have to love it.

It is only the excesses of competitive sports, the monomania and overheated aggression, that I find turns me off. Two men battering themselves bloody, or four men carrying off a linebacker who has just broken his neck, make me shield my eyes, for they are miniatures of the blood and gore of battle that has broken the human spirit for millennia. In their slogans (that a tie is like kissing your sister and winning is the only thing) they come close to the ugliest feature of biblical religion: the oxymoron called "holy war."

Ecstasy

I have to say, of course, that the nature which God has created is no stranger to blood and gore. I have to say also that there are evils which seem impervious to any solution other than crushing their spine. But I do not like the fixation on such evils that I have perceived in the scowl of an Indira Gandhi or the hawkishness of a Margaret Thatcher. They strike me as opportunities lost or capitulations made—places where Lady Wisdom must be weeping. The Jerry Falwell raised on football, chubby-cheeked and full of more than the bible, epitomizes much that I think has gone wrong in the relations between sports and religion. The militant religious fanatics, ecumenical in their distortion of their traditions, should all be forced to run marathons or punch bags until their arms drop. If competitive sports can siphon off violence or destructive aggression, let's hear it for competitive sports. If sports further can open realms of exstasis, places where the spirit jaunts to better realms, let's ponder an athletic spirituality.

My own preference is for participation and exercise, so let me first reflect on the ecstatic potential in these. Participation in sports, as in education, brings charges of energy and emotion that mere spectatorship seldom can. What one feels comes from what one is doing, and what one feels has a natural release in sweat, strain, and effort. If the sport is a team matter, there can be bonding and the sense of losing (and finding) oneself in a larger entity.

Our society is such a stranger to profound experiences of community that the temporary fusion of nine players into a beautifully functioning whole can seem a preview of the church triumphant.

In exercise, both in running and simulated cross-country skiing, I have learned things about the embodiment of the self and the Christian faith that otherwise I could only have conjectured. We are animals who need to race and jump. We would be less neurotic if we trimmed our lard and suffused our lungs. To Aquinas' recipe for relieving depression (prayer and a hot bath), I would add a vigorous workout. Had Tom himself done more of that, he might not have spilled over his cincture or died at forty-nine. The Word did become flesh. God has made us considerably different from the angels. We don't fully appreciate this until we like to sweat. If our ladies can only perspire, and even then can barely wait to get to their deodorant, we don't have a feminist Christianity.

The ecstasy of big-time spectator sport, vicarious and manipulated as it tends to be, first strikes me as quite problematic. I have been in a crowded basketball arena listening to a state official conflate sports, religion, and Americanism into a fervent attack on the Iranian fanatics. I started looking for jackboots and listening for "Deutschland uber Alles." But I have also enjoyed the spectacles of the Olympics and marveled at the perfect performances of Mark Spitz, Eric Heiden, and Carl Lewis. When sport transcends the big bucks and the TV hype, it can show us incarnate spirits achieving wonders. I love the perfect body of the mature Nadia Comanesci, the graceful power of the mature Martina Navratilova. Where one was flat as a boy and the other was round as a dumpling, both have become gorgeous specimens, aglow with an animal beauty that makes blusher superfluous and foundation perverse.

This is the ecstasy I find redeeming big-time spectator sports: now and then one can see humanity fully alive (Irenaeus's definition of God's glory). I don't think that the occasional glimpse we get justifies what the coaches and the networks subject us to. I don't think the rare time of perfection blocks out the regular babble and trivia and violence and manipulation. But I do think we should applaud grace wherever we find it. And I do think the men and women to whom God has given superb physical talents or athletic skills should be encouraged and applauded. It pains me that musicians and poets equally gifted should be so much less appreciated. I think the financial side of big-time spectator sports is a triumph of Satan. Yet despite that, now and then I find myself in front of the tube cheering, and I think I hear God joining in.

Evangelicalism and the Revitalization of Religious Ritual in Sport

Shirl J. Hoffman

According to historians, sport arose as a religious rite, but has long since been secularized (Guttmann, 1978). Yet there is underway in the athletic subculture what appears to be a genuine religious revitalization movement that seeks to convert sport performances to religious rituals. For some time the disproportionate numbers of religious athletes in big-time sport have been a matter of curiosity to social commentators, as have their eagerness to make public announcements about Divine Providence having played a hand in delivering a home run or a touchdown for their team. This extrinsic appropriation of religion to serve very practical ends, along with its trite and superficial descriptions, has led many to conclude that this represents the sum total of the theology of the sports-faith movement, and that the athletes have managed to put their theology at a considerable distance from their athletic experience.

Such a view denies the keen interest among Christian athletes who sincerely attempt to relate their religious beliefs to their athletic experiences. More importantly, it overlooks a relatively recent innovation in their theological conditioning, the increasing tendency to conceive of their performances as spiritual events, acts of worship which are intended first and foremost to glorify God.

Pete Brock, a 6'5", 260 lb. lineman for the New England Patriots, became a Christian in 1978, an event that changed his entire approach to professional football: "I now approach Sunday afternoons as a worship service," he says. "The Bible tells me, 'Present your bodies as a living and holy sacrifice, acceptable to God, which is your spiritual service or worship.' God has blessed me with a large body, great strength and the ability to play this difficult game. My responsibility is to play to 100% of my ability as a way of thanking Him for what He's done for me" ("Testimony," p. 2). Nancy Richey retired from the professional tennis tour in 1978, partly because of her age, but mostly because she found it increasingly difficult to reconcile her competitive emotions with her new-found Christian faith. "I had problems relating tennis to Christianity,'' she said. ''When I stepped onto a court I felt I was in an isolated area and the Lord was outside of that (area). I knew hating my opponent was not a Christian view.'' Thanks to some counseling from evangelist Tom Skinner, sometime chaplain for the Washington Redskins, Ms. Richey returned to the tour with a new perception of the significance of tennis in her spiritual life. ''I saw that tennis could be an act of worship and that I should try to make each shot as perfect as I could,'' she said. ''I'd never looked at tennis as an act of worship'' (''Tennis Pro'').

As described by these athletes, this form of athletic worship is different from the pragmatic religiosity of the locker room or the ''good feeling gospel'' glorified by the Sheehanites. Their talk is of a genuine worship, objectively discharged and borne of a shared religious belief system. Provided the athlete's heart is fixed on God, sport performances of almost any variety can be transformed into symbolic spiritual offerings in which the quality of the performance (the ritual form) and the motivations of the performer are considered more important than the euphoria generated by the experience.

Obviously these Christian rituals are different from the rites enacted at ancient Olympia. Not only were the Grecian athletic festivals pagan (from the Christian view), they were communal rites as well. The games transformed the stadium into a temple, bound participants and spectators in a religious ideal, reaffirmed their peculiar destiny and pledged their allegiance to Zeus. But the evangelical athletes talk of a more personal ritual: the contest isn't sacred, the individual performances are. Nancy Richey may deliver her blistering serve with a deep sense of spiritual purpose, but she realizes that most spectators and opponents don't share in the ritual experience. Hers is a private rite, publicly displayed in what often is an unholy sanctuary. Likewise when Pete Brock, in a spirit of percussive piety, blasts defensive targets onto their backsides, the ritual takes place as part of a pluralistic spectacle, the religious character of his act no doubt lost on his unfortunate victims. And, in light of its lurid history, one has to wonder if anything could transform Shaeffer Stadium into hallowed ground.

Not that privatization of athletic rituals renders them less authentic than the communal rites of the ancient games. Worship rituals are most commonly group exercises, but not exclusively so. Individualized forms of worship are relatively recent arrivals in the process of religious development, the notable example being the ''liturgy'' ushered in by the Protestant Reformation. When it tore down the barriers Medieval theology had interposed between the sacred and secular domains of life, post-reformation Calvinism broadened enormously the scope of Christian worship. Priests were no longer needed as mediators between God and worshippers. Common labor and the creative efforts of the Christian's hands could become consecrated offerings of praise and thanksgiving simply on the basis of the spirit and manner in which they were offered. To paraphrase Max Weber, ''All the world became a cathedral and every believer a priest.''

And so it has continued. Modern evangelicals take to heart St. Paul's admonition that everything they do should resound to the glory of God (I Cor. 10.31), work and play in worldly environments just as surely as hymns and prayers in the sanctuary. Ask a group of good Presbyterians the old catechismal query, "What is the chief end of man?" and they likely will respond with the words of the Westminster confession, "To glorify God and enjoy Him forever." Ask a group of evangelical athletes, "Why do you play sports?" and there is a good chance they will echo the words of former Pirate Manny Sanguillen, "I just want to glorify God, that's why I play ball" ("The Happiest Man in Town"). Neither the drunk on the bleachers, the blabbering broadcasters in the booth, nor the screaming coach, red-faced with jugular bulging, may appreciate the spiritual significance of the moment, but that in no way prevents Christian athletes from sanctifying a limited space in the stadium, symbolically endowing a heroic act with spiritual significance, and treating it as a ritual of worship.

If this trend among evangelical athletes constitutes the genesis of a genuine revitalization of religious ritual in sport, what are the chances that it will stimulate a reconceptualization of the meaning of sport among those in the burgeoning evangelical community who share the athletes' theological convictions? I believe the chances are not good, for one very critical reason. In presuming to appropriate sport as a ritualistic medium the Christian athletes confront an inevitable antinomy: Christian thought and sentiment shape the symbolic significance attached to athletic performances, but the ethos of modern sport has shaped its mode of expression. The result is a sharp disjunction between sentiment and symbol, between devotion and deed; a strange disparity between the heart-felt desires of the athlete's soul and the formulae which comprise the ritual act. This dialectic between the form and substance of the "athletic offering" has created sharp conflicts in the minds of Christian athletes, such that anyone wishing to make sense out of contemporary evangelical sportsthink must first understand it as an inspired, though unsuccessful, attempt to synchronize these disjunctive elements of ritual.

The Evangelicals' Conflict of Conscience

The conflict is recognizable on two fronts. The first concerns the athletes' attempts to deal with a suspicion (if not belief) lurking deep in the evangelical conscience, that sports are generically deficient as ceremonial substance. They are widely accepted as legitimate pastimes justifiable on sound utilitarian grounds, but on the whole there is little appreciation in the evangelical community for sport *qua* sport. Sport is for modern day evangelicals very much like it was for the congregation of Robert Higgs's boyhood church: "a wild animal, spirited, beautiful, but dangerous if one came too close" (Higgs, p. 62).

Since the mid-sixties, the editors of *Christianity Today*, the most influential and widely read evangelical periodical, have consistently bestowed their blessings on sport, but rarely without an accompanying caveat, "not to get carried away" or "not to overdo" the amount of time devoted to sports. Interestingly, the same concerns are not expressed about literature, philosophy, art, or classical music, traditionally viewed as experiences of a higher order. Somehow the souls of huffing, puffing, sports-playing brothers and sisters seem caught up in what is altogether too physical and superficial to inspire feelings of gratitude and reverence.[1] "Among the various activities we can relax with,'' reminded the editors of *Christianity Today*, ''athletics are low on the scale of demonstrable religious significance'' (''Sport: Are We Overdoing It?''). Most evangelicals may prefer basketball to Beethoven, baseball to Botticelli, and boxing to Bach, but deep in their hearts they know which is the more worthy spiritual offering.

Rough edges between the attitudinal correlates of competitive sport and the basic requirements for Christian worship create the second and most intractable source of conflict. Church tradition and scriptures quite clearly teach the importance of purity in expressive acts symbolically offered as rituals of worship. The New Testament Christians were just as concerned about the acceptability of their symbolic offerings as the Old Testament priests and prophets were about the purity of their animal sacrifices. Under most circumstances Christians wouldn't think of consecrating acts of robbery, murder and raw violence as worship, nor would they condone worshippers enacting the liturgy while harboring feelings of jealousy, hate, or the unquenchable thirst for revenge.

Yet anyone close to the sports scene knows that competition, even between the most amiable opponents, often becomes a rite of unholy unction, a sacrament in which aggression is vented, old scores settled, number one taken care of, and where the discourteous act looms as the principal liturgical device. Even in contests played in the shadow of church walls—the church league softball or basketball game—tempers can flare and the spiritual graces of compassion and sensitivity can place second to ''winning one for good ole' First Baptist.''

The psychological dimension of competition has always been a touchy subject among evangelicals, most of whom downplay its importance in the competitive process, and for good reason.[2] Any objective appraisal of the competitive process will reveal it as a social interaction driven entirely by the spirit of self-promotion. This is not an anomaly or a description of the competitive urge gone berserk. *This is the way it has to be.* Self-promotion is the lifeblood of competitive games. Those who would give the game an honest try (and this is widely held to be a spiritual duty of the Christian athlete) must make a sincere effort to win, and within the context of the game ''trying to win'' means promoting one's own (or team's) interest at the expense of the opponent's interests.

In a spirited but frank defense of competition, sailor Stuart Walker avowed that good competitors should ''. . . feel no concern for the opinion and feelings of others. . . .'' The lack of concern for the feelings of competitors is useful because it eliminates one distraction. ''If you don't care what the other fellow thinks, you can tack on him wherever you wish'' (Walker, p. 46). After all, said Walker, ''competition is not Christmas'' (p. 47). As a way of underscoring the common sense in Walker's philosophy, consider a sympathetic tennis player who constantly worried about the detrimental effects of her serve on her opponent's performance and, in a gesture of sympathy and good will, decreased is velocity and spin and placed it conveniently in the center of the service area. Not only would she win few championships, she would be ridiculed (even by her opponent) as a dangerous subversive, a spoil-sport who violated the unwritten contract by not giving the game an honest try.

Just as surely as sympathetic instincts can douse the fires of competition, a cool, calculated insensitivity toward opponents can fan them into a blaze. The so-called "killer instinct"—an instrumental affectlessness that enables a player "relentlessly and without inner prohibition or a sense of guilt to keep the pressure on his opponent while achieving victory . . ." (Beisser, p. 161)—is widely believed to be indispensable for athletic success. In an analysis of winning and losing attitudes among athletes, sport psychologist Bruce Ogilvie reported: "Almost every truly great athlete we have interviewed during the last four years representing every major sport has consistently emphasized that in order to be a winner you must retain the killer instinct" (Ogilvie, p. 37).

Testimonials to its importance appear regularly on the sports pages. Following Notre Dame's 1973 win over Pitt, Irish quarterback Tom Clements was asked by reporters if he "had consoled or felt any compassion" for Pitt quarterback Billy Daniels. After all, they had been friends in high school. "I didn't have any sympathy for him during the game," said Clements. "You never have any sympathy for an opponent" ("Playing Games"). Because such hard-nosed indifference doesn't always come naturally, the coaching fraternity has devised rituals to insure that sympathetic instincts don't get in the way of competitive fervor. The most common is to separate competing teams in the hours before a contest lest the social interaction promote friendly feelings. In the 1973 Fiesta Bowl which paired Pitt against Arizona State, the players were scheduled to attend a pregame steak-fry as part of the bowl festivities. Arizona State coach Frank Kush was upset. "You can't tell the kids that they're going up against a bunch of ogres, then have them sit across the table from the opponents at a banquet and find out that they're really pretty nice guys" ("Kush Puts the Kibosh on Camaraderie").

Coaches like Kush don't settle for mere affectlessness; how much better feelings of sympathy can be controlled if opponents are viewed as dangerous enemies. It is a trick employed by many superior athletes. Jimmy Connors's meteoric rise to the top in professional tennis was accompanied by a brash demeanor that shocked the traditional staid tennis aristocracy. He berated officials, made obscene gestures, and openly chided his opponents. Said Connors: "Maybe my methods aren't socially acceptable to some, but it's what I have to do to survive. I don't go out there to love my enemy, I go out there to squash him" (Tutko, p. 37). Interestingly, Connors was replaced by John McEnroe as America's number one player. Not only did McEnroe have a better serve but he had an even greater indifference to the feelings of his opponents. Meanwhile tennis players like Vijay Amritraj seem hamstrung by their decorous behavior. "Pancho Gonzales (his coach) keeps telling me I am too polite," says Amritraj. "He says I don't have the killer instinct" (Warner, p. 69).

Even coaching legend Vince Lombardi saw the need to conjure up "competitive animosity" toward the opponent during the week before the big game, a belief captured in his oft-quoted remark, "To play this game you must have that fire in you and nothing stokes that fire like hate." There is clinical evidence to show that Vince wasn't just talking through his helmet. In a study of differences between habitually successful and unsuccessful competitors, Francis Ryan, former psychologist and track coach at Yale, discovered that good competitors used their opponents as temporary enemies while poor competitors, "rather than whipping up their anger to meet the competitive challenge, did everything possible to maintain an atmosphere of friendliness with their opponents, doing everything possible to avoid recognizing the contest as a competitive one" (Ryan, p. 130). Psychologist Arnold Beisser observed essentially the same phenomenon in his examination of one of America's (pre-1967) tennis personalities. "As a tournament would progress and he could see who his next opponent would be, he would undergo a strong personality change toward that opponent. He would avoid his potential opponent and not speak to him. If, as was inevitable, they met socially, he would glare angrily and utter hostile and sarcastic remarks" (Beisser, p. 157).

The inherent tension between the kind of mindset associated with competitive success and the Christian ethic has surfaced in several recent incidents. The evangelical movement in professional sports has flourished in large part with the blessings of the sports establishment, but when athletes get too religious, owners and coaches get nervous. The fear seems to be that it will smother the fires of competition and chill hot sporting blood. In 1979, the Pittsburgh sportswriters publicly wondered if hard-hitting Steeler All-Pro safety Donnie Shell's performance slump was the result of his recent conversion to Christianity ("Johnson May Replace Gentleman Shell"). In Toronto, Maple Leafs owner Harold Ballard traced the decline in performance of first round draft choice Laurie Boschman to the day he started studying the Bible. Jean Pronovost also worried the Calgary Flames when he got religion, not so much for its effect on his play—he is not a fighter—but for fear it might spread to his teammates (Donovan, p. D-1). Several years ago, the San Francisco Giants, called "The God Squad" by local reporters, endured criticism that linked their ineffective play to the unusually large number of active evangelicals on the team (Vecsey, p. S-1). And Kent Benson, center for the Detroit Pistons, also labors under the dark shadow of a Christian witness: "There are still those in the pros and media who believe my faith has hampered my play," he says. "'You're too gentle,' they say, 'not aggressive enough'" ("God Made You Tall For A Reason").

Not surprisingly, the collision of Christianity and competitive ethics has produced ambivalence in the evangelical conscience which invariably surfaces when athletes talk about applying their religious beliefs to competitive sport. Asked how he blended football with faith, former Cincinnati Bengal Ron Pritchard said, "As far as being challenged physically, I'm probably not at the point where I can turn the other cheek all the time. I'd like to be able to say: 'Hey God loves you and I love you and I'll see you later.' But I'm not there yet, but with God's help I'll make it some day" (Diles, p. 115). Doug Plank, hard-hitting defensive back for the Chicago Bears, calls his athletic and religious life a paradox: "As a Christian I learn to love, but when the whistle blows I have to be tough. You're always walking a tightrope" (Warner, p. 18). The trick to walking the tightrope (which few seem to have mastered) is to temper competitive enthusiasm with just the right amount of spiritual grace, engendering the requisite competitive disposition without marring one's Christian witness.

This, then, is the plight of evangelical athletes: wanting very much to ritualize their performances as acts of worship, yet not entirely sure that sport is worthy of sacred offering, and even less certain about the competitive social dynamic in which it is embedded. The question nags at the subconscious: "Is sport a tribute or a temptation, a unique liturgy to symbolize Christian sentiment or a close brush with perversity?" Is it a "rite" or a "wrong"?

Resolving Conflicts Over Sport's Frivolity

In a desperate attempt to harmonize these disjunctive elements of ritual, evangelicals have concocted a locker room religion, not so much orthodox evangelicalism as a hodgepodge of Biblical truths, worn-out coaching slogans, Old Testament allusions to religious wars, and interpretations of St. Paul's metaphors that would drive the most straight-laced theologian to drink. The most popular doctrine in locker room religion, bar none, is "Total Release Performance," promulgated throughout the evangelical network by The Institute for Athletic Perfection. By employing a slick bit of theological open-field running around the Pauline athletic metaphors and ethical exhortations contained in I Corinthians 10:31 and Colossians 3:23, the Institute has derived the teaching that God's acceptance of an athletic performance as a spiritual offering depends upon the athlete's love for Christ and the intensity with which the athletic performance is executed. In a total release performance the two are related. "The quality of an athlete's performance can reveal the quality of his love for God," says IAP President Wes Neal (Neal, p. 59), and the quality most valued is intensity, the same kind of intensity that Jesus had—"His total concentration toward accomplishing His Father's purpose" (p. 48). There is, in this ingenious attempt to purge sport of its frivolity and increase its worth as a spiritual offering, the strong scent of 19th century Kantian thought, the Protestant-based notion that the intrinsic importance of an act is directly related to the level of effort required to perform it.

Total Release Performance (initiates refer to it simply as "T-R-P") has become a familiar watchword for evangelical athletes, a ritual for identifying the faithful. Shouted across lines of scrimmage or whispered in the huddle, "T-R-P" is a cosmic energizer, the athletic equivalent of the Pentacostal's "Praise the Lord" or the Baptist's "Amen," a three-consonant condensation of Christian theology applied to sport. So forcefully has the doctrine behind the motto shaped the beliefs of Christian athletes, they rarely talk about sport as worship without mentioning the critical contingency of total release. Pro footballer Archie Griffin paints crosses on his shoes and wristbands as a reminder that he is playing to glorify Christ and not himself. Says Griffin, "All you can ask of yourself is that you give 110%. I want to please Christ, and I can't be happy if I'm giving any less than that" (Smalley, pp. 38, 40). Steve Bartkowski, quarterback for the Atlanta Falcons, believes, "It gives God glory when you prepare yourself and exhaust every physical capability that God gives you" (Jansen, p. 37). Seminarians, marathoners and authors of a small tract "No Fading Wreath," Jeff Wells and John Lodwick agree. "God is not glorified," they say, "when we do not use all the athletic ability He has given us" (Wells & Lodwick, p. 38).

Love and intensity of play often are coupled with thankfulness, taking the form of "Praise Performances," the purpose of which is to "express your love and gratitude to God for who He is and what He has done" (Neal, p. 75). Belting another person around on a football field may seem an odd way to express your love to him or to the Almighty, but when sport frames the totality of one's social and religious lives the incongruities are scarcely perceptible. In what may be the most puzzling theological conundrum to come out of the movement, former Los Angeles Ram Rich Saul once warned his Christian opponents, "I'm going to hit you guys with all the love I have in me" (Warner, p. 279).

Not long after he had joined the Cincinnati Bengals, Anthony Muñoz, a 6'6", 278 lb. offensive tackle, lost his motivation to play football, wondering if he might better serve the Lord in another capacity. He sought spiritual counsel from Wendell Deyo, a regional representative of *Athletes in Action*, a sports outreach ministry of *Campus Crusade for Christ*. The encounter, as described in a recent book published by the organization (Joe Smalley, *Heroes of the NFL: Exciting Stories of Faith From Football's Top Superstars*), shows how aggression can be theologized into the natural handmaiden of a loving and thankful sport:

> "Anthony," Wendell said, "you've got every reason to play and be motivated. For you football can be a way to worship the Lord. . . . As Christians, we're to present our bodies as a living holy sacrifice." He reminded Anthony of the Old Testament sacrifices the Israelites made: "They gave the very best they had and sacrificed it. The Apostle Paul is urging us to do the same thing, but he is urging us to give our very lives and bodies. And whatever we do, Paul tells us in Colossians 3:23 to do our best, to work heartily, as for the Lord rather than men. . . . Well, you can worship God—you can thank Him—out there on the field. You're a football player, Anthony. God gave you your body and ability for a reason. The more aggressively you play, the more intensity you play with—the louder you're saying 'Thank you' to God. You can whisper it, say it out loud, or you can shout it. But ask yourself out on that field tomorrow: How loud am I saying 'Thank you' to God through my performance?" (p. 25)

Before leaving, Deyo encouraged Muñoz to meditate on some specific scriptures and to think of something that he could thank God for during the game the following afternoon. Muñoz decided, "I'm gonna thank God for my mother today. Nobody's done more for me." According to the author, "nothing better tells the story of Anthony's performance that afternoon than the NFL films. Deyo had a chance to view part of the game action on Monday. On at least half of the dozen plays he watched, Muñoz literally drove his man off the screen—nearly off the field a few times!" (Smalley, p. 26) Even his normally unimpressable coach, Forrest Gregg, was impressed. "I want you to know that in all my years of involvement in football on every level, I have never seen one man dominate everybody put over him the way Anthony did yesterday" (Smalley, p. 27).

Total release requires an expense of physical sacrifice, pain and suffering. It thrives on the belief that the most redeeming spiritual qualities of sports, those which instruct the heart and make true worship possible are those requiring *ascesis*. Perhaps it is only natural that athletes baptized in the ritual waters of weight training and wind sprints and for whom the pain of physical exertion is the doorstep to athletic excellence, could also be led to view *ascesis* as the doorstep to spiritual enlightenment. Originally used by Plato and Aristotle to refer to the discipline of athletic training, the term was injudiciously applied by Clemens of Alexandria (something of a sports fan) to the Christian life. He described the Christian life as *ascesis* and depicted the patriarch Jacob as an ascetic. The modern evangelical athlete has, in a manner of speaking, picked up Clemens's fumble and run with it.

As a result, for many in the sports-faith movement, *ascesis* is the single most important link between sports and the Christian faith. Pain and discomfort are not incidental conditions of sport competition, they are central, the indispensable relish for mellowing the raw taste of pleasure. They bind together the fabric of faith, life and competitive sport, a point emphatically put by author Gary Warner in his book, *Competition*, the most comprehensive statement of the evangelical position on athletics:

> When the apostle Paul says "I press on," he doesn't need to explain. It is the process of faith, life, and competitive sport. Anyone who has ever played football at any level will not soon forget two-a-days in August. The heat, the weight and rub of equipment, the screams of distended muscle fiber, legs like anvils, lungs burning like the inside of a dry kiln, the taste of sweat, home for a lunch of iced-tea—and throwing it up. Fun? No. Anyone in the affirmative is a masochist. Why does one endure? There are reasons, but fun is not one of them (p. 75).

Pain is not the only schoolmaster. Hard work teaches too. The struggle to refine skills and survive the awesome tests of the arena also strengthens Christian character and provides the essential backdrop to worship. Sport has its light moments and its tense moments; moments when players effortlessly *give* themselves to the game and stern moments when they must *apply* themselves to the game. For Christians seeking spiritual payoffs from sports, stern moments requiring application clearly are the most important, and according to Warner, they also are the most morally enlightening:

> When it begins to hurt, when one must elect to sacrifice and make deeper commitment, when defeats mount, when pressure and stress crest, those who choose "playing" over "competing" can sit this dance out. And whereas I advocate recreational play over brutalizing, self-destroying competition with all its harmful attitudes and perspectives, one must acknowledge that at certain points, endurance being one of them—competition can instruct us and complete us in ways play cannot (p. 72).

When those whose enthusiasm for the sporting life runs deeper than their theological insight attempt to convert sport to a religious ritual, a blurring of critical distinctions between the sacred and secular domains is virtually guaranteed. The result is that invariably sport is given more than its due. For example, in the following passage from Wells and Lodwick's "No Fading Wreath" one easily could get the impression that discipline, whether mastered on the athletic field or in the prayer cell, leads inescapably to the soul's salvation:

> The athlete of God experiences pain, just as all dedicated athletes do. However, the pain in a workout or race proves to be beneficial for the future. Hebrews 12:11 states: "All discipline is painful rather than pleasant. Later it yields the peaceful fruit of righteousness in our lives." Discipline is worthwhile by virtue of what it produces in our lives (p. 42).

One of the chief architects of this brand of theological sport-think is former Cleveland Browns defensive end, now globe-trotting evangelist, Bill Glass, whose series of books targeted at youngsters are models of athletic-theological metaphors gone awry. In one of his most recent books (*Expect to Win*, 1981), Glass blends machismo with spiritual imagery to draw a startling parallel between his fights in the pits and the theology of redemption:

> I would look down to the inside and here he'd come, charging at me, weighing about 270, and almost three feet away. His teeth were gritted, and his head was wagging from side to side. I got the distinct impression that he intended to do me no good. . . . The only thing I could do is exactly what I didn't want to do, face that big guard head on, right in the middle. Now that's not comfortable, and it's bone-shaking and traumatic. But if I was going to stop him, that was the only way I could do it. This was precisely the way it was for me when I was introduced to Jesus Christ in high school. He said to me, "I am the Way, the Truth, and the Life, and no man gets to God but by Me" (p. 51).

The epitome of this attempt to detrivialize sports is to envision the athlete's suffering in the same light as Christ's suffering at Calvary. More than one Christian athlete claims to have mustered up the will to endure by reminding himself that "Christ was not a quitter." In one of several case studies described in Neal's *The Handbook on Athletic Perfection*, a wrestler who had been "trying to give a total release of (himself) to perform like Jesus" but hadn't been wrestling up to his potential in a tournament, discovered that he "had taken my eyes off Him," thinking instead about his competitors; the next day he "took [his] eyes off the number of competitors and who [his] opponents would be and committed each one as a love expression to the Lord." Reflecting on the tournament championship he eventually won, the wrestler pondered the similarities between his performance and Jesus' suffering at Calvary: "I learned that I had to do the same thing Jesus did when He went out to finish the task His Father had called Him to do" (p. 64). Here, one has to admit, is dramatic and forceful imagery that elevates enormously the importance of sport, an athletic ritual for celebrating the very centerpiece of Christian theology.

Resolving Conflicts Over Competition

It hasn't been as easy for the evangelicals to purge athletic rituals of the contamination of competition as it has been to purge them of superficiality. Reconciling the ethos of modern sport with Christian theology is difficult, especially for those constrained by the principles of logic, but when love of sport teams up with religious conviction, history has shown that logic often is relegated to the bench. One way evangelicals have sought to sanctify competitive sport has been to view it through the finely ground lenses of instrumentalism; to ignore the ethical (interpersonal) issues of competition and look for more pragmatic reasons for competing, concentrating instead on the evangelistic potential of sport. In a society which attaches inordinate significance to competitive success, winning in athletics offers a visible platform from which athletes can publicly declare their witness. Record-setting Walter Payton of the Chicago Bears says he "realized in my second year that for me, performing well on the field and doing well as a professional football player made little kids look up to me. God enabled me to communicate with them. I found out that this was the way Christ wanted me to spread His message. My professional performance is God's way of using me to reach out and touch kids and bring them to Christ" (Smalley, p. 49). Turning in stellar individual performances, as Payton consistently does, increases his evangelistic potential to be sure, but it would be raised even higher if the Bears could put together a Super Bowl season. As Roger Staubach, reflecting on the Cowboys' win over Miami in the 1972 Super Bowl, said: "I had promised that it would be for God's honor and glory, whether we won or lost. Of course the glory was better for God and me since we won, because the victory gave me a greater platform from which to speak" (Roberts, pp. 117-118).

When victory becomes theologically significant even those reluctant to pray for victory can be convinced it is the right thing to do. Tom Landry, former coach of the Dallas Cowboys, normally takes a dim view of praying to win but allows that it may be appropriate ". . . in circumstances where it is important for Christians to have an excellent platform to witness for God" (Boone, p. 228). In 1980, Muriel Brier, a veteran golfer on the LPGA tour, told a reporter for Campus Crusade's *Worldwide Challenge* how, after a long winless drought, she asked the Lord for a win ("Blessing Indeed," p. 4): "It was hard for me to do but I had the confidence it was God's will to bless my golf game for His honor and glory." After sinking the putt that won the tournament for her team, she proclaimed: "I give total credit to the Lord for the victory." Not only do such public proclamations following a win fulfill the mandate of Christ's great commission to "go into all the world and preach the gospel," they constitute important rituals in their own right, rituals which anchor the athletes' belief system in the euphoria of the moment and provide them an opportunity to explain to their fans the private spiritual significance of their athletic performances.

But by using sport as a net to catch sinners' souls the evangelicals exacerbate rather than assuage the nagging conflicts. When sport is harnessed to the evangelistic enterprise, evangelicals become as much endorsers of the myths reinforced by popular sport as they do of the Christian gospel, and this results in a strange confusion of symbols. Sport, which celebrates the myth of success, is harnessed to a theology which consistently stresses the importance of losing. Sport, which symbolizes the morality of self-reliance and teaches the just rewards of hard work, is used to propagate a theology dominated by the radicalism of grace ("The first shall be the last and the last first"). Sport, a microcosm of meritocracy, is used to celebrate a religion which says all are unworthy and undeserving.

The contradictions notwithstanding, theologizing about sport as religious worship obviously has helped evangelicals come to grips with their involvement in a social institution that enjoys a rather awkward relationship to the Christian gospel. But one has to wonder why they have chosen to organize their worship ritual around evangelism and a rather minor *ethical* concept (the Christian responsibility to work diligently) while ignoring *theological* constructs which could more securely link the ritual to Christian theology. Why, for example, haven't they organized the athletic liturgy around the principle of grace, the fundamental Christian doctrine which teaches that humankind was secured by God in an act of unmerited favor? Surely, no doctrine lies closer to the heart of historic Christianity. Or why haven't they considered sport as an expression of the divine spark called play, and ritualized it as a celebration of humanity's status in the divine order? Where else but at play can we exude what Father Hugo Rahner called "a lightness and freedom of the spirit, an instinctively unerring command of the body, a certain neatness and graceful nimbleness of mind and movement" through which we "participate in the divine" and achieve "the intuitive imitation and the still earth-bound recovery of an original unity [we] once had with the One and the Good" (p. 11). What a dramatic departure from the meritocratic glorification of human effort that undergirds the doctrine of Total Release Performance and the calculated technology of mass evangelism.

It is hard not to be suspicious, not so much of sincere Christian athletes who say they worship through sport, but of a sports establishment who, more than anyone else, seems to benefit when sports are appropriated as religious ritual. In his book *Identity and the Sacred*, Hans J. Mol noted that social institutions typically sacralize (that is, attribute sacred significance to) beliefs and values regarded as essential for the group's survival. In the jungles of high-level competition, it is no secret that survival depends on winning, and somehow it seems too happy a coincidence that giving an all-out effort is considered to glorify God but also helps you win championships; or that winning improves one's evangelistic potential but also moves your team up in the standings.

There is, of course, a way out for the evangelicals, a way they can more closely align their athletic rituals to the sentiment and beliefs they wish to express, a way to cancel inherent contradictions between faith and action, belief and liturgy, a way to insure that the seeds of the movement will lead to a reconceptualization of the meaning of sport in the Christian life. This would quite obviously require them to build a new sports ethic from the ground up, an ethic that places a premium on the Christian distinctives of submitting ends to means, product to process, quantity to quality, caring for self to caring for others. An ethic, I'm afraid, that would never lead to the Super Bowl, but then the Super Bowl has never been good Christian liturgy anyway. That sports can and should be played as expressions of Christian sentiment is a radical notion, one I find both logical and practical, but only as the ritual allows itself to be shaped by the religious beliefs that give rise to it. It is a notion the sports establishment, with its appetite for production and commercial gain, has every reason to fear, because to approach sport as a medium for expressing Christianity is, like the Christian message itself, an invitation to renewal.

Bibliography

Beisser, Arnold. *The Madness in Sports*. New York: Appleton-Century-Crofts, 1967.

"Blessing Indeed." *Worldwide Challenge*, May 1980, p. 4.

Boone, Pat. *Pray to Win: God Wants You to Succeed*. New York: G.P. Putnam's Sons, 1980.

Bright, Bill. "That Winning Spirit." *Athletes in Action Magazine*, 6 (Fall, 1984), p. 21.

de Menasce, Jean. "The Experience of the Spirit in Christian Mysticism." In *The Mystic Vision*, Joseph Campbell, ed. Princeton, NJ: Princeton University Press, 1968, p. 344.

Diles, Dave. *Twelfth Man in the Huddle*. Waco, Texas: Word Books, 1978.

Donovan, Dan. "Bible Big Help in Saving Dion." *Pittsburgh Press*, 17 January 1982, p. D-1.

Glass, Bill. *Expect to Win*. Waco, Texas: Word Books, 1981.

"God Made You Tall For A Reason." *Worldwide Challenge*, April 1982, p. 55.

Guttman, Allen. *From Ritual to Record*, New York: Columbia University Press, 1978.

"The Happiest Man in Town." *Worldwide Challenge*, August 1973, p. 33.

Higgs, Robert J. "Muscular Christianity, Holy Play, and Spiritual Exercises: Confusion About Christ in Sports and Religion." *Arete: The Journal of Sport Literature*, 1:1 (Fall, 1983), pp. 59-85.

Jansen, Al. "What's So Different About Steve Bartkowski?" *Worldwide Challenge*, December 1981, pp. 35-37.

"Johnson May Replace Gentleman Shell." *Pittsburgh Press*, 19 October, 1979, p. B-3.

"Kush Puts the Kibosh on Camaraderie." *Pittsburgh Post-Gazette*, 19 December 1973, p. B-2.

Mol, Hans. *Identity and the Sacred*. New York: Free Press, 1977.

Neal, Wes. *The Handbook on Athletic Perfection*. Prescott, Arizona: Institute for Athletic Perfection, 1975.

Ogilvie, Bruce. "The Unconscious Fear of Success." *Quest*, 10 (May, 1968), pp. 35-39.

"Playing Games." *Pittsburgh Post-Gazette*, 12 November 1973, p. B-2.

Rahner, Hugo. *Man at Play*. New York: Herder & Herder, 1972.

Roberts, Michael. *Fans*. Washington, D.C.: The New Republic Book Co., Inc., 1976.

Ryan, Francis. "An Investigation of Personality Differences Associated with Competitive Ability." In *Psychosocial Problems of College Men*. Bryant M. Wedge, ed. New Haven: Yale University Press, 1958, pp. 113-139.

Smalley, Joe. *Heroes of the NFL: Exciting Stories of Faith From Football's Top Superstars*. San Bernardino, Calif.: Here's Life Publishers, 1983.

"Sport: Are We Overdoing It?" *Christianity Today*, 11 August 1972, p. 23.

Steere, Douglas. *Work and Contemplation*. New York: Harper, 1957.

"Tennis Pro." *Worldwide Challenge*. March 1980, p. 16.

"Testimony." *Winning* (Newsletter of Pro Athlete's Outreach), January 1981, p. 2.

Tutko, Thomas & William Burns. *Winning is Everything and Other American Myths*. New York: Macmillan Publishing Co., 1976.

Vecsey, George. "Religion Becomes An Important Part of Baseball Scene." *New York Times*, 10 May 1981, p. S-1.

Walker, Stuart. *Winning: The Psychology of Competition*. New York: W.W. Norton & Co., 1980.

Warner, Gary. *Competition*. Elgin, Illinois: David C. Cook Publishing Co., 1979.

Wells, Jeff & John Lodwick. "No Fading Wreath." In *Exhilaration: The Inspirational Side of Running*. Zola Levitt, ed. Wheaton, Illinois: Tyndale House Publishers, Inc., 1979, pp. 35-47.

Notes

1. The same sentiment is expressed, though for different reasons, by Higgs. "God's work is to be done in the world but God himself must be approached in reverence, silence and stillness" (p. 65). And again, "The holy by contrast is sought in solitude usually with the seeker sitting still, very still" (p. 72). I would argue that the physical actions of sport should not rule out contemplation akin to worship. A kinetic meditation which opens one up to the underlying meaning of things, known to mystics as "the rest most busy." Mystic Jean de Menasce once noted: "Contemplation at its height is not distinguished by a non-activity which immures it in solitude; it carries its cell inwardly" (p. 344). Philosopher Douglas Steere gives the point even stronger emphasis in his important little book *Work and Contemplation* (p. 33):

    > True contemplation does not deny that it enjoys large type and a general margin around the pages, a *Zimmer mit Balkan*, a house with a porch and perhaps even some freedom from noise. . . . But true contemplation can read the scriptures in a vest pocket edition with no margin at all, can be housed in a cubicle or dormitory or the upper berth of a trailer, can suffer year after year what seem to be unbearable denials of quiet and privacy and leisure, and yet be most intensely operative.

2. A favorite approach has been to stress the Christian's obligation to attain excellence and to describe competition as merely an adjunct that helps athletes achieve it. Some spiritual leaders closest to the movement go so far as to

describe competition as a gift from God. Bill Bright, founder and president of Campus Crusade for Christ International, an organization which sponsors national and world class sport teams under the banner of *Athletes in Action*, recently did in an editorial in *Athletes in Action Magazine*. "Does the Bible, then, teach that competition is wrong? Is it unspiritual to want to rise to the top, to excel? Far from being harmful, competition is a gift of God. Therefore, I do not disagree, as some do, with people who pray to win or succeed. Obviously, while Christian players on opposing teams may pray for a victory, only one team can win. But that does not mean God is put on the spot. Christians should pray to be the best they can be for the glory of God" (p. 21).

Prayers work best when players are big.
Knute Rockne

All this seems to argue, on the one hand, that the same temperament inclines people to sports as inclines them to the anthropomorphic cults, and on the other hand that the habituation to sports, perhaps especially to athletic sports, acts to develop the propensities which find satisfaction in devout observances.
Thorstein Veblen

At worst, religion is just one more means by which coaches can keep players busy and in line. (If there were no God, head coaches would have to invent one.)
Roy Blount, Jr.

I think this is where football and Christianity have a very close relationship, because to live a Christian life a person has to be just as disciplined in the things he does as a player does to be successful in football. We feel we can build character and develop good traits in athletes and this is why I think an athlete is such a great candidate for Jesus Christ.
Tom Landry

Part III
Religion in Sport

The Demon Deacon of Wake Forest University and
the Duke Blue Devil of Duke University.

Twice each summer in the Italian city of Siena, a horse race is run around the city's central plaza. The race, called the Palio, is a vestige of the Middle Ages and is held each summer in honor of the Virgin Mary. Days before the race, the Palio banner bearing an image of the Virgin is paraded through the streets and down the aisle of the church where it is blessed at the altar by the archbishop. Palio means "piece of cloth," and the Palio banner is the only official prize in the race. On the day of the race, jockeys representing the city's *contrade*, or civic organizations, lead their horses to the altars of their respective *contrada*'s chapels where a priest blesses the horse and jockey in a brief ceremony described by Dundes and Falassi (1975) as follows:

(priest)	Our help is in the name of the Lord.
(response)	Who made heaven and earth.
(priest)	O Lord hear my prayer.
(response)	And let my cry come on to You.
(priest)	The Lord be with you.
(response)	And with your spirit.

Let us pray:

O God, our refuge and our strength, source of our devotion, accept the humble prayers of your Church and grant to us in full that which we ask in faith.

O God, You are the benefactor and protector of mankind; You who made man in your image, guard and protect and defend your servant [name of jockey] from the possible dangers of the coming race.

Accept O Lord, our prayer and in your beneficience let your blessing fall upon [priest makes the sign of the cross] him and upon this horse; and through this blessing may they be safe and protected from the approaching dangers and from any harm; through the intercession of blessed Anthony and of [the name of the patron saint of the *contrada*]. Through Jesus Christ our Lord.

[The priest sprinkles holy water on the jockey and horse]

May the benediction of God almighty [priest again makes the sign of the cross] the Father, the Son and the Holy Ghost, fall upon you and remain with you always. (Response-Amen).

[Name of horse] and [name of jockey], go! and return victorious!

After the horse and jockey have been blessed, the race begins. Passions run high, fueled by long-standing rifts between *contrade*, many of which have survived for centuries. Bribery, cheating, and violence are integral components of the event. Jockeys beat the horses and beat each other with whips; injuries are commonplace. The conclusion of the race brings weeping, revelry, and usually fighting. The winning jockey and his *contrada* join in a parade to the church for much singing of thanks to the Virgin Mary for her role in the victory, followed by a party that lasts through the night. Members of the losing *contrade* have been known to hunt down their jockey and beat him if they felt the jockey had taken a bribe or had not done all he could do to win. Even patron saints are not immune from the crowd's vengeance. Once, having endured a long losing streak, the *contrada* of Chiocciola tossed a statue of the patron saint of horses, St. Anthony, down a well in disgust, earning them the name *affogasanti*, literally, the drowners of saints. Thirty years later still without a win to their credit, the women of Chiocciola sensed a connection between their treatment of St. Anthony and their string of bad luck at the race-course and pulled the statue out of the well. Chiocciola won the next Palio.

Religion in American Sports

The Palio strikes Americans, unfamiliar with its bizarre mixture of religion and sport and its gracing of ignoble conduct with the highest blessings of the church, as a preposterous welding of crass and deceitful manipulations with the holy orders of the church and as a profanation of sacred places. Religion seems wholly out of place here, strangely adapted to an occasion that in many of its manifestations is antithetical to the religious life. A priest blessing a horse in a chapel or blessing the jockeys who are arranging bribes and preparing to do violence to their fellow competitors is more a parody of religion than true religion itself. Yet, in the words of a citizen who has never known Siena without the Palio, it is simply "a contest in the art of living in a world that is complex, contradictory, part good, part bad, part chance, part skill and where prayers and ruses can go hand in hand" (Tanner, 1979, p. A2).

Anthropologists have long appreciated the ease with which people ignore the most intimate and prevalent features of their own culture. That same ethnocentric impulse often blinds Americans to the paradoxes and unlikely pairings of symbols that are woven into the warp and woof of their sports and games. James Michener watched American football for years, but it wasn't until he viewed sport with a sense of the anthropologist's detachment that he apprehended the way religion and other aspects of culture were all made part of the spectacle:

It was during a Monday-night NFL half-time show that I first became aware that football games had become a heady mix of patriotism, sex, violence and religion. A bloody first half had barely ended when hordes of personnel flooded the field, carrying flags, and trumpets and small cannon, and rifles, and Bibles. They were joined by eighty-six scantily clad girls in age groups ranging from fourteen years old to twenty-five. This was a combination of American values hard to beat, with marines and rabbis and priests adding sanction to the affair. It was difficult, at times to tell whether I was in a strip-tease show, an armory, a cathedral or a ball park. (1976, p. 475)

Even sports fans intimately familiar with American sport fail to appreciate the permeance of religion and religious symbolism and its similarities with the Palio, perhaps because they lack the fresh perspective that comes from emotional distance. Americans may not lead their horses to a chapel before a race, but more than one horse in the Derby has been prayed over and prayed for, and priests and chaplains have blessed baseball bats and dedicated the hallowed ground of stadium and arena. Prayer, both individual and corporate, sincere and comedic, graces the playing fields of our land. That of clergyman Richard J. Bailer, delivered before a Miami Dolphins-Cincinnati Bengals game, stands as testament to the spirit of carnival even more than does the priest's blessing of the horse and jockey in the Palio:

Creator God: Father and Mother of us all: We give you thanks for the joy and excitement occasioned by this game. We pray for the physical well-being of all the gladiators who run the gamut of gridiron battle tonight. . . . but knowing that the tigers are voracious beasts of prey, we ask You to be especially watchful over our gentle dolphins. Limit if You will, the obfuscations of Cosell's acidulous tongue, so that he may describe this night truly and grammatically as it is. . . . A great game, in a great city, played before Your grateful children, on whom we ask peace and shalom. Amen. (Michener, 1976, p. 476)

American coaches, who would find ridiculous the practice of raising Palio banners with images of the Virgin, nevertheless tack religious sayings on locker room bulletin boards as a matter of course and frequently dispense so much gospel to their players (often in required doses) that the practice in public universities and schools has been challenged on legal grounds (Monaghan, 1985). American athletes may not march en masse to the church after a big victory, but they paint crosses on their athletic footwear, shave crosses on the backs of their heads, print scripture verses on T-shirts, cross themselves before free throws, and kneel in the end zone after scoring touchdowns. Americans, who might view as bizarre the Palio custom of jockeys visiting churches in preparation for violence and skullduggery, find nothing unusual about converting professional football and baseball locker rooms into pregame chapels for players each Sunday or of asking 300,000 people, many already in a drunken stupor, to bow their heads in prayer as a clergyman asks for divine protection of men who, in the name of sport, are about to race their cars around the Indianapolis Speedway at speeds in excess of 200 miles per hour.

As the jockeys of the Palio consider the contest's outcome to be a matter of divine intervention, so do many American athletes. Both may request divine assistance in the contest, and both are careful in postgame celebrations to thank the Almighty for the win. Many famous professional athletes grant postgame interviews to reporters only on the condition that they first be permitted to publicly affirm their religious views, a practice that has prompted reporters to click off their tape recorders until the ''God-talk'' has finished. Some athletes, adhering to a sketchy theological determinism, accept a defeat as coming at the hands of God as surely as does a win. In one celebrated case in professional baseball, Bob Knepper, a pitcher during the 1979 season for the San Francisco Giants, gave up a game-winning home run and later credited it to ''God's will.'' Knepper's comment added to the suspicion widespread among local sportswriters, that the Giants (known at the time as ''the God-squad'' because of all the outspoken religious players on the team) were substituting divine providence for good hard effort and old-time competitive fire.

A further example was witnessed by those tuned to the televised boxing match between Marvin Frazier and Larry Holmes in which Holmes knocked out Frazier in the first round. Answering NBC sportscaster Dick Enberg's question about how the knockout occurred, Frazier replied: ''First I give praise to my Lord and Savior Jesus Christ for giving me the opportunity to be a witness for him . . . well, uh . . . I went out and I was slipping to the left, slipping to the right, when I slipped back to the left he caught me with a good shot. I thought I could recuperate, but it wasn't in the Lord's will for me to recuperate.''

Spectators at the Palio join in the religious celebrations as do American fans. American spectators, especially college students, paint their faces with school colors or with images of the school mascot, practices reminiscent of tribal religious customs. Neither is it unusual for fans to pause before a game in a moment of silent tribute to some recently departed hero, although Americans have to go some to catch up with the fans of England's Liverpool Football Club who arrange to have their ashes strewn on the home field as part of the funeral service, hoping to remain attached to their team in death as in life (Elias & Dunning, 1986).

Just as obvious as the Palio's use of religion is religion's use of the Palio, principally as a reminder of the importance of religion and assuring it a central role in Siena's most popular cultural event. And while the church tacitly sponsors the Palio, there is no indication that the church attempts to moderate the excesses of the event, including either the bribery or the violence. So too, American churches have long appreciated the effectiveness of sports in promoting the church, not just as a tool for luring youngsters to religious activities or for molding character and values in accord with religious teachings. Big-time sport has helped religion, especially Protestant evangelical religion, to achieve social respectability in a new way. Rather than distancing itself from sport on moral grounds or challenging its hallowed status in society, the more constructive approach by the church has been to use sport to a positive end. As a result, big-time sport is now one of the most popular vehicles for evangelizing athletes and their followers, and athletes have been willing partners in lending their celebrity status to gospel causes. Recognizing the influence athletes wield as magnets for religious causes, professional and college athletic teams have been targeted for special evangelistic attention by such groups as Sports Ambassadors, Sport Chapels, Inc., Athletes in Action, Pro Athlete Outreach, and the grandaddy of them all, the Fellowship of Christian Athletes. Never has so much religious ammunition been spent by so many big (religious) guns on so few targets.

The sport-religion knot is drawn especially tight at church-related schools and colleges where much of the social life centers on athletics. For years, Notre Dame football was the prototype for blending Christianity, education, and hard-nosed play into its institutional fabric. Now, however, most Catholic colleges are known for their basketball teams. Three of the four finalists in the 1985 NCAA tournament were Roman Catholic colleges, and a Catholic school won the championship in both 1984 and 1985, albeit largely on the efforts of talented black Protestants. Unfortunately, while publicly emphasizing their institutions' roles in integrating religious values with higher education, these schools have been noticeably silent concerning the moral crisis in college athletics, not unlike the priests who reign benignly over the Palio. Such hypocrisy has not escaped the keen eye of sports' analyst Frank Deford:

While big-time basketball is indisputably a rotten borough, Catholic schools have hardly been shy about residing there. When it comes to morality, they often seem to ask more of their students than of themselves. . . . Questions about the direction of big-time intercollegiate athletics are regularly brought up by Catholic school presidents when they gather together, but apart from perfunctory nods toward goodness and light, no strong moral protests ever seem to be publicly ventilated. (1989, p. 68)

Not to be outdone, Protestant colleges have begun in recent years to move their athletic programs to center stage. The smaller evangelical Christian colleges in America have banded together in the NCCAA, National Christian College Athletic Association, complete with its own set of regulations and national play-offs. Many of these Christian schools aspire to even more ambitious goals. Evangelist Oral Roberts sought publicity for his university by moving the basketball team rapidly to NCAA Division I status and demonstrating that ORU could compete with the bigger schools. He also showed that like its larger church-related counterparts, Southern Methodist and Texas Christian, ORU was not immune from NCAA investigations and sanctions. Recently, ORU's basketball exploits have taken a back seat to Liberty University's football program where fundamentalist President Jerry Falwell pushes to accomplish one of his life goals for the school: fielding a football team that can beat Notre Dame. Summarily dismissing his very successful football coach for reasons no better than that the more popular former coach of the Cleveland Browns was available to coach the team, Falwell determinedly has set his sights on producing a football team that can popularize his school and its conservative religious message. The Liberty team sports a flashy evangelism that at one point included scripture-emblazoned towels draped from the athlete's pants during warm-up drills, a practice that eventually was banned by the NCAA. What the NCAA has not banned is the team's custom of witnessing to opponents after the game. According to their star player: "We each pick out a player, maybe the guy on the other team who plays the same position. We explain how we played for the Lord. We ask, 'If you died tomorrow, do you think you would go to Heaven?'" (Montville, 1989).

Viewed objectively, the interpenetrations of American sport and religion are every bit as incongruous as the Sienan Palio. Religion is serious and solemn, and concerns things eternal; it acknowledges human weakness and dependence, it inspires contrition and adoration. By comparison, sport is frivolous, amusing, and concerns things ephemeral, manifesting itself in acts of confidence, domination, and not infrequently intimidation. It impresses us as not of the same stripe as music, dance, or art, cultural performances that mix more solubly with religion; sport lives on a different existential plane.

It is in the ethical sphere that the incongruities of the sport-religion mix appear most glaring. For too much of its history, sport has provided escape from the confines of an uptight religious establishment, rather than being a natural concomitant. Overlaying one with the other virtually guarantees incongruities every bit as striking as those evident in the Palio. One can imagine the reactions of a citizen of Siena upon discovering that "The Fighting Christians" of Elon College, North Carolina, reside only a few miles down the road from "The Demon Deacons" of

Baptist-supported Wake Forest University; or consider the images brought to mind by sports page headlines announcing "St. Francis thrashes St. Joseph" or the reaction to boxers (among the most ostensibly religious of athletes), who acknowledge the Almighty's help in pummeling an opponent unconscious. In 1990, after beating Mike Tyson bloody to claim the heavyweight championship, Buster Douglas credited God for the victory and went on, as if to acknowledge the human limitations of his pugilistic powers, to tell reporters that he was afraid of only one man, Jesus Christ. Against the background of physical intimidation and life-threatening injury so much a part of modern sports, implicating the divine, even indirectly, seems presumptive, a point not lost on a Liberty University running back who told the Washington Post: "We can reach people Dr. Falwell can't reach. Of course, it's hard sometimes to show them the love of Christ after we've beat them up and down the field. You say, 'Hey, Jesus loves you,' and they don't exactly understand" (Jenkins, 1985).

Why Sport and Religion?

Why do we mix religion with sport? What is there about religion that lends itself so readily, albeit so awkwardly, to athletics? And what is there about sport that predisposes religion to embrace it, even at the risk of compromising its purity? As we saw in Part I, similarities exist between the two, similarities in form and function, similarities in their power to galvanize a community of adherents around a set of values, to incite fanaticism in "believers," to instill respect for the power and importance of ritual, and to speak to the human spirit in unique and meaningful ways. Perhaps the incorporation of religion in pregame and half-time pageantry as Michener (1976) described can be accounted for on the basis of such similarities, but the deeper interpenetration of sport and religion is more difficult to understand.

The value of sport in polishing religion's social image, in lending it relevance and social currency, and as Flake (1984) has noted, in providing a masculine ethic to balance Christianity's largely feminine American heritage are rather easily recognizable features of this interplay. But the strength of the relationship suggests more profound factors—for example, the potential for sport to symbolize certain cultural aspects of the nation's public Protestantism. As Eitzen and Sage contend, the emergence of sport in North American society owes in large part to the dominance of Protestant Christianity, which taught values consistent with the fundamental doctrine of North American sports ideology:

> If we place the values inherent in the Protestant ethic and the ideology of sports side by side, it immediately becomes apparent that the two are congruent; that is, they share a significant equivalence. Without attempting to claim a causal link between the two belief systems, it does seem possible to suggest an elective affinity between them. Success, self-discipline, and hard work—the original tenets of the Protestant ethic—are the most valued qualities of an athlete. (1986, p. 149)

Merging shared values from these two influential aspects of the culture is mutually reinforcing to each and provides participants with a world view that can be used to rationalize participation in sport regardless of the rough edges that might emerge in the ethical realm. Sufficiently secularized, a result of both religious and nonreligious forces, these values have enormous appeal to athletes, even those from diverse religious backgrounds. Thus, any disproportionate representation of religious athletes may simply be a reflection of the selective attraction of sports for individuals already predisposed to the values shared by both realms.

This may be true especially of athletes from more conservative evangelical traditions, who Quebedeaux (1978) identified as being united if not in theology, then in their love of sports and appreciation for its power to build character, and who Yankelovich (1981) identified as the last bastion of social support for the traditional virtues of self-denial and self-sacrifice in every facet of daily life. If there is a universal doctrine among Christian athletes, it is that their performances must be worthy of God's blessing, meaning that the highest level of skill and effort of which an athlete is capable must be brought to bear on the athletic event. This has led to an enfringement of work values on play such that essentially nonproductive features of daily life (including leisure-time pursuits) are endowed with a spiritually inspired vocationalism. The hallmark of the Christian's work is that it is done "as unto the Lord and not unto men"; consequently, vocationalized sport provides occasions not only for public display but for acting out and testing this theological truth with a clarity and vividness not possible in the normal pursuit of most professions or trades.

Adding to this is an impulse contained in traditional Protestantism, which has been described by Albanese (1981) as activism, "a spiritual style that puts its premium on public and expressive behavior," an intrinsic valuing of doing, acting, and moving, in which "to be active is to be oriented rightly in the world" (p. 255). In this regard, sport and especially sport spectacles possess an enormous capacity to ritualize and to underscore in a metaphorical sense certain theological truths, something intuitively recognized by those religious athletes who affix to their athletic wear scripture verses such as: "I have fought the good fight, I have finished the race, I have kept the faith" (2 Timothy 4:7). Coupled with activism is a mental and spiritual reductionism evident in both sport and conservative Protestantism (Albanese, 1981); it is embodied in the former as clear and unambiguous rules and in the latter by a theology that leaves little room for doubt and uncertainty. Like activism, reductionism may have paved the way for the integration of sport and religion. Thus, at the subliminal level, sport may speak in theological ways to certain athletes, a point made by Peter Heinegg in describing the clarity and sense of justice served by sports rules:

> Sport eliminates the suffering caused by the randomness of existence—the loose ends and ragged edges, the imbalances and anticlimaxes of everyday life. All men are aesthetes to some extent: they fly from the messiness of sick room, bedroom, factory, and market place to the artificial neatness of the playground. (1976, p. 155)

Any case to be put for the integration of sport and religion on grounds of shared values may be vulnerable to claims that the value structure of young conservative

Protestants may have changed over the past several decades. In his exhaustive study of the values of evangelical college students, James Hunter (1987) points out that the inner worldly asceticism so fundamental to the internalization of the Protestant values (the competitive pursuit of success and conformance to rigorous moral codes) hinges on a personal ethic of self-denial, self-discipline, and self-mastery. However, his data, and that provided by others, show clear trends among this cohort of young evangelicals in precisely the opposite direction: toward virtual veneration of self, as exhibited in deliberate efforts to achieve self-understanding and self-fulfillment. In addition, rather than renouncing social practices traditionally judged by this group to be sin, the trend among their sample was toward accommodation to the cultural norm. All of which led Hunter to the conclusion that "industriousness, competitiveness, vocational discipline, and the like continue to carry only marginal moral value and no spiritual value for the Evangelical" (p. 72). If Hunter's interpretations are accepted, explanations based on a shared set of values reminiscent of the Protestant work ethic no longer may account for the pursuit of sport by the young religious players. One is left then to conjecture that sport, at least for the committed athletes and their followers, gains status among this religious group for precisely the opposite reason—that sport for them becomes a means of holding up and celebrating virtues long since moderated by theological revisionism and diminished in their daily lives.

Finally, the synthesis of sport and religion may reflect in some indirect sense their shared cultural root in the human experience of play. A commonly held theoretical position is that sports arose as religious ritual to influence the gods and to promote fertility and an abundant harvest (Brasch, 1970). Their association in rites of worship, although altered in form and substance, extends into the Middle Ages (Henderson, 1947) where sports were embedded in the holy festival along with the singing, dancing, and telling of stories that helped participants position themselves as part of a cosmic story and historical setting ("somewhere," as theologian Harvey Cox, 1969, suggested, "between Eden and the Kingdom of God"). The decline of festivals in modern religious life has been associated with a denial of an innate, divinely ordained aspect of human nature, the capacity to be *homo festivus*. Some see in the rise of sport, especially sport spectacles with their tailgate parties, victory celebrations, communal sufferings, and rehashing of athletic exploits, an attempt to fill some primordial void in the human condition. George Stoddard is supposed to have maintained that Americans need football weekends because there is no other equivalent of the feast days associated with the ancient religions, prompting one writer to suggest that deep reasons may exist for placing the football season at harvest time (Cady, 1978).

Sport, Religion, and Magic

The importance of religion in assuaging the fears and anxieties of a people confronted with the contingencies of natural disasters and the uncontrollable forces of nature is generally accepted by theorists (Wilson, 1982). For individuals who have organized their lives around faith and belief in an all-knowing, all-powerful deity with whom they can enjoy a direct and personal relationship, seeking solace from that deity in times of great stress is not only understandable but an eminently rational act. On the same basis, the prevalence of religion in sport may be accounted for, not to ward off natural disasters (although players and fans might consider the loss of a big game precisely that!) but to deal with uncertainty. Parsons found uncertainty to be a principal stimulus of religious activity, especially in situations in which "there is a strong emotional investment in the success of certain human endeavors, where energy and skill undoubtedly count for much, but where unknown and/or uncontrollable factors may and often do intervene to upset any 'reasonable' balance between action and success" (1952, p. 293). No matter how capable the farmer, a flood can wipe out the crops; regardless of the skill of the athlete or team, the odd bounce of the ball or a bad break in the game are humanly unpredictable or uncontrollable factors that can result in defeat or personal injury. In such cases, religion helps athletes adjust to the strain occasioned by the uncertainty of the contest and, as Parsons noted, provides an opportunity to act out some of the psychological products of the strain and bolster self-confidence. It provides "a protection against allowing the risk of failure to lead to a fatalistic discouragement, the attitude that since success cannot be assured, it is no use trying at all" (Parsons, 1952, p. 294).

Parsons (1952) was of the opinion that in times of emotional frustration over failure to achieve some expectation in which one has a deep emotional investment, magic becomes continuous with religion. And nowhere are the boundaries between religion and magic more blurred than in rituals performed in the face of the tortuous anxiety that afflicts athletes confronted with the uncertainties of sport competition. Although anthropologists and sociologists are far from agreed as to the differences between magic and religion, they are generally agreed on the importance both attach to supernatural powers. Religion typically is described as different from magic in that it is concerned with the ultimate or holy as an end in itself rather than as a tool, its rituals are conducted for intrinsic rather than extrinsic purposes, and it fosters a binding together of individuals in a community, unlike magic, which knows of individual "clients" but rarely congregations (Durkheim, 1954). Nottingham characterized the major difference between the two as follows: "Religion's goals are oriented to the non-empirical, the other-worldly, the supernatural. Though religion is often concerned with the physical and social welfare of human beings, it always has a transcendental point of reference. This is not true of magic. The ends the practitioner of magic seeks are in the everyday human world" (1954, p. 35).

In modern conceptions of religion, which incorporate tests of the powers of religion in the practical matters of everyday life, the distinction between the two is much less clear. Barbara Hargrove (1979) noted that some ministers denounce the use of religious talismans or prayers for what seem like magical ends—health, success, or winning a game—while others rely on practices such as laying on of hands to heal the sick, promoting religion as the key to financial success, or blessing the handkerchiefs of the faithful in order to ensure health. Theologian James Gustafson has written persuasively on this point, contending that today as much as in ancient times, religion (like magic) is sought for its utilitarian value: "Religious belief, trust, and practice, are offered as useful instruments for getting on well in the business of living, for resolving those dilemmas that tear individuals and communities apart, and for sustaining moral causes, whether they be to the right, the left or in the middle. Both individual pieties and social pieties become instrumental not to gratitude to God, the honor of God, or service of God, but to sustaining purposes to which the Deity is incidental, if not something of an encumbrance'' (1981, p. 18).

The use of religion in sports, including instances of prayers before games or crossing oneself before a free throw may be the most visible manifestations of this blend of magic and religion. Pregame prayers have been found to be common among college athletes and coaches, more than half of whom assume the prayer will affect the game's outcome (Marebeto, 1967). The continuity between these religious practices and magic can be seen when special powers are attributed to the person offering the prayer. During the 1978 football season, when the Houston Oilers visited the Pittsburgh Steelers, they recruited a local minister to deliver the pregame talk and prayer. Following the Oiler's upset of the previously unbeaten Steelers, the minister's currency increased to the point that on the Oilers' return trip to Pittsburgh for the division play-offs, both teams vied for the minister's prayers. The minister opted to pray for the Steelers, who then won, extending his streak to 2-0! Athletes frequently interweave superstitions and traditional religious rituals. During his tenure at the University of Tennessee, record-holding place-kicker Carlos Reveiz was known for his superstitions, including sitting in the same seat on the bus and wearing new shoes every second game (Cohen & Moschella, 1985). Before going onto the field he would pace the sidelines uttering: "Help me Lord, help me Lord." His on-field ritual he described as follows:

> I put the tee down, clap twice, back away and get in my stance. My holder Ricky, says "Ready," and I shake my head. While the ball is being snapped, I say "Help me Lord, help me Lord, help me Lord," and then I kick it. (Cohen & Muschella, 1985, p. 3C)

Determining the boundary between magic and religion in instances where religion is valued primarily for its utility is not always an easy task.

Those close to the athletic scene understand that pregame prayers often are quite sincere, not occasions for asking for a victory as much as asking God's presence and blessing on the event. Athletes who have integrated religion into all aspects of their lives and who customarily pray before important events in their lives also are likely to pray before a big athletic event in which their performance will be viewed and evaluated publicly and in which the prospect of physical injury looms on the horizon. Yet even the sincerest form of prayer has a psychological payoff, and when offered before athletic contests it can be a powerful mechanism for dealing with pregame anxiety.

Articles in Review

Allan Guttmann's article, excerpted from his book *From Ritual to Record*, provides a cursory examination of the relationship between religion and sport from ancient to modern times. According to Guttmann (and a host of other historians), sport once had religious meaning for participants. In fact, it was originally incorporated as an element of religious ritual such as to be indistinguishable from it. Although religion continues to pervade modern sport, in Guttmann's view it is more like an adornment than a phenomenon having symbolic significance. Sports remain essentially secular events in spite of their religious trappings. In proclaiming the secularization of sport, Guttmann implies that religion and religious themes no longer influence attitudes toward sport or how sport is organized, managed, or celebrated, although he acknowledges the possibility that sports may be a kind of secular faith.

Hoffman's essay, "Recovering a Sense of the Sacred in Sport," considers whether Guttmann is correct in assuming that forces of secularism have made it impossible to reclaim sport as a mode of religious expression. Describing many examples of religious-linked ritual in sport, Hoffman concludes that, unlike authentic religious rituals, most have their bases in a utilitarian end (usually victory). Moreover, most of the rituals lack any direct symbolic connection to a coherent religious belief system. The door is left open, however, for the possibility that sport may be an effective human experience for expressing general religious sentiment.

Carol Flake's paper has been excerpted from her book *Redemptorama: Culture, Politics and the New Evangelicalism*, a penetrating analysis of the accommodation of modern evangelicalism to the culture in which it presently thrives. She concentrates on the use of sport by the evangelical community to counter the prevailing and troublesome feminine strains that threatened to undermine the masculine mystique, long a part of the Protestant tradition. The "muscular Christianity" of the 1800s, with its dual themes of moral development and manliness, has been the object of a number of serious studies, but its reemergence in contemporary evangelical culture has been largely neglected. Reiterating the theme underscored by Deford (1976), Flake shows how establishment evangelicalism appropriated sport, not to tame its passions or modulate the fanaticism of the spectator nor to hold spiritual values in clear view, but as a member of its team. Her essay underscores the point that sport's use of religion, like religion's use of sport, is almost always self-serving. It is a matter of the sport establishment recognizing that religion, properly tailored and regulated, can further the team's goals, whereas the religious establishment has come to realize that sport, especially when freed from the controls and influence of the church, can make religion respectable in a way that few other segments of society can. And the key to achieving both ends is athletic success.

Those interested in studying the relationship between sport and religion will find journalistic accounts such as Lori Rotenberk's "Pray Ball" to be helpful in disclosing the personal reactions of athletes and pointing up issues. Such accounts tend not to be widely circulated, hence the decision to include one of them here. Rotenberk's article concentrates on the pervasiveness of religion in professional baseball, a topic also receiving excellent coverage from *New York Times'* sportswriter George Vecsey (1981). Linda Kay's "When Christianity Goes into the Locker Room" (1982), Dennis Collins's "Nearer My God to the Goalline" (1978), and Jane Leavy's "The Lord and the Locker Room" (1988) all offer valuable insights into the sports-religion movement in baseball as well as in other sports.

In "Are You Blocking for Me Jesus?" historian James Baker, reflecting on the interpenetration of sport and religion, ponders the potential of football as a metaphor for the Christian faith. In the process, he describes the efforts of some to manufacture the metaphor in a way that always reinforces the dominant secular values of American society more than the pointed though less popular themes emphasized by Christian theology.

As this section demonstrates, the use of religion by athletes often is indistinguishable, in a scholarly sense, from the use of magic. The topic of religion, magic, and superstitions in sport is given splendid coverage by Eitzen and Sage (1986); their chapter on religion and sport is required reading for anyone researching in this area. Gmelch's (1971) study of magical practices in baseball has attained the status of a classic in the field, if only because there are few competing entries. Gmelch tested Bronislaw Malinowski's (1948) hypothesis that magic is more likely to flourish in the face of anxiety and uncertainty than where people can exert control over events. He compared the incidences of magical practices among batters and pitchers (where uncertainty is high) with such practices among fielders for whom the game presents far less uncertainty. True to expectations, he found a higher incidence of taboos, fetishes, and superstitions among hitters and pitchers. Although witchcraft and sorcery are not uncommon in the athletic practices of other cultures (Fox, 1961; Scotch, 1969; Stevens, 1988) and are becoming a topic of increasing concern in international competition (such as the World Cup), they have yet to become a pervasive feature of American sport.

Two articles concerning magic and superstition in sport have been included in this section. Mari Womack's analysis of magical rites in "Why Athletes Need Ritual: A Study of Magic Among Professional Athletes" classifies magical practices into preparatory, day-of-the-game, activity-specific, and rites of protection, as well as determines why athletes engage in such rituals. Jack McCallum's article, "Green Cars, Black Cats and Lady Luck," is a humorous but informative description of the superstitions of athletes and coaches, some of whom prefer to think of their rituals as "routines" rather than superstitions. McCallum's is good companion reading for Womack's anthropological analysis.

References

Albanese, C.L. (1981). *America, religions and religion*. Belmont, CA: Wadsworth.

Brasch, R. (1970). *How did sports begin?* New York: McKay.

Cady, E.H. (1978). *The big game*. Knoxville: University of Tennessee Press.

Cohen, M., & Moschella, N. (1985, December 31). Vols' Reveiz can't kick superstition. *Cape Coral (Fla.) News-Press*, p. 3C.

Collins, D. (1978, November 19). Nearer my God to the goalline. *The Washington Post Magazine*, pp. 12, 15, 19.

Cox, H. (1969). *The feast of fools*. Cambridge, MA: Harvard University Press.

Deford, F. (1976), April 19). Religion in sport. *Sports Illustrated*, pp. 90-92, 95-99, 101.

Deford, F. (1980, March 3). A heavenly game? *Sports Illustrated*, pp. 59-70.

Dundes, A., & Falassi, A. (1975). *La Terra in Piazza*. Berkeley: University of California Press.

Durkheim, E. (1954). *Elementary forms of the religious life*. Glencoe, IL: Free Press.

Eitzen, D.S., & Sage, G.H. (1986). *Sociology of North American sport* (3rd ed.). Dubuque, IA: Brown.

Elias, N., & Dunning, E. (1986). *The quest for excitement*. New York: Blackwell.

Flake, C. (1984). *Redemptorama: Culture, politics and the new evangelicalism*. New York: Doubleday.

Fox, J.R. (1961). Pueblo baseball: A new use for an old witchcraft. *Journal of American Folklore*, *74*, 9-16.

Gmelch, G. (1971, June). Baseball magic. *Transaction*, **8**, 39-41.

Gustafson, J.M. (1981). *Theology and ethics*. Oxford: Blackwell.

Hargrove, B. (1979). *The sociology of religion*. Arlington Heights, IL: Harlan Davidson.

Heinegg, P. (1976). Philosopher on the playground: Notes on the meaning of sport. *Southern Humanities Review*, **10**(2), 153-156.

Henderson, R. (1947). *Ball, bat and bishop*. New York: Rockport Press.

Hunter, J.D. (1987). *Evangelicals: The coming generation*. Chicago: University of Chicago Press.

Jenkins, S. (1985, October 5). Liberty U. hits first saves later. *Washington Post*, pp. B1, B5.

Kay, L. (1982, October 17). When Christianity goes into the locker room. *Chicago Tribune*, p. 4-1.

Leavy, J. (1988, July 28). The Lord and the locker room. *The Washington Post*, pp. D1, D8.

Malinowski, B. (1948). *Magic, science and religion*. Glencoe, IL: Free Press.

Marbeto, J.A. (1967). *The incidence of prayer in athletics as indicated by selected California collegiate athletes and coaches*. Unpublished masters thesis, University of California, Santa Barbara.

Michener, J. (1976). *Sports in America*. New York: Random House.

Monaghan, P. (1985, September 9). Religion in a state-college locker room: Coach's fervor raises church-state issue. *The Chronicle of Higher Education*, p. 37.

Montville, L. (1989, November 13). Thou shalt not lose. *Sports Illustrated*, pp. 82-86.

Nottingham, E.K. (1954). *Religion and society*. New York: Random House.

Parsons, T. (1952). Sociology and social psychology. In H.N. Fairchild (Ed.), *Religious perspectives in college teaching* (pp. 293-299). New York: Ronald Press.

Quebedeaux, R. (1978). *The worldly evangelicals*. San Francisco: Harper & Row.

Scotch, N.A. (1969). Magic, sorcery and football among Zulu: A case study of reinterpretation under acculturation. *Journal of Conflict Resolution*, *5*, 70-74.

Stevens, P. (1988). Table tennis and sorcery in West Africa. *Play and Culture*, **1**, 138-145.

Tanner, H. (1979, August 20). Medieval pageantry and skulduggery at the Palio of Siena. *New York Times*, p. A2.

Vecsey, G. (1981, May 10). Religion becomes an important part of baseball scene. *New York Times*, p. S1.

Wilson, B. (1982). *Religion in sociological perspective*. New York: Oxford University Press.

Yankelovich, D. (1981). *New rules*. New York: Random House.

From Ritual to Record

Allen Guttmann

Primitive cultures rarely have a word for sport in our sense.[1] If we hold strictly to our definition of sport as a nonutilitarian physical contest, we may be tempted to say that primitive men had no sports at all. Carl Diem's monumental world history of sports begins with the bold assertion, ''All physical exercises were originally cultic.''[2] Plentiful evidence exists to document the claim that primitive societies frequently incorporated running, jumping, throwing, wrestling, and even ball playing in their religious rituals and ceremonies.

Ethnographers have done a great deal of work on the games of the American Indians, especially of the Plains Indians who were the last to fall under the cultural influence of their conquerors. In his enormous compendium, Stewart Culin writes:[3]

Children have a variety of other amusements, such as top spinning, mimic fights, and similar imitative sports, but the games first described are played only by men and women, or youths and maidens, not by children, and usually at fixed seasons as the accompaniment of certain festivals or religious rites. . . .
In general, games appear to be played ceremonially, as pleasing to the gods, with the object of securing fertility, causing rain, giving and prolonging life, expelling demons, or curing sickness.

Culin's collection of ethnographic information does not, with rare exceptions, actually elucidate the religious nature of the games, but an excellent example is available from a later account.

The Jicarilla Apaches of the Southwest used ''sports'' in conjunction with solar-lunar symbolism as part of a yearly fertility rite. Apache myth dramatizes the delicate balance between the two main sources of food among Plains Indians. Animal sources were associated with the sun, vegetable sources with the moon. ''The sun is connected with the animal and the moon with the fruit because the sun is a man and the moon is a woman.''[4] This dualistic conception of natural order is one that

143

Claude Lévi-Strauss and many other anthropologists posit as an inevitable facet of *la pensée sauvage*. Writing about the Timbira Indians of Brazil, Käthe Hye-Kerkdal emphasizes the connection between the sport and the worldview: "Athletic contests and the dualistic social organization of primitive peoples can be characterized as two different representations of a polarized picture of the world (*eines polaren Weltbildes*)."[5] The enactment of the dualistic myth which interests us at present is a kind of relay race in which all males participated at least once between puberty and marriage. One side represented the sun, the other side the moon. The race was governed by complicated rituals. Abstinence from meat and from sexual intercourse was required prior to the race. The track was called "the Milky Way" after the heavenly path over which the sun and the moon had originally raced. The "Milky Way" connected two circles around whose circumference small holes were dug, clockwise, into which the leaders of the two sides, praying all the while, dropped pollen. Trees were then planted in the holes. This and other rituals were accompanied by drums representing the sun and the moon, by flags, dances, songs, a feast. The race itself was on the third day of the festival, at which time a fire was ignited in the center of each circle. The boys were painted, pollened, adorned with feathers, and led to their circles by two young girls carrying an ear of corn in one hand, an eagle feather in the other (symbolizing the two sources of food). Four old men paced out the track, then came the race itself. The ceremony was clearly more important than the question of winning or losing. The leaders ran first, followed by the others in no particular order. Some ran four or five times, but everyone ran at least once. Dances and another feast followed the conclusion of the race.[6]

A second example of cultic sport is not, strictly speaking, drawn from a primitive society, because the Zulu soccer players of Durban, South Africa, are members of a transitional culture between tribal and modern social organization. Their game, soccer, is the most widespread of modern ball games, but their perception of the game assimilates it to a way of life anything but modern. Zulu soccer teams play by the rules of the International Football Association and the desire to perform well can lead to behavior which directly violates Zulu custom. A coach or trainer, for instance, may strike an older player—a clear instance of an imperative of modern sport overriding a traditional tabu. Other aspects of the "soccer culture" are contributions of the Zulus themselves. There is a preseason and a postseason sacrifice of a goat. Pregame ritual requires that players, coaches, and dedicated supporters of the team spend the night before a game together—sleeping in a huge group around a camp fire. All are naked, but there are no sexual relations. A witch doctor, called an "Inyanga," makes incisions in the knees, elbows, and other joints of the players (very much like the medicine man in the ritual ball game of the Cherokee Indians). The players are also given a purifying emetic. On the day of the game, there is a procession, a movement in tight formation with each man touching those adjacent to him. The Inyanga administers magic potions. When the team is unsuccessful, it is the Inyanga, rather than the coach or manager, who is replaced.[7]

My examples demonstrate the concurrence of sport and religious cult, but Carl Diem's comment implies not merely the possibility but also the inevitability of this concurrence. His generalization forces an implied question upon us. Is sport among primitive peoples invariably a part of religion or is there an independent sector where sports are simply a part of secular life? The question supposes that primitive people have a secular life, which some authorities deny, arguing instead that primitive religious life was coterminus with culture. The question has a special significance in light of our preliminary paradigm of play-games-contests-sports. If we decide that sports among primitive peoples were always sacred, always part of cult, then we are forced to the somewhat curious conclusion that they had no sports at all in our sense because their physical contests were religious in nature and thus in an extended sense utilitarian. They were for an ulterior purpose—like assuring the earth's fertility—rather than for the sheer pleasure of the activity itself.

But is Diem right? I think not. From ethnographic reports we can document many instances of cultic sports, but we cannot meaningfully stretch the term "religion" to the point where all human behavior falls within the sphere of the sacred. Children wrestling or casting spears at a target? It is difficult to think of their actions as part of a cult. Although Käthe Hye-Kerkdal's account of the arduous "lograces" of the Timbira Indians of Brazil makes clear the cultic significance of many of the races, *some* of them seem to have been secular activities pursued for their own sake.[8] Dogmatic proclamations of negative universals ("Primitive peoples have *no* secular sports") are unwise. Nonetheless, Diem's overstatement contains an important truth—sports, as opposed to "physical exercises," may indeed have entered the lives of primitive adults primarily in conjunction with some form of religious significance. It is a fault of our own pervasive secularism that we tend to underestimate the cultic aspects of primitive sports.

Among the most thoroughly documented and intensively studied of all religious sports was the ball game of the Mayans and Aztecs, whose complex civilization we can classify as ancient rather than primitive. Although my subsequent discussions of ancient sports will concentrate on classical antiquity rather than on the distant pasts of China, India, and other "non-Western" cultures, the prominent place of the Mayan-Aztec ball-court game in anthropological literature, plus the intrinsic interest of the activity, justify the use of this example.

Behind the game itself was the myth of twin brothers whose names appear in various transliterations. The brothers left their mother's house in order to challenge the gods of the underworld in a game of football (actually soccer of sorts). They lost and paid the mythically predictable price of defeat—death. The head of one brother was placed in a tree, where a young girl happened upon it. From the mouth of the head spurted a stream of seeds which impregnated the girl, who removed to the house of the twin's mother, where she bore children. They grew to youthful manhood and challenged the gods at football and, again predictably, won. Whereupon the heads of the twins rose to the heavens and became the sun and the moon.[9]

The archeological evidence for this sun-moon myth can be found in the more than forty ball courts which have been located in an area stretching from Arizona to Guatemala and Honduras. Considered as symbols of the heavens, the ball courts are invariably within a temple complex, the best preserved of which is at Chichén Itzá in Yucatán. In Aztec times, the game itself was under the protection of the goddess Xochiquetzal, but the stone rings through which the ball seems to have been propelled were carved with the symbols of Quetzalcoatl, the famed plumed serpent. To these and other gods, thousands of human sacrifices were offered annually, some of them in direct connection with the ball game. Whether the losing players or the winning ones were sacrificed is unclear, but we can safely assume that the requirements of the contest *qua* contest doomed the losers rather than the winners. In either event, the archeological evidence indicates clearly that the game was quite literally for life or death. Each of the six reliefs at the great ball court of Chichén Itzá shows the decapitation of a player. On the whole, details about the actual playing of the game are meager and much disputed, but Spanish observers of the sixteenth century clearly saw the religious nature of the activity and one of them noted, "Every tennis-court was a temple."[10] The Spanish authorities banned the game—if game it was.[11]

Although Greek sports may be conceived of as the ancestors of modern sports, the physical contests of Olympia and Delphi were culturally closer to those of primitive peoples than to our own Olympics. The relative familiarity of Greek culture and the revival of specific track and field sports in our own time act to obscure fundamental similarities between the sports of the Athenians and those of the Apaches and Aztecs. The problem is only in part a lack of information. Book XXIII of the *Iliad*, containing the funeral games celebrated in honor of the slain Patroclus, is merely the first, and most important, of numerous literary texts which are the heritage of every educated person. Athletic encounters depicted on Greek vases remain a part of the aesthetic experience of Western man and Myron's *Discus Thrower* must rank among the best known statues ever sculpted. Although our knowledge of Greek sports is marked by many lacunae, the problem is less one of information than of interpretation.

The Olympic games, like the Pythian, the Isthmian, the Nemean, and the Athenaic, were sacred festivals, integral aspects of the religious life of the ancient Hellenes. In the words of one scholar, "The Olympic games were sacred games, staged in a sacred place and at a sacred festival; they were a religious act in honor of the deity. Those who took part did so in order to serve the god and the prizes which they won came from the god. . . . The Olympic games had their roots in religion."[12] The games at Olympia were in homage to Zeus. Those of Corinth—the Isthmian games—were sacred to Poseidon, while Apollo was worshipped by the runners and wrestlers of Delphi and Nemea. (See table 1.)[13]

The exact history of the origins of the Olympic games is unknown and in all likelihood never will be known. It is thought that Olympia was first sacred to Gea, goddess of the earth. Greek legend told also of Pelops ("producer of abundance") and of his suitor's victory in the chariot-race against Oenomaus, father of Hippodamia. It was said that Herakles inaugurated the games at the tomb of Pelops, who was considered to have been brought back to life by the sacrifice of a boy. Defeat in an athletic contest was thus the symbolic substitute for sacrificial death. (Contemporary football coaches who liken defeat to death are better anthropologists than they realize.) Since Herakles had been a Minoan fertility god whom the conquering Greeks demoted to a demi-god and hero, the fertility myth is the common thread of every version of the founding of the games. By classical times the games were

Table 1   Greek Athletic Festivals

Festival	Place	God Honored	Branch or Wreath	Intervals (years)	Founded (B.C.)
Olympic	Olympia	Zeus	olive	4	776
Pythian	Delphi	Apollo	bay	4	582
Isthmian	Corinth	Poseidon	pine	2	582
Nemean	Nemea	Apollo	parsley	2	573

marked by a kind of syncretism—the altar of Gea remained as one of the four at Olympia, the funeral rites of Pelops were celebrated on the second day of the games, and the great sacrifice to Zeus took place on the third day. The purpose of the games remained cultic, religious. The athletic events were "held in order to persuade the god to return from the dead, to reappear in the form of a new shoot emerging from the dark womb of the earth into the light of day."[14]

The time of the games was as sacred to the Greeks as the place. The games occurred at the time of the second or third full moon after the summer solstice, and three heralds went forth to announce an Olympic truce. The athletes gathered at the nearby town of Elis and spent thirty days in final preparation for their exertions, after which came a two-day procession with much religious ceremony to the actual site on the river Eurotas. Because of the sacred nature of the games, women were excluded even as spectators, except for the priestess of Demeter. The games expanded over time from the simple stade race (one length of the stadium) in 776 B.C. to an elaborate program of foot races, chariot races, boxing, wrestling, a combination of boxing and wrestling known as the *pankration*, discus and javelin throwing. There were contests for boys as well as men and, from 396 B.C., contests for trumpeters and heralds. According to most accounts, the fifth and last day was devoted entirely to religious ceremony. There was a banquet, the gods were solemnly thanked for their sponsorship of the games, the winners were awarded olive branches cut from the sacred grove of Zeus by a boy whose two parents were still alive. The religious character of the Olympic games was never in doubt, nor was that of the other "crown" games (thus named because the victors were crowned with olive, bay, pine, or parsley wreaths).

With this information in mind we can return to the contention of Frayssinet that sports are forms of artistic expression. "The study of various Greek religious ceremonies teaches us that one can always please the gods by offering them . . . music, dance, poetry, drama and athletic contests."[15] The "crown" games, and many hundreds of local games, were indeed a way to please the gods, but this fact should not incline us to the conclusion that sports are one with music, dance, poetry, drama, and the other arts. The relationship of sport and art among the Greeks was the opposite of that suggested by Frayssinet. To the degree that Greek athletic festivals were religious ritual and artistic expression, they had a purpose beyond themselves and ceased to be sports in our strictest definition of the term. The closer the contests came to the status of art, the further they departed from that of sport.

The Olympic and other "crown" games were sacred festivals, and athletic events were often endowed with religious significance; but we can nonetheless detect among the Greeks the emergence of sports as a more or less secular phenomenon too. The remark of a German scholar is relevant. "When one speaks in this context of 'secularization,' one does not mean that an originally religious phenomenon becomes worldly but rather that an athletic game (*sportliches Spiel*), originally laden with religious significance, concentrated itself upon its own essential elements—play, exercise, competition."[16] This is what happened. Sports gradually became a part of the ordinary life of the *polis* as well as a means of worship. That Greek society generally valued physical excellence is obvious from any examination of Hellenic civilization. Cities gloried in the athletic victories of their citizens, rewarded the victors materially with large pensions and other benefits, honored them in legend, in the form of statues, and in some of the greatest poetry ever written (the Olympic odes of Pindar, for instance). Socrates, who had participated in the Isthmian games, admired physical excellence and scorned those who took no pride in their bodies. Even Plato, who never wavered from his conviction that the world of pure ideas was of a higher order than the sphere of the corporeal, had been a wrestler in his youth and had won prizes at the Pythian, Nemean, and Isthmian games. And in *The Republic* he insisted upon the importance of gymnastic exercises for both men and women. Ordinary citizens emulated the achievements of the most gifted and no city was without its athletic facilities. We can be sure that those who exercised in the gymnasium did not neglect to offer libations to the gods, but we can nonetheless detect the secularization of sport.

Roman society continued and accelerated the tendency. The Romans were given neither to athletic competitions nor to athletic festivals. They believed in physical fitness for the ulterior end of warfare. In his classic study of sports and antiquity, E. Norman Gardiner wrote, "The only athletic events which interested them at all were the fighting events, wrestling, boxing, and the pankration."[17] Roman moralists tended to mock the degeneracy of those who revealed an interest in Greek athletics. "The Greek principle of a harmonious development of the body, and a striving for bodily beauty and grace, was considered effeminate."[18] Not even Scipio Africanus, the famous conqueror of Hannibal in the Third Punic War, was immune from the verbal darts of his fellow citizens when he appeared at the gymnasium in Greek clothing. Not even the imperial prestige of Augustus was sufficient for him to establish "isolympic" games patterned on the Greek model. Such festivals as existed were usually occasions for Roman spectators to watch Greek athletes from Pergamon, Antioch, or Alexandria. More typical for Roman tastes than races or the discus were the gladiatorial combats which date from the funeral celebrations for the father of Marcus and Decimus Brutus in 264 B.C. It is common knowledge that gladiatorial spectacles reached bestial enormity by imperial times. Whatever religious significance remained was apparently overshadowed in the eyes of the mob accustomed to bread and circuses and blood.

In their secularism as in most of their other characteristics, modern sports are closer to the Roman than to the Greek model. It is, indeed, precisely this pervasive secularism which made modern sports suspect in the view of many religious leaders of the seventeenth through the nineteenth centuries. After long and stubborn opposition to the allegedly misplaced emphasis on the body symbolized in Greek athletics, both Catholicism and Protestantism have worked out a *modus vivendi*, a kind of concordat, with modern sports. Theologians now repudiate the harsh condemnations of earlier generations and blame Platonism and Neo-Platonism for the ascetic strain in traditional Christianity. Churchmen now seek eagerly to establish the harmony of modern sports and Christian doctrine.[19] The Cathedral of St. John the Divine in New York has a stained-glass window depicting baseball and other modern sports, the Fellowship of Christian Athletes endeavors to leaven the hard ethos of football and basketball and hockey with the words of Jesus, and in a popular song of the 1970s, the singer asks, in a refrain, that Jesus drop kick him "through the goal-posts of life."[20]

There is, however, a fundamental difference between obligatory pregame locker-room prayers and the worship of the gods by means of an athletic festival. For the Jicarilla Apache running between the circles of the sun and the moon or the Athenian youth racing in the stadium built above the sacred way at Delphi, the contest was in itself a religious act. For most contemporary athletes, even for those who ask for divine assistance in the game, the contest is a secular event. The Sermon on the Mount does not interfere with hard blocking and determined tackling. Religion remains on the sidelines.

Unless sports themselves take on a religious significance of their own. One of the strangest turns in the long, devious route that leads from primitive ritual to the World Series and the *Fußballweltmeisterschaft* is the proclivity of modern sports to become a kind of secular faith. Young men, and many no longer young, seem quite literally to worship the heroes of modern sports. Journalists, referring to the passion of the Welsh for rugby or the devotion of Texans to football, speak of sports as the "religion" of the populace. "Sport," says an Australian authority, "is the ultimate Australian super-religion, the one thing every Australian believes in passionately."[21] Pierre de Coubertin, founder of the modern Olympic games, spoke reverently of the "religio athletae" and the French version of Leni Riefenstahl's monumental documentary film of the 1936 Olympics was entitled *Les Dieux du stade*. Michael Novak's ecstatic homage to the joy of sports contains a reference to baseball, football, and basketball as a "holy trinity." He goes on to maintain that sports are "secular religions, civil religions. . . . The athlete may of course be pagan, but sports are, as it were, natural religions."[22] If we shift our attention from philosophic ecstasy to sophomoric irony, we can consider the name given by the students of Notre Dame University to their library's mosaic of Christ with upraised arms: "Six Points."[23]

Whether or not one considers the passions, the rituals, and the myths of modern sports as a secular religion, the fundamental contrast with primitive and ancient sports remains. The bond between the secular and the sacred has been broken, the attachment to the realm of the transcendent has been severed.[24] Modern sports are activities partly pursued for their own sake, partly for other ends which are equally secular. We do not run in order that the earth be more fertile. We till the earth, or work in our factories and offices, so that we can have time to play.

Notes

1. See Hans Damm, "The So-Called Sport Activities of Primitive People," in *The Cross-Cultural Analysis of Sport and Games*, ed. Günther Lüschen (Champaign, Illinois: Stipes, 1970), pp. 52-69. Many anthropologists deplore the term "primitive" because of its ethnocentric connotations. Unfortunately, none of their suggested alternatives seems wholly satisfactory and I fall back upon the layman's term, although I do not use it in order to make moral judgments.

2. *Weltgeschichte des Sports*, 3rd ed., 2 vols. (Frankfurt: Cotta, 1971), 1, 3.

3. *Games of the North American Indians* (Washington: U.S. Government Printing Office, 1907), pp. 31, 34.

4. Quoted in Morris Edward Opler, "A Jicarilla Apache Ceremonial Relay Race," *American Anthropologist*, 46 (1944), 78n.

5. "Wettkampfspiel und Dualorganisation bei den Timbira Brasiliens," in *Die Wiener Schule der Völkerkunde Festschrift*, ed. A. Haekel, A. Hohenwart-Gerlachstein, and A. Slawik (Vienna: Verlag Ferdinand Berger, 1956), p. 509.

6. Opler, "A Jicarilla Apache Ceremonial Relay Race," 75-97.

7. N.A. Scotch, "Magic, Sorcery and Football Among the Urban Zulu," *Journal of Conflict Resolution*, 5 (1961), 70-74. Scotch's experiences among the Zulu seem to have led to conclusions about baseball; see William A. Gamson and N.A. Scotch, "Scapegoating in Baseball," *American Journal of Sociology*, 70 (1964), 69-72. For other examples of the blend of primitive and modern, see J.R. Fox, "Pueblo Baseball: A New Use for Old Witchcraft," *Journal of American Folklore*, 74 (1961), 9-16; Eugene H. Freund, "The Transition of a Fertility Rite to an Indigenous Spectator Sport," *Quest Monograph*, no. 16 (June 1971), 37-41; "Orioles in 'Spirited' Race," *New York Times*, September 16, 1975.

8. "Wettkampfspiel und Dualorganisation," pp. 504-33.

9. Walter Umminger, *Supermen, Heroes and Gods*, trans. James Clark (New York: McGraw-Hill, 1963), pp. 71-72.

10. Quoted in W.A. Goellner, "The Court Ball Game of the Aboriginal Mayas," *RQ*, 24 (May 1953), 164.

11. The best studies of the game are Goellner, *ibid.*, pp. 147-68; Walter Krickeberg, "Das mittelamerikanische Ballspiel und Seine Religiöse Symbolik," *Paideuma*, 3 (1948), 118-90; Theodore Stern, *The Rubber-Ball Games of the*

Americas (Seattle: University of Washington Press, 1949), pp. 34-45, 50-71; Kurt Weis, "Die Funktion des Ballspiels bei den alten Maya," *Die Soziologie des Sports*, ed. Günther Lüschen and Kurt Weis (Darmstadt: Luchterhand, 1976), pp. 115-129.

12. Ludwig Deubner, quoted by Ludwig Drees, *Olympia: Gods, Artists, and Athletes*, trans. Gerald Onn (New York: Praeger, 1968), p. 24. A contrary view appears in E. Norman Gardiner, *Athletics of the Ancient World* (Oxford: Clarendon Press, 1930), pp. 32-33.

13. Data for the table were derived from Gardiner, *Athletics of the Ancient World*, pp. 33-37; H.A. Harris, *Greek Athletes and Athletics* (London: Hutchinson, 1964), p. 36.

14. Drees, *Olympia*, p. 31.

15. Pierre Frayssinet, *Le Sport Parmi les Beaux-Arts* (Paris: Arts et Voyages, 1968), p. 27.

16. Hans Kamphausen, "Traditionelle Leibesübungen bei autochthonen Völkern," *Geschichte der Leibesübungen*, ed. Horst Überhorst, 6 vols. (Berlin: Verlag Bartels und Wernitz, 1972), 1, 69.

17. *Athletics of the Ancient World*, p. 49.

18. Peter L. Lindsay, "Attitudes Towards Physical Exercise Reflected in the Literature of Ancient Rome," *History of Sport and Physical Education to 1900*, ed. Earle F. Zeigler (Champaign, Illinois: Stipes, 1973), p. 179.

19. See Alois Koch, *Die Leibeserziehung im Urteil der antiken und frühchristlichen Anthropologie* (Schorndorf: Karl Hofmann, 1965); Ralph B. Ballou, Jr., "An Analysis of the Writings of Selected Church Fathers to A.D. 394 to Reveal Attitudes Regarding Physical Activity," *History of Sport and Physical Education*, ed. Zeigler, pp. 187-99; Georg Söll, "Sport in der katholischen Theologie des 20. Jahrhunderts," *Sport im Blickpunkt der Wissenschaft*, ed. Helmut Baitsch (Heidelberg: Springer Verlag, 1972), pp. 43-63; Rüdiger Schloz, "Probleme und Ansätze in der protestantischen Theologie," *Sport im Blickpunkt der Wissenschaft*, pp. 64-83.

20. See Frank Deford, "Religion in Sport," *Sports Illustrated* 44 (April 19, 1976), 88-102; Deford, "The Word According to Tom," *Sports Illustrated*, 44 (April 26, 1976), 54-69; Deford, "Reaching for the Stars," *Sports Illustrated*, 44 (May 3, 1976), 42-60.

21. Keith Dunstan, *Sports* (North Melbourne: Cassell Australia, 1973), p. 1.

22. *The Joy of Sports* (New York: Basic Books, 1976), pp. xiv, 18-19, 34.

23. Dan Jenkins, *Saturday's America* (Boston: Little, Brown, 1970), p. 88.

24. See Martin Hörrmann, *Religion der Athleten* (Stuttgart: Kreuz Verlag, 1968).

Recovering a Sense of the Sacred in Sport

Shirl J. Hoffman

One of the more remarkable twists in the historical evolution of sports has been its curious relation to the religious life of those most enamoured by it. In its earliest versions, sport was liturgical; it embodied expressive rites enacted to please the gods and bring fertility, rain, or cures for the sick. Sports entered the lives of primitive adults, says historian Allen Guttmann, "primarily in conjunction with some form of religious significance" (1978:19). Over time, however, sport became warped by converging forces of specialization, rationalization, bureaucratization and quantification, so warped in fact, that contemporary societies find it difficult even to imagine any substantive commonalities between it and the practice of religion.

It remains a topic of serious debate as to whether the forces of secularism have so demythologized sport that it cannot be reclaimed as a legitimate ritual for expressing religious sentiment. That modern athletes worship at the altar of production and achievement is as obvious as their disdain for Grantland Rice's sentimental adage that "how you played the game" is the ultimate criterion of victory. On the other hand, there is a trend detectable in some parts of the athletic community toward reconceptualizing sport as a mode of religious expression, a faint hint that the cycle of human history eventually may rejoin that which earlier generations viewed as natural companions.

This essay is an examination of the trend toward conceptualization of sport as religious ceremony, a clarification of what should and should not be considered part of the movement, and why the modern attempt to revitalize religious ritual in sport falls short of the ancient ideal.

It is important to distinguish authentic signs of a revitalization from those that are not. It hardly takes a cultural historian to appreciate the abundance of religious trappings in American sport, and one needn't sit through six showings of *Chariots of Fire* to recognize that of all religions, a pietistic, sentimental derivative of Christianity seems to be the athlete's favorite. Evidence can be assembled from almost any stratum of sport competition, from Junior High basketball and Pop Warner football to big time athletics. At American Catholic universities, a coarse pragmatic version of the faith has always been kept close to the playing fields and at the hundred or so small unheralded Protestant ("Christian") liberal arts colleges that dot the land, athletics assume an exaggerated importance, spicing up what some consider to be a rather restricted campus social life.

Like his predecessors, Jerry Faust, the current Notre Dame football coach, mixes piety with hot sporting blood in fairly equal proportions, decorating locker room walls with athletic-religious slogans and encouraging his players to say "Hail Marys" at crucial points in a contest ("Moeller Wins Without Faust," 1981). At the small Christian colleges, religious gestures often are expanded to include the audience. Pregame prayers offered over the loudspeaker implore God's blessing on the contest and ask His protection on the players. In this small circle of colleges, this pregame ritual presumably stamps the contest with a distinctive "Christian" label. Not that a congregational prayer diminishes in any way the importance attached to winning. There may not be bowl games or big TV contracts in the offing, but bragging rights are up for grabs and, of course, publicity. Winning the national basketball or soccer championship of the NCCAA (National Christian College Athletic Association) offers a rare (and perhaps the only) opportunity for these small institutions to showcase their athletic and academic programs at a national level.

Along with publicity, theological symbolism implicitly is associated with winning at these small schools. Several years ago Liberty Baptist College's famous chancellor, Jerry Falwell, shared his goal for the football program at LBC with reporters from *60 Minutes*: "To build champions for Christ," puzzling but popular imagery that makes up in holy zeal for whatever it may lack in theological clarity. Oral Roberts, president at the small Oklahoma university that bears his name, justified the school's move to NCAA Division I basketball on grounds that it would provide visibility for the school's theological position, and was careful to point out: "Just playing the game is not enough. It's all right to lose some but I'm not much for losing. We're geared up for winning here" (Boyle, 1970:64). Let Ohio State win for its student body or Notre Dame for its loyal alumni, Liberty Baptist, ORU, and their sister institutions will win for the Lord. Presumably the Lord likes to see his favorite team win, and trouncing the heathens from the state college up the road proves, in its own inexplicable way, that the institution's position on theology was right all along.

Clearly, the most remarkable mix of sport and religion has been managed at the highest levels of competition, particularly in the professional ranks. Ecclesio-jock organizations like Fellowship of Christian Athletes and Pro Athletes Outreach flourish. Informal Bible studies for players and their wives are commonplace. Most professional football teams now arrange for *ad hoc* chaplains to lead in prayer before each game and sometimes compete for the services of the same minister. Players on every major and minor league baseball team attend Sunday morning services arranged by Baseball Chapel, where total attendance is estimated to exceed 1,000 players per week (Carvalho, 1984). Never has so much evangelical ammunition been directed by so many at so few.

Apparently it has paid off. Professional football and baseball teams sparkle with what seems to be a disproportionate number of evangelical Christians. Roy Blount, Jr., claimed that so many Christians had invaded big-time sports that when he set out to select an "All-Religious Team" and an "All-Heathen Team" to compete in an imaginary "Christians vs. Lions Bowl" he couldn't find enough genuine heathens to field a squad (Blount, 1976:111). No closet Christians, these athletes. They take any opportunity to identify themselves as believers, attributing their athletic success to Divine Providence. The ubiquitous, unsolicited, postgame theological endorsement—"First of all I just want to thank the Lord for the win and give Him all of the credit"—has become a familiar feature of locker-room interviews, a custom that hasn't set all that well with a religiously indifferent press. An *Oakland Tribune* sportswriter, assigned to cover a week-long road trip with the notoriously religious San Francisco Giants, returned home numbed by the experience: "It's terrible," he said. "For almost every interview you had to go through ten minutes of religion first" (Collins, 1978:12).

From an historical perspective it can be argued that these are little more than elaborations of a trend long a part of American sports. Athletics always has had its share of religious types, foxhole converts mostly, pious and repentant in the gut-wrenching moments before a big game, destined to backslide as soon as the ball is put into play. In many locker rooms, prayer has become the ultimate psych-up. Football coaches, even those whose personal approach to life and sports runs hard against the grain of The Golden Rule, have been known to require their players to pray before games, a bit of hypocrisy not lost on former Michigan State coach Duffy Daugherty who reportedly quipped: "All those coaches who require pregame prayers for their players ought to be made to attend church once each week."

It has been my impression that pregame piety usually runs in direct proportion to the importance of the contest, the anticipated size of the audience and the probability that participants will suffer pain and injury. For the latter reason, football players tend to be more prayerful than basketball or tennis players, and boxers, for obvious reasons, are the most prayerful of all. Indeed, some of the best boxers to have entered the ring may be destined for sainthood. It was fighter Carmen Basilio's trademark to enter the ring, drop to his knees, eyes fixed on the ceiling of the arena, and offer a prayer—whether for protection or victory was never made clear. When Sugar Ray Robinson beat him into bloody submission to capture the crown, it seemed appropriate that the new champ accept the sacerdotal obligations that went with the title. Robinson didn't let us down, taking care in post-fight interviews to publicly thank "Reverend Johnson and Reverend Williams" who, as it turned out, had been praying for him throughout the fight. In what probably was the most publicized post-fight religious statement by a boxer (and one clergy have tried for decades to forget), Floyd Patterson credited the Lord with helping him flatten Archie Moore to win the heavyweight championship. "I could see his eyes go glassy as he fell back," said Patterson, "and I knew if he got up again it wouldn't do him any good. I just hit him again and the Lord did the rest" (Day, 1957:59).

Recent fighters have concocted more imaginative rituals. According to his manager, Gerry Cooney and he embrace each other and recite the *Lord's Prayer* in unison before each fight. When the prayer is finished the manager, in benedictory tones, says: "Let's go in there and get this man out of the way. Let's kick his butt" (Norman, 1981:32). One of the more puzzling, if not theologically complex incidences, occurred when heavyweight Mike Weaver, hopelessly behind on the judges' scorecards, made a miraculous comeback to knock out John Tate in the last round of their 1980 Championship fight. Weaver told reporters that he had been reciting the Twenty-Third Psalm since the beginning of the 14th round. Not only that, tucked inside his left shoe, apparently to cover all the theological bases, was a star of David given to him by his pastor ("Hercules Was a Myth," 1980).

Hundreds of examples of the way religion and religious ritual permeate sport could be cited, but using athletic achievements to publicize Christian education, to validate a theological position, or whiten the dirty linen of big time athletic programs hardly qualify as authentic religious ritual. Neither do self-serving prayers prompted by panic. Seeking God in a pinch or trying through pious pregame demeanor to tilt the cosmic odds in one's own favor, no more converts a football game into a sacred rite than desperate supplications by sweaty-palmed infantrymen at Normandy turned World War II into a religious festival. As Professor Guttmann put it: "There is a fundamental difference between obligatory pregame locker room prayers and the worship of gods by means of an athletic festival. . . . For most contemporary athletes, even for those who ask for divine assistance in the game, the contest is a secular event" (Guttmann, 1978:25).

The motives of a modern day coach like George Allen, who insists on locker-room worship services for his players on game days because it does more "to produce togetherness and mutual respect than anything else I've found in 21 years of coaching" (Levitt, 1972:33), can hardly be confused with those of the Jicarilla Apaches who ran the circles of the sun or the Athenians who ran in the stadium at Delphi above the sacred way. There is a big difference between the pragmatic appropriation of religion as a sort of cosmic ergogenic aid to maximize outcomes and the sacred appropriation of sport to symbolically express religious emotion and belief. In the first instance religion is pressed into service for sport, while in the second, sport serves religion. In the jungles of big-time athletics you had better put your religion in proper perspective.

It's difficult to say whether the demise of religious ritual in sport is the result of specific alterations in the structure and meaning of sport, or simply is fallout from what anthropologist Mary Douglas described as a general "revolt against formalism" (Douglas, 1970:18), an explicit rejection of rituals on a much larger social scale. Perhaps liturgist Romano Guardini was correct in his assessment that "man in this industrial and scientific age, with its new sociological structure, is no longer capable of a liturgical act" (Guardini, 1964:239). Yet, for those willing to take a closer look faint signs of what appears to be the genesis of a revitalization of religious expression in sport can be seen on the horizon, signs that Guttmann has overlooked.

The most obvious is the growing number of athletes who talk about the existential implications of their performance, bona fide jocks who seem more concerned with sport as a medium for opening mind and soul to new spiritual vistas than with appropriating religion as a bandage "to protect a soul made bloody by circumstance."

The horde of Sunday morning joggers immediately comes to mind, ascetic adherents of *cultus aerobicus* who claim to have found on the roads passing by the church what they could never find within its walls.

If there is a high priest of this religion of the roads it has to be George Sheehan, cardiologist, philosopher, author, and reigning guru of the middle-aged jogging set. He had his own conversion of sorts during a particularly consciousness-raising run: "Running that day became for me, as I'm sure it has for others, a mystical experience, a proof of the existence of God" (Sheehan, 1978:230).

Runners by nature are introspective and perhaps naturally inclined to metaphysics, but they don't have a monopoly on mystical encounters. Athletes from a broad range of sports, from mountain climbing to basketball, from surfing to tennis, have reported making supernatural-like contacts during their performances.

Reflecting on the uniformly sacred tone of these testimonials, Howard Slusher, in *Man, Sport and Existence*, considered them "too close to the religious to call (them) anything else" (Slusher, 1967:127).

It's impossible to say whether jock-theologians like Sheehan, as they push through pain barriers of physical exertion, have been truly grasped by a sense of the Ultimate or simply dizzied by one too many laps around the track. Mystical encounters are inherently private experiences, unobservable, difficult to verify and almost impossible to interpret. Higgs has noted how easily athletes can confuse *natural* mysticism, a self-expanding experience, with *spiritual* mysticism, a contraction of self in the presence of the Almighty (Higgs, 1983:80). After all, even St. Theresa of Avila, one of the great Christian mystics, was never really certain her vivid apprehensions of the Trinity were inspired by God or Satan (St. Theresa, 1930:171).

Yet, supernaturally inspired or not, mystical encounters cannot be considered rituals of worship, at least insofar as the term "worship" is understood by students of religion. Worship rituals may or may not induce a sense of the holy presence, but they are fundamentally behavioral, not emotional experiences. "Ritual," says theologian Harvey Cox, "does for movement what language does for sound; transforms it from the inchoate into the expressive" (Cox, 1969:87).

The transformation derives its power, not from moods or feelings but from the personal motivations of the worshippers and intricate symbolic connections between the movements of the ritual and the religious belief system in which the ritual is embedded. Admittedly, moods also are part of worship but, as historian James Hitchcock notes, "of the two, moods are more evanescent and unreliable, motivations are deeper and more enduring and do not necessarily have to do with feelings" (Hitchcock, 1974:50). In this sense, Christian worship is inherently rational. True worshippers understand, if only at a superficial level, why the rituals are performed, what the ceremonies celebrate and, most importantly, are able to articulate the motivations that give rise to their ritual acts.

It is this critical connection between ritual and belief system, the grounds for commitment to the inner reality symbolized by external gestures, that is missing in most athletes' accounts of mystical religious experiences. A runner may describe a marathon as "a worship experience" but one is left to guess what might be the symbolic connections between the ritual of running and the religious system of which it is a part. If running truly is worship, what eternal verities are expressed in the synergistic churnings of arms and legs, in the incessant pulsation of Pumas on pavement? Do liturgical interpretations change with a change in running style? Does the spirited bounce of a trained athlete, for example, signal different spiritual realities than a fat man's waddle? Does running uphill have a sacred significance that running downhill does not?

These are not insignificant questions. Anthropologists and historians have typically used "ritual" to mean "an agreed upon pattern of movement" (Mitchell, 1977:x). In religious ritual the external qualities of the performance must conform to divine prescription in order to be efficacious. Yet for all the worship talk that creeps into the vocabularies of modern Sheehanites, one cannot help being struck by their contempt of external ritual forms. In the rush to phenomenology they have subordinated motivation to moods and liturgical form to private experience. All of this leaves one wondering why runners who claim to have caught a glimpse of the Divine Presence while running up the side of Pike's Peak or swimming the English Channel couldn't just as easily have seen Him while walking behind their lawn mowers or soaking in the bathtub.

None of this is to ignore the potential of athletic performances for expressing religious sentiments. It has never been clear to me how my Protestant progenitors (and many contemporaries) could consecrate the gestures of artists and musicians, in some cases viewing them as virtual artpaths to God, yet not sense the same potential for religious expression in athletic performances. After all, when the ark of the covenant was brought into Jerusalem, scriptures say that David, "danced before the Lord with all his might" (II Samuel, 6:14). On the surface at least, there seemed to be no good reason why the same jubilation couldn't have been expressed by throwing the javelin or running 1500 meters.

To suggest, however, that sports possess salvational powers or that they embody anything other than a dimly reflected glory runs the risk of humanizing the sacred, gutting it of its autonomy, and reducing it to merely a projection of human aspirations. Not only this, it threatens to burden a fascinating human experience—made all the more fascinating for the freedom and lightness of spirit it entails—with some weighty cosmic baggage.

References

Blount, Roy, Jr. "Temple of the Playing Fields," *Esquire*. (December, 1976):111-113; 198.

Boyle, Robert H. "Oral Roberts: Small but OH, MY." *Sports Illustrated*. (November, 1970):64.

Carvalho, John. "Leading the League in Scores." *Athletes in Action Magazine*, 6 (Fall, 1984):4.

Collins, Dennis. "Nearer My God to the Goal Line." *The Washington Post Magazine*, 19 (November, 1978):12, 15-19.

Cox, Harvey. *The Feast of Fools*. New York: Harper & Row, 1969.

Day, John. "The Lord Did the Rest." *The New Yorker*. (27 July, 1957):58-59.

Douglas, Mary. *Natural Symbols*. New York: Random House, 1970.

Guardini, Romano. "A Letter From Romano Guardini." *Herder Correspondence*. August 1964, 239.

Guttmann, Allen. *From Ritual to Record: The Nature of Modern Sports*. New York: Columbia University Press, 1978.

"Hercules Was a Myth, But I'm Not." *Sports Illustrated*. (14 April 1980):20-21.

Higgs, Robert J. "Muscular Christianity, Holy Play, and Spiritual Exercises: Confusion About Christ in Sports and Religion." *Arete: The Journal of Sport Literature*, 1 (Fall, 1983):59-85.

Hitchcock, James. *The Recovery of the Sacred*. New York: Seabury Press, 1974.

Levitt, Zola. *Somebody Called Doc*. Carol Stream, Illinois: Creation House, 1972.

Mitchell, Leonel. *The Meaning of Ritual*. New York: The Paulist Press, 1977.

"Moeller Wins Without Faust." *The New York Times*. (8 November 1981):S-13.

Norman, Michael. "The Rise of Gerry Cooney." *New York Times Magazine*. (9 August 1981):23-26; 30-34.

Sheehan, George. *Running and Being: The Total Experience*. New York: Warner Books, 1978.

Slusher, Howard. *Man, Sport and Existence*. Philadelphia: Lea & Febiger, 1967.

St. Theresa. *Interior Castle*. London: Thomas Baker, 1930.

The Spirit of Winning:
Sports and the Total Man

Carol Flake

Upon the fields of friendly strife are sown the seeds that, upon other fields, on other days, will bear the fruits of victory.

Douglas MacArthur

If Jesus Christ were alive today, he would be at the Super Bowl.

Norman Vincent Peale

The militant trumpet blares of masculine superiority that periodically has announced the resurgence of conservative Christianity in America have not managed to obscure the uneasiness men have felt about the influence of women and about their own roles in the church. During the late nineteenth century, for example, the preponderance of women in the church pews and at the cash registers of popular culture caused a backlash. As historians Ann Douglas, Jackson Lears, and others have suggested, the apparent collusion of women and liberal ministers in appropriating the subject of morality created a hostile defensiveness and a muscle-flexing bravado among men who felt excluded or alienated from the sentimental pieties of the church—and of popular culture as well. One could not have Little Eva and hunting trophies too. As one scholar put it, ''In its very success, middle-class culture had come to seem stifling, enervating, effeminate, devoid of opportunities for manly heroism.'' Conservative preachers as well as restless spirits like Teddy Roosevelt hailed the virtues of the martial spirit, the cleansing power of muscular Christianity. In this view, the feminine influence might be uplifting, but too much of it was dangerous.

Traditionally, women simply have been more at home in church than men. For one thing, they seem to get along better with preachers. Even the homeliest preachers have had a better way with women than with men—always a cause for suspicion in the mind of a jealous husband. In the nineteenth century, when revival fervor was causing such stirring in the pews, there were a number of cases of preachers being shot or tarred and feathered by husbands who did not share their wives' uninhibited piety.

Historian Donald G. Mathews related in his fine book *Religion in the Old South . . .* that a preacher named John Tanner ''once baptized a woman who had for a long time wanted to join the church, but whose husband—a 'great persecutor,' one clergyman called him—had persistently and stubbornly refused to allow it. Finally, during a revival, she gathered up her courage, related her experience of grace to the church, asked to be admitted into the community of faithful people, and was baptized. Her husband's fury was so intense that months later he deliberately intercepted Tanner on the way to meeting and shot him in the thigh with a horse pistol.''

Jealousy, however, was not the most troubling emotion that men associated with preachers. Worse still was guilt. Traditionally, most of the vices put on parade from the pulpit were those that tended to lure husbands rather than wives away from respectability: drinking, gambling, whoring, cursing, immoral conduct. If a man didn't feel the watchful eye of God upon him as he struggled against temptation, he could certainly sense the accusing eyes and hear the wagging tongues of his fellow church members.

Even for men who welcomed the moral constraints offered by the church, there were other emotional difficulties to overcome. There has always been something of the spiritual panderer in the revival specialist who acts as go-between urging the union of Christ and soul. The great evangelists of the sawdust trail, and the Super Savers who succeeded them, used the pulpit as a cosmic stage, upon which they stalked and sweated, working their congregations to the burning edge of agony and surrender. While women could swoon or weep, joyously weak-kneed, during the sermon, guilt-wracked men knelt grim-lipped, their wills bent like birches in the wind, ready to snap back upright after the service. Even in the livelier pentecostal sects, except for the snake-handlers, women were more demonstrative in their worship, trembling and shrieking unashamedly when possessed by the Holy Ghost.

The central evangelical experience of yielding to a superior being was a humbling experience for man; how could he surrender himself emotionally without losing his manhood? It was the genius of evangelical preachers to make the born-again experience seem a masculine rite of passage. Christianity was like a team, an army, into which one was initiated, with Jesus as the commander. That was a kind of subordination men could understand. For women, Jesus could be a comfort and a constant companion, but for men he was more like a boss. Or a coach.

The God Squads

Sports were an inevitable addition to male-dominated multiministried churches. During the rise of Moral Majority, when it seemed that there were fewer and fewer arenas in which men could assert their manhood without women trying to muscle in on the action, it was crucial for men to maintain control of the churches as a preserve of masculine power.

If the model fundamentalist woman of the Falwell era was a positive-thinking house-wife kneeling in a negligee at the altar of masculinity, the ideal evangelical man was a tireless athlete who exerted his competitive spirit for God, country, and business. While the aspiring Total Woman studied to weaken her will, the total Christian male practiced getting tough for Jesus. It was time for tough love for one's family and tough luck for one's competitors. The paradigm for the Christian life was no longer the pilgrimage but the game, played by the rules of St. Paul and Vince Lombardi.

The resurgence of evangelicalism in America had brought with it a revival of muscular Christianity and a return to the social Darwinism of the athletic arena. Jesus the teacher had become Christ the competitor, as in the film version of *Elmer Gantry*, when Burt Lancaster avowed to a barroom full of backsliders that Christ was the greatest quarterback who ever lived. From the pulpit, preachers prayed for winning seasons, sprinkling their sermons with so much athletic symbolism that they sometimes sounded like color commentators on TV sports broadcasts. Straining for sinewy images, they fused athletic and religious symbolism in crude metaphysical conceits reminiscent of country singer Bobby Bare's mock-sincere rendition of "Drop-Kick Me, Jesus, Through the Goalposts of Life."

The character-building benefits of sports could be obtained by spectating as well as participating. Rather than trying to lure the more fervent fans in the congregation away from the worship of their sports idols, the wilier preachers managed to merge the altar with the scoreboard, so that Jesus was never the loser. Many churches were virtual cheering squads for their local teams. The pastor of the Second Baptist Church of Houston, for example, knew better than to force his congregation to choose between the pew and the bleachers. During the football season, the most devout Oiler fanatics could attend the special "Oiler Service" at 8:30 a.m. so they wouldn't be late for the kickoff at the Astrodome. No less accommodating was the Reverend W.A. Criswell of the First Baptist Church of Dallas. One year, when the Dallas Cowboys were scheduled to play in the Super Bowl at a time that overlapped with the regular Sunday Service, the church elders considered delaying the service. Instead, they taped the game on a Betamax, and the congregation adjourned to the cavernous church basement after the sermon to watch the playback.

Participating in sports was not only good, clean American fun; it was a means of firming up one's fortitude to do battle with the moral flabbiness and easy physical gratifications associated with contemporary culture. There was no room for gender doubt or socialist anarchy on the football field. Infusing the pep talks of preachers and high school coaches alike was the credo that one could effect a moral regeneration of school, church, community, and country by going all out to win football games, track meets, golf tournaments, and the game of life itself. Implicit, too, in the evangelical enthusiasm for sports was an ambivalence about the growing prosperity and physical comforts of churches and individuals alike. There was always the danger of growing "soft" in one's complacency when church pews and hardships were cushioned. Sports represented a return to an older ascetic/martial ideal of harsh conscience, selfless duty, and strict discipline.

Although a few hardy souls pointed out that athletes now hied to the highest bidder, and pro clubhouses were corporate countinghouses, it was difficult to argue that sports were a pagan endeavor. Many of the biggest gladiators were Christians. By 1980, there were almost as many chapters, ''huddles,'' and local fellowships of the nationwide Fellowship of Christian Athletes (FCA) as there were pro, college, and high school football teams. Devout players had organized specialized prayer groups within every professional sport, and on many teams the Bible-toters outnumbered the infidels. Baseball players could attend Baseball Chapel meetings, while bodybuilders could join the International Fellowship of Christian Iron Men, and golfers could pray together during Professional Tour Chapel. Secular humanism seemed to be as rare on the gridiron, the green, and the baseball diamond as on the battlefield.

Such devotion above and beyond the call of duty was the inspiration for the character of Dr. Tom Bennett in Peter Gent's novel *North Dallas Forty*. Bennett had ''set out to fulfill the bargain he had made with the Lord. In an even swap with God for salvation and its Puritan ethic ramifications, Doctor Tom swore an oath to the Lord Almighty on the blood of the crucified Christ that he would carry the mantle of Christianity without recompense to a congregation that desperately needed his divine guidance. He chose the National Football League.''

>   *God loathes mediocrity.*
>   Gary Player

I was neither shocked nor baffled by the notion of a double ministry to body and soul, since my own conversion experience at the age of nine had been inspired by an all-pro lineman named Bill Glass who was touring the Texas revival circuit during his off-season. Glass, a part-time seminarian who was then a starter on the Detroit Lions, had appeared as valiant as Samson to a dreamy young girl in a small town where pep rallies weren't much different in spirit from worship services and football players were pampered like gods. As the biggest celebrity to hit town that year, Glass had an immediate edge over the local pastor, Brother Johnny, whose red-faced fervor was considered excessive by the younger members of the congregation. Glass's huge body, its heroic massiveness looming over the pulpit, had seemed a bulwark against doubt and pain. As he described the sweat and blood of the crucifixion, the supreme sacrifice, his shoulders hunched as if in anticipation of the snap of the ball from center, he seemed strong enough to have borne the agonies of Golgotha, strong enough to have deflected a legion of Romans. Glass merged with my Sunday school image of a mild and merciful Jesus, and I saw an invincible redeemer who not only understood my weaknesses but who could fight my battles for me.

>   *I ran on, and as I ran, I made a prayer; it wasn't theological either, I tell you*
>   *that. I said, ''God, if you ever helped mortal man, help me to get that ball!''*
>   Billy Sunday

Glass, in fact, was a latter-day proselyte of the cult of the Christian athlete that peaked early in the century with the career of William A. ''Billy'' Sunday, the baseball-player-turned-evangelist. As his biographer William T. Ellis described him, Sunday "was a man's man. His tabernacle audiences resembled baseball crowds in the proportion of men present. . . . Sunday talked religion as he talked baseball. His words smacked of the street corners, the shop, the athletic field, the crowd of men." Rescuing the Bible from women and overly refined preachers, Sunday restored the masculine aura to Christ and delivered Christianity to the businessmen and bully pulpits of the land.

For social critic Thorstein Veblen, who regarded both the sporting and the religious temperaments as predatory, the Christian athlete had represented a juncture of two kinds of barbarism. But for conservative Christians, the cult of the arduous life was a means of resolving the old Puritan squeamishness about sports; it was a way to embrace both asceticism and sheer physicality. As he strived mightily, the muscular Christian did not have to doubt either his masculinity or his faith.

Originally, the Puritan ethos had precluded any sort of games. A code called The Book of Sports, which promoted games on Sunday, was made into law by James I and Charles I as a means of counteracting Puritan influence. Play-hating Puritans in Massachusetts and Connecticut banned dice, cards, quoits, bowls, ninepins, "or any other unlawful game in house, yard, garden, or backside," singling out for censure "the Game called Shuffle Board, in houses of Common Intereinment, whereby much precious time is spent unfruitfully." But as the character ethic evolved from the Puritan work ethic, competition became a kind of test to weed out the weaklings from the ranks of the elect. Competition built character, and winning, like wealth, was evidence of God's blessing.

Not long after Sunday's career began to decline, legendary Notre Dame coach Knute Rockne took up the banner of Christian competitiveness. Like Sunday, he spent countless afternoons addressing business-luncheon audiences about the need for strenuous competition in a world going soft. A late convert to Catholicism, he brought a plain Protestant pragmatism to his pep talks. He had a patented "fight talk" that he delivered in his high, rasping voice to Studebaker salesmen, emphasizing that the "trouble in American life today in business as well as sports is that too many people are afraid of competition. They are unwilling to make the sacrifice that means achievement and success." One had to bite the bullet and win one for God, the Gipper, and the GNP.

Sanctified Sweat

For many Christians, athleticism was itself becoming a kind of religion, with its own kind of grace. By the 1970s, self-fulfillment, along with fame and money, had supplanted sportsmanship and self-sacrifice as the supreme values of athletic diversion. Catholic author Michael Novak argued in his book *The Joy of Sports* that sports were "natural religions," with baseball, football, and basketball a kind of "holy trinity." One could imagine the Pittsburgh Steeler fullback ricocheting toward eternity near the goal line, just as the Jicarilla Apache had run between the circles of the sun and the moon in the desert and the Athenian youth had raced for

Apollo in the stadium above the sacred way at Delphi. According to Novak, American sports fans ought to have recognized that they were performing a kind of sacrament, for sports brought to men's lives—whether they were players or spectators—the kind of experiences once provided mainly by religion. Sport, like religious transport, was a means of transformation that brought the Christian into contact with the ultimate. "Church and stadium alike are places of renewal, recreation, and sanctity," opined Charles Prebish, associate professor of religious studies at Penn State University.

> . . . [W]rite the vision . . . that he may run that readeth it.
>
> Habakkuk 2:2

The notion of running one's way to glory received a big boost in 1981 with the movie *Chariots of Fire*, choreographed to the transcendent pounding of composer Vangelis's synthesized score. In the Oscar-winning film, Eric Liddell, that other great Christian athlete of the early twentieth century, was portrayed reverently by actor Ian Charleson as the first proponent of the runner's high. Liddell, a bandy-legged little Scotsman who won the 400-meters competition in the 1924 Olympics, ran like a mad priest, his head flung back in blind volition, feeling God's pleasure.

Liddell found no contradiction between running fast and witnessing for Christ. In the film, he tells his doubtful sister, who wants to drag him off to missionary work in China, "God made me for a purpose. He also made me fast. Not to run would be to hold him in contempt." Yet Liddell ultimately obeyed a higher calling and became a missionary. Shortly after his triumph in the Olympics, he left for China, where he died a few years later in prison.

Despite the valiant Scot's example, few Christian athletes have stopped competing before age dictated a change in vocation. (An exception was boxer George Foreman, who had a vision of Christ in 1977 after losing a bout to Jimmy Young on St. Patrick's Day. Subsequently he put his gloves away and founded his own church in Houston.) Born-again athletes have tended to use sports as their pulpit, applying the principles of sportsmanship to the Christian life. Particularly effective for many years in winning converts were the Athletes in Action, who began operating as a branch of the Campus Crusade for Christ, competing as a kind of paraprofessional league but usually managing to score a high percentage of wins against secular teams who deigned to play them. However, their effectiveness in converting teenagers seemed dependent on their ability to deliver points. Said an AIA basketball player, "It's important for us to win, not because God wants winners, but because Americans do." Players for the AIA, he said, were out to prove that Christians were not "Casper Milquetoasts."

Born-again athletes who remained on pro teams had even stronger incentives to bolster the image of Christians as tough customers. In the film based on Peter Gent's *North Dallas Forty*, the pious second-string quarterback (whom some people took to be a thinly disguised Roger Staubach) was portrayed as a sniveling hypocrite, and the team's sanctimonious chaplain bumbled around the locker room, an oblivious missionary surrounded by bloodthirsty savages in pads and bandages.

That skeptical attitude toward pious players survived even as Christians on many teams began to outnumber the secularists. Baltimore Orioles manager Earl Weaver reportedly once queried a born-again player caught snoozing on first base what the Bible had to say about base-running. And in 1978, the San Francisco Giants were nicknamed the God Squad when pitcher Bob Knepper was said to have attributed a game-losing home run scored against him to God's will.

New York *Times* sportswriter George Vecsey interviewed a number of Giants players who had become concerned about the potential complacency of their born-again teammates, but most expressed grudging admiration for their Christian colleagues. Fritz Peterson, a member of Baseball Chapel in the Chicago area, heatedly denied the placidity sometimes attributed to devout players, claiming that "if Jesus Christ was sliding into second base, he would knock the second baseman into left field to break up the double play. Christ might not throw a spitball but he would play hard within the rules."

So many of the hardest hitting, meanest swinging, longest striding, and straightest shooting superstars in pro sports were born-again testifiers that any lingering notions of the pacifying effect of prayer should have been dispelled. Included on the roster of devout Christians were then-Yankee Tommy John, marathoner Alberto Salazar, '76er Julius Erving, Steeler Terry Bradshaw, Oiler Earl Campbell, and Patriot John Hannah. Hannah, who had been dubbed the greatest lineman in the history of the NFL by *Sports Illustrated*, gained a certain notoriety when he passed out New Testaments instead of cigars to Pro Bowl players when his child was born.

The Faith Factor

When one considered the factors of demographics, stress, and peer pressure at work in the lives of athletes, it seemed inevitable rather than strange that pro players were converting in such numbers. Athletes tended to come from the same geographic and economic sectors that produced the greatest proportion of evangelicals in America. Growing up in a lower-middle-class family in a small town in the South, Southwest, or Midwest increased the odds that one would become either an athlete or an evangelical, or both. And born-again experiences in the general population tended to occur during times of duress or "identity crisis," often during adolescence or middle age. (Jimmy Carter's conversion experience after losing the governor's race in Georgia was a case in point.) For athletes, who lived through a prolonged adolescence and then faced retirement at thirty, those vulnerable times of passage were compressed and intensified.

Players who neglected their educations for workouts, who had been primed for physical prowess like prize bulls, tended to have limited intellectual and emotional resources and little real-world experience to draw on when they could no longer cut the mustard. When troubled, rather than making visits to the psychiatrist's couch or taking mystical journeys to the East, they were more likely to choose the source of relief closest to home.

According to evangelical writer Bob Hill, who interviewed dozens of born-again players for his book, *The Making of a Super Pro*, many players, suffering from boredom and loneliness, tried every avenue to oblivion and returned to the religion they knew as kids because it offered more permanence. For some players, it seemed, Christ was the ultimate placebo. They called on Jesus as the perfect coach with the perfect game plan, the valiant lineman who could block out a path for them, the omniscient spectator whose love and enthusiasm never faltered. A sentiment I could well understand, from my own brief vision of Jesus as hulking rescuer.

Most players, in fact, found their religiosity to be an asset rather than a liability. Faith helped them to conquer fear, weariness, slumps, and negative attitudes. In his book *The Power of Positive Thinking*, Norman Vincent Peale recounted the time major league pitcher Frank Hiller restored his strength during a game on a blisteringly hot day by repeating Isaiah 40:31 over and over again: "But they that wait upon the Lord shall renew their strength; they shall mount up with wings as eagles; they shall run, and not be weary; they shall walk, and not faint."

Ultimately an athlete's ability to produce those wondrous moments of deliverance in a game was as much a mystery as his inability to do so. There was a certain fatalism involved in fondling a favorite bat or praying for relief from a slump like a farmer praying for rain. Although practice, technique, and strategy obviously affected probability in a game, winning often seemed a gift of grace, a power that could come and go like a deity's whim.

Apparently, there were many kinds of fortitude to be gained from one's faith. For John Hannah, it was consistency. Hannah related: "When I have a right relationship with Christ, I have found that I can play the game more relaxed and make fewer mistakes." A born-again bodybuilder used Christ to muster his motivation: "I didn't feel like working out today. But I felt the Lord's will come over me and I knew I had to come to the gym." Golfer Larry Nelson used Christ to calm his nerves: "I went into the final round of the Inverrary Classic in Florida with a three-shot lead. I could have worried about losing, but for the first time as I went into a situation of this type, I felt buoyed up with God's peace. No longer looking over my shoulder, I went on to win my first tournament on the PGA tour."

Some athletes sought not only peace but perfection from their Bible studies. Former athlete Wes Neal, who worked for several years with the athletic-ministry branch of the Campus Crusade for Christ, founded the Institute for Athletic Perfection with the premise that biblical principles were the ideal foundation for athletic training. Neal, who had been traveling the country with an evangelistic weight-lifting team, found himself asking, "How do I lift weights the way God wants me to lift them?" Turning to the Bible, he found that there were specific answers to such questions. He compiled in a training manual a list of Bible verses that seemed to apply directly to various dilemmas in the life of an athlete, including anger, depression, money, and team spirit. Under the section for contract negotiations, he referred the athlete to Luke 3:14: "And the soldiers likewise demanded of him, saying, And what shall we do? And he said unto them, Do violence to no man, neither accuse *any* falsely; and be content with your wages."

This blunt directive was seldom followed, of course, in the NFL or in any other league, for that matter. An exception was Steve Largent, a receiver for the Seattle Seahawks, who announced during the summer of 1982 that he felt obligated to honor his contract with the Seattle club even if the NFL Players Association called a preseason strike. "God's word calls a contract a vow," said Largent. "I've made a vow with the Seahawks that I will play football with them for three more years."

Dietrich Bonhoeffer, a German Christian hanged for his resistance to the Nazis, said, "When Christ bids a man come and follow him he bids him come and die." To be a Christian means giving up a comfortable position on the sidelines and getting in the game.

Bill Glass, *Don't Blame the Game*

Wes Neal was not the only contemporary ex-athlete to devise a precise formula for a winning attitude. One of the best-known motivators in the business was Bill Glass, my erstwhile hero. Glass now worked as a freelance chaplain (he was never formally ordained), operating various crusades from his headquarters in a shopping mall in Midlothian, Texas, about sixty miles southwest of Dallas. He was in constant demand as an inspirational speaker for prison groups, Baseball Chapel, and various NFL clubs. He often spoke to the Dallas Cowboys before their games, and once he was asked by both the Cowboys and the Los Angeles Rams to speak in chapel before an important game. He had written a number of books, including a volume called *Expect to Win*, in which he offered specialized variation of Peale's positive-thinking strategy, a kind of mind-over-muscle mental judo adapted to the needs of the Christian athlete/achiever.

Anxious to meet Glass again so many years after succumbing to his testimony, I arranged an interview at his Midlothian headquarters. When he strode into his small suite of offices on a warm autumn morning, he was genial but distracted. His daughter was sick, and he had to depart shortly for a board of directors meeting for Baseball Chapel. He was almost as big as I remembered him, the shoulders and mouth as broad, the hands as huge. When I reminded him of that long-ago crusade at the then-small Baptist church in my hometown, he smiled wryly. "How could I forget Brother Johnny," said Glass. "I used to make fun of him. I'd imitate him, the way he used to say 'Beloved' ''—Glass pursed his lips and stretched out the syllables. "But he was no dummy," Glass added quickly in response to my startled look. "If his message was simplistic, it was because the congregation expected it."

Had that pulpit-pounding approach gone out of style, then?

"Maybe, but I still don't have much use for unemotional preachers. The churches that have the ministers who *believe* the gospel are growing—it doesn't have anything to do with education or intelligence. I'm more stimulated myself by a sophisticated approach, but the preachers who choose an intellectual method are from churches that are dying. When it comes to pro ball, most of the players are college graduates. But the theoretical, abstract preacher—they don't want to hear it. They say, 'Tell me about something that's real to *you* or don't waste my time.' ''

How did he himself preach to athletes?

"When I speak to a team before a game, I find that I'm talking a Christian line, but I'm also talking motivation. I know that most players aren't into a heavy spiritual content, so you don't preach a sermon like you would in church. I talk about how I used to get myself ready before a game; it's the Christian power of positive thinking. I have a computer-like subconscious that's going to operate the way I program it. I can't say I'm gonna ask God to bless me professionally unless I'm willing to do the preparation."

In addition to its practical value, then, for pregame psyching up, what did Christianity have to do with sports—why, in his opinion, were so many athletes professing born-again experiences and joining groups like the FCA and Baseball Chapel?

"When I first started going to seminary, there wasn't much interest on the team in chapel, but there were a number of players who grew up in Christian homes. The groundwork was there. By the time I retired, there were twenty to twenty-five players who would come to chapel regularly. It's the same with other teams."

"I think sports have gotten tied into religion because with sports everything is more stark, more dramatic than in everyday life. Are you going to make it, or aren't you? You might get the snot knocked out of you at any time. It's a very existential experience, right out there on the edge, being tested every week, when you're only as good as your last game. You get it every week—three different film angles on everything you do, right there on the instant replay; you can't fake it. It's a highly pressurized existence. Our society is drawn into sharp contrast: if you're pagan, you're very pagan. It's either 'I'm gonna be a committed Christian' or 'I'm gonna overdose.' A player gets to feeling he can't handle it, and he finds God, sex, or drugs."

How did he apply his theories to his own life?

"When my son Bobby developed a hip infection that kept him out of sports for two years, I told him, 'You can either say you're gonna learn from this and let it be a source of strength, or you can nurse, rehearse, and curse the problem.' It's like Rafer Johnson, who was born with a club foot. You can't read a biography about a famous person that they didn't have a problem to overcome; momentum makes you an achiever. I never pushed my boys—I didn't want them to play in Little League, where the coaches all play Vince Lombardi—but it's in the Scripture that whatever you do, you do it with all your heart. The bottom line is that Bobby is now playing for Baylor, and my oldest son made the cut for the Cincinnati Bengals."

Christian and pagan athletes alike had long sought some form of grace under pressure. Glass seemed to be suggesting that Christian faith offered, in practical terms, a detachment from anxiety that allowed the athlete to perform at his peak. Choosing Christ over sex and drugs, then, was a matter of choosing the better opiate—or at least the better bromide. Faith acted as both an upper and a downer, as a spur to achievement and a painkiller for failure. For Glass, however, faith seemed primarily a stimulant for success.

When it comes to religion, I am not a scrambler. As an athlete I have gone somewhat against the grain. . . . I have been tabbed a gambler on the field. . . . But I pray to God I will never gamble with my immortal soul.

Roger Staubach, *First Down, Lifetime to Go*

If ever a team had been an arm—or army, perhaps—of Christian boosterism, it was the Dallas Cowboys in the seventies, with Roger Staubach's Hail-Mary passes, Tom Landry's computerized sense of calling, and the First Baptist Church's team spirit. Shortly after I spoke with Bill Glass, I drove to Dallas to ask Staubach and Landry about the connection between Christ and victory. Although Dallas was not generally known for the kind of rabid rooting that characterized the Luv-Ya-Blue boosters of Houston, the entire city was bestirring itself to pay tribute to Staubach with a gala in Texas Stadium that very week. As I listened to radio announcements of the event, which was to be hosted by Bob Hope and Suzanne Somers, I felt as though I had secured an audience with Captain America, the avatar of lost American ideals.

Although Staubach had descended to the realm of lesser mortals since his retirement by selling land, investing in fried-chicken franchises, advertising cheap slacks and Rolaids, and campaigning for Ronald Reagan, I was still a little apprehensive about meeting him. As I waited in his new real estate office in a sleek, smoky-glass building in north Dallas, I was surrounded by the evidence of America's approval. Next to the huge "NFL Player of the Year" gladiatorial bronzes on his desk was a fan's football to be signed, a stack of fan mail to be answered. On the walls were permaplaqued awards, corporate testimonials, an engraved Optimists Creed. On a shelf was a still-cellophaned set of *Conflicts of the Ages* from Pacific Publishing. On a coffee table were back issues of *Texas Realtor* magazine. It seemed that here was a man who had it all—his faith, the adoration of millions of fans, an old-fashioned family, a heroic career completed while he was still in his prime, a lucrative new career and elegant office in a woodsy plaza only minutes away from the Cowboys' headquarters.

It was all too perfect. It was easy to see why fans in other cities resented the Cowboys. Washington writer George Gildea had exhibited that admiring rancor in the September 1980 *D* (Dallas's city magazine): ". . . it's not simply that the Cowboys are good. It's that they seem to be above the battle. It's the shift in the shotgun and then a cute double reverse to avoid the grimy doings at the line of scrimmage. It's a preoccupation with excessive display, like picking up 30 yards at a clip and not even getting their uniforms mussed. Those beautiful uniforms. Those beautiful cheerleaders. Those beautiful computers . . . America's team. Disgusting. . . .''

I had seldom cheered for the Cowboys, for reasons along those lines, but I had watched their games whenever I could, even after I left Texas, and often found myself anticipating Staubach's last-minute rescues. His ability to deliver two-minute-warning miracles seemed a mystical deviance from the Cowboys' programmed game plan—he seemed the spirit in the machine. A fervent Catholic, a gambler with an utter reverence for authority, he had adapted to the Cowboys' computerized Protestant ethos without losing his faith in intercession. He was the obedient officer who executed orders like an automaton and then found it within himself to lead an unbidden kamikaze charge. His autobiography, *First Down, Lifetime to Go*, published by Word Inc., in 1974, was the account of a dutiful son, dutiful husband and father, dutiful soldier, dutiful Catholic, and dutiful quarterback—constantly driven, almost despite himself, by a competitive urge.

Staubach arrived at his office in a dark pin-striped suit, offering a polite apology for being late and a firm handshake, despite the dangling, useless pinky on his passing hand, one of the stigmata from his NFL career. But it didn't take long to place him on the defensive. Although he knew that I had come to talk about religion, Staubach seemed eager to dispel his super-Christian image. I asked him what he thought about the film version of *North Dallas Forty* and the character of the Bible-gripping quarterback. "What bothered me," he said irritably, "was the hypocrisy of the character. I wasn't the type to bring a Bible into the locker room—I would have been laughed out of there. I'm a very fierce competitor—I've been known to play hurt—and they had the guy in the movie crying. I never was a pansy they made that guy out to be."

Had his religious faith frequently caused him to be misunderstood?

"I really get bored with that goody-two-shoes image people have of me, like that *Sports Illustrated* story leading off with me in the confessional. I don't want to be tabbed that way— life isn't all gloom and doom if you're a Christian."

Why, then, had he just rewritten his autobiography for Word, Inc., a religious publishing house?

"Word wanted to redo the book because of the good seasons I'd had since the first one. But I didn't want to write just a Christian book, with my faith as a cross or shield in front of me—I wanted non-Christians to read it, too. The new book will make me more of a three-dimensional person; it talks about some of the unpleasant things in my career, like the fistfights I had with Clint Longley."

How did he relate his religious beliefs to things like money, competition, and success?

"Even if I was a non-Christian, I'd be a competitor. I had it inside me when I was growing up. But I'm not a knockdown competitor in business. I recently went to a Christian conference on how to handle money—I do think it's okay to have money. I know there are people starving while I'm sitting here, and we could live on less than we do. But as long as money doesn't become the bottom line. I never had an agent, for instance. And even the apostles weren't perfect—they were fickle. We don't have the opportunity ourselves to stick our hands into the wounds."

What did he think about players who regarded their win-loss records as a matter of divine intervention?

"I'm not into that, into saying that everything is God's will. Let's say that there's thirty Christians on a bus, and it goes over a cliff. The two that survive say 'Thank the Lord.' Or there are people who say 'When I found the Lord we won the district championship.' I don't think it works that way. You have to look at the permanence of Christianity and not get too literal or fundamental. But then there are things you can't explain, like Cheryl Prewitt, Miss America, whose leg grew two inches to make it normal."

What about allegations that the Cowboys put pressure on players to conform to an all-American Christian image?

"It comes down to skills. If you can produce, they don't care what you are. If you try, the management will work hard for you. It's a bunch of ---- that Thomas (Hollywood) Henderson was cut because he didn't fit the image. Look what happened to him at San Francisco after he left the Cowboys. If he had been cut for that reason, I would have been the first to object. Landry would keep an atheist on the team who mouthed off every Sunday as long as he produced.''

The team itself is a fiction and playing for B.A. made it all the more obvious to me. Team success to B.A. meant personal success. But it wasn't winning that B.A. cared about; or football, or God; it was how those things combined to make him successful.

Peter Gent, *North Dallas Forty*

I spoke to Tom Landry himself at Cowboy headquarters only a few minutes after I left Staubach's office. Although it was the day before a big game with the Redskins, he seemed relaxed, even avuncular. Landry indoors, minus all-weather hat and earphones, was taller, huskier, and friendlier than I anticipated after watching him on television. He carried himself like a five-star general on holiday. I felt as though I must be hallucinating the kindly twinkle in his eye. Yet it was easy to imagine powerful and tender egos alike being battered into obedience against that granitic self-confidence.

Landry, a Methodist, was always willing to talk about faith and fortitude. He spent a good deal of his spare time with the FCA. ''I talk to high school and junior high school audiences,'' he said, ''trying to relate athletic qualities with spiritual qualities—the similarities between being a Christian and being an athlete. I think our country is in trouble—we're too soft. If you avoid disciplining a youngster, he'll never have character; he'll turn to escapism to handle adversity. St. Paul himself was a sports spectator; he used athletic terms. I talk about the four points of faith, of training, of goals, and commitment, about being a champion on the field and a champion for God.''

''Most of us fail to fulfill our potential because of our own doubts and anxieties—a Christian is relieved of a lot of the anxieties that hold back an athlete. The champions don't fail in those difficult moments. I think Roger Staubach's faith enabled him to do what he did in the two-minute period; he knew he could handle it whether he won or lost.''

Did some players use their faith simply as a good-luck charm or as good PR?

''We're all guilty of using our faith as a crutch. Sometimes it's because of lack of maturity. But it all comes down to performance. I've had to cut some great Christian players, and it hurts, but I can't go by my personal feelings.''

How did he reconcile his faith with the competitiveness and violence of sports?

''Christ ran the money changers out of the temple, and he showed strength in adversity, as well as gentleness. A contest is a learning and a teaching experience. If you go out and win, you're teaching the opposition something. If you say you can't play within the rules and play a tough, punishing type of game, you can't play as a Christian. We try to eliminate the vicious side of the game, but you have to punish the opposition.''

Did he have a conversion experience, and did it change him radically?

''I had studied management and industrial engineering before I became a Christian—I'm very method-oriented, and that hasn't changed. But all my life I thought all I had to do was be a great athlete and a great coach. I was a churchgoer, but I wasn't really a Christian. I was never really committed to Christ until I was thirty-three. I went to a Bible-study group because some friends had invited me, and I was ripe for it. It wasn't as though I was down and out, because I had just had a great season. I came to it as a winner. A calmness and a peace came over me rapidly.''

"I hope I can be an example. My ambition is to bring people to Christ. It's the only thing. Even the Super Bowl is a platform for that.''

In 1924, illustrator Warner E. Sallman was asked by Dean Sellers of the Chicago Art Institute to create a "virile, manly Christ." Sallman's portrait of a robust, strong-jawed Jesus, minus halo, which first appeared as a charcoal drawing in an issue of the Covenant Companion, *became the prototype for pinup icons of Jesus. "No pale, anemic Christ is this," Sellers is reported to have said.*

Landry's reference to the ''softness'' in the American character was familiar. Like Billy Sunday and Knute Rockne, he was speaking in the standard rhetoric of the character ethic. The fear of softness was a common sentiment among American leaders, from coaches to presidents. Even John F. Kennedy resorted to such a rationale when he promoted ''vigah'' and created the President's Council on Physical Fitness. The assumption was that a nation's very spirit, its strength and stamina, could be tested through the speed of its sprinters, the heft of its shoulders.

But for many conservative Christians, sports were the showing forth of a system of social Darwinism that decreed the survival of the fittest on the field, on the job, in the marketplace. As these Christians pursued more aggressive policies in every arena, there was little opportunity for turning the other cheek or celebrating the meek. Bill Glass admitted in his book *Don't Blame the Game* that he had felt a twinge of concern when he blindsided a rookie quarterback and knocked him cold, yet he concluded, ''The weak shouldn't play in the first place. . . . Being rough, tough and aggressive doesn't mean you don't care about your opponent as a human being.''

The bottom line for Tom Landry, as for any nonreligious coach, was winning, not testing character. Despite Landry's avowal that competing built character, self-reliance, and sound judgment, he seldom let Staubach call his own plays. Like a cautious business executive, he relied on statistics to reduce the element of chance in every game. Moreover, Landry wasn't averse to a little non-Methodist hocus-pocus in pregame preparation if it gave his team any sort of edge. The Cowboys frequently found themselves guinea pigs for a variety of performance-enhancing techniques, including being dunked in sensory-deprivation tanks and being conditioned by instant-replay reinforcement.

Landry's authoritarian approach seemed to give new credence to the neo-Marxist critics who had argued in the sixties that athletes were pawns in the hands of a power structure composed of retired athletes and businessmen, and that sports helped to socialize fans and players alike into accepting the rules of the game and the system, upon which they had no influence. Certainly, athletics had consistently been in the service of conservative ideology in America. Sports appealed to fans from nearly every social class or political persuasion, but as James Michener admitted in *Sports in America*, "The athlete and his coach move in a world of conservative values and are surrounded by conservative types. Very few Democrats among the alumni have private jets, or good jobs to dispense, or the spare cash to endow athletic scholarships."

During the Vietnam War, sports events were often the occasion for patriotic gestures. While flags were burning on campuses, they were being waved on football fields. Former pro Dave Meggyesy charged in his exposé, *Out of Their League*, that "A military aura surrounds football. Not only in obvious things like football stars visiting troops in Vietnam, but in the language of the game—'throwing a bomb,' being a 'field general,' etc., and the players' obligation to duty. The game has been wrapped in red, white, and blue."

For we wrestle not against flesh and blood, but against principalities, against powers, against the rulers of the darkness of this world, against wickedness in high places.

St. Paul

Although Tom Landry admitted to me that he doubted whether God actually took sides in a football game, Christian athletes, like the legions of Moral Majority that were besieging Congress and the courts, seemed confident that the best defense of the faith was the offense. They seemed to have lost sight of the clear lines of battle laid down in the very Scriptures they cited so often. St. Paul was indeed fond of athletic images. But he always tempered his rather Roman enthusiasm for contests of will with the Christian reminder that worldly victories were fleeting and laurel leaves withered. The real battle was against the weaknesses of one's own flesh, not that of one's competitors or even of one's enemies.

The savior Bill Glass used to talk about in revival meetings resisted the temptations of worldly success: power, money, renown. The savior Glass described in those simpler days understood failure; he was the champion of the poor and the powerless, of those who had never won, at least in worldly terms. Yet it seemed that Christian athletes, like the new evangelical activists and the new Christian capitalists, were not prepared to wrestle against the principalities and powers; they were too eager to bear the banners and wear the uniforms of success.

Note

On the alienation of men from female-dominated church and culture: see Douglas, *Feminization*; Jackson Lears, *No Place of Grace: Antimodernism and the Transformation of American Culture 1880-1920* (New York: Pantheon, 1981); Alan Trachtenberg, *The Incorporation of America: Culture and Society in the Gilded Age* (New York: Hill & Wang, 1982).

References

"In its very success . . .": Trachtenberg, *Incorporation*, p. 141.

John Tanner and the jealous husband: Donald G. Mathews, *Religion in the Old South* (Chicago: University of Chicago Press, 1977), p. 103.

Dr. Tom Bennett's bargain: Peter Gent, *North Dallas Forty* (New York: William Morrow, 1973), p. 27.

"God loathes mediocrity." Quoted by Bill Glass in *Don't Blame the Game* (Waco, Tex.: Word Books, 1972).

"I ran on . . .": Quoted by William G. McLoughlin, Jr., in *Billy Sunday Was His Real Name* (Chicago: University of Chicago Press, 1955), p. 28.

Sunday as "man's man": William T. Ellis, *Billy Sunday: The Man and His Message* (Chicago: The Moody Press, 1959), pp. 25 and 59.

Puritan ban on sports: Foster Rhea Dulles, *America Learns to Play* (New York: Appleton-Century-Crofts, 1940), p. 6.

Rockne's fight talk: Robert Harron, *Rockne: Idol of American Football* (New York: A.L. Burt, 1931), p. 27.

Sports as "natural religions": Michael Novak, *The Joy of Sports: End Zones, Bases, Baskets, Balls, and the Consecration of the American Spirit* (New York: Basic Books, 1976), p. xiv.

"Church and stadium alike . . .": Charles Prebish, *New York Times*, January 17, 1982.

Fritz Peterson on sliding: George Vecsey, *New York Times*, May 10, 1981.

Interviews with born-again players: Bob Hill, *The Making of a Super Pro* (Atlanta, Ga.: Cross Roads Books, 1979).

Hannah on consistency: Quoted by Bob Hill in *Christian Review* 7, no. 8.

Born-again bodybuilder: Quoted in *Us*, May 25, 1982.

Golfer Larry Nelson: Quoted in *Christian Life*, August 1982.

"How do I lift weights . . .": Wes Neal, *The Handbook on Athletic Perfection* (Milford, Mich.: Mott Media, 1981). p. ix.

Steve Largent's vow: Quoted in *Christian Life*, July 1982.

"When it comes to religion . . .": Roger Staubach, *First Down, Lifetime to Go* (Waco, Tex.: Word Books, 1974), p. 280.

Warner E. Sallman's head of Christ: Cynthia Pearl Maus, *The Church and the Fine Arts* (New York: Harper & Row, 1960).

"The athlete and his coach . . .": James Michener, *Sports*, p. 265.

Meggyesy's exposé: Dave Meggyesy, *Out of Their League* (Berkeley, Cal.: Ramparts Press, 1970).

"For we wrestle not . . .": Ephesians 6:12.

Pray Ball

Lori Rotenberk

Above, the organ plays *"Take me out to the ball game . . .,"* while below, in the clubhouses of the great American stadiums, the chaplains stand.

The shower drains and weight machines are their pulpits, half-clad ballplayers, the flock. Surrounded by the *clink* of cleats, the *bonk* of the Louisville Sluggers, and the strings of profanity, they wind up for their pitch. The delivery is pure heaven as it curves and drops low for a strike landing smack in their mitts.

I can do all things through Christ who strengthens me. That's Philippians—not Phillies—4:13.

And from Chicago to Cincinnati, from Pittsburgh to St. Pete, baseball players bow their heads in worship, God's message belting forth from the storage rooms, trainer's rooms and locker rooms cum chapels:

"No men, the diamond is not sacred ground. Remember, the world doesn't revolve around this here little ball. There is only one Perfect Player, one True Game Plan. So, hit the dust, break up the double play. Get the team a run, but give the Glory to God!"

And thus ends Baseball Chapel, a 20-minute pre-game exercise of faith performed in ballparks nationwide each Sunday by an estimated 4,000 major and minor league players, coaches, trainers and managers. They even hold Bible studies once a week at home or in hotels on the road. Wives of the Montreal Expos have started their own Bible study.

Yea verily, testimony indeed that the Lord has a seat in Sky Box and he carries a locker-room pass. A religious revival—though often the center of controversy—gradually is sweeping baseball.

"I think some people are going to be surprised that there is this side to a ballplayer, this side to the sport," says Philadelphia Phillies pitcher Don Carman. "For people only see what is in the papers. Neither baseball chapel nor Bible study makes for good headlines."

Players on each team who serve as chapel leaders report about half of each team's roster participate in the non-denominational services led by local chaplains or players. Even Billys—Graham and Carter—have stood before the clan for a service, says Van Crouch, chaplain to both the Cubs and Sox, "that should be as much fun as the best bar in town—only filled with a different spirit!"

While everything from football to Foosball now operate ministries, chaplains who make the rounds to other sports find baseball draws the most participation. Players say the word spreads quickly because of the close fellowship of teammates, who spend nearly half a year together.

"When someone you admire finds faith in Jesus valuable, you are more likely to adopt it," says Martin E. Marty, professor of the history of modern Christianity at the University of Chicago. "If a farm kid comes up and really admires the clean-up hitter who speaks up for his religion, this kid might well take a second look at the faith he left behind. . . . Is it not better that players are hooked on Jesus rather than addicted to drugs?"

It was infielder Johnny "Peaches" Werhas whom pitcher Frank Tanana watched closely when both were with the California Angels. "I was one of those guys who joked about John going around with his Bible, but I knew he had something I lacked," says Tanana, now leader of the Detroit Tigers' chapel. "He showed me in scripture what God's plan was for me and asked if I wanted to become born again that afternoon. I told him no, I had a lot to do that day."

Among those who are outspoken in their faith are the Tigers' Frank Tanana and his manager, Sparky Anderson; the Twins' Greg Gagne, the Pirates' Gary Redus, the Brewers' Paul Molitor, the Astros' Bob Knepper, and the Reds' Nick Esasky. In Chicago, there's Sox Bill Long and coach Cal Emery and Cubs Andre Dawson, Scott Sanderson, Rick Sutcliffe and Vance Law. In New York, there's Gary Carter, all-star of the Mets. Out west, you have Seattle's Alvin David and Harold Reynolds, San Diego's Eric Show and Jimmy Jones. The list goes on.

They want to tell of how they once worshipped baseball, and now worship Christ.

"I thought being a major league ballplayer was everything, that it was what heaven and earth and happiness was all about," says the Rangers' Jim Sundberg, who caught for the Cubs.

"Then another player had me read Hal Lindsey's *The Late Great Planet Earth*. It scared me to death. I found there is more of a purpose to life than baseball, and I don't want to be left behind. I've always been a winner."

Players often are called to the Christian lecture circuit. Yankee Tommy John has appeared on TV's "700 Club." Others have appeared with Evangelist Pat Robertson on his show. Sundberg once appeared on the "Jim and Tammy Bakker Show."

Christian players make this point: If they can use their name and uniform to promote Gatorade and Goodyear, *why not God?*

Skeptics question players who claim a great hit was an act of God. And wonder how God decides whether he's for the hitter or pitcher that particular day.

Or, for that matter, if God even cares about baseball.

Dugout theologian Sparky Anderson, a regular chapel attendee, says, "No, I do not believe God cares about baseball. If he did, you would never have a loser. I am suspicious of guys who think that by attending chapel it is going to help them with their baseball.''

The Twins' Gagne says, ''We know what you are apt to be thinking. Another superstition. Another white line [not to be crossed].''

They've been called a bunch of easily influenced, uneducated rubes from Class B towns. They are occasionally asked: How can a player who pitches inside call himself a Christian?

Of the rare razzing by teammates, Sox pitcher Rick Horton says, ''There are always a couple of guys who like to kid you. But most of the time it is just typical baseball banter that goes on in the dugout. It certainly is not like other persecutions that Christians have dealt with throughout the ages.''

Standing in Wrigley Field, a gold crucifix around his neck, the Expos' Tim Burke says he understands when players shun chapel guys. ''If guys aren't interested in the Lord and have nothing to do with chapel, that is OK,'' Burke says. ''That is where they are at. I was certainly there for 22 years and I didn't really care about Him either.''

The Mets' Ron Darling says although he ''is not a big fan of organized religion . . . I don't knock these guys. I say if it works for them, it is wonderful. Baseball is a very lonely and trying experience, and going to baseball chapel on Sunday can be one of the best ways to handle that.''

Once, the only time the Lord's day and baseball was spoken in one breath was in reference to Billy Sunday, a hard-drinking outfielder for Cap Anson's Chicago White Stockings. A man to live up to his name, Sunday retired in 1891 from Philadelphia to become an evangelist and lead thousands down his famous ''Sawdust Trail.''

But it was a man who spent a goodly portion of his life reporting about ballplayers who baptized Baseball Chapel.

Watson ''Waddy'' Spoelstra was a hard-drinking Detroit News sportswriter gone good. One Sunday Spoelstra saw how difficult it was for players to attend services when he accompanied Yankees Mickey Mantle and Bobby Richardson to church, and witnessed mayhem in the pews as fans passed their bulletins down the rows for autographs.

Games scheduled on the Lord's day also hampered church-going ballplayers. So Spoelstra and a chapel speaker, Sam Bender (now Midwest coordinator for Baseball Chapel) suggested to baseball commissioner Bowie Kuhn that chapel might work at the park. They said it was already happening in football.

Kuhn opened the doors and in 1973 the New York-based umbrella organization of Baseball Chapel Inc. was formed. Its current president is former Yankee Richardson, who along with teammate Tony Kubek were dubbed ''The Milkshake Twins'' for their clean living, non-drinking baseball lifestyle.

Baseball Chapel, funded by fans and players, provides about 200 speakers nationally for team chapels. Proceeds from its quarterly 8,000-circulation newsletter, ''Baseball Chapel News,'' go toward operation costs, and the Danny Thompson Award is given during the All-Star Game to the ballplayer who best exemplifies the Christian lifestyle. This year's recipient was Mets catcher Gary Carter.

The Minnesota Twins became the first team to hold park chapels, led by Al Worthington and Jim Kaat. The Cubs soon followed with chapel leaders Don Kessinger and Randy Hundley and with the benign approval of manager Leo Durocher, known for what was called his "unselfconscious and creative use of profanity." P.K. Wrigley not only promoted chapel, but he footed the bill for a Sunday chapel brunch.

"Chapel services grew by leaps and bounds. I still find it hard to believe how widespread it is," Spoelstra, now 78, says from his Florida home. "Years ago you could count the guys on one hand. They were closet or secret service Christians. The focus on religion in baseball is increasing. The image of the tobacco-chewing and hard-living kind of player will be replaced by one who is upbeat and intelligent and whose career and future just happens to be baseball."

Now 15 years after its start, chapel not only is in every park but is gaining hold in the minors, where an estimated 80 percent of the players attend services held in dugouts, bleachers or in right field, says Rip Kirby, Minor League Baseball Chapel coordinator, headquartered in Knoxville, Tenn.

"Most of the kids who come to us are Catholics and there is always one Born Again on which to build a nucleus," Kirby says.

The idea is to catch them in the minors and the Lord uses us to send them up to the majors, which is chocked full of Christians," Kirby says. "Enough so that if we wanted, we could franchise a Christian ball team, a real quality team that could win the World Series every year—an awesome team with Dave Winfield and Don Mattingly . . ."

Generally, an athlete's first encounter that ties religion to sports is through college organizations such as Fellowship of Christian Athletes.

Professional sports ministries are flourishing. Among them are Athletes in Action, and Unlimited Potential, which sends ballplayers around the globe to preach God to youngsters. Former Miami Dolphin Norm Evans operates Pro Athlete Outreach, which offers Christian baseball cards. Each card is a palm-sized trifold that includes a color photo of the player and opens to his testimony and verse. Testimony, but no gum.

David Burnham, chairman of the International Sports Coalition, reports that there are 200 former athletes active in ministries, and the numbers are expected to increase.

As more players assert their faith in the locker room and on the field, management sometimes wonders if religion is getting in the way of work. Or if they even want the image of the Christian ballplayer on their club.

Ted Turner, owner of the Atlanta Braves, is said to be comfortable with the squeaky-clean, milk-drinking image. Turner said of well-liked Mormon Dale Murphy, "He's the original Mr. Goodie Two-Shoes. He makes Steve Garvey look evil. The man doesn't drink, doesn't smoke, doesn't even drink Coca-Cola. If God comes back, he's coming back as Dale Murphy."

Tom Trebelhorn, manager of the Brewers, believes spiritual ballplayers perhaps make better husbands, better fathers and better athletes because they don't have problems taking them away from the game.

But Phillies manager Lee Elia is said to teeter more toward anti-chapel when the team is on a losing streak. Although he says, "If the guys benefit from the service, they can have it," he recently moved chapel up an hour to ensure it didn't interfere with batting practice.

Former Baltimore managers halted chapel in the minors for four years, preferring "the guys keep their minds off God and on baseball," says one coordinator. "But it was OK for them to be obsessed with girls and food and cards. So what we did was meet them in their hotels or meet them for breakfast."

But the Tigers' Anderson, who often holds chapel in his office, sees religion and baseball complementing one another.

"Chapel—it is good, for it keeps all of us in a reality while we play a game that is all superficial show business. . . . But sometimes I think the speakers stink. They give a lot of rah rah and those rah rah guys don't do it for me. Just tell me what things are. Don't take me back to the time of Moses. Talk to me about the brave, the believers."

OK, Sparky. Believers like Pat Kelly, who hit a three-run homer in the bottom of the fifth in the 1979 playoffs. As he rounded the bases he pointed toward the sky, and yelled "I live to glorify God!" Like Gary Carter, who after winning the '86 World Series went before the cameras to say, "My only dream was to give glory and praise to Jesus Christ."

Or Giant Dave Dravecky, who last October paused after becoming the fourth pitcher in history to pitch a two-hitter in a championship series. "If I could put Jesus Christ into my shoes, he would be the most aggressive and intense performer on the field," Dravecky said. "He would win every time."

The organ pipes forth from the East Coast to the West. The Brewers' Paul Molitor lowers his head for the anthem, saying quietly to himself, "I am blessed to be a major leaguer, and I give thanks." Don Carman steps to the mound for the Phillies and pauses: "Hey, it's me. Here I am again. I just wanted to thank you for all that has happened. . . ."

At the plate a player makes contact. He steams around the bases and his bat rolls in the dust. On it he has inscribed:

*Do you know that in a race, all the runners compete, but only one receives the prize? So run that you might obtain it—*1 Corinthians 9:24.

Are You Blocking for Me, Jesus?

James T. Baker

It's a game, yes—and much more: a school for life, a cultic celebration. Football, I mean. It is what we are and what we will be. Passionate involvement with football begins for most American males in grade school; for a few, it culminates in playing with the National Football League; for most, it eventuates in watching the NFL on TV from an easy chair.

Let me make my own position clear: I may presume to comment on the game and the society it mirrors, but I am no disinterested, dispassionate critic. For years I thought I was. I arrogantly declined to attend the local high school and college games; and with eyes narrowed and brows aloft I flipped from the Thursday, Friday, Saturday, Sunday and Monday TV battles to the public broadcasting channel for a film by Ingmar Bergman or a lecture from Chicago on recent trends in Bulgarian poetry. But last fall, when after ten or more long, sad seasons of mediocrity and travail my own alma mater—Baylor, home of the fighting Bears—began winning a few games, something surprising and a bit frightening happened to me. A flame I thought long dead came leaping up to thaw my cold heart.

At first I just checked the Sunday papers for scores—still detached, uncommitted. But then I found myself collecting news features, the longer and more fantastic the better, about the Cinderella team of the Southwest Conference. Before long I was hanging out at the faculty lounges bragging to the boys about how the old green and gold had disposed of last week's opponent. And when at the end of three months of glory I was forced to see those brave colors stomped flat in the Cotton Bowl in Dallas by Penn State, I was so disconsolate that I couldn't eat or sleep.

I was, I am, a man as other men.

'In Town' and 'In the Field'

I suppose it's natural for an American male to love the national sport. It's hard to overcome conditioning. People create games of real life—as lumberjacks invented logrolling, cowboys rodeos—and pass on through their games the rules and values and dreams of their lives. Football is rooted in our deepest psyche; it replays our experiences as a people.

Baseball, that pleasant anachronism we play in the dog days when we have time to catch our breath and dream of the dusty past, was once our game. It was played on long, slow, warm Sunday afternoons. There was little danger of injury to undermanned teams. There were no time limits to interrupt or hurry the ritualistic chewing and stretching and scratching, because the cows could always wait another hour. Team play was less important than individual skill and power. Discipline mattered less than heart. But even then it was obvious that people had more fun "in town" than "in the field." We all wanted to be "in town."

Football was born and grew to maturity, as did the modern age, in those burgeoning industrial towns, once the farmer's dream, now the urbanite's reality, where people were and are expendably plentiful and time artificially, efficiently restricted. Its fast pace, its strict discipline, its controlled brutality were all perfectly tailored to the needs and style of a society where it is not heart but guts that matter. For half a century now, football has been telling us who we are and what we will be. We made it, now it makes us.

Vietnam: Not Our Kind of Football

It probably even helped us win those two world wars, both fought as if under a referee's eye along well-defined lines, according to established rules, mostly fair and sportsmanlike (if entirely without moral conscience). And of course the game was ended before anyone got bored or hungry or lost too much time at the mill. We fought as football had taught us; convinced that the side with the better players and coaches and training had won, we came home happy champs, worried only by the fact that somewhere along the way we had misplaced the trophy.

Our football mentality may even partially explain why we fell so colossally on our faces in Vietnam. 'Nam just wasn't our kind of game. The opposition, the red team, wouldn't play by the rules. They showed no signs of shame or repentance when our coach called them bums. We found ourselves losing, though the statistics and even the scoreboard showed us winning. In the confusion our game plan went awry, and we didn't know how to correct it without using strategy that would make bums of us. The battle went on and on without a timekeeper and with less and less hope of a final gun. Our own cheering section began rooting for the other side. Rookies refused to report to camp. An impossible situation.

And so, after a long afternoon's journey into night, butting our heads against first one goalpost, then the other, we had to admit that the opponent wanted the game more than we did, that in fact they had more guts, and as the sensible team we were, we began to take ourselves out of the chaotic field "with honor." We sent in a few expendable substitutes and agreed to keep supplying uniforms and paying rent on the stadium. We told the subs it was their game to win or lose, wished them luck, and got on the bus and left for the hotel. We just hadn't played enough cricket to learn patience or enough soccer to be able to bring order out of chaos *in medias res*.

But we are still football people. Vietnam, embarrassing as it was, did nothing to diminish our faith in or devotion to the game. The 'Nam game was a fluke. We weren't up for it. It had nothing to do with us as a team or with our rules or style of life. Rocky Bleier might be cut down in Vietnam, but back in the civilized world he could still lead the Steelers to the Superbowl. And now that it's Monday morning and the sun is shining, things are looking up. It was just a bad game. Wait'll next week.

Metaphors for the Faith

For years now, certain sages have been calling football America's newest indigenous religion; and the more I watch it, the more I tend to agree. It certainly has all the trappings of a cult: colored banners, armies of good and evil, fanatic supporters, the cosmic sphere, even its own miniskirted vestal virgins to fan the flames. And far more important than these superficialities, it acts as a religion by teaching its followers how to order their personal and professional lives. For those who play, it is an educational act, an immersion in truth. For the rest of us, who are too small or too clumsy or too old to play and have to watch from the stands or before television screens, it is not unlike a Latin high mass performed by professionals for the edification and instruction of those deemed by the Heavenly Commissioner unworthy to participate personally.

Thoroughly American, it shows us American men, in its colorfully dramatic way, that in our drab lives we can best succeed by becoming expert specialists, by playing sensible odds, and most of all by occasionally running a gutsy risk of injury. The American dream, conceived by pioneers, redefined by immigrants, taught to the next generation by football, seems to be that by the age of 30 any young man, given lots of hard work and a little luck, can be both rich and crippled for life.

And even more authenticating is the fact that football's teachings are borrowed from the "wisdom" of the ages and that it passes that wisdom on to a new age in a manner that the people of the new age can understand and accept. Thus the dream of today's young American man, reared in the religion of the gridiron, is not very different from that of the young Roman legionnaire or the young medieval crusader or, more important, of the young European immigrant to the new world, his own ancestor. He believes that sacrifice and specialized daring lead to wealth and glory. He works for wealth and honor, the spoils of war.

Yet strange as it seems, though a new religious expression of some rather old verities has sprung up in our midst, no Christian theologian of any real merit has made any significant effort to make of football—and the wisdom it seeks to transmit—a metaphor for the faith. It has of course been said—as many said of Platonism and later Aristotelianism and more recently existentialism—that because football is not of truly Christian origin it is essentially irredeemable; it could not bear the weight of the gospel; it would by mere association pervert the Good News and make it Bad. But as Augustine, Aquinas and Tillich have demonstrated, those who said that of the other systems were wrong, and so too probably are those who say it of football. To tell the story through the language and categories of football would in all likelihood be no less profitable than St. Paul's attempt to liken the Christian disciple to a Roman soldier or the early missionaries' attempt to portray Christ as a divine tribal chieftain and the rock generation's creation of *Jesus Christ Superstar*.

Another typically American and equally barbaric cultural phenomenon once thought irredeemable, the western movie, has indeed provoked a new and intriguing and perhaps even legitimate Christian theological expression. Chaplain Wesley Seeliger of Texas A&M University, aroused and inspired by the "Gunsmoke" craze of the '60s, wrote a compelling little book called *Western Theology* (Forum, 1973) in which he showed how the American obsession with the 19th century trans-Mississippi west could be used as an occasion, and the western a medium, to teach the Christian faith. He made a plea for what he called pioneer religion—in which God the trail boss and Jesus the scout lead the church, a covered wagon always on the move, as the minister dishes up for the pioneers fresh meat brought in by the Holy Spirit—over settler religion in which God the mayor and Jesus the sheriff run the church as a courthouse and the minister-banker protects the interests of the religious establishment.

A bit campy, perhaps a touch heretical, but on the whole a refreshing and creative response to a phenomenon clearly understood by the masses yet considered by professional theologians too mundane to touch. A valiant effort. Unfortunately no one with Mr. Seeliger's imagination has yet tackled football.

Winning With Jesus

Which is not to say that no one has tried. It's just that those who have been willing to give it a try have either misunderstood the game or misinterpreted the faith. They have been a bit off-base or, I should say, offsides. Anyway, they have failed to score.

Arnold Mandell, who for two years held the unique office of psychiatrist to a professional football team, has found that the position a player fills on a squad is dictated as much by his personality as by his physical endowments. The most articulate and at the same time the most religious of all players, for example, the potential theologian of the team, is the quarterback. And so it would seem that from one of the many Fellowship of Christian Athletes passers, from a Staubach or a Tarkenton, one of those handsome guys who go around telling church camps how it feels to win with Jesus, would have come at least the raw materials and perhaps even the incipient form for a football theology. But in my vain search for such materials and forms, I have found among the golden boys a distressing theological superficiality. God is a *great* general manager. Jesus is a *terrific* coach. Life is a *terrifically great* game if you're playing for Those Two. It's OK to gamble on fourth and one, but don't gamble with your soul. And that's about it.

Perhaps this can be explained by Mandell's discovery that quarterbacks are the most intensely conservative members of the team, Joe Namath notwithstanding. They follow game plans. They do as they're told. They don't think daringly unless a daring play is sent in from the sidelines. They are settlers, not pioneers. They are uncreative.

What we probably need, if Mandell's categories are accurate, is a theologically sophisticated wide receiver, the most daring man on the field. But wide receivers are loners, a bit paranoid, and they don't like to talk in public about matters as intimate as religion. Besides, they're usually the team bad boys, and theologians must be holy. Offensive linemen are holy, always ready with a smile, extroverted, protective of their fellow players—but not very penetrating: more bishops than theologians. Defensive players are penetrating but notoriously demonic, and they have all kinds of trouble constructing things. They'd much rather tear them down.

So the job has been left to a rather odd assortment of men, amateurs either at the game or the faith, who have tried with very little success to make sense of matters too deep for them.

Average Christian Carries the Ball

The first person I know of who made a stab at it—a pioneer in the truest sense—was a young entrepreneur from Waco, Texas, who in the early '50s put out a long-playing album that revolutionized American sermon illustrations. It was a drama-tized allegory, complete with sound effects, of the football game of life. If I remember correctly, Average Christian carried the ball and Jesus the head coach picked him up after every nasty spill and encouraged him on to the eventual touchdown. All very emotional; all very profitable for the young entrepreneur. Simply a renovation of the old baseball game-of-life allegory, it hit the market at a time when football's popularity was on the rise, and it proved a tremendous success. The young man made enough money to start his own recording and publishing company. He scored.

There was never any question as to where he got the idea. He had listened to a decade or more of Baylor University's football-playing ministerial students. They were once legion, as they doubtless will be again now that Baylor is once again a power. They fanned out from Texas to every corner of the country bearing their various versions and interpretations of the game. Perhaps the most famous of these—a college All-American, a professional defensive lineman, a seminary gradu-ate—was Bill Glass. He's still around today, still playing to packed houses all over the nation.

Mr. Glass spoke to the Baptist World Congress in 1965, and his most memorable sermon illustration left the Americans in the audience laughing and the foreigners confused. He explained in great detail that just as a defensive player must get past a certain blocker to get to the quarterback, so must every man go through Jesus to get to God. I must confess I was as confused as the Africans and Russians. It made little sense unless Jesus is a barrier to be jumped or knocked down and God an opponent to be sacked.

But it all seemed clear enough to a good portion of the crowd. The meeting was, after all, held in Miami's Orange Bowl. Perhaps those who laughed so heartily had heard such homilies before and grown accustomed to the logic. You can hear them at summer camps any year. They are usually handed out by religious athletes who— I'm guessing here—spent more college hours on the field than in the library. A paragraph from a recent *Christian Athlete* article by Kent Kramer amply demonstrates what I mean:

> The Christian faith is not a rose garden. It's something like third and two with Green Bay's Dave Robinson as linebacker and the play coming over me at tight end. Man, you've got to fire up and help get that first down.

Footballing the Word

But pro linemen aren't the only ones with the spunk to make fools of themselves. A few ministers have tried their hands at footballing the Word as well. Their motives are beyond reproach, their efforts courageous and sometimes even imaginative—but such strange results!

One pastor in British Columbia sent his bread-and-butter play in to the *Christian Athlete*. It appears to be a sermon outline. According to his diagram, the defensive line in the Christian's life is made up of Fear, Sin, Satan, Despair, Worry and Separation. The linebackers are Sorrow, Tribulation and Unbelief. Deep backs are Darkness and Death. The offensive line is Love, Joy, Grace, Christ (?), Hope, Peace and Faith. The quarterback is Prayer, the blocking backs are Resurrection and Light, and the ball carrier is "You, the Redeemed."

The pastor explained:

> Jesus Christ is the center of this big play. He snaps the ball to Prayer and then brings down Satan. Prayer calls the signals, hands off to Redeemed and takes worry out of the play. Faith removes unbelief; Peace overcomes tribulation; Hope blocks despair; Grace covers sin; Joy erases sorrow; Love casts out fear; Light wipes out darkness; Resurrection overcomes the last enemy death; and Redeemed scores.

He adds: "Separation is no threat in this play." The end zone is marked "Eternal Life." A dark line marks Redeemed's certain pathway there, untouched by a single hostile arm.

There are some interesting points in this little allegory. Christ as offensive center instead of coach or quarterback is brand-new so far as I know and should remain popular as long as Gerald Ford does. Mandell says in his study that the offensive lineman, especially the center, is unselfish—sacrificial, even—but he is also terribly undramatic, as indeed Ford is (as Christ isn't). On the whole, though, it all seems too easy. Every blocker gets his man. Every victim stays down instead of jumping back up to try again as fierce competitors are trained to do. No penalty calls halt the play, not even when Grace holds Sin until the play is past and Love uses his hands to cast out Fear. And while the point about Separation's being no threat to Redeemed may be comforting to us all, it becomes allegorically suspect when it requires a defensive end to stand stock-still while across the field a cocky halfback threads his way through falling bodies to paydirt.

With its ease and smug self-assurance the whole business reminds one of a certain life insurance company's recent TV ad in which a balding, middle-aged family man without pads runs behind one pro line of beefy huskies through another equally beefy line to the security of an end zone free of financial worries. We have to wonder how many new policies such sermons sell.

A Theology for Failure

And so it goes. Despite some admirable efforts—and some not so admirable—past attempts to make football a motif for the faith have fallen somewhere between faintly amusing and hilarious. Or, if you take them seriously, between vaguely threatening and downright sinister. They have all missed the goal by yards. I have run across a few other ideas: one writer suggested celebrating communion by sharing your dog and suds with a bleachermate. But mostly it's been one big goose egg.

But why? Is it because the football field is indeed an inappropriate arena for the Word? If so, then perhaps the society which it mirrors is too.

Is it that there is simply no one around who understands both the game and the faith? Perhaps that is part of it. But surely there are enough intelligent Christians around, even among football fans, to have produced one decent apologist. Superstar ball stands waiting to be an inspiration.

Or does the problem go deeper? Could it be that the game is indeed a good motif, better than most of our day, but that no one has been willing to admit what it is really saying to us? So far we have looked for the new theology to come from winners: the successful football-playing preachers, the victorious products of the game, or theologians who are themselves successful in the modern game of life. Maybe it's time we got our message from today's Christ and his disciples.

If I read his story correctly, Christ was one who stood—and no doubt still stands—over against rather than in support of the game of his day. By the standards and rules of his time, he was a loser, and perhaps he still would be, still is. Yet through his "failure" he brought, and still brings, hope to all those knowingly or unknowingly victimized by the game. Even Superstar, glamorous as he was, didn't get to ride the bus back to the studio. So how could Christ be coach of the year and his followers all-pro? Wouldn't Christ and his disciples today be more like Rod Serling's battered and self-sacrificing prizefighter in *Requiem for a Heavyweight* than like the quarterback of the Superbowl champs?

Maybe the real message of the game *is* being preached, but by a voice we don't really want to hear. Perhaps it is saying that as in every other age Christ is the one who exposes the violence and exploitation of our crassly commercial game of life and through his subsequent rejection by the powers-that-be dramatically illustrates his message of freedom to those who couldn't see or hear it any other way.

Maybe what our age and its game are finally forcing upon us is a Christ symbol modeled on that half of our population most visibly victimized by and hostile to the game, whether on TV, in the stadium, or in the marketplace.

Maybe it's time for us to explore the implications of a female Christ.

Why Athletes Need Ritual:
A Study of Magic Among Professional Athletes

Mari Womack

Al Hrabosky, pitcher for the Kansas City Royals, is known to baseball fans as "The Mad Hungarian." Hrabosky's reputation is partly due to his elaborate pitching routine.

Before an important pitch, Hrabosky turns his back on the batter and stalks toward second base. He stares toward center field while the umpire and 40,000 fans yell at him to "Throw the ball!" Hrabosky then goose-steps back to the mound and glares at the batter. He swings his left foot back and forth across the pitching rubber, takes off his hat with his left hand and wipes across his head with his right forearm. He jerks his head up and down, and from side to side. Finally, he pitches.

The sports pages frequently refer to the "personality quirks" or "superstitions" of professional athletes, because they make good reading. There is increasing evidence that they make good sense as well.

In this paper, I propose to discuss these behaviors as ritual, and I will attempt to explain why the athletes persist in using ritual even though they are products of a culture in which such practices are referred to derisively as "superstition," and even though team psychologists may sometimes try to persuade them to give them up. My analysis is based on several years of intensive interviews with and observations of professional athletes in baseball, football, hockey, basketball and tennis.

I chose to study professional major league athletes because the highly stressful environment and social complexity of professional sports interaction epitomizes conditions under which anthropologists would expect to find ritual. Before I proceed to a discussion of ritual in sport, however, I would like to offer a definition of ritual and a summary of anthropological explanations for ritual.

What Is Ritual?

A clear definition of ritual is essential to studying ritual outside the religious context, because it is the means by which behaviors are included or excluded. In their book on secular rituals, Moore and Myerhoff have written, "The looseness of the concept of ritual . . . is a serious obstacle to investigation of the subject" (1977:21).

Ritual has been variously defined in anthropology. Durkheim (1968) defined ritual as a set of practices through which participants regulate their relationship to the sacred. Leach (1966) said that ritual is "Behavior which . . . serves to 'communicate' information . . . and behavior which is potent in itself in terms of cultural conventions of the actors but *not* potent in a rational-technical sense." He added, "A ritual sequence when performed in full tends to be very repetitive."

Victor Turner defines ritual as "prescribed formal behavior for occasions not given over to technological routine, having reference to beliefs in mystical beings or powers" (1967:19). Anthony F.C. Wallace (1966) writes of ritual as "complex, stereotyped sequences." Tambiah writes, "Magical acts are ritual acts . . ." (1973:199). Friedrich defines ritual as "any prescribed, formal behavior that is not essential to technical or practical affairs" (1966:192). Firth writes that ". . . a special character of ritual is its reserve, its apartness, its 'sacred' quality" (1973:176). However, he hastens to add, "The 'sacred' in my view is not a necessary criterion in the definition of ritual . . . There can be secular rituals . . ." (1973:176). Gluckman and Gluckman, however, distinguish ritual from ceremony on the basis that ritual involves beliefs in occult powers (1977:233).

In spite of the limitations of these definitions, several key concepts emerge. I have attempted to summarize these concepts in my operational definition of ritual. Ritual is:

1. Repetitive—It occurs again and again in a given context, and/or certain elements tend to be repeated throughout the behavioral sequence.
2. Stylized—It is formal, rather than spontaneous.
3. Sequential—There is an orderly procession from beginning to end. Transposition of elements within a ritual is thought to diminish its efficacy.
4. Non-ordinary—It is distinct from ordinary mundane activities and/or is not essential to technical performance. "Actions . . . used are extra-ordinary themselves, or ordinary ones are used in an unusual way, a way that calls attention to them and sets them apart from other, mundane uses" (Moore and Myerhoff 1977:7).
5. Potent—It is believed to be either innately powerful, or powerful in controlling supernatural beings or forces.

On the basis of the last criterion, I was able to distinguish ritual from such behaviors as habit and practice, which are stylized and repetitive, but which are not considered to be innately powerful. I have also excluded such behaviors as the practice in baseball of shaking hands with teammates after getting a home run or drenching the team manager with champagne after winning the pennant. I follow the lead of Gluckman and Gluckman in characterizing these behaviors as ceremony. I do so reluctantly, because these are important customs, that serve some of the functions which I will attribute to ritual.

At the same time, such distinctions should not be arbitrary, but should be based on logical differences which become evident in the data, and which are consistent with previous analyses of the phenomena. The presumed "potency" of ritual on the part of participants has been an important factor in ritual studies, and a concept regarding the potency of ritual has emerged in my discussions with athletes about their own behavior. For example, an athlete may say of a ritual, "It works."

How Ritual "Works"

Although, by definition, ritual is not essential to technical performance, anthropologists have offered impressive evidence of the impact of ritual on human affairs, in both the psychological and sociological realms. Malinowski (1927: 1948) argued that ritual or magical behavior is associated with high-risk activities, with risk being expressed in terms of physical danger to the participants or possibility of failure of the enterprise. In the context of sport ritual, Gmelch (1971) supports Malinowski's contention. He determined that magical behavior in baseball is associated with the high-risk activities of pitching and hitting, rather than with the low-risk activity of fielding.

Fortes (1936) acknowledged the element of uncertainty associated with ritual. However, he maintained that ritual is not concerned with the safety of individuals, but with the security of the group. Hilda Kuper (1945) stressed the importance of ritual in defining social roles and reinforcing social stratification. Following the line of Fortes and Evans-Pritchard (1940:16f), Gluckman and Gluckman wrote "the most fruitful form of interpreting ritualization has been to see it as the acting of the conflicts which lie deep in the structure of society itself . . ." (1977:232).

Mary Douglas (1966) suggested that ritual can be used to deal with areas of psychic danger, as well as with physical danger and threat of deprivation. She pointed out that ambiguity is threatening, and is typically dealt with through elaborate ritual or by taboo. Victor Turner (1967) wrote that rituals can be a means of communicating to the individual society's expectations of him, and of forcing him to order his thinking in ways which are acceptable to the society of which he is a part.

Geertz (1965) stated that rituals are effective in social control because they induce moods and motivations. Ritual is also an important communication device because it conveys information succinctly and emphatically. The communicative aspect of ritual is significant in sports. Renee Van fraechem-raway (1976), a French investigator, wrote that in sports, "le geste," or movement, is the medium of communication rather than "la parole," or speech.

Professional Sports Interaction

Professional major league team sports provide an ideal laboratory for the study of ritual, because the conditions of social complexity, ambiguity and risk are accentuated.

The athlete engaged in professional team sports is "owned." Terms associated with the contractual agreement between the team and the player reflect "ownership," rather than an employer-employee relationship. The player can be "traded," "bought" or "sold." Implicit in this contractual agreement is that the movements of the player are determined by the demands of the team. The player can be transported to play an out-of-town game, or he can be "traded" to another team, and, thus, be required to move to another town to fulfill the terms of his contract. This enforced mobility makes it difficult for the player to form stable social bonds outside the team.

Pressure to "succeed" is intensified for professional athletes. The values of the dominant society relating to achievement are supported, but opportunities are limited and the time span for achievement of career goals is compressed. The competition among professional athletes is severe, so that very few "make it" at all. In addition, the career of an athlete is comparatively short. And injury could mean a premature end to a promising career.

The team is the center of intense competition-cooperation relationships. Competition is basic to professional sports. However, competition must be directed against the opposing team. The athletes must cooperate with members of their own team to win games and also because teammates provide the only constant and reliable source of social interaction. The necessity for directing aggression against the opposing team and cooperating with teammates is complicated by frequent trades among major league teams. Today's teammate may be tomorrow's opponent, and vice versa. Thus, the player's loyalty must be to the team, not to individual players on the team. In all team sports, "team spirit" is considered essential to playing the game.

Professionals in sports recognize the importance of psychological well-being to athletic performance. Sport psychologist William P. Morgan (1974) wrote, "Mental health plays an important role in athletic success," and, further, ". . . psychological stability is a prerequisite for consistent success in the high-level athlete."

Yet the life of a professional athlete is characterized by uncertainty along at least three dimensions:

1. Potential for "success" within the context of the game.
2. Potential for "success" in terms of life goals.
3. Potential for establishing a viable network of social interaction.

The athlete is faced with the necessity of maintaining emotional "stability" for maximum performance on the one hand, and he must deal with conditions of prolonged uncertainty and stress on the other. Ritual can be a behavioral means for resolution of this conflict.

Ritual in Sports

Rituals used by professional athletes may range from a two-minute prebatting sequence to an elaborate ten-hour pregame complex. Based on the context in which they occur, I have devised the following typology of ritual in sports: initiation rites; preparatory rites (day-of-the-game rituals, pregame rituals, and activity-specific rituals); and rites of protection. *Initiation rites* may be considered under the heading of what Victor Turner calls life-crisis rituals, "designed to mark the transition from one phase of life or social status to another . . ." (1967:7). Turner writes, "These 'crisis' ceremonies not only concern the individuals on whom they are centered, but also mark changes in the relationships of all the people connected with them . . ." (1967:7).

In the instance from sports which I am about to cite, the initiation rite does not mark a change in status per se, but a change in affiliation. In hockey, it is the custom to shave new members of the team from head to foot. For a discussion of the symbolic sexual significance of hair, I refer you to Leach (1958). However, I would like to quote Raymond Firth in his work on "Hair as a Private Asset and Public Symbol." Firth says:

. . . deliberate shaving of the head, or close cutting of the hair, has taken on a ritual quality, intended to mark a transition from one social cast to another, and in particular to imply a modification in the status or social condition of the person whose hair is so treated . . . in most general terms shaving the head is a sign of *tristitia* (sadness) . . . of diminution of the self . . ." (1973: 288-290).

I quote this passage from Firth because it is consistent with the way the hockey players themselves talk about the shaving ritual, as a way of bringing the new player under control. When the player has not been shaved, the other players may taunt him about it whenever he behaves in a way that inconveniences other members of the team.

Preparatory rites consist of rituals that precede and may be directed toward influencing the outcome of a scheduled event. These are perhaps the most neglected rituals in the anthropological literature, in terms of analysis. This is in spite of the evidence that preparatory rites are found in most societies. Hilda Kuper discusses preparatory rites for the Swazi king as a means of emphasizing status. In his paper on war, John Kennedy comments, "Almost all groups perform a series of rituals before they join the enemy in battle which sometimes go on for days or even weeks in advance. We may call these preparatory rituals" (1971:48). Further, Kennedy says, "the training of modern soldiers has a ritualistic character" (1971:56).

Kennedy attributes the use of prebattle rituals to a necessity for overcoming fear and repugnance for killing:

Often these emotion-arousing rituals have the effect of irrevocably committing the individual to bravery and self-sacrifice . . . The great ritual effort to induce commitment may be seen as culturally developed means for overcoming the subconscious repugnance to killing as well as for reduction of fear" (1971:49-50).

The value of ritual in coping with prebattle stress is perhaps evident, although we may argue with Kennedy's contention that men have "a subconscious repugnance for killing." However, I think the dramatic link between fear of death and ritual may lead us to overlook some more subtle aspects of preparatory ritual that are more readily observable in preparatory rituals in sports. Although sport has been called ritualized warfare and, as I have said previously, danger of injury is clearly present in sport, *Webster's New Collegiate Dictionary* defines sport as "a physical activity engaged in for pleasure."

It is a matter of conjecture whether professional athletes play for pleasure, but, the point remains, they *choose* to play. I will now cite some instances of preparatory rituals in sports, and then will discuss a recurring theme among athletes: the relation of ritual to performance in the game.

Day-of-the-game rituals. Most professional athletes have elaborate day-of-the-game "routines," which they think help their game. Many of the athletes I have talked to would feel anxious or uncomfortable if they were forced to vary their ritual, because they think it would "throw their game off." This type of ritual is described by hockey player Dennis Abgrall:

> . . . when you win, you try not to change anything. Nothing. You do everything exactly as you did the whole day of your win. Beginning from the time you get up, was your window/door open? Get up on the same side of the bed. Eat the same meals, at the same places—home or at the same restaurant—nothing extra. If your salad was dry, order it dry again; if you had a large milk, then again; if your steak was ordered medium, then again; no dessert, and so on. You leave at the same times, take the same routes, park in the same place, enter through the same door, and prepare for the finale—game time—with the accent on precision.

Tommy Lasorda, manager of the Dodgers, confirms that this kind of ritual is common in sports. "If we won the game the night before, I try to do everything the same way. But I don't get to the point of wearing the same clothes, like some do."

Not all day-of-the-game rituals are as elaborate as that outlined by Abgrall, but many of the elements mentioned come up repeatedly in interviews. Eating habits and precise ordering of the route to the game are described by baseball players, football players, basketball players, and hockey players. There is a great deal of consistency from sport to sport.

In all cases referred to in this paper, the participants perceive a direct link between the behaviors and the outcome of the game. Note that, in the examples given by both Abgrall and Lasorda, the activities are based on what the participant did the last time the team won.

Sometimes rituals fail. When the team has a losing streak, or when the athlete goes into a slump, ritual may be renegotiated. When asked what happened when he went into a slump, one athlete replied, "I don't change my main ritual." But he went on to say that he experimented with his "other" rituals.

Although ritual is marked on the day of a competition game, it is not commonly associated with practice games. Athletes often mention that there is something "special" about the game, as opposed to practice, even though the form of play may be similar. It is considered important for an athlete to play in games frequently to maintain his skills. Practice is not enough to maintain the "competitive edge."

Sometimes, the team may regulate day-of-the-game behavior for the athlete. This is especially prevalent in football. In baseball, basketball and hockey, the player is often left to his own devices on the day of a game. However, it is customary on some football teams to check the entire team into a hotel the night before a game. This is true for "home" games as well as for "away" games. The day of the game may begin with vesper services, and communal meals may be served that day. When I asked one coach why football teams regiment the day of the game more than do teams in other sports, he replied, "Football is only played once a week. The other sports are played almost every day so the players stay psyched up."

This very satisfactorily illustrates the importance of formalized activities on the day of the game to being "psyched up" for the game. However, I think regimentation in football is also related to the way the game is played. Football has been called the "only team sport." Sharing meals and other activities on the day of the game encourages members of a football team to identify with the group.

Pregame rituals. A player may have a precise routine that he follows between the time he arrives at the playing arena and the beginning of a game. These routines order and control the critical period of time just before a game. Pregame rituals need not be elaborate.

Some hockey players dress the entire left side of their bodies first—socks, skates, kneepads, etc.—before dressing the right side. Football players want to be taped the same way as long as they are winning. If they go into a slump, they may vary the pattern until they come out of the slump.

As you can see, pregame or day-of-the-game rituals usually consist of ordinary behaviors, which are stylized and regimented, or exaggerated, until they take on ritualistic characteristics. In any cases when I could not determine that the player attributed magical power to the behavior, I excluded it from the study.

Activity-specific rituals. Al Hrabosky's routine, which I described at the beginning of this paper, is an example of a pitching ritual. Some batters tap the plate with the bat every time before batting. There is a utilitarian explanation for this, in that it helps the player position himself in relation to the plate, but "rational" explanations do not account for the precise sequencing and timing of plate tapping.

One of the more interesting aspects of these preparatory rituals, from the anthropological point of view, is that they are performed by the participant alone, which virtually eliminates sociological explanations. A more satisfactory explanation may be offered by the athletes themselves, when they talk about getting "psyched up" for the game.

"Psyching up" is not simply a matter of achieving maximum excitement. The player must be fully alert, but if his excitement or anxiety is not brought under control, he may make errors during the game.

As may already be apparent, ritual is ideally suited to promote this state of controlled excitement. Malinowski (1931) writes that ritual allays anxiety and inspires confidence. Radcliffe-Brown (1939) counters with the argument that anxiety is frequently experienced when a customary ritual is *not* performed. Homans suggests that "There is . . . evidence from our own society that when ritual tradition is weak, men will invent ritual when they feel anxiety" (1941). I would suggest that the exaggeration and routinization inherent in ritual focuses the attention of the participant on the task at hand and prevents energies from being diverted to nonproductive distractions.

Rites of protection, according to my typology, differ from preparatory rites in that they are directed toward controlling vague, undefined, and potentially threatening events or situations. These types of rituals are more diverse than the rituals mentioned previously, but they typically deal with areas that are important to the game. In baseball, the foul line is the dividing line between a "foul" or a "fair" ball, and an inch one way or the other could decide the outcome of a game. Thus, according to anthropological theory, it should be sacred territory, associated with ritual and taboo. This is, in fact, the case. Some players always step over the foul line with the left foot first. For some players it is taboo to step on the foul line.

According to sports lore, some playing positions have more rituals associated with them than others. In baseball, pitching and hitting are more likely to be attended by ritual than fielding. This has been demonstrated in research on baseball magic by anthropologist George Gmelch (1971). Gmelch claims his findings support Malinowski's contention that risk is the primary factor in ritual, because pitching and hitting are "riskier" than fielding. Pitchers are considered to be the most superstitious of all baseball players.

In hockey, the goaltender might be considered a liminal figure,[1] because he guards the goal. He is the last line of defense in preventing the other team from scoring. The "special" nature of the goaltender is often remarked upon by other players. It is a custom in hockey for players to tap the goalie's kneepads with the hockey stick before each period of the game, or before the game. Goaltenders are considered to be more "superstitious" than other hockey players.[2]

Fetishes are commonly found in sports. Some Rams players tape medallions inside their shoes. They are not allowed to wear medallions around their necks, because of the danger of injuries.

Playing equipment and protective gear are important to the outcome of the game and the safety of the player, and these items figure prominently in sports magic. One quarterback for the Dallas Cowboys has been wearing the same shoulder pads for years. The same player used to wear only black shoes. However, once he tried wearing white shoes and played an outstanding game. Now he wears only white shoes.

Numbers are important because they can become part of the player's identity. "Buck" Buchanan says a football player will usually try to keep the same number he had while in college. "If possible, we give it to him," he says. If a veteran member of the team already has that number, the rookie must settle for some other number. Baseball player Reggie Smith had Number 7 when he was with Boston and the St. Louis Cardinals. However, when he went to the Dodgers, Steve Yeager already had Number 7 and refused to give it up. Smith took Number 8 instead. The highest honor a baseball team can bestow on a player is to retire his number when the player retires.

Athletes do not typically form ritual bonds with other individual teammates, although they may have rituals addressed to the occupant of a given position. Players are traded frequently, so that ritual bonds with a specific other player may be disrupted when either of the players is traded. However, football and hockey players develop close ritual bonds with individual trainers. They may insist on being worked on by a specific trainer, and many share a pregame ritual with that trainer. This is hardly surprising, in view of the fact that the trainer, even more than the team doctor, is in charge of the player's physical well-being. By the time a player sees the team doctor, he has usually already sustained an injury. However, the trainer is supposed to keep the player in good condition so that he can play well and avoid injury.

One of the more interesting rituals I learned about concerned a ritual shared with a trainer and was told to me by Dave Schultz, formerly a defenseman with the Los Angeles Kings hockey team. In hockey there is a specialized type of defenseman, known as an "enforcer" or "policeman." It is the enforcer's job to see that players on the opposing team do not unnecessarily "rough up" his teammates. Naturally, the enforcer is likely to be involved in fights on a regular basis. Dave Schultz was an enforcer for the Kings. He shared a ritual with John Holmes, which included having Holmes tie down the back of his jersey, so that it couldn't be pulled over his head when he got into a fight.

Taboo, or avoidance behavior, is an important part of sports ritual. A classic taboo in baseball is the one against saying "no-hitter" during a no-hit game. Most goaltenders in hockey don't like talking about a shutout before a game, or when a shutout is in progress. It is taboo for a baseball player to throw a bat down in such a way that it lands across another bat. Rogie Vachon will not allow the defensemen on his team to sit with their hockey sticks crossed.

Athletes are often reluctant to talk about their magic. They often begin by saying, "I'm not superstitious," then go on to describe a complex system of ritual, fetish and taboo. One reason for the reluctance to talk about ritual is that our society has cultural sanctions against "superstitions." "Science" has taken on an almost mystical value for us, and we like to think of ourselves as "rational." Also, ritual is hard for anyone to talk about because it is an intensely personal experience. As Ken Locker put it, asking players about their "superstitions" is "like asking them what brand of shorts they wear." Finally, ritual or magic is nearly always accompanied by taboos against "naming" it. Ron Cey said, "If I told you about it, it wouldn't work."

Conclusion

I have not described these rituals because of their entertainment value—although they are definitely interesting—but to give an idea of the scope and the circumstances under which ritual occurs in sport. I think the data I have included are sufficient to indicate that ritual behaviors of professional athletes form a coherent, even prag-matic, complex.

I will not postulate a single, illuminating explanation for ritual in sports. It is unlikely that any single explanation can account for the persistence of ritual among professional athletes, or, indeed, for the persistence of ritual in any case. There are likely to be multiple explanations, with emphasis shifting depending on the instance and the form of the ritual involved. One of the characteristics of ritual is that it is efficient and can achieve several ends at the same time. For a clear understanding of ritual, it must always be studied in its context.

Based on my data, and taking into consideration previous anthropological analy-ses of ritual, I would suggest that ritual is important to sports interaction in the following ways:

1. Ritual helps the player focus his attention on the task at hand. It can be used by the player to prevent anxiety or excessive environmental stimuli—such as the chanting of fans—from interrupting his concentration.
2. Ritual can signal intent to the other team. Specifically, ritual can be used to "threaten" the other team.
3. Ritual provides a means of coping with a high-risk, high-stress situation.
4. Ritual helps establish a rank order among team members and promotes intra-group communication.
5. Ritual helps in dealing with ambiguity in interpersonal relationships, with other team members, and with people on the periphery of the team, such as management and the public.
6. Ritual is a "harmless" means of self-expression. It can be used to reinforce a sense of individual worth under pressure for group conformity, without endangering the unity of the group.
7. Ritual directs individual motivations and needs toward achieving group goals.

Obviously, rituals are no substitute for ability. Pitcher Bruce Sutter says, "You can't just take someone out of the stands and put him out there to pitch. A ritual doesn't help you if you can't pitch." But a well-disciplined, highly-conditioned athlete may use rituals to screen out distractions and order his world so that he is free to concentrate on the game.

For some time, a number of psychologists have been developing ritualistic forms of psychotherapy. These are popular—and often effective—because they offer a means of regulating our lives in a productive and meaningful way. However, as scientists, and students of behavior, we cannot claim to comprehend our subject as long as we continue to ignore the capacity of human beings to create individually significant ritual forms.

Notes

This study could not have been completed without the cooperation and assistance of members of the following professional athletic teams: Los Angeles Dodgers, St.

Louis Cardinals, Chicago Cubs, New York Yankees, Los Angeles Rams, Dallas Cowboys, Green Bay Packers, Los Angeles Kings, Portland Trailblazers and Los Angeles Strings.

1. See Victor Turner (1967; 1969) for a discussion of liminality.
2. The "superstitious" nature of goaltenders is not entirely due to their liminal status, however. Goaltending is literally the most dangerous position on the team, in terms of injury. It is the goalie's job to stop a hockey puck that may be traveling from 90 to 120 miles an hour.

Bibliography

Douglas, Mary
    1966   Purity and Danger. London: Routledge and Kegan Paul.
Durkheim, Emile
    1968   Les formes elementaires de la vie religieuse. Fifth edition, Paris: Presses Universitaires de France.
Firth, Raymond
    1973   Symbols, Public and Private. London: Allen and Unwin, Ltd.
Fortes, Meyer
    1936   Ritual Festivals and Social Cohesion in the Hinterland of the Gold Coast. American Anthropologist 38:602.
Fortes, M., and E.E. Evans-Pritchard
    1940   Introduction. In African Political Systems, M. Fortes and E.E. Evans-Pritchard, eds. London: Oxford University Press for the International African Institute.
Friedrich, P.
    1966   Revolutionary Politics and Communal Ritual. In Political Anthropology. Marc J. Swartz, Victor Turner and Arthur Tuden, eds. Chicago: Aldine.
Geertz, Clifford
    1965   Religion as a Cultural System. In Anthropological Approaches to the Study of Religion. Michael Banton, ed. London: Tavistock.
Gluckman, Mary, and Max Gluckman
    1977   On Drama, and Games and Athletic Contests. In Secular Ritual. Sally F. Moore and Barbara G. Myerhoff, eds. Amsterdam: Van Gorcum, Assen.
Gmelch, George J.
    1971   Baseball Magic. In Conformity and Conflict. James P. Spradley and David W. McCurdy, eds. Boston: Little, Brown.
Homans, George C.
    1941   Anxiety and Ritual: The Theories of Malinowski and Radcliffe-Brown. American Anthropologist 43:164-172.
Kennedy, John G.
    1971   Ritual and Intergroup Murder: Comments on War, Primitive and Modern. In War and the Human Race. Maurice Walsh, ed. New York: Elsevier Publishing Co.

Kuper, Hilda
1945 An African Aristocracy: Rank Among the Swazi of The Protectorate. London: Oxford University Press for the International African Institute.
Leach, Edmund
1958 Magical Hair. Journal of the Royal Anthropological Institute 88:147-164.

1966 Ritualization in Man. In Philosophical Transactions of the Royal Society of London. Series B. 251 (722): 403-408.

Malinowski, Bronislaw
1927 Coral Gardens and Their Magic. London: Routledge and Kegan Paul.

1931 Culture. In Encyclopedia of the Social Sciences. Seligman and Johnson, eds. London: Macmillan.

Moore, Sally F., and Barbara G. Myerhoff
1977 Secular Ritual. Amsterdam: Van Gorcum, Assen.
Morgan, W.P.
1974 Selected Psychological Considerations in Sport. Research Quarterly 45: 324-339.
Radcliffe-Brown, A.R.
1939 Taboo ("The Frazer Lecture"). Cambridge: University Press.
Tambiah, S.J.
1973 Form and Meaning of Magical Acts: A Point of View. In Modes of Thought. Robin Horton and Ruth Finnegan, eds. London: Faber and Faber.
Turner, Victor
1967 The Forest of Symbols, Ithaca, New York: Cornell University Press. 1969 The Ritual Process: Structure and Anti-Structure. Chicago: Adline.
Van Fraechem-Raway, Renee
1976 Etude de la personnalite sociale du sportif en fonction de la structuraltion de son equipe. International Journal of Sport Psychology 7:169-186.
Wallace, Anthony F.C.
1966 Religion: An Anthropological View. New York: Random House.

Green Cars, Black Cats and Lady Luck

Jack McCallum

The next time you're at a baseball game, watch the first base coach to see if he kicks the bag before he enters the coach's box each inning. Now, he may kick the bag because he has nothing else to do, a frequent problem for first base coaches. More likely, though, he kicks the bag because he feels that, if he doesn't, all sorts of bad things will happen. Runners will get picked off. Or runners will get thrown out trying to stretch a single into a double. Or runners who beat throws to first will be called out by a diabolical umpire. Or, if he's the New York Yankees' first base coach, he will get word that George Steinbrenner wants to see him after the game.

The next time you see Mario Andretti, hand him a green pen and ask for an autograph—then duck. He may throw the pen to the ground. He may throw *you* to the ground. Like many race car drivers, Andretti considers the color green more of a threat to his well-being than Turn 1 at Indy.

The next time you're around Buffalo Bills quarterback Jim Kelly before a game, you may find you want a quick change of company. Why? Because Kelly may suddenly bolt from his seat, rush to the bathroom and force himself to vomit. He has been doing this since his days at East Brady (Pa.) High, not because a physician or trainer told him it would help relieve pregame jitters, but because Kelly feels it brings him luck. "I don't eat a pregame meal," says Kelly. "I rent it." Ugh!

In the world of sports, superstition isn't all rabbit-feet and four-leaf clovers. Sometimes, in fact, it's octopuses, as it is at Detroit Red Wing hockey games. The tradition of throwing octopuses onto the ice started at the old Olympia in 1952, when a seafood merchant named Peter Cusmano tossed one out, reasoning that its eight tentacles would help the Wings achieve the eight victories (in two series) they needed to win the Stanley Cup. Sure enough, Detroit won, and its fans never forgot. When the Red Wings, who now play in Joe Louis Arena, qualified for the play-offs last season for only the fourth time in the last 16 years, down came the octopuses. Some eager fans even throw them during the regular season. That's not superstition, however—it's mass hysteria.

Your basic, run-of-the-mill superstitions usually don't cut it with athletes. Take the case of former New York Yankee pitcher Bob Tewksbury. One of the first things Tewksbury did last season after he learned he had been demoted to Columbus was kick his lucky rabbit-foot across the locker room. However, when athletes indulge in superstition, it generally involves something stronger and more unusual than mere rabbit-feet. Marvin Johnson, three times a light heavyweight champion from 1978 to '86, for instance, never washed in the 24 hours before a fight. Now, *that* was a strong superstition.

Superstitions have been around since the dawn of man—we know this from cave drawings showing Neanderthals stepping carefully over foul lines—but athletes probably do as much as anyone to perpetuate superstitions in this enlightened age. There are several reasons for this. Superstitions tend to be passed down from one generation to the next through the strong oral tradition of the locker room—in between dirty jokes, of course. Athletes, too, seem largely unburdened by the commonly held assumption that superstition is mumbo jumbo that doesn't work. And some athletes turn to superstition for the same reasons that others turn to religion or drugs—to relieve pressure, to convince themselves that results are predetermined, to take the fear out of the unknown.

"A superstition is a way to get through a tough situation," wrote Carol Potter in *Knock on Wood*, a 1983 book about superstitions. For the athlete, superstitions are a crutch, a secret weapon, a way to get that little edge. And a superstition can't fall out of, say, Joe Niekro's pocket on the mound, the way an emery board can.

Much as they might indulge their superstitions, however, athletes, coaches, team executives and other sporting types rarely admit that they are superstitious. They prefer to talk about "habits" or "routines." New York Giants coach Bill Parcells is a classic example. Each morning when he's not on the road, Parcells follows this "routine": He drives from his house in Upper Saddle River, N.J., to Elmer's Country Store for a cup of coffee and then stops by Christiana's Coffee Shop in nearby Wood-Ridge and picks up two more containers of coffee to drink in his office at Giants Stadium in East Rutherford.

Now, one might assume that Parcells simply likes the coffee brewed by those two establishments (which happens to be true). But a routine becomes a superstition when someone believes that he must follow it to have good luck, or that bad luck will come knocking if he doesn't. Put Parcells in that camp. He doesn't want any of his players or staff to precede him into the locker room, and he always wants to see the same three players—Phil Simms, Brad Benson and Chris Godfrey—before he sees anyone else. He'll never pick up a penny that has tails facing up. He collects brass statues of elephants—20 of them adorn his office—but only elephants whose trunks are pointing upward.

Parcells should be in baseball. Superstition envelops that game like a shroud. It's bad luck for a pitcher to strike out the first batter. Never mention a no-hitter in the dugout. Don't cross bats. Don't wash your uniform or change your sanitary socks during a winning streak. Step over the baseline, not on it. The fans get involved too, joining the seventh-inning stretch to bring good luck to their team. Let's be careful, however, to exclude from the list of venerable baseball superstitions such modern gimmicks as the Homer Hankies that were waved by Minnesota Twins fans during last year's World Series. Anything invented since 1950 and done by more than, say, 100 people at a time isn't a superstition. It's an effort to get on national TV.

Why is baseball so rich in superstition? Probably because it's older than most American sports and is so enmeshed in folklore. Many early baseball players weren't the most educated of men, and the idea of rubbing a bat with a hot towel to get out of a slump seemed more effective than, say, adjusting your stance. Remember, back then there were no videos, nor analytical batting coaches like Charley Lau to talk about "a tension-free swing." Even Christy Mathewson, a college man, wrote in his 1912 book *Pitching in a Pinch*: "[A jinx can] make a bad pitcher out of a good one and a blind batter out of a three hundred hitter."

Some superstitions are endemic to baseball, but others were simply adapted to the sport from sources lost in the murky depths of time. Stepping over the foul line is no doubt an offshoot of the old childhood superstition that says, Step on a crack, break your mother's back. That superstition, incidentally, can be traced to the belief that a crack represented the opening of a grave, and to step on that crack meant you might be walking on the grave of someone in your family. Ask a base coach about this sometime and notice how he nods his head in pensive accord before he spits tobacco juice on your shoes.

The idea of not bathing during a hot streak is an offshoot of the centuries-old superstition about washing away good luck. According to Raymond Lamont Brown, author of *A Book of Superstitions*, Welsh miners never washed their backs for fear that the roof would fall in on them. Though the percentage of Welsh miners on their roster was small, the Salt Lake Trappers of the Class A Pioneer League adopted the no-wash superstition last summer during their 29-game winning streak, a professional baseball record. No player washed his socks, and some washed nothing at all. When their streak finally ended with a 7-5 loss to the Billings (Mont.) Mustangs on July 27, the rest of the league was relieved in more ways than one.

Even what appears to be a contemporary display of ritualism (not to mention bad taste) might be an update of an ancient superstition. Like one of those ancient tribal warriors who wore amulets to please the gods, former major league infielder Tito Fuentes hung as many as a dozen chains around his neck, and each had to be perfectly aligned before he would step into the batter's box. A man of many superstitions, Fuentes also named one of his sons Clinch because he was born on Sept. 29, 1971, the day before Fuentes's team, the San Francisco Giants, clinched the National League's Western Division title. "If we had made it to the World Series and he had been born then, I was going to name him W.S.," said Fuentes.

Wade Boggs of the Boston Red Sox could match any of the old-timers superstition for superstition. Eating chicken every day barely scratches the superstitious surface for Boggs, whose game-day routine makes a guy like Parcells seem positively spontaneous. Here's the Boggs Log for every Red Sox home night game:

- 3 p.m.: Leave apartment for Fenway.
- 3:30: Sit in front of locker and change into uniform.
- 4:00: Go to dugout and sit down.

- 4:10: Warm up arm.
- 4:15: Take grounders for 20 to 25 minutes.
- 4:35 or 4:40: End grounder drill by stepping on third, second and first (in that order). Take two steps in first base coaching box and lope to dugout in four steps, preferably hitting the same four spots every evening. Get drink of water. Jog to centerfield for meditation.
- Just before infield practice: Stand or sit in runway between clubhouse and dugout and toss ball against wall.
- 7:17: Do wind sprints.
- While in on-deck circle: Arrange pine tar, weighted doughnut and resin in a precise way and apply them in that order.
- Upon stepping into batter's box: Draw a *chai*, the Hebrew symbol for life.
- After that: Hit the ball where it's pitched—and where they ain't—whenever possible.

"Everybody has a routine," says Boggs. "Mine just takes five hours."

Far fewer superstitions have found their way into football, possibly because, philosophically, its confrontations take a much more direct approach than baseball's. Instead of, "Hey, fellas, let's mix the bats up to change our luck," football players tend to say things like, "Hey, fellas, let's get out there and punch their faces in!" The less subtle the sport, the less room there is for superstition. Remember, this is just a theory.

Confrontation—that's what football players thrive on, but of course there are exceptions. On Friday, Nov. 13, 1987, a stray black cat strolled into the Denver Broncos' practice facility. Five days earlier the Broncos had lost 21-14 to the Buffalo Bills to fall 2 1/2 games behind the San Diego Chargers in the AFC West. The Broncos decided to keep the cat to see if it would change their luck. Obviously, they were going against the grain of conventional superstition. (Actually, black cats were considered lucky in ancient Egypt. It was only during the witchcraft-mad Middle Ages that black cats got a bad rap.) Anyway, when Denver won its next four games, Quatro, as the cat was called, became a good-luck charm.

Many football superstitions involve equipment. Jim Kelly, he of the pregame retch, will use only black laces in his rib protector and will lace it only from top to bottom. One of his offensive tackles, Joe Devlin, feels that any cosmetic alterations made to his equipment are bad luck. One day Devlin came in to find that Dave Hojnowski, the Bills' equipment manager, had cleaned his helmet. Devlin went outside and beat it against a curb to restore its battle-worn look. His head was reportedly not in it at the time.

Many football players let only certain trainers tape them, and only at certain times and in a certain pattern. Denver quarterback John Elway always has offensive guard Keith Bishop sign in for him on the pregame list that goes up in the Bronco locker room of those who want to be taped. Million-dollar quarterbacks can do stuff like that. And some quarterbacks are even superstitious about other quarterbacks. Kelly, for example, refuses to watch game films with his backup, Frank Reich, for fear that if he does, Reich will play in a game other than one in which the Bills are far ahead late in the fourth quarter—a game in which Kelly is injured, for instance.

When John Madden coached the Oakland Raiders, he never let his players leave the locker room to start a game until running back Mark van Eeghen had burped. (This ritual was known as the pregame "Buick.") Perhaps Madden was aware of ancient aural superstitions, such as the wailing of a banshee, which foretold death in Gaelic culture. More likely, though, van Eeghen's burp was somehow just pleasing to Big John's ear.

An inordinate number of basketball superstitions center on clothing. Take that awful brown, red and blue crewneck sweater that St. John's coach Lou Carnesecca wore for good luck during the 1984-85 season. Though it can be safely said that Carnesecca has never exactly fled the spotlight and that the garment in question was good for attracting the public's attention, Carnesecca was, no doubt, sincerely superstitious about wearing it while his team was winning 13 in a row. But Carnesecca put it away after Georgetown dashed the sweater's winning streak in a game during which Hoyas coach John Thompson wore a T-shirt designed to look like the horrible sweater.

Kansas coach Larry Brown also has several superstitions involving fashion. He always wears a University of Kansas pin on his lapel and tucks a white handkerchief into his breast pocket. He will never again wear the same suit and tie that he wore during a loss. For a long time paisley ties were verboten on the Jayhawk bench because Brown was wearing one when he lost his first game at Kansas five years ago.

In addition to his sartorial superstitions, Brown shaves in the same pattern each morning. He will tape his pregame radio show only inside arenas, since the Jayhawks once lost after he had taped the show in a lobby. Kansas players must leave the floor to return to the locker room with just under 10 minutes showing on the pregame clock. And Brown must touch each assistant before the tip-off, just as Egyptian pharaohs touched hunchbacks for luck centuries ago.

Two young members of the Indiana Pacers, second-year forward Chuck Person and rookie guard Reggie Miller, zealously cling to superstitions that started in their high school days. Miller wears tape on his left wrist for luck. He also wears tape on his right wrist but, he says, "only to keep my shooting hand straight." He has two sweatbands over the tape on his left wrist but none over the tape on the right, because he feels it would throw his shot off.

Person's superstition is much sweeter—he must have two candy bars before a game. They may be two KitKats, two Snickers or one of each, but he has to have two of them. Before the Pacers' opening game in Philadelphia this season, Person was sitting on the team bus ready to leave for the Spectrum when he realized he didn't have his lucky bars. He fast-broke back into the hotel gift shop, bought them and got back before the bus departed.

John Wooden, the legendary UCLA basketball coach, is one of those who insists that he had routines, not superstitions. Call them what you will. Wooden could be counted on to turn toward his wife, Nell, who always sat in the same seat at Pauley Pavilion, and give her the high sign with his right hand, just before the tip-off. And during the game he always clung to a rolled-up program. "I wrote my game notes on it," he says, routinely.

But Wooden would have a hard time explaining away one of his lesser-known rituals as routine. On his daily walk around the UCLA campus he would look for hairpins on the ground. When he found one, he would stick it in a tree. "There's a tree trunk on campus stuck full of hairpins," says the Wizard. "It must amaze people when they come upon it." Oddly enough, Adolph Rupp of Kentucky, another renowned college basketball coach, also used to scour the ground for hairpins. And these are two guys whose teams were known for their heads-up play.

Pins have always been considered magical, probably because they are made from shiny material. The rationale for picking up hairpins, writes Potter, "dates back to the days of witchcraft, when it was believed that witches used odd bits of metal to cast magic spells. If you didn't pick up a fallen pin, a witch might." As the rhyme goes: "See a pin and pick it up/All the day you'll have good luck." With a life-time winning percentage of .813 in 40 years of high school and college coaching, Wooden certainly had his share of lucky days.

Aside from baseball players, no group of athletes is more superstitious than hockey players, particularly goalies. Former Vancouver Canucks goalie Cesare Maniago had lucky socks. Gary Smith, who played for several different NHL teams, would remove all 30 pounds of gear and put it back on again between periods. Even Ken Dryden—lawyer, author, intellectual, consumer activist—superstitiously avoided watching the referee make his pregame inspection of the goal judges' lights. "I just consider it unlucky to see the red light before the game," Dryden once said.

Other hockey players, forwards especially it seems, are superstitious about the route they skate in pregame warm-ups. Former Buffalo Sabre forward Craig Ramsay explains his, ahem, routine: "I'd stay near the boards and not touch any lines. Then on the first pass I'd go between the face-off dot at center ice and our logo. The next time through, I'd go between the other side of the logo and the big face-off circle. It was quite involved." And just about everyone whacks the shin pads of the goalie before a game.

Wayne Gretzky has undoubtedly influenced hundreds of junior players to tuck the right side of their jersey behind their hip pad, something the Great One has done since long before he was so great. It's pure superstition, unlike, say, Boston Celtic Larry Bird's practice of rubbing his hands on his sneakers, which, he says, actually gives him "a better feel" for the ball.

But Gretzky is not in the same league as former All-Star center Phil Esposito, now the general manager of the New York Rangers. Espo rose to the top of the superstition game during his playing days. He posted countless good-luck charms around his locker (a hemlock sprig, a shamrock, etc.). He always followed the same pattern of dressing. He always took his gum from a new pack and his tape from a fresh roll. And he was a strong believer in one of history's most storied superstitions, the evil eye, or *malócchio*, as it was known in the Italian neighborhood of Sault Ste. Marie, Ont., where Espo was raised. If Espo cast his evil eye on someone, so he believed, bad luck would surely follow.

Esposito has grown no less superstitious in his executive days, and the same can be said of his boyhood chum Lou Nanne, a former Minnesota North Star forward and defenseman and, until last week when he resigned, that club's general manager. Nanne suffers—or at least he did suffer—from something that might be called superstition sickness. During the final weeks of the 1986-87 season, when the North Stars were playing so poorly that they ultimately failed to qualify for the play-offs, Nanne lost 12 pounds in 10 days. His superstitious rituals and agonizing obsessions, coupled with his team's failures, were the primary cause.

Even Nanne can't remember all the superstitions he followed. He left his office only through a certain exit. He changed seats in the press box after every goal scored by the opposition, circling his new chair four times before sitting down. Conversely, when things were going well for the Stars, he sat immobile even if his leg went to sleep. He drove himself crazy trying to remember what sport coat he had worn with what shirt and tie when the Stars had won a certain game months earlier.

Cases of irrational belief in omens of misfortune (albeit less extreme than Nanne's) can be found throughout the wide world of sport. Witness the following:

• The all-time superstitious tennis player was probably Art (Tappy) Larsen, the U.S. champion in 1950. Larsen selected a daily lucky number and changed his clothes that number of times. He also clung to the belief that a good-luck eagle resided on his left shoulder. He got his nickname from his conviction that good luck would follow him if he tapped on objects. During matches he tapped the baseline, tapped the umpire's stand, tapped the net with his racket. Sometimes he even tapped his opponent. He has a modern-day counterpart, of course, in John McEnroe, who has tapped a watercooler or two.

Many golfers are superstitious about color. This is only natural, since golf is the sport for human peacocks. Hubert Green avoids yellow, which, according to ancient superstition, is the color of jealousy, inconstancy and treachery. Judas is frequently shown dressed in yellow. Unfortunately, Green, like so many golfers, likes green. As a public service we would like to remind golfers that green is unlucky because it's the color of gnomes and leprechauns. So put away all those lime-green pants, lime-green shirts, lime-green golf shoes, lime-green golf bags, lime-green golf hats, etc. It's considered particularly bad luck to wear green to the christening of a child, though one can't imagine who would do that except for a golfer en route to an early-afternoon tee time.

Golfers are also frequently superstitious about coins. Jack Nicklaus once said that he didn't "feel secure" unless he started a round with three pennies in his pocket (and something more than that in his bank account). Al Geiberger always marked his ball on the green with a penny, and if he was playing well, he made sure the same side was always up or that Lincoln's eyes always pointed toward the hole.

• Most of boxing's superstitions have to do with hexes and curses and are frequently more prefight hype than anything else. But oldtimers swear that the late cornerman Benjamin (Evil Eye) Finkle had magical powers. Finkle was noted for three curses: the Whammy, the Zinger and the Slobodka Stare. Finkle earned his reputation in 1937, when he worked middleweight Solly Krieger's corner during his upset of Billy Conn.

The contemporary fighter best known for his superstitions is former lightweight champion Livingstone Bramble (now known as Ras-I Aluja Bramble). Funny, but all his witchcraft and voodoo didn't do him much good against Edwin Rosario, who took his title.

• Andretti's fear of green, shared by many other auto racers, may stem from a couple of sources. Ray Gilhooley was driving a green Isotta at Indianaplolis during the 500 in 1914, when he blew a tire and lost control; Joe Dawson, trying to avoid Gilhooley, drove his car into the wall and was badly hurt. Indy historian Bob Laycock says that another explanation goes back to the early days of racing, when the natural vegetation surrounding the course made green cars hard to see. A more mystical interpretation holds that driving a green car means you will soon by lying under green sod.

That superstition itself is dying—Mario's nephew John Andretti, for example, is one of the top drivers whose cars have a lot of green on them—but still, the late Jimmy Clark of Great Britain is one of the few to win Indy in a green car (in 1965). Clark later died during a Formula Two race in Germany. The car he was driving that day was gold and red.

• The Spectrum in Philadelphia may have been home to more pregame superstitions than any arena in the country. The NHL Flyers may have started it all on Dec. 11, 1969, when they played a tape of Kate Smith belting out *God Bless America*. They had remarkable success in games at which Smith sang, particularly in 1974 and '75, when they won Stanley Cups. Even after she died, more than a year ago, Smith continued to serve as Lady Luck for the Flyers. Before Games 3 and 6 of last season's Stanley Cup finals against Edmonton, the Flyers played a tape of Smith's *God Bless America*, and on both occasions, they scored come-from-behind victories. Smith's record at the Spectrum, live and on tape, stands at 58-9-2.

Superstitions like these will always have a place in sport, if only because an athlete's life-style makes him vulnerable to them. "Athletes do the same thing day after day," says Nanne. "They practice at the same time, they eat at the same time, they play at the same time. Important parts of their lives are very ordered, and so, perhaps, they want to bring that same kind of order into every aspect of their lives. Little rituals become little obsessions. Obsessions become superstitions."

Cincinnati Reds reliever Rob Murphy has a little obsession that even a superstitious turn-of-the-century ballplayer might have looked at askance: He's convinced that wearing black silk underwear helps his pitching. (At least two other major league pitchers share Murphy's attachment to a certain undergarment: Houston Astros space cadet Charlie Kerfeld often wears a Jetsons T-shirt on the mound, while Montreal pitcher Bryn Smith wears one bearing the logo of the rock group Rush.) Murphy relies on the silk undies only while he's in action. "Right now I'm wearing an ordinary pair of J.C. Penney cottons," said Murphy during a recent interview. But, since he's a frequently used reliever who's never sure when manager Pete Rose is going to call on him, he puts on his silk skivvies at the ballpark 162 times a year.

"I look at it as my security blanket," says Murphy. "You can't see them. Nobody but me knows they're on. But they're important. I have certain things I do to get ready for the game—go over the hitters, warm up, etc.—and putting on the underwear is part of that, part of my mental preparation."

What loyalty. What devotion. What faith. Bet you'd stick with the black-undies routine even if your pitching started going bad, right Rob?

"Are you kidding me?" said Murphy. "I'd take 'em off in a minute."

"For what did you pray?"
"I pray nobody get hurt. Then I pray it be a good fight."
"Don't you ever pray to win?"
"No, I would never do that."
"Why not?"
"Suppose I pray to win. The other boy, he pray to win too. Then what God gonna do?"
Beau Jack

Oh Lord, the hatred that fills the stadium frightens me. I am unable to understand such demonic exercises in a world already filled with an abundance of dispair. Please offer me light. Amen.
Jerry Pyle

How can religious people reconcile their beliefs with the violence in football? How can we have a minister give a prayer in the locker room before the kickoff? It's like having the priest say a few words just before the lions come out to eat the good Christians.
Thomas Tutko and William Burns

I firmly believe that if Jesus Christ was sliding into second base, he would knock the second baseman into left field to break up the double play. Christ might not throw a spitball but he would play hard within the rules.
Fritz Peterson

Part IV
Sport, Religion, and Ethics

The public doesn't believe that one athlete in a hundred before and after a big game can take prayer seriously.

Frank Deford

Ethics and Sport

Ten minutes remained in the 1969 Spanish Football (soccer) league championship game played before 80,000 screaming fans in the enormous Bernabeu Stadium in Madrid. With the game scoreless, Pedro Zamballa, right wing for one of the teams, skillfully maneuvered the ball near the opponent's goal and prepared to shoot from fairly close range. Readying himself to defend Zamballa's impending shot, the goalkeeper on the other team viciously collided with one of his own teammates; so forcefully, in fact, that both fell to the ground injured and unconscious. Facing a defenseless goal, Zamballa could have scored easily. Instead, he did a remarkable thing. He deliberately kicked the ball wide of the goal and over the end line. Zamballa's team eventually lost the game by a score of 1-0. His refusal to score a goal well may have cost his team the championship.

Zamballa's conduct was both criticized and praised. His fans and teammates denounced his seemingly charitable act: "Zamballa is paid to shoot goals, not to make gifts to the other side," they said. "What would happen if every footballer and every athlete declined when the fancy took him, to score, or to seize a chance of winning, even if he were responding to the dictates of his conscience?" On the other hand, The International Committee on Fair Play honored his conduct by presenting him with an award "for reflecting all that is finest and purest in sport." However, even the committee was ambivalent, noting that Zamballa's act constituted "an extreme case of fair play" and that making the award did not imply that "in similar circumstances every player should necessarily behave in the same way" (Frost & Sims, 1974, p. 89).

Was Zamballa's decision right or wrong? Should he have been given the sportsmanship award or dismissed from the team? Where does one start in assessing the morality of Zamballa's act? What factors should be taken into consideration in deciding whether it was good or bad conduct? One way is to apply what ethicists call a formalist approach, which attributes primary moral significance to the motives underlying an act rather than to its consequences. Although we don't know what prompted Zamballa's act (he said only that he followed a natural impulse not to score in the situation), a host of different motivations and intentions might be hypothesized. His action may have been prompted by deep sympathy and concern for the injured athletes. Thus, to attempt to score in the face of their suffering would have been to blatantly disregard their plight and symbolically, if not literally, to value the game, specifically victory in the game, above the physical welfare of one's fellows.

On the other hand, Zamballa may have refrained from scoring because he was acting in concert with gamblers whose money had been bet on the other team, or his act may have been a calculated attempt to attract national attention to himself. In the former instance, his conduct would have been judged dishonest, even treasonous; in the latter, his action could be considered a case of "grandstanding," engaging in self-promotion at the expense of his own team's chances of winning the contest.

Even the best intentions do not always produce good consequences, thus one might opt for a different method of analysis, a teleological approach in which the consequences of an act rather than the intentions that give rise to it become the primary consideration. One consequence of Zamballa's act was that he denied his team a chance to win a contest in which they had invested deeply in terms of time, effort, and emotion. In choosing not to score a goal, he contributed directly to the misfortune and displeasure of his teammates. Some might contend that Zamballa failed to honor a commitment implicitly made to his teammates by virtue of his membership on the team, which was that he would try his best to win the contest. So, too, a perceptive and objective opponent might question Zamballa's conduct on grounds that it violated an implied contract presumed to exist between the two teams, a contract guaranteeing that each would try their best to win within the rules, thereby assuring each team of a good and enjoyable contest (Pearson, 1973; Simon, 1985). The individual who does not try to win is a spoilsport who threatens the very life of the contest.

On the other hand, one might justifiably argue that Zamballa's act led to an overall "good" that superseded either of these negative considerations. His magnanimous act entailed great personal sacrifice; it graced the contest with nobility and a lofty vision of humanity, reminding all that the game should never be valued above concern for the welfare of its players. It could be argued that his act may have inspired others to display similar behaviors in the broader sphere of society. Yet, even if it could not be shown to have any instrumental value, it might still be looked upon as an intrinsic good in its own right because it underscored, in a symbolic way, the notion that people need not be slaves to a social convention or to the dictates of the masses.

This scenario from a soccer game illustrates the rich context sports offer for studying the ethics of human behavior. Sports are rule-governed activities in which players, by virtue of participating in the game, consent to abide by established regulations. Yet opportunities abound for circumventing the rules, deliberately and secretly, with an intent to deceive (cheating). Sometimes rules are violated intentionally with no intent to deceive. For example, in sports such as basketball, soccer, or hockey, players commonly commit physically harmless, intentional fouls within full view of the game officials as a strategic maneuver to stop the game clock or prevent a score. Although widely accepted as an effective game strategy, the practice of intentionally fouling opponents raises some interesting ethical questions (Fraleigh, 1984).

In addition to being rule-governed, sports also are competitive contests in which each team or individual attempts to gain for self or for the team a prize available only to one. As such, they hinge upon the expectations that individuals will act in their own best interests at the expense of others. Having begun a game, it is the object of players to secure for themselves the joy of victory, which can be attained only when one's opponents are forced to taste the bitterness of defeat. Unless players commit themselves to an all-out effort to win the contest (or put another way, commit themselves to ensuring that the opponents, not they, come out on the short end of the score), sports lose their structure and meaning.

On the other hand, while competition sustains the contest, it also threatens its extinction if not checked by adherence to the rules. The same power that envelops, absorbs, and transports athletes and spectators, thus giving rise to claims for its status as a religion, can be the same power that moves athletes to do the "unreligious" (unethical) act. Sport fuels what John Sisk (1973) labeled "fanatic potential," and the only buffers against this potential are the rules of the contest, the referees who enforce them, and whatever real-world values are brought to the game by the players and the spectators. When the urge to win exceeds the strength of will to abide by the rules of the contest or to follow a higher path of conduct prescribed by the players' inner convictions, unethical conduct is the result.

Although the official rules of a contest offer the most obvious reference point for evaluating ethical conduct in sport, they do not define its limits. Athletes enjoy a remarkable range of freedom to act unethically within the framework of the rules. Decisions regarding whether or not to attempt to intimidate an opponent psychologically or physically, how to react to defeat or victory, how viciously one should tackle an opponent in football, whether or not to help an opponent to his feet, whether or not to expose one's body to physical harm, or whether or not to exploit an opponent's injury are examples of ethical decisions not covered by the simple prescriptions of the rules. It may be the case as well that the rules of a sport such as boxing or football may permit conduct that a player finds morally unacceptable. In such cases, strict adherence to the rules by the player may raise as many ethical questions as a blatant disregard for them. Thus, conscientious players may find themselves in situations where an ethical commitment to play to win must be balanced against an equally strong commitment to honor a personal code of conduct. When the athlete's code of conduct is more restrictive than that required by the rules and more restrictive than the ethical code honored by one's opponent, that athlete may be forced to compete on a very unlevel field. And in cases where a sport is structured so as to require conduct that an athlete considers to be morally reprehensible, the ethical decision for that player may be to refrain from participating.

Among the considerations that guide ethical conduct in such sport situations, social custom and self-interest may be the most influential (Fraleigh, 1984). When social custom is the authoritative basis for action, a practice becomes the standard of conduct simply because "everybody does it," often without consideration of its legal or moral implications. Social scientists have produced evidence suggesting that the subculture of sport can create its own moral code. For example, as athletes become immersed in the cultural context of competitive sports, they appear to become more receptive to rule violations and increased violence (McIntosh, 1979). Empirical data also suggest that as youngsters gain more experience in competitive sport programs (even those sponsored by the Catholic Youth Organization), they adopt an ethical code with respect to sports that differs from that of athletes with less experience. This code places increasing importance on winning relative to playing fairly (Mantel & Vander Velden, 1974).

An example of the extent to which the sports culture can shape ethical conduct can be seen in how players react to injuries that they inflict (unintentionally) on others. From their earliest years athletes are taught that injuries, whether to one's self or to one's opponents, are "all part of the game." The phrase is broadly interpreted to mean that athletes who inflict injuries on another (provided, of course, that no illegal measures were employed) are not morally responsible for the consequences of their actions. Presumably, no one is responsible for the pain and suffering of the injured party. The depth of conviction with which this belief is held by the athletic community was illustrated in a highly publicized incident in which a professional football player presumed that he was in some way responsible for the injury suffered by the man he knocked down. During the 1989 professional (American) football season, New York Jet Freeman McNeil accidentally shattered the left knee of his opponent while legally blocking him. In an unusual gesture of sympathy and remorse, McNeil took himself out of the game and for 10 minutes knelt on the sidelines with his head down as teammates tried to console him. After the game, with tears in his eyes he personally apologized to his unfortunate victim. Reacting so sensitively violated an unwritten code among professional athletes that forbids expressions of sympathy for an opponent. In fact, his conduct earned him a sharp reprimand from his coach, who told reporters, ''I understand his feeling, but that's the way the game goes. Obviously, it [allowing his remorse to affect his play] was not a good thing . . . and he realizes that'' (Newman, 1989, p. 112). Freeman eventually felt pressured to deliver a public apology for ''not staying focused'' and for ''not being a leader.'' As one critic perceptively noted, ''For a while there, it looked as if McNeil might be a leader *because* of how bad he felt. Instead, all the normal rules remain suspended. Play ball'' (Newman, 1989, p. 112).

Self-interest may be the most prominent reason given for human action in sport, if only because the essence of the game involves promoting one's own ends relative to one's opponents. In such cases, athletes' decisions are based entirely on what they find pleasurable in the short term or most compatible with their life goals and aspirations in the long term. Usually self-interest in athletics is expressed in self-serving behaviors that maximize chances for winning. Actions are judged good or moral because they further the ends to which the athletes are committed. For example, players fake injuries in order to stop the clock because in the short term it increases the possibility that they may win the game and in the long term may further their chances of attaining a higher national ranking (Fraleigh, 1984). Similarly, the growing tendency for athletes to rely on anabolic steroids often is defended on grounds that if such practices lead to improvements in performance, they should be permitted.

Religion and Ethics

These are but a few examples illustrating the rich context for ethical decisions sport offers participants. Although it is impossible here to cover in any complete way the broad and complex topic of ethical considerations in either sport or religion, it will be helpful to provide some background to the readings in this section.

Sport philosophers may like to think otherwise, but ethical decisions in sport, like ethical decisions in most of life, rarely are anchored in a formal moral philosophy, nor are they organized around such primary values as reason, love, nature, pleasure, or self-realization. Often, ethical decisions are made without any conscious point of reference; in some instances, they are made on an ad hoc basis with little evidence of consistency from decision to decision. Less frequently, ethical decisions are framed in general social and philosophical world views, such as Marxism or existentialism. The athletic reform movement of the 1970s, popularized by Jack Scott (1971) and the Institute for the Study of Sport and Society, was an example of how a social-political perspective can influence a proponent's public ethical positions on competitive sport.

It should be recognized that religious views also may be subject to modification by an individual's social, political, and economic philosophy. For example, at the extreme ends of the continuum of modern religious thought, both conservative (the new Christian right) and liberal (liberation theology) Christian views share a proclivity for incorporating heavy concentrations of social and political philosophy into their theologies such that it becomes difficult to separate ethical views based on *religious* beliefs from those representing an amalgam of religious and secular beliefs (Hargrove, 1979). It should be noted also that people may disguise as religion (sometimes unconsciously) their social and political ethics in order to lend a sacred force to their own views (Yinger, 1961).

For most people, religion is more than a social, philosophical, or world view, and it is more than merely adhering to the prescriptions of an eternal order. Nevertheless, religion does have as one of its central features a code for guiding human conduct that derives from the religion's belief or doctrinal system. In fact, religion and religious beliefs probably have a more general and pervasive influence on the ethical decisions of the population at large than do formal philosophical systems (Titus & Keeton, 1973, p. 218), which is not to imply that religion is essential to moral conduct or to overlook the fact that religions may prescribe actions that are immoral.

In religion-based ethical schemes, questions of right conduct are related to beliefs about the nature of humanity and the nature of the universe. In this sense, secular ethical schemes share the general character of religious schemes. As the esteemed theologian-ethicist James Gustafson noted, there is a way in which all practical moral questions, if pursued to their logical ends, require some reflection that, if not explicitly theological, at least is the secular equivalent of it (1981, p. 71). Yet religion-based ethics involve more than extrapolating from general notions regarding the meaning of life. What is real and true is expressed by acting in accord with eternal truths. Morality that is based in religion traces ethical issues, problems, and questions to some ultimate origin and relates goals and purposes for conduct to some ultimate reality. Theologian Reinhold Niebuhr expressed the relation this way: "The ultimate moral demands upon man can never be affirmed in terms of the facts of human existence. They can be affirmed only in terms of a unity and a possibility, a divine reality which transcends human existence" (1935, p. 50).

Thus, there is an expectation that some clear correspondence will be evident between the nature of religious beliefs and quality of moral conduct. Conformity to a particular moral code often is used to distinguish the faithful from the unfaithful. Usually, decisions about right conduct are centered in beliefs about God and God's relation to the world, unlike "secular" ethics where the individual is regarded as the ultimate center of value. Moreover, religion-based ethics have an affective component often lacking in objective, secular, ethical analyses. Beliefs (that sense of intellectual assent to and use of formal moral doctrines and dogmas) provide a rational basis for the moral act, but faith (a sense of deep personal trust and reliance upon the wellspring of the human spirit) provides the motivation to act. Gustafson (1981) described a theocentric ethics as not just something cerebral, but visceral.

Religion-based ethical approaches range from legalistic systems framed in dogmatic moral codes emphasizing obedience to some ecclesiastic or divine authority to more flexible systems in which theological principles are used in a less specific sense to guide moral reasoning. In legalistic systems, actions are judged less by engaging in reflective moral reasoning or examining the consequences of an act, than by literally applying a strict set of divine commands or theological statements that prescribe moral conduct. In such systems, frequently referred to by ethicists as "Divine Command Theory," acts are likely to be judged intrinsically moral if they meet the prescriptions of religious doctrine. For example, the widespread tendency for Christian athletes to view it as their ethical responsibility to play as intensely as possible, without viewing sport or their performance in terms of the broader social and moral context is an example of this approach to religious ethics. Because their views are based on interpretations of biblical injunctions such as: "Whatever your task, work heartily, as serving the Lord and not man" (Colossians 3:23), there is no need to consider the more practical parameters of their conduct.

Less fundamentalistic approaches may be rooted in identical theological doctrines but based on a more flexible (less literal) approach to ethical analysis. For example, Christian evangelical (as opposed to fundamentalistic) traditions tend to recognize divine authority but also recognize the pitfalls of applying too literal and too simplistic interpretations of biblical injunctions to complex individual and social problems. There is a recognition that the Christian ethical heritage is largely a story of accommodations, debates, unresolved questions, and variations stemming from attempts to apply the principles to ever-changing social situations. In such cases, general theological principles are used to guide analyses of specific problems, along with reflective moral reasoning that takes into account the consequences and implications of an act.

Sport, Religion, and Ethics

To refer to Christian ethics or Buddhist ethics or humanist ethics suggests that some distinctive quality or form or behavior exists that is conditioned by a belief system that justifies the characterization (White, 1979). In American sports, religion-based ethics are most notable in their Christianized form, although the spectrum of positions this provides is expansive. In fact, those who believe a Christian approach to ethical analysis imposes an unnecessarily limiting analytic perspective will be surprised in their reading of this section to encounter the enormous variety of ethical positions on sport that have their roots in Christian theology.

Given the power of religious belief to influence ethical positions on sex, crime, abortion, and political affiliation (Batson & Ventis, 1982), it should not be surprising to learn that religion also might modify ethical approaches to sport. Over the centuries, major denominations of Protestantism have espoused well-defined ethical positions on leisure, amusement, recreation, and sport. From the time of the Protestant Reformation to the latter part of the 19th century, sport was more likely to be the object of criticism than of praise by clerics (Hogan, 1967). The grounds for criticism were ot always the result of dogmatic narrow-mindedness as many appear to believe but frequently the result of a careful analysis of the nature of sport in popular culture as it stood in relation to a clearly delineated theology. Violence, destruction of friendships, fanaticism, exposing one's body unnecessarily to physical injury, and using sport to escape the more pressing responsibilities of Christian citizenship all were targets of criticism. Concerning the latter, few ministers of the mid-19th century were able to imagine any convincing reasons to justify participating in sport; in light of widespread poverty and suffering in the industrialized communities, most viewed it as a waste of God-given time. Church members inclined to spend some free time watching professional baseball games were confronted with a theologically poignant question: "Are Christians the followers of the Savior, at leisure so that their work is done long before the sun is set? Do they perform all that is needful for the young, for the aged, for the church, for the world . . . ?" ("Amusements," 1867, p. 417).

As sport grew in popularity, resistance from American churches declined, and they gradually came to embrace sport as a wholesome activity that could be used to further the goals of religious education and evangelism, a phenomenon Page referred to as "the basketballization of the churches" (1952). By the 1970s, Protestantism and Catholicism had become the strongest lobbies for organized sport in the country, seemingly oblivious to the ethical problems discussed in the national press (Deford, 1976). Although sport occasionally is criticized on religious grounds (Bianchi, 1972; Pyle, 1972; Schmidt, 1982), modern attempts to apply religious ethics to sport are more likely to stress athletes' obligation to play to the best of their abilities (Neal, 1975), to emphasize parallels between sports and religious living (Warner, 1979), or to promote the importance of harnessing the popularity of sport for evangelistic purposes (Ardnt, 1982) than to encourage athletes to challenge popular credos and forms of sport competition.

There have been few investigations concerning the role religious beliefs play in shaping ethical views on sport. Two recent empirical studies have sought to clarify the connection.

In an unpublished study (Hoffman & Luxbacher, 1983), undergraduate students who were classified as high or low in Christian religious belief on the basis of scores on a doctrinal orthodoxy inventory were compared in their responses to an ethical-choice-in-sport survey. One of the vignettes to which the students indicated their degree of approval was the conduct of Zamballa. Additional questions required students to rate their level of approval under four hypothetical situations: if Zamballa's team had been ahead by a score of 4-0 when he refused to shoot at the goal; if his team had been behind 1-0; if the game had not been a championship; and if it had been an informal contest played on a vacant lot in front of no spectators. The hypothetical situations were designed to increase or decrease the cost of Zamballa's decision in respondents' minds.

Students who were high in religious belief recorded higher levels of approval for Zamballa's conduct across all but one of the contexts than did the low religious-belief students. The single exception was the hypothetical situation that placed Zamballa's act in an informal game played on a vacant lot in front of no spectators; both groups indicated high approval of Zamballa's action in this situation. Also, the ratings of Zamballa's conduct by high religious-belief students were relatively stable across hypothetical situations, whereas the ratings by low religious-belief students declined when Zamballa's team (hypothetically) was behind and increased when his team was ahead. Although the findings were far from conclusive, they hint that ethical norms for students of high religious belief may align more closely with the Golden Rule (do unto others as you would have them do unto you) than do the schemes of the students of low religious belief.

A second study examined the relationship between competitive orientation and religious orientation (Kelley, Hoffman, & Gill, 1990). Here the ethical theme was imbedded in respondents' views of the purpose of athletic competition. Three orientations were possible: competitiveness, an enjoyment of striving in competition; goal, a focus on personal goals and standards; and win, a focus on outcome and success in competition. An intrinsic religious orientation (one that valued religion without regard for its usefulness) was associated more closely with competitiveness and goal than with win orientations, while precisely the opposite effect was observed for students with an extrinsic religious orientation (one that valued religion for its uses). Furthermore, stepwise regression analyses showed athletic experience and extrinsic religious orientation to be the strongest predictors of a win orientation, whereas orthodoxy (strength of belief in traditional Christian religious doctrines) was a major predictor of the adoption of a "goal orientation."

Although the trend in this study was not strong, and it is unknown whether the behavior of the students in athletic settings parallels their expressed preferences, such empirical data suggest nevertheless that what people believe religiously may affect how they think about sport and, ultimately, how they may conduct themselves in sport situations.

Articles in Review

Each article in this section deals in some way with the relationship between ethical judgments in sport and religion. In "Sport: Morality and Ethics," Howard Slusher challenges the feasibility of a religion-based morality as a guide to conduct in sport. He believes that religion holds up ideals of human perfection by legalism and by external absolutes that deny athletes the opportunity to be "authentic." According to Slusher, morality in competitive sport should be free and guided by feelings that reside within the individual. In fact, the instinctive nature of ethical decisions in sport do not allow for reflective moral reasoning; hence, gut reactions constitute a more authentic moral response than some internal struggle to adhere to a higher, absolute, external standard. Slusher's argument for a relative rather than an absolute ethics reflects an existential-based ethical system that is reminiscent of the "situation ethics" popularized by theologian Joseph Fletcher (1966). Somewhat like Michael Novak's (1976) celebration of man's imperfection as revealed in sport, Slusher argues that the highest morality in sport is the honesty to confront both the inherent pragmatism that underlies our games and the fact that we really don't expect players of games to demonstrate the high ideals traditionally associated with sportsmanship.

In "Sport, Religion and Human Well-Being," Brian Aitken traces theological problems, and ultimately problems in sport, to a contemporary view of humanity as *homo faber*, or man the worker. It is a mindset that fuels an incessant quest for victory and triumph over others and is despiritualizing and alienating in its effects. Aitken asks how sport might be converted from an experience of alienation to an experience of liberation. His answer is to recast our view of humanity, replacing *homo faber* with theologian Sam Keen's (1969) model of *homo temptestivus*. *Homo temptestivus* is "timely man," who resists the tendency to be totally absorbed by the productive ethic of *homo faber*, yet resists totally rejecting it. *Homo temptestivus* is the ethical person, who like Slusher's moral athlete knows instinctively how to act in any given situation. The key is to oscillate between the Apollonian extreme of discipline, order, and reasonableness and the Dionysian extreme of spontaneity, feeling, and wonder, giving vent to each when appropriate. Thus, the tendency to give into the game's fanatic potential will be delicately balanced by a certain detachment, yet without dismissing the game as unimportant and turning it into spontaneous, frivolous play.

A more explicit guide to integrating sport and religion-based ethics is provided by Arthur Holmes in "Towards a Christian Play Ethic." Holmes's essay is one of the most articulate attempts to apply evangelical Christian theology to play (see also Robert K. Johnston's *The Christian at Play*, 1983, and Gordon Dahl's *Work, Play and Worship*, 1972.) Holmes identifies sport as one species of the larger family of play and defines play as an attitude of mind rather than a specific activity. Somewhat like Aitken, Holmes rejects the views of humanity as *homo faber* or as *homo ludens*; unlike Aitken, he rejects any notion of redemptive or salvific powers of play. The distinctive character of humans is that they are *homo religiosus*. Consequently, their play as well as their work must be lived in responsible relationship to God. This relationship becomes the reference point for examining all ethical problems in sport. In applying the standard, Holmes raises questions about injurious forms of sport, sport that is destructive of the environment, or sport that dehumanizes.

Michael Kerrigan's article appeared originally in a special issue of a leading Catholic journal (*New Catholic World*) devoted entirely to sports and was intended to enlighten the laity concerning Pope John Paul II's pronouncements on the role of sport in the Christian life. What readers may find striking is what often is characterized as a heavy Protestant strain in John Paul's arguments for sport. Michael Novak (1976) has described Catholics as valuing sport intrinsically as part of the natural human spirit, unlike Protestants who value sport as a means to improve the efficiency of work. The Catholic tradition, claims Novak, values sport for its own sake.

Yet the distinction may be less pronounced than writers such as Novak have presumed. As Kerrigan's summary indicates, although John Paul pronounces clearly in sport's favor, he appears to value it for what traditionally have been considered Protestant reasons: fitness, psychological well-being, friendship, and the integration of body and spirit. Suggestions that athletic values mimic those taught in the New Testament and appropriation of St. Paul's athletic metaphors as a biblical sanction of sport reflect familiar themes in the largely Protestant sport-religion movement. On the whole, Kerrigan's summary discloses no unique delineation of a ''Catholic'' position on sports, at least as that position can be differentiated from a Protestant view. In this respect, sport may be much more ecumenicized within religious circles than has been assumed.

The remainder of the articles in this section deal with specific ethical issues in sport and represent an enormous range of ethical opinion as it is informed by religion.

Coach Tony Simpson's article, ''Real Men, Short Hair,'' demonstrates that religion-based fanaticism can lead in many directions. Simpson's article was written in the early 1970s when the authoritarian practices of coaches were coming under fire and long hair on men was associated by the athletic fraternity with a socially and politically liberal and rebellious subculture. The article illustrates the absurd lengths to which theological presuppositions can be applied in defending the authoritarian role of a coach or the masculine ethic in sport that Carmody (1986) has so eloquently questioned.

Boxing, because violence and physical incapacitation play a central role in its conduct, has attracted the criticism of theologians and ecclesiastics more than any other sport. Perhaps the most public declaration of boxing's immorality by a cleric was Richard A. McCormick's article (1979), originally published in a national sports magazine. A more recent denunciation of boxing as ''pugilistic pornography'' appeared in the Protestant journal *The Christian Century* (Weaver, 1982). These articles have explored in full the religious grounds for objecting to boxing. The article included here, ''Death in the Ring: A Pastoral Dilemma'' offers a different perspective. Originally published in the Catholic periodical *America*, the article describes the struggle of one priest in reconciling his objections to a violent sport and his pastoral love for the killer.

Until his death, Herbert W. Armstrong was the influential leader of The Worldwide Church of God—a religious organization with an international outreach through radio, television, a college, and a publishing arm that produces *Plain Truth*, the magazine from which his short article has been excerpted. Armstrong shows keen insight into the ethical problem of competition and questions it on explicit theological grounds. Applying the basic biblical principle, ''Love thy neighbor as thyself,'' he singles out sports in which competitors attempt to gain an advantage at the expense of their opponents, especially those involving physical contact, as particularly troublesome ones for those athletes who desire to apply God's law in sport.

The concluding article in this section, ''Nimrod, Nephilim, and the Athletae Dei'' by Hoffman, examines the issue of physical violence in sport in relation to the popular practice by Christian athletes of describing sport as a form of religious expression. Hoffman shows how religious expression and experience are linked inextricably to ethical considerations and contends that modern forms of athletics deny athletes access to deep spiritual meaning because of the way the body is perceived and used. Relying on insights from the original athletae Dei—the ancient hermits of the Western desert—about the power of their surroundings to facilitate inner dialogue as a source of understanding, Hoffman challenges modern Christian athletes to seek athletic contexts where their religious aspirations can be realized.

References

Amusements, (1867). *New Englander*, **26**, 417.

Ardnt, R. (1982). *Winning with Christ*. St. Louis: Concordia Publishing House.

Batson, C.D., & Ventis, W.L. (1982). *The religious experience: A social psychological perspective*. New York: Oxford University Press.

Bianchi, E. (1972). Pigskin piety. *Christianity and Crisis*, **32**(2), 31-34.

Carmody, D.L. (1986, July/August). Big-time spectator sports: A feminist Christian perspective. *New Catholic World*, pp. 173-177.

Dahl, G. (1972). *Work, play and worship*. Minneapolis: Augsburg.

Deford, F. (1976, April 19). Religion in sport. *Sports Illustrated*, pp. 90-101.

Fletcher, J. (1966). *Situation ethics*. London: SCM Press.

Fraleigh, W.P. (1984). *Right actions in sport*. Champaign, IL: Human Kinetics.

Frost, R.B., & Sims, E.J. (1974). *Development of human values through sport*. Washington, DC: American Alliance for Health, Physical Education, Recreation and Dance.

Gustafson, J.M. (1981). *Theology and ethics*. Oxford: Blackwell.

Hargrove, B. (1979). *The sociology of religion*. Arlington Heights, IL: Harlan Davidson.

Hoffman, S.J., & Luxbacher, J. (1983). *Competitive attitude and religious belief*. Poster presentation, North American Society for Psychology of Sport and Physical Activity, East Lansing, MI.

Hogan, W.R. (1967). Sin and sports. In R. Slovenko and J.A. Knight (Eds.), *Motivations in play, games and sports*. Springfield, IL: Charles C Thomas.

Johnston, R.K. (1983). *The Christian at play*. Grand Rapids, MI: William B. Eerdmans Publishing Co.

Keen, Sam (1969). *An apology for wonder*. New York: Harper & Row.

Kelly, B.C., Hoffman, S.J., & Gill, D.L. (1990). The relationship between competitive orientation and religious orientation. *Journal of Sport Behavior*, **13**(2/3).

Mantel, R.C., & Vander Velden, L. (1974). The relationship between the professionalization of attitude toward play of preadolescent boys and participation in organized sports. In G. Sage (Ed.), *Sports in American society* (2nd ed., pp. 172-178). Reading, MA: Addison-Wesley.

McCormick, R.A. (1979). Is professional boxing immoral? In E.W. Gerber and W.J. Morgan (Eds.), *Sport and the body: A philosophical symposium* (pp. 258-263). Philadelphia: Lea & Febiger.

McIntosh, P. (1979). *Fair play: Ethics in sport and education*. London: Heinemann.

Neal, W. (1975). *The handbook of athletic perfection*. Prescott, AZ: Institute for Athletic Perfection.

Newman, B. (1989, October 16). Remorse? Not in the NFL. *Sports Illustrated*, p. 112.

Niebuhr, R. (1935). *An interpretation of Christian ethics*. New York: Harper and Brothers.

Novak, M. (1976). *The joy of sports*. New York: Basic Books.

Page, C.H. (1952, March). Bureaucracy and the liberal church. *The Review of Religion*, pp. 147-148.

Pearson, K.M. (1973). Deception, sportsmanship and ethics. *Quest*, **19**, 115-118.

Pyle, J. (1972, January). Sports and war. *The Christian Athlete*, pp. 3-9.

Schmidt, T. (1982). Time to kick football out of the Catholic schools. *Catholic New Times*, **6**(3), 3-7.

Scott, J. (1971). *The athletic revolution*. New York: Free Press.

Simon, R.L. (1985). *Sports and social values*. Englewood Cliffs, NJ: Prentice-Hall.

Sisk, J. (1973, March 2). Hot sporting blood. *The Commonweal*, pp. 495-498.

Titus, H.H., & Keeton, M. (1973). *Ethics for today* (5th ed.). New York: Van Nostrand.

Warner, G. (1979). *Competition*. Elgin, IL: David C. Cook.

Weaver, C.E. (1982, November 17). Pugilistic pornography. *The Christian Century*, pp. 1156-1157.

White, R.E.O. (1979). *Biblical ethics*. Atlanta: John Knox Press.

Yinger, J.M. (1961). *Sociology looks at religion*. London: Macmillan.

Sport:
Morality and Ethics

Howard Slusher

Philosophy has always been interested in exploration of the "good life." Given the absolute thinking of the idealists, man's behavior has been often measured against a scale of perfection. This system of thought has undergone some marked discussion and alteration among scholars from many disciplines.

Sport has been duly involved with this very same argument. At times one would think that "philosophy of sport" and sportsmanship are one and the same. From the time a child is old enough to play with other children, he soon learns about *sportsmanship*. Yet a review of the literature indicates that perhaps theory and practice are greatly removed from each other.

No doubt part of the problem rests in the "realistic" expectations of the participant. It has been fairly well demonstrated that individuals might well *know* the "correct" pattern of behavior; but indeed they act another way. However, a second and greater problem exists—namely, is there such a thing as *the* correct or right way? If there is, one must conclude that an independent system, divorced from the environmental forces that man is subjected to, is in operation. Unless we assume this form of "super-structure," or inner voice, we must give up the ideal of an absolute morality. If it does not come from this basic source, the chances are good that it does not exist at all.

When considering the *existence* of ethics, it is most direct to perceive them from a sociological viewpoint. To develop ethics from the basis of a deity is neither convincing *nor* desirable. It simply becomes a merry-go-round of perfection. To assume the role of the freedom of man, within his environment, might well be the place to start. The importance of freedom in sport can hardly be overemphasized. To consider a morality divorced from freedom is simply not just. Since the very meaning of the term *absolute* indicates the existence of an ultimate *beyond* the validity of man, it appears fruitless to pursue the end of absolute ethics. This is not to indicate we should not be concerned with "right" and "wrong." But the search for value structures is not one of looking for the perfect, which is not really attainable. Certainly our world of sport asks for an evaluation, based upon a standard, which greatly goes beyond the powers of man to fulfill. No one person should assume a perfection, or be troubled that he has not reached it.[1]

Of course this does not indicate that we do not work for the best. But it is more important to recognize that the ideals of life must be adjusted to the capacities of the performer within the structure of his world. It is indeed dangerous and rather foolish to urge the absolute heights of perfection in a survival world of action. This, again, does not mean we neglect value theory or a high sense of ethics as much as we develop them realistically.

In a sense, values become a map. The ones we hold did not suddenly develop; rather, they were developed out of many years of experience. To think about them and develop relative structures is all one can ask of man. And certainly of the participant in the world of sport can be expected no more or less than this.

When looking at sport, one is generally tempted to focus at "situations" and deduce ethical structures from these happenings. The problem with this method is that it produces only general guidelines for the individual but does not resolve the problems in the "gray" areas of life. How does man resolve the choice between two "goods"? Frequently, the answer is resolved in terms of the "greater" good. Yet this complete discussion comes close to employing an externalized structure. In the sport situation the ethical question is usually resolved during the "action." These are usually emotional times. Traditional ethics would ask the man of sport to beware. Yet I think it is here that the decision tends to be *easiest*. Simply, man needs to listen to the inner forces that direct one. Let no one be deceived. These "inner forces" are not an ultimate power. They simply represent man's feelings. Again, we face a constantly recurring theme; namely, that man is not all rational. Thus, why be afraid to let our "guts" speak for us? If man is to be *really* free in his choice, it is important to recognize that the "rational" part of man might well be greatly influenced by his previous experiences. Therefore, he might not be, indeed, as "rational" as he thinks he is.

The world of sport is often a lonely existence. Perhaps this is the way it best be if man is really to develop a theoretical value structure with some degree of "honesty." It would seem that when man is alone, his actions reflect a normative basis that is as "free" as one could hope it to be. Man, as he exists, demonstrates his value structure. If he argues with the official, holds an opponent illegally or covertly manipulates a situation in his favor, he determines the realm of ethical basis. Some might see this as some form of anarchy; however, it is quite the contrary. In truth, since man develops the criteria for morality, he is thereby *responsible* for these standards of action. It is again important to stress that man comes to sport with a prior value structure. In an emotionally charged setting, which sport frequently is, man makes decisions based upon the dynamics of the situation. It is little wonder that the sport situation acts as a type of "projective" instrument, telling a man and all the world about his basic morality. It is entirely proper that values accruing in action should be judged as authentic, for often it is not until man acts that we really know personal fact from fiction.

From the prior discussion it can be seen that morality is not a listing of rules for each and every situation that may possibly confront man. Rather, morality is to be viewed as a type of "promise in process" that one makes to himself. The parameters are certainly broad; and transfer is assumed. Thus, a difference is viewed between moral "law" and the application. It is in the world of sport that man is constantly reminded not only of the variance in application but in the law itself. Football coaches, for years, have developed the ethic that one does not "run the score up" on an opponent. The idea is simply when you "have enough," you do everything within your power not to let the other squad look too bad on the scoreboard. This might well look like a principle of "sportsmanship," but in truth it is founded on the "Golden Rule"—namely, the next time the "tables may be turned"; don't do anything that is going to hurt you tomorrow. If one looks at the pure facts of the situation, man is being highly immoral. He is thus curtailing, voluntarily, his own performance. To do this because of a "point spread" is illegal. To do the same act because of survival is morality. Relativity? Situational ethics? I am afraid so.

Of course one might say, "This is all well and fine but because this is the way things *are* does not mean this is the way things *should* be." But indeed it *can* be no other way. Man's experience is all we know. This does not imply objective cognition as much as it demands honest subjectivity. Again the term *honest* implicates man's responsibility for choice.

Sport is integrally concerned with the business of achieving. And in so doing, the act must be one of volition in order to be truly moral. It appears this is the only way that man can really maintain the freedom that is rightfully his. In truth, the ability for man to escape his immediate world and therefore *to free* himself *for and into* freedom is one of the enticing elements of sport. It is perhaps *the* true morality of sport. Certainly it appears that sport, itself, does not possess a moral structure. To confuse the element of "sportsmanship," for example, as *belonging* to sport appears to be a stretch of the imagination. When one's actions are "sporting," he is not necessarily reflecting the essence of sport. In reality he is acting as one would expect any civilized individual to behave. Perhaps our acute awareness of this cultivated action in sport is but an indication that we really *don't* expect man *to be human* in the sport situation. For certainly I expect the same form of behavior from my opponent in tennis as I do from my business competitor. If there were not a certain degree of honesty and respect for the general rules of civilization, sport, as well as all mankind, would become quickly anarchistic (Umminger, 1963). Perhaps this is what is meant by "gamesmanship and one-upsmanship."

To speak of ethical choices in sport it becomes necessary to understand the experiences within which these decisions must be made. Value decisions are partially dependent upon the analysis of the existing time. To talk of absolutes is to admit to a static world when the evidence that constantly confronts us indicates profound change. It seems only justified that the conduct of man in sport be evaluated in keeping with the "changing times." The very essence of sport, as a collection of dynamic events involving the participation of man as both object and subject, speaks to the commitment to the transitional nature of man; and therefore available to the subjective. Absolute values, in sport, are simply an attempt to hold onto a "neat" world, one in which we are all allowed "to keep our cool." The determination of any value decision is to utilize *both* reason and emotion.

To even hint that the "Christian ethic" is to be maintained in modern sport is to contradict the very existence of sport as we know it. At the risk of sounding greatly "used," I must indicate that in sport, traditional *Christian ethics are dead.* One simply cannot expect two tennis players to place their shots in such a position, provided they did possess the necessary skill, as to assist in the increased development of the opponent. This is simply not the *reason* for sport as we know it today. The name of the game *is* win. Any effort to read in the noble aims of the naive is to be unjust with what is. Grantland Rice was noble, but wrong, when he indicated they remember you for "how you played the game." They remember you for sixty-one home runs, 9.1 seconds in the 100-yard dash, 18-foot vaults, four-minute miles and over one-hundred stolen bases. Achievement, conquest, victory, and performance—these *are* the heroes and the gods of sport. Mr. Durocher, in saying that "nice guys finish last" might not have been right, but that is only because he confused values with placement.

The real world is revealed to real people and sport offers dividends to the realist. The man of sport makes both rational and irrational decisions. Reality is treated cognitively only if it is *practical.* Values indicate man's *feelings* and his prejudices. Because his decisions are founded on internal aspirations, makes them no more meaningless than those developed scientifically—*provided* they bring about expected achievement.

In an analysis of the sport situation, man typically makes the emotional decision. When the choice is made *in action*, it tends to be an inner reaction. Therefore, the obvious conclusion one must reach is that the man of sport is both more and less moral than his fellow man. He is "more" moral because he trusts his impulses and tends to minimize rational conditioning. However, he is less moral in that he tends to make an *unexamined* choice. It has always been my *personal* feeling that sport is *not* the place to teach moral virtue. Choice in sport tends to be pragmatically oriented. To consider that man will weigh "druthers" on the basis of responsibility of the authentic life is a bit naive. Again, morality and immorality are not based on an absolute scale, but are *situationally relative.* Their validity is grounded in concern and responsibility in an *authentic* existence.

On Ethics. Modern life is new dynamic. The advent of modern science and technology, coupled with shifting populations and rapidly altered social codes, has renovated the citizen of the latter half of the twentieth century. To assume that man will act as he did yesterday is to demonstrate an unrealistic outlook germane to today's culture. From a simplified and relatively quiet past man has passed to a quickly changing society of dynamic dimensions.

In the sport situation a slightly different picture is presented to the participant. There is extensive "security" offered to the man of sport because the sport scene is one of *order*, even if it is not idealized. Man learns *what* the rules of the game are. During the contest the rules remain fixed and decisions become a matter of "living-up" to the known. Man comes to sport from a fickle society of changing mores and fluid traditions. Now, present in sport, he faces a cosmos of regulation.

The security he lost in "real life" is quickly regained in a stable world of sport. Not only does he *know* for "sure" what is expected of him, but now he has a group of officials, umpires, commissioners, and the like to make certain he remains within the rules. Deviation is permitted but one soon learns *just* how far one can stretch the rules.

Unlike the "real world," where conscience has been transformed from a mediator between id and ego to law itself, and where action is evaluated on the utilitarian functional scale, sport attempts to make man adhere to predetermined ethical constructs (needless to say this is not always carried out). During the sport event the performer is asked to evaluate or at least be cognizant of each happening, in keeping with rules, as an occurrence which has its roots in prior happenings. Thus, not only is there security in the known, but there is security in the comparison. Unlike the decisions he is asked to make in a social setting, which calls for him to evaluate events as unique phenomena, thereby each standing on its own, the man of sport can look toward objective and rational order. He can determine the "norms" and make his own decision within the context of an "absolute" system. In social settings, decisions may agree with morality. But if they do, it is purely tangential to the act of immediacy. In sport the immediate must comply with the rules. This type of forced security makes an "artificial" world of *sureness*, if not comfort. It is "nice" to have an established order; at least it is consoling to know where one stands.

In place of fuzzy standards determined by a cross between ideals and norms, sport affords *deduction* in a *realistic* sense. It admits the abstract of the common good (sport even demands officials to "interpret" same), thereby necessitating man to be aware of the "higher and inner voice," while it asks him to act on an individual value bringing about a "good" for personal existence rather than an abstract omitting evaluative feedback. In this way previously established false images of good and bad are avoided. Sport thereby combines the paradox of the polar extremes of absolutism and relativism. It is interesting to note that professional wrestling, once a sport, now an "exhibition," always provides this dimension of polarity. There is always the "good guy" against the "bad guy." It is of interest that "good" normally gets defined in keeping with "clean" or ethical, while "bad" is synonymous with "dirty" and therefore unethical. Perhaps professional wrestling needed "to be arranged" so that the naivete of life could be demonstrated in "sport." Is it not the "Batman" of sport? Namely, the sublime highlights the foolish reality!

It must be pointed out that rules in sport are more than guides for decision. They actually direct the *way* of doing things, if not the choice of doing. The participant is usually suppressed by a God-like official, who, rather than provide an image of the "loving father," becomes a dogmatic legislator (the umpire is *always* right). In a manner of speaking, every personal decision must be interpreted in keeping with that which will be made by the official. Likewise the man of sport really does not need to develop his own ethical existence. The rulers of sport do this for him. This is much different from everyday life where man must "go by" the rules of the social order much like the rules of the game. The difference rests in the immediate response. In life man is *eventually* "ruled on," but he does not live with a *constant* whistle to remind him of what he *should be* doing. Pragmatic rationale, and not morality, undergirds the real ethical choice in sport.

In reality, sport does not really concern itself with absolute, for if it did it would relegate itself to an abstract audience. It must consider *hic homo* (concrete man) rather than *homo ut sic* (abstract man) (Poppi, 1957, pp. 3-63). The *practical* way is neatly woven together with *traditional* regulations to form a basis for *ethics*. Thus, in a way, the sportsman is truly representative of Nietzsche's *Superman*. Static morality is present, yet personal existence is that which ultimately gives causation to decision. Each decision is based on *the* happening along with the *emotional* determinants of the individual. Through development of the spirit and emotion an ethic of absolutism is tempered from "formalism" to relativism. As an area greatly involved with *system* and conversely dependent upon individual existence, sport calls upon regulated freedom and relative choice to develop an ethic that above all is *workable*.

It must be emphasized that the *basis* of morality is in the *authenticity* of man. Once the participant *examines* his life, he commits himself to a constant search, not for truth, but to the *meaning* of truth. Since sport is a dynamic and changing situation, and there is no established order of values, it follows that moral decisions are founded on a system of *relatives*.

Do these normative structures have an objective? Is there a target man can shoot at? The answer is both yes and no. If one perceives a goal as a stationary archery target, the answer is an unequivocal no. Again, the very nature of a changing environment and a developing man necessitates a modulating structure. Thus, if morality is viewed as a system of "audibles" in football, man might well make appropriate decisions. The quarterback will call a play in the huddle. This decision is based on numerous factors including the expected defensive alignment of the opposition. When standing at the line of scrimmage, prior to the snap of the ball, the quarterback may well see a different situation from the one he thought would exist. To run the same play as called in the huddle is sure defeat. To perceive the different environment, to be flexible enough to alter and decide on a new "play" are the marks of a *winner*. Man must learn to react to the situation. For the quarterback the goal is victory; for man it is a meaningful life. Morality must not only be true to the situation, it must also allow for purpose to man's life.

In this light it can be seen that a relative ethic is not, if authentically derived, a symptom of ambivalence or moral seasickness. Situational morality is not an attempt to avoid problems; rather, it is an effort to have man face the realities of life. If anything, sport "teaches" man it is life that must be faced as it *really* is in existence. One cannot run away or deceive oneself in sport or in life. Self-deception might work for a while, but only a short while. Meaning is diffused and life becomes a *nothingness*. Our safeguard is human concern for being. To say it will *work* is to fuse the pragmatic and the idealistic into the unreal. We have to evidence, in any sense of the word, that this "new" system will contribute to a higher level of life. Yet to *settle* for what we have is to admit our destiny. I, for one, am willing to place my faith (concern) in man rather than believe (statement of probability) in the supposed "goodness" of man. We must ask the man in sport to risk *defeat* (after all it is only a *game*). He must be willing to say *no* to his conscious, as a rational power, and beat down the false self. Once rid of the demigods of societal influence, namely "MEPSKY" (M is for money, E for energy, P for power, S for Sex, K for knowledge and Y for youth), man can use this new found *freedom* truly to actualize the self. No doubt this requires extensive self-regulation.

I have not attempted to show the possible causation of human morality. Morals, like life, might be a product of qualities. But so what? What is important is their existence. They are present. To admit their existence is not to confirm their absoluteness. But rather to implicate the evolutionary dimension which is demanded by the nature of the modern world. In truth, it appears that man's insistence upon absolute structures is an attempt to mirror symbolically man's uncertainty, his insecurity, and his incessant attempt to achieve peace the "easy way." But to settle for the unreal is not to bring peace but to bring a sword.

To look at the "lessons" of sport in this way is to question the basic meaning of human existence. It places great importance as to the *basis* of value decisions. Is sport simply a *battleground for human conquest*? Or is it possible, through the use of freedom, to make choices leading to authentic *being*? To be tied to "a power beyond" might well cause man to rationalize and sublimate *what he is doing*. To live a false life, when real self is "good," is unexcusable. I see great potential for achieving this end in most situations in sport. Simply, it lends itself to this form of ethic. But it will not come until the performer becomes aware of the relationship of his action to the authentic self. In so doing he must renounce prior conditioning and search for meaning in each activity of life. To not search in this manner is to play the game (of life or sport) without any *extensive* purpose. If man acts without being "bugged" by the attempt for constant meaning, then life and sport might well be, as Sartre indicates, *absurd*. But it is not life or sport that *is* absurd. They are *nothing*. They don't exist without man. It is in man's hands to make each act meaningful. He is morally *free* to do so. If he does not, then he must shoulder the responsibility for *making* it absurd. Man, therefore, *creates* sport. Through a relative value structure he *re-creates* the life process. He makes sport, again and again, what it potentially is. To say any more is not necessary.

Morality as an Intimate of Sport

Working within the structure of *personal concern* the morality decisions that face man in sport are most personal. They provide the *intimate* fiber of communication between man and the activity. In order to actualize the ethic man must ask where he *is* within the totality of the sport experience. For all of life begins and ends with what he experiences in existence. If one espouses the thesis that you "treat your opponent as you would desire to be treated," then the *meaning of the truth* of that statement is a dependent variable. Its validity is determined by the *intimateness* of man to the experience.

The word "intimate" is being used to connote that which is beyond human thought. The value is not achieved, *really*, if man just *thinks* that is the way to act. Or even if he says that is the way I would like to be treated. This quality of the "intimate" goes into the depths of existence and certainly extends itself beyond modern Christian Ethic. The implication is that man *cares*, not merely intellectually, but with an involvement that extends to the very root of his personhood. If man is not treated in this manner, one is not *just* disappointed, he becomes *nauseated*. He *suffers* because his involvement was more than what was stated—it was *all* of life. Sport is, generally, an act of initial volition. Man participates with *all* of his complexities. This completeness leads to a seriousness of involvement. Only too often the "intermediate" goal of victory blinds man from seeing the eventuation of his participation. To become intimate is to initiate morality. Real morality cannot be achieved until man is willing to *risk* his self in the sport experience.

In achieving this morality man cannot treat man according to usual role expectancy. One does not treat one as an umpire, bowler, boxer, jockey, skier, or basketball player. One is treated *intimately*, as an *individual*. Too often, in our complicated and mass culture of mechanization, we forget that man is not a collective noun. He is a person with a unique identity. Sport must be wary that, in its zest for *ends* and results that are indicated on the scoreboard, man is not relegated to a *mean*. Again, I trust this thought is in keeping with Buber's moral imperative:

> One cannot treat either an individual or a social organism as a means to an end absolutely, without robbing it of its life substance. . . . One cannot in the nature of things expect a little tree that has been turned into a club to put forth leaves. (Buber, 1953, p. 17)

The *intimate* relationships of sport provide the raw material for the most "humane" of all ethical structures. However, one must wonder if the potential is being realized or prostituted. The question is not one of the normal means/ends dichotomy. No matter how good or bad is either the means or ends, man is *immoral* if he attempts to structure any form of dualism which segments, and thereby injures, the authentic existence of man. Our experiences and our goals need be one. Our dreams and our realities need be fused. To say they *are* not is to admit *reality*. To say they *cannot* is to admit *defeat*. We might make choices that are less than what we would hope them to be. But we must not close our eyes and our hearts to those that are *not* chosen. An ethic of *existence* is personal; it is intimate. In sport man can free himself *in* the closeness of another: in his relations with man, in his empathy for skill development, in his appreciation of dedication. All these qualities *bring* him closer to the door of being. Whether he *enters* into life or stays behind a closed partition is a matter of *choice*. A choice of none less than life or death, for man and sport.

In making the choice we cannot run away from the obvious question. Is the authentic life both "good" and "right"? When man is trying to find *real* self in the world of sport, does the *sport* itself encourage man in a world of good and right? The subtle differentiation between "right" and "good" affords insights into the sport situation as an arena for the development of *being*. Choices are difficult to make when the scope of the question is clear. But in the complexity of the sport world we are talking of another issue. It is easy to see how man could "settle" for a world of absolutes. When life becomes intimate, man needs to deal with the "gray areas.'' Black and white will not do. The importance of *relatives* becomes both obvious and terrifying. But now the decisions cannot be avoided. They are close. They are intimate. How do you regulate between the good of the team and the rightness of man? It might be right for man to hunt (the deer will be injured due to overpopulation is the usual reason that is given); but few would say it is good to kill a defenseless animal. Hopefully the reader is not expecting any type of ethical panacea. The only answer I know is that man must do what *he* feels is good. Values and ethics, as moral derivatives, need be unclouded so that man can act with a decisiveness that indicates position and reflection. But this is only the start. For the more immediate and intimate man becomes to sport, the greater will be the effort to reach the zenith.

Allowing for the Existing Morality

Morality is directly related to its environment. However, this does not mean the social matrix always affords assent to the expressed value. Since the realm of sport is atypical from many other endeavors of life—one would expect a varied ethic. That is to say, it is hard to believe that one would even dream that the sport participant would exhibit the same value structure on the gridiron as he does when visiting friends. Each situation calls for its own judgments. This is not to say that this system of relatives is right or wrong. But it does say that it is internally consistent with prior analysis. We might not like ourselves for making certain value decisions. Nevertheless, man makes the choice. Yet, it has been my impression that educators, laymen, sportswriters, and sometimes even coaches act surprised and even shocked when a value is demonstrated that is contrary to the Judea-Christian Ethic. All of this in spite of the accepted thesis of spiritual ethics.

This expressed horror is not naiveté. In fact, it is more probably a reflection of associated guilt which is manifested in another. Any individual who has been around football for any period of time knows that ''elbows fly'' on the first play from scrimmage. This is when each man tells his opponent ''who is boss.'' Yet let a player get ''caught'' for punching and everyone exhibits great shock. ''How could such a nice boy do a thing like that? Why he goes to church every Sunday.'' Yes. But this is Saturday. And on Saturday the name of the game is *kill*. Do we really expect him to practice the Ten Commandments in front of 60,000 people? I think not. We might *like* him to. But we don't *expect* him to. Yet overtly we give the impression that the morality of sport is identical to the morality of the choir. It seems it is high time we either change the nature of sport (which is highly unlikely), or stop the hypocrisy and *admit* to ourselves the existing ethic. To condone, covertly, and punish, overtly, is not my idea of authenticity.

Our expressed purpose and preference in sport is clear. It is not comradeship, self-discovery, or aesthetics. I don't care what the ''level'' of participation is—be it six-year-olds or sixty-year-olds—man plays to succeed. And success is measured by pushing the other guy down, just a little, so that you, as you harness the forces of nature, climb a little higher. Each time we climb a little higher. Each child learns that some day if he works hard and is lucky (but he also learns he has to *make* his own "breaks"), he might grow up to be the champion.

The athlete *knows* the acceptable moral code; however, within this frame he might make many varied value decisions. While he might select to play professional baseball as opposed to seeking a college education, it is not an unethical decision. It is simply an expressed preference. This is what he *likes*. Values are *not* moral imperatives. Since man is *not*, in any sense, forced into action, it would seem wise that we make room for the values we locate in sport. Again, no one is saying this is what we *want*. All that is being said is this is what *is*. Let us not make the mistake of so many who preceded us. Let us recognize *situations* in sport as they exist; and let us stop in the game of self-deception. No life could be more immoral than where one refuses to be aware of his own existence.

Note

1. For a most interesting "lay" discussion on contemporary values see, "On Having a Sense of Values," The Royal Bank of Canada, Monthly Letter. December, 1962.

References

Buber, M.: *I and Thou*. (R.G. Smith, Trans.), Edinburgh, T. & T. Clark, 1953.
Poppi, A.: Le Morale de Situatione. *Miscellanea Francescana*, **57**, 3-63, 1957.
Umminger, W.: *Superman, Heroes and Gods*. (J. Clark, Trans.), London, Thames & Hudson, 1963.

Sport, Religion and Human Well-Being

Brian W.W. Aitken

Introduction

North Americans have entered upon a love affair with sports. Given the time, money and emotion that we invest on a plethora of sports, one might go further and suggest that sport is rapidly becoming a new cultural religion in North America. Many factors have contributed to this apotheosis of sport. The most obvious of these is a combination of rising personal affluence and mushrooming free time. In an age of leisure sport has replaced work as a central life interest. Another factor is the disappearance of the Puritan detestation of games and amusements. In a sports-crazy society few of us feel that an involvement in sports is a "fearfull Ingratitude and Provocation unto the Glorious God" [2]. But perhaps the most powerful stimulus to the enthronement of sport atop the hierarchy of American activities has been the widespread belief that sport functions as a primary reinforcer of social values and goals. Sport in our culture gives support and sanctification to the North American belief that achievement, success, hard work and discipline are the chief ways to godliness. To put this somewhat differently, sport helps to define our personal identity by supplying us with an appropriate image of what it means to be human. Of course, in a pluralistic society there are many images which shape our behavior. And as writers like David Riesman (*The Lonely Crowd*) and Charles Reich (*The Greening of America*) have shown, images of man are always in a state of change. Nevertheless, it is my belief that there is one image which has come to dominate and to shape the behavior of industrial man, namely, that of *homo faber*, man the fabricator. As Keen puts it, "The image of homo faber is the key to the contemporary identity . . . the central organizational image of modern man" [6]. According to this image, man must pursue the *vita activa*, and the goal of all his activity is the fabrication of a world and the fabrication of himself. To put this in religious language, *homo faber* in the absence of religious belief attempts to save himself. Sport in North America not only reflects these promethean aspirations of modern man, but it also tends to support and give credence to the view that "man is the measure of all things."

The Folly of Homo Faber

The *homo faber* image of man has had both a positive and negative effect on the quality of human life in modern industrial society. It was the birth of the *homo faber* image that freed Western man from religious and political tutelage and permitted him to take charge of his own destiny. And certainly man's view of himself as a maker or fabricator has been the major dynamic in the development of a technological society which in turn has bestowed upon man so many indisputable blessings. Mesthene lists some of the fruits of man's "tool making":

> What is new about our age . . . (is that) our technical prowess literally bursts with the promise of new freedom, enhanced human dignity and unfettered aspiration [9].

Yet at the same time the *homo faber* image of a man has created in industrial man a profound sense of alienation. It seems that the more industrial man has assumed control over his exterior world, over his body and his own behavior, the more he has lost touch with his own interior. This despiritualization of industrial man has been extensively documented and analyzed by a great variety of writers for over a century. Marx, for example, writing in the 19th century, warned that industrial-capitalistic society had made man into an economic commodity and Emile Durkheim spoke of the experience of *anomie* or the lack of inner values and norms. In this century the nature of man's alienation has been further dissected from many different perspectives. Fromm suggests that modern man experiences himself "as an impoverished thing, dependent on powers outside himself" [3]. Arthur Koestler calls modern man "the ghost in the machine." Albert Camus has vividly portrayed modern man as a "stranger," and theologian Harvey Cox claims that technological society has perpetrated "a seduction of the spirit." But perhaps the writer who has most poignantly explained the nature and origins of modern man's alienation is Horney, who suggests that alienation results from a deeply imbedded and unresolved neurosis. The neurotic individual is one who devotes all his energy and imagination toward the creation of an "idealized image" of self rather than toward the realization of the actual potential of the self. The neurotic person is driven by a constant search for glory and this search manifests itself outwardly in an inordinate striving for perfection, an insatiable need to excel at everything and by a desire to gain a vindictive triumph over others in every human relationship. The result of this drive for self-glory is self-hatred and self-contempt because of the neurotic individual's failure to live up to the idealized image of himself. What the neurotic personality lacks, argues Horney, is an appropriate sense of his own limitations.

> Every neurotic is loath to recognize limitations to what he expects of himself and believes is possible to attain [4].

This analysis of the neurotic personality gives us a lucid picture of the inner side of alienation. Furthermore, it exposes the folly of *homo faber*. Underlying the *homo faber* image of man is an unwillingness to accept the real self with its limited potential, combined with a neurotic desire to achieve the ideal of the perfect. The tragedy of *homo faber* is that in attempting to be godlike, *homo faber* loses contact with his finite but unique humanness.

In a culture dominated by the *homo faber* image of man all human activity becomes a source of alienation. But sport in particular seems to be an alienating force. And the element in sport which most exacerbates alienation is winning. Of course, winning is an essential component of sport. No matter what the level of sport there is always present a desire to achieve a good or better outcome. Yet in contemporary sport we are confronted with a perverted or alienated form of winning. Today winning does not involve just the desire to demonstrate a superiority of skills which is a normal goal of any game; rather, it involves an inordinate desire to win in an absolute sense, a desire to dominate, to obliterate, to wipe out the opponent. Winning in our contemporary sports reflects a desire to achieve a vindictive triumph over the opposition.

This alienated form of winning is particularly manifested in professional or highly organized and competitive amateur sport, or in what physical educators and sports' sociologists term "athletics." "Athletics," according to Keating, "is essentially a competitive activity, which has for its end, victory in the contest, and which is characterized by a spirit of dedication, sacrifice and intensity" (unpublished data). In athletics at all levels there is much evidence for believing that Vince Lombardi's often quoted proclamation—"Winning isn't everything—it's the only thing"—has become a statement of faith. And it is my opinion that most of the other vices connected with contemporary athletics, which have been extensively catalogued by writers like Paul Hoch, Leonard Schecter, Bob Lipsyte, Dave Meggyesy, Bruce Kidd and John MacFarlane, all have been accentuated by the inordinate desire to win, to achieve a vindictive triumph over the opposition. Drug abuse; the taking of bennies before and tranquilizers after the game; excessive commercialization, the buying and selling of players in a fashion reminiscent of a cattle auction; the specter of violence, the brutal intimidation of an often superiorly skilled opponent—all have been prompted by the increased pressure to win an ultimate victory. Even the increased technologicalization of sport can be interpreted in the same light. Today athletes more than willingly submit themselves to new sports techniques: the time study of performance, power skating, isometric exercise programs, or use the latest scientifically refined equipment. (Who can forget the science fiction costumes designed by Messerschmidt of the German bobsledders at last winter's Olympics!) Why? The answer is obvious: to enhance their chances of winning. Unfortunately, not everyone can be a winner. Even perennial winners suffer an occasional defeat. Muhammad Ali has blown a fight or two, Secretariat suffered at least one loss in his career and the Montreal Canadians do manage to lose at least a handful of games each season. The tragedy of the modern athlete is that he is not prepared to accept and live with defeat. Defeat or failure evokes feelings of frustration, doubt, anxiety and self-contempt, and these feelings in turn only tend to further aggravate the basic drive toward self-glorification. But in the process the game is destroyed. The modern athlete, obsessed by the desire to achieve his idealized image, has no qualms about circumventing the rules of the game. Cheating is condoned and violence is tolerated, if the goal is victory.

But winning in this perverted or alienated form characterizes not only athletics but sport in general. According to Keating, sport is a broader reality than athletics. Sport "is a kind of diversion which has for its direct and immediate end, fun, pleasure and delight, and which is dominated by a spirit of moderation and generosity" (unpublished data). In a society of rapid change which makes personal identity extremely tenuous, in a society where high-powered advertising pushes an idealized image of self in order to sell more goods and services, even the Saturday sportsman is driven to seek an ultimate triumph. In playing our games we all nourish fantasies of playing pick-up hockey like Bobby Orr, making a curling take-out like Hec Gervais or putting like Jack Nicklaus. But our own limited skills waken us rudely from our pipe dreams resulting in feelings of frustration and self-contempt which manifest themselves outwardly in a great variety of unsportsmanlike conduct, i.e., the breaking of curling brooms, the hurling of golf clubs or arguing with the umpire or referee.

It must be noted that this perverted or alienated form of winning characterizes not only the participants in sports but the spectators as well. The average fan (the term fan is, after all, an abbreviation for fanatic) seeks not just entertainment but a satisfaction of his inner drive for perfection, success and absolute victory. This perhaps explains the inordinate identification we make with sports heroes in our culture. Through our favorite sports stars and teams we vicariously achieve the self-glory we never experience in everyday life. As a New York sports reporter put it in a moment of self-reflection:

> For 27 years I have designated certain athletic teams as extensions of myself, their defeats and victories are my own and at age 34 there is little I can do about it [10].

No area of sport today then is exempt from this perverted or alienated sense of winning. All sport consequently exacerbates modern man's alienation from his real self. What John McMurtry says of pro football can be applied to all sport: "Pro football is a sick society's projection of itself into public spectacle" [8].

The Case for Homo Tempestivus

Sport, however, need not be a primary agent of alienation in human life. On the contrary, sport can liberate men to experience human wholeness. Maheu eloquently lists the possibilities for human well-being implicit in sport.

> Sport is an order of chivalry, a code of ethics and aesthetics, recruiting its members from all classes and all peoples. Sport is a truce; in an era of antagonisms and conflicts, it is the respite of the gods in which fair competition ends in respect and friendship. Sport is education . . . that of character. Sport is

culture because it creates beauty and above all, for those who usually have the least opportunity to feed upon it [7].

Sport can create human well-being or wholeness in a great variety of ways. But for sport to have this liberating impact on human life, what is required a priori is for modern man to adopt a new image of man or a new understanding of what it means to be human. As I have mentioned, it is the *homo faber* image of man which is at the root of modern man's alienation. But this does not mean that this image of man should be discarded completely. The *homo faber* image of man does point to something essential in human life. We are born to create, to fabricate and to do, but not exclusively. It seems to me that the *homo faber* image presents us with too limited a view of man. Man has other needs to be satisfied if he is to be authentically human. It is my belief that we need to develop in our culture a more holistic view of man, if he is to experience a measure of well-being.

In theological circles the writer who provides us with the most comprehensive analysis of authentic humaneness is Keen, who states that authentic man is best understood as *homo tempestivus*, the timely, seasonable or opportune man [6]. *Homo tempestivus* combines the virtues of two modes of being in the world which were first articulated by the classical Greeks. One is the Apollonian way, which incarnates all those virtues which were associated with the god Apollo. The Apollonian way is characterized by the ego, reasonableness, order, discipline and balance. The Apollonian man is driven to create order and meaning out of the chaos of experience. He needs to know and to control in order to gain security. The Apollonian way is the dominant thrust in the *homo faber* mentality; they share the same desire to fabricate a meaningful world. But the Apollonian mode of being contains a virtue which is totally lacking in the *homo faber* mentality, namely, balance. Writes Keen, "Wisdom or authentic life in the Apollonian tradition consists of learning the rules and boundaries, and distinguishing with clarity between that which belongs to mortality and that which is immortal, between the knowable and the unknowable, the possible and the impossible, man and God" [6]. In short, the Apollonian way always strives toward the mean. The Socratic admonition "nothing in excess" is the categorical imperative.

The second mode of being in the world is the Dionysian way. In the pantheon of Greek gods Dionysus was a wild and mysterious god associated with wine, feasting, fertility and change in general. The Dionysian way espouses those virtues avoided by the Apollonian way: ecstasy, license, revelry, feeling and wonder. Wisdom in the Dionysian tradition involved an openness to novelty and to a diversity of experiences and, most importantly, an unwillingness to accept any limitations. Where the Apollonian mode of being fears and attempts to order chaos, the Dionysian mode of being affirms and celebrates chaos.

Both of these modes of being in the world, according to Keen, have serious defects and, if followed exclusively, can lead to pathological behavior. The Apollonian model can create in an individual feelings of captivity, limitedness and impotence. In seeking order and security, the Apollonian man forfeits freedom and spontaneity. The Dionysian model, on the other hand, can lead to feelings of anomie, grandiosity, limitlessness nd omnipotence. The Dionysian man lacks an internal order and a healthy sense of limits.

These two models of human life are of course perennial, and they often conflict. The current conflict between the so-called counter-culture—espousing feeling, "doing your own thing," being open to new experiences—and the mainstream of contemporary society—advocating order, security and conformity—is an example of the perennial conflict between these two modes of being. Keen's point is that authentic human life can be experienced only if a delicate balance is struck between the two models of behavior. But the question is how? "How is it possible to combine the virtues of Apollo and Dionysus within a single model of man" [6]? The answer, according to Keen, is that we must see time and not space as the primary organizing principle in human experience. Time, he argues, is the primary context in which we live out our lives. And it is because time is the stage of human life that Keen believes the image of man as *homo tempestivus* is so evocative. *Homo tempestivus* is the timely or opportune man. He has the sense to do the fitting or timely thing at each moment. The fitting thing might involve ordering, fabricating or limiting oneself, but it also might mean enjoying, celebrating or letting things happen. *Homo tempestivus* can act in either an Apollonian or Dionysian way; the determining factor is what the present moment demands. The writer of Ecclesiastes (3:1-4) has captured well the wisdom of *homo tempestivus*.

> For everything there is a season, and a time for everything under heaven . . .
> a time to break down and a time to build up, a time to mourn and a time to laugh.

Homo Tempestivus **and Liberation**

Keen's notion of *homo tempestivus* offers us a profound insight into the nature of man. It offers a model for behavior which can help men to achieve a measure of wholeness. With respect to sport I believe that this image of man as *homo tempestivus* can liberate sport to be sport. As I have stressed, sport in itself is not alienating; sport has become a major dehumanizing factor because of the kind of culture we live in. In North American society we impose on sport the values and ideals implicit in the workaday world. This is not to suggest that sport can ever function exclusive of society. I hold to an integrationalist view of society and human life. Each component of any society is to some extent a microcosm of the whole. Nevertheless, in our society, the dominant forces, captured in the *homo faber* image of man, tend to destroy the reality and essence of sport. *Homo tempestivus* is a liberating image of man because the timely or opportune man is free to participate in sport for its own sake. Sport, after all, is a form of play and what Huizinga suggests of play is also true of sport. "Play . . . is a free activity standing quite consciously outside 'ordinary' life as being 'not serious.' . . . It is an activity connected with no material interest, and no profit can be gained by it. It proceeds within its own proper boundaries of time and space according to fixed rules and in an orderly manner" [5].

Homo tempestivus has the sensitivity to know when to play, when to drop the cares of the everyday world and to enter into another realm and accept its specific rules and realities. But this is not to say that in playing sports *homo tempestivus* rejects one of the two modes of being that shape his identity. Playing should not be identified exclusively, as it so often is, with the Dionysian mode of being in the world. Every human activity, sport included, requires a balance between these two modes of being if it is to provide a sense of well-being. Sport does involve a discharge of emotion, spontaneity, exuberance and letting go (of rationality), but it also can involve a creation of and a willingness to accept order. It involves an acceptance of limits, but at the same time an openness to new experiences. In other words, both the Apollonian and Dionysian modes of being should function in sport and this applies to both the athlete and to the casual sportsman. The athlete needs to balance his discipline, regimentation and drive for victory with spontaneous and exuberant play, and the sportsman needs to balance his spontaneous and nonserious play with some acceptance of rules, meaningful competition and some desire to improve his skills. Without this balance sport can become a dull and perhaps dehumanizing experience for both.

Homo tempestivus always seeks the mean between extremes and this has some interesting ramifications for winning. As I have argued, winning is an essential part of sport. As Weiss has pointed out, from the beginning of time men have involved themselves in sport and been absorbed by it because it is one of the few areas of life which gives every man an equal chance of attaining a limited degree of excellence [11]. Winning in contemporary sport, however, has as its goal not just the achievement of a limited degree of excellence, but the achievement of an absolute, unlimited victory. It seems to me that the *homo tempestivus* image of man can liberate us from this perverted and alienated sense of winning. *Homo tempestivus*, the timely man, seeks a balance between doing too much and not achieving enough. Once again, whether *homo tempestivus* is involved in athletics or casual sport he strikes this balance. The athlete by definition attempts to excel, to win the contest, but he does not attempt to win an ultimate, cosmic victory because he knows he cannot be God. The casual sportsman, on the other hand, is not satisfied with spontaneous or undirected play. He does compete in the game in a less skillful and more relaxed way than the athlete, but he plays with the knowledge that in playing the game to the best of his ability he can experience a measure of victory. The *homo tempestivus* image of man then can liberate sport to be sport and, in so doing, it permits sport to convey on human life a measure of wholeness.

But the *homo tempestivus* image of man has one last ramification. I believe that it can not only liberate sport to be sport, but that it also can liberate men for religion. *Homo tempestivus* does not impose the reality of the workaday world on the game; he is free to experience the game as another world, as an extraordinary happening. Berger has perceptively captured this extraordinary or religious dimension of play. He writes:

When one is playing, one is on a different time, no longer measured by the standard units of the larger society, but rather by the peculiar ones of the game in question. In the 'serious' world it may be 11 a.m., on such and such a day, month and year. But in the universe in which one is playing it may be the third round, the fourth act, the allegro movement, or the second kiss. In playing one steps out of one time into another. . . . In other words, in joyful play it appears as if one were stepping not only from one chronology into another but from time into eternity [1].

In other words, in playing, suffering and our movement toward death seem to be bracketed and suspended for the moment. And the joy one experiences in this situation is apprehended "in a barely inconceivable way, as being a joy forever" [1]. Because authentic sport gives to us this experience of an extraordinary time, it can act as a "signal of transcendence"; it can give to us a ground for believing that there is a mysterious reality at the foundation of human experience and that this reality is trustable.

References

1. Berger, P.: A Rumour of Angels. Pelican, 1969, pp. 76-77.
2. Dulles, F.R.: A History of Recreation: America Learns to Play. Appleton, Century, Crofts, 1965, p. 18.
3. Fromm, E.: The Sane Society. Fawcett, 1955, p. 114.
4. Horney, K.: Neurosis and Human Growth. Norton, 1950, p. 50.
5. Huizinga, J.: Homo Ludens. Beacon Press, 1950, p. 13.
6. Keen, S.: An Apology for Wonder. New York: Harper and Row, 1969, pp. 117, 153, 196, chap. 6.
7. Maheu, R., cited by McMurtry, W.: Report on the Investigation and Inquiry Into Violence in Amateur Hockey, August 1974.
8. McMurtry, J., quoted by Hoch, P.: Rip Off the Big Game. Doubleday-Anchor Book, 1972, p. 8.
9. Mesthene, E.: What Modern Science Offers the Church. Saturday Review, Nov. 19, 1966, p. 30.
10. Schwartz, J.: Harper's Magazine, May 1973.
11. Weiss, P.: Sport: A Philosophical Enquiry. Southern Illinois University Press, 1969.

Towards a Christian Play Ethic

Arthur F. Holmes

A citizenry unprepared for leisure will degenerate in prosperous times. That, says Sebastian De Grazia, is what happened to ancient Sparta.[1] Ours is an increasingly leisured and playful society. Four-day work weeks, once beyond the wildest dreams of labor, are now becoming a reality. Early retirements are common: some retirees find new careers, while others lapse into an idleness relieved only by fishing or television. Expensive sports like skiing, once the preserve of the rich, have become commonplaces of popular culture. Since the 1960s, the traditional work ethic has been challenged by an idea of play not yet embodied in a clearcut ethic. Self-indulgence and narcissism have therefore come to mark the games people play.

On the other hand, workaholism blights the home, even work, and life itself. We need recreation and the capacity to enjoy life. But we are caught between the two extremes of self-indulgent play and compulsive work, and have no adequate map of the road we should tread.

Christian ethics rests on Christian theology and a Christian understanding of human persons as God made us to be. In proposing a Christian play ethic, then, I want first to point out various kinds of activity that play includes and how pervasive the idea of play has become, then to inquire about the place of play in relation to the nature of man, and finally to identify some needed ingredients in a theology of play. My thesis will be that play is best seen as an attitude, a state of mind, rather than as a distinguishable set of activities, and that the separation of work from play is a historical disjunction consequent upon the fall.

I. The Pervasiveness of Play

Playing with words can help us make the point. We play *with* words and play *on* words. We play with ideas, play music, play ball, play back, and play the fool. We have playboy, playbills, play therapy, play-schools, and playsuits. We playact, play down, play up, play off and role-play, until we are quite played out—or else out-played by others.

Two kinds of play emerge in this list. The first includes games, sports, and athletics (play with words, play ball, etc.), and others where the play occurs for the sake of something else (e.g., play school, play therapy, play with ideas). The second includes art, imagination, and fantasy (e.g., play music, playbills, role-play), in which play becomes aesthetic activity. But some examples (e.g., play back, play down) fit neither of these two categories but are metaphors that can function in almost any area of life.

Consider some related concepts, brothers and sisters of play, and cousins by the dozen: leisure, free time, recreation, relaxation, games, sport, humor, jokes, teas-ing and pleasing, fun and pun, contests and competitions, joy, adventure, pageant, festivity, celebration, ritual, imagination, contemplation, fantasy, myth, drama, art, creativity. Notice that sheer frivolity, utter waste, complete idleness and indolence, if relatives at all, are the prodigal children of play, the black sheep of the family. Even the term "vacation," taken literally as "emptiness," is a misfit here in com-parison with the literal meaning of "holi(holy)day."

The relatives who are in good standing, however, fall into several groups: not only games and art, but also celebration, ritual, festivity. Play then takes at least three cultural directions: first, games, sport, and athletics (notice the increasing organization, technique, and professionalization in that trilogy); second, art, drama, fantasy (notice here the increasing creativeness and play of imagination); third, festivity, ritual, and celebration (notice how they all replay the past, but with in-creasing structure). The three are not mutually exclusive. There is art in sport, and ritual too. But our point is that we play both for present enjoyment (games), and in creating new worlds of experience (art), and in reliving the past (celebration). That is indeed pervasive.

Academic disciplines tell a similar story:

in anthropology, we have Huizinga's *Homo Ludens*,
in sociology, Goffman's dramaturgical theory of the roles people play, and the sociology of sport,
in economics, money games and "playing the market,"
in political science, the presidential "race" and its "front runners" with their "game plans,"
in psychology, there is Freud on dreams and play,
in education, we read how children learn through play,
in history, Erasmus' *In Praise of Folly*, a title that puns on its dedicatee, Sir Thomas More (Greek, $m\bar{o}ros$ = fool), the imaginative author of *Utopia*,
in literature, we have Hesse's *Magister Ludi*, Sartre's *Les Jeux Sont Faits*,
in philosophy, Wittgenstein introduces "language games,"
in mathematics, we find game theory,
in religion, the theology of play.

Here we find not so much kinds of play-activity, but rather interest in play and analogues to it, even extensions of it, in every area of inquiry. Someone has suggested that play is the root metaphor that gives overall meaning to life in the mythologies of our day. "All the world's a play, and all the men and women merely players," said Shakespeare, and "each one in his time plays many parts." Play pervades every department of life, and cannot be kept on the fringes. Playfully man acts in everything he does.[2]

Play is thus all-pervasive, and extends beyond isolable kinds of activity. It does not lie just on the fringes of life, as if games were spare parts we don't really need in the main business of life. On the contrary, we work playfully, joke with colleagues, and tease an audience along. The old disjunction breaks down.

II. Play and the Nature of Man

In the light of play's pervasiveness, what shall we say about its proper place and purpose in human life? Two antithetical attitudes exist. Some see play as essential to human nature, even the defining characteristic of man. He is *homo ludens*, and his kinds of play distinguish him from other animals. Leisure, says Joseph Pieper, is the basis of culture, and sociologist Sebastian De Grazia documents this thesis at great length.[3] Piaget finds play essential to the cognitive development of children.[4] Harvey Cox claims that essential to retaining our humanity is the festivity that links us to our past, and the fantasy that links us to possible futures.[5] But some have outdone themselves: Nietzsche went so far as to reduce all of life and thought to masks in a play, taking nothing seriously except the will to power—in effect, the will to win—so that all of life is a biologically driven powerplay. The flower children of the '60s said it more ironically, and today it is a self-infatuated narcissism that speaks. On this view everything is play, self-centered play, but still no play ethic exists.

On the other hand, man is defined as *homo faber*, the maker of things. Work, not play, is the meaning of life. Play may indeed provide an escape valve to help us work harder when vacation ("empty") time is over. But then nonproductive play becomes productive in the end. We commercialize sport and bring the latest medical technology to heighten athletic prowess, until the human meaning of play is forgotten in the technology of medics and trainers. Bruce Haley traces this trend among nineteenth century Victorians, who required sports in school "for moral self-improvement." The battle of Waterloo was won on the playing fields of Eton. Meanwhile a wealthy playing class absorbed itself in such games as war and mercantilism as well as in field sports and athletics. Their pursuit of more wealth, said Ruskin, was a game "absolutely without purpose." London, the center of British finance and commerce, became "a great city of play; very nasty play, and very hard play. . . . a huge billiard table without the cloth, and with pockets as deep as the bottomless pit."[6] They turned play into work, and work into the worst of play, with unbridled competitiveness.

The lack of playful play is evident today in the Vince Lombardi slogan, "winning isn't the main thing, it's the only thing," a slogan that at times seems true of the political and business worlds as well. Institutionalized play is no longer festive and free, but has become big business. Play for its own sake seems to have lost meaning, as if, in the words of Bernard Shaw, "hell is an endless holiday: nothing to do, and plenty of money to spend on doing it."[7] So really work is all that counts.

This attitude may have arisen in reaction against the overplayfulness of Romanticists, themselves in reaction against the Enlightenment's rule of reason in all of life. But *homo faber* is a child of the industrial revolution, close kin to technologism, scientism, positivism, liberalism, utilitarianism, where the "ism" marks a value judgment of an exclusivist sort. Today's *homo faber* has inherited these reductionist extremes, to the loss of imaginative play and the celebrative spirit. He has little room either for playful work or for playful play, for work has swallowed up play.

Sam Keen contrasts *homo faber* and *homo ludens* as the Apollonian and Dionysian views of life.[8] For the former, life is all work, ruled by reason, law, and order, and play is only a means to that end. For the latter, life is all play, ruled by feeling and sensation, given over to life's enjoyments.

In Christian perspective, however, the meaning of being human is found in neither work nor play. In the final analysis man is neither *homo faber* nor *homo ludens*. So it is not play that will rehumanize work, but something more basic than either that rehumanizes both work and play. The task of a play ethic is not to revert to Aristotle's nonproductive activity, and separate work from play as in his aristocratic society where slaves worked while the wealthy could enjoy unproductive leisure. Play is not the key to being human, but being human is the key to play.

Man at the heart of his being is *homo religiosis*, his life to be lived in responsible relationship to God, and it is worship that is his most distinctive activity, not work and not play. Of course there are aspects of play in the celebration of worship, but more fundamentally it is the religious nature of man that gives purpose and meaning to both work and play. This must ground our play ethic, for a responsible relationship to God includes play. Hence we need a theology of play, to see more fully its purpose in relationship to God.

III. Theology and Play

Three ingredients for a theology of play stand out in my reading of Scripture. More may well be needed; in fact, it would be valuable not only to consider how each classical topic of systematic theology bears on the subject, but also to review the social history of Old Testament Israel with this in mind. My three ingredients, then, are only a beginning.[9]

1. *The analogy to play in God and his activity.* Play cannot be forced, but in order to be truly playful it must be voluntary and with a free spirit. Yet those very characteristics mark the activity of God. The eternal Trinity before creation was, from the *homo faber* standpoint, strangely unproductive: the divine being enjoyed leisure for eternal conversation, with endless time to imagine possible worlds that might or might not be created.

The "work" of creation itself was not necessary, neither logically required nor morally obligatory nor economically needful nor inwardly compulsive, but was voluntary and entirely free. God did not have to create at all, let alone to create the actual worlds he made. He created things, we are told, for his own pleasure. And on the seventh day he rested and enjoyed its goodness. The work of redemption too was voluntary and freely engaged in, not forced on God by an economy out of control. No necessity, internal or external to God, drove him to it. God redeems for his own glory and pleasure.

Calvin calls the world the theater of God's glory. So perhaps Shakespeare was right, and all we men and women are merely players, playing our many parts for God's pleasure and honor. The chief end of man, according to the Westminster divines, is to *glorify* God and *enjoy* him forever. Life, then, is celebration.

At the New York World's Fair in 1965, Jesus was depicted in *The Parable* as a pathetic clown. At first I reacted negatively. Gradually I saw: he wanted to make people laugh, by turning their usual values upside down and dancing to a different tune. With playful innocence he became the butt of others' jokes—and eventually of their sadistic turns.

This theme appears in *Ecclesiastes*. Amid the frustration and apparent emptiness of life, the enjoyments of life are still God's gifts. "There is nothing better for a man than that he should eat and drink, and find enjoyment in his labor. This . . . is from the hand of God" (2:24). "I command enjoyment, for man has no good thing under the sun but to eat, and drink, and to enjoy himself" (8:15). The New Testament likewise talks of joy in life and work, of serving with gladness. Its ideal of servanthood is not one of maximizing productivity, but of the liberty to serve joyfully, even playfully, from the heart.

2. The *Sabbath*. For one day in seven, the people of God were told to forget their work and *rest* in God's gracious provision. Even in the wilderness, where subsistence depended on collecting manna before it rotted, the day of rest applied. It was a holiday, holy before God, not a "vacation." Celebrating God's creation and his deliverance, the people gathered festively to recall the past and to anticipate the future which Sabbath rest prefigured. Because of God's provision, work need not be compulsive. Ultimately life depends on God, not on our work.

Likewise for one year in seven the land was to lie fallow, at leisure, unproductive, resting in God's provision and anticipating his kingdom. The Sabbath pictured life in a time frame between creation and the *eschaton*, a life embraced by God. Hence there need be no fear of wasting time in celebrating; nor need we take ourselves too seriously.

The same idea appears in God's words to Job, when everything seemed lost and all the fruits of his labor gone.

Behold, Behemoth, which I made as I made you: he eats grass as an ox. . . . he is the first of the works of God. . . . the mountains yield food for him, where all the wild beasts *play*. Under the lotus plants he lies. Behold, if the river is turbulent he is not frightened. (40:15-23; italics added)

It is a picture of leisure and play replacing fear of what will happen if we are not productive, a picture echoed by the birds and the lilies of the Sermon on the Mount which neither toil nor spin. For *homo religiosis* too, meaning and hope in life are not focused in work. We can afford to rest and play.

William Henry Davies, intentionally or not, suggests the same idea in a poem I was forced to learn as a boy in school.

What is this life if, full of care,
We have no time to stand and stare,
No time to stand beneath the bough
And stare as long as sheep and cow,
No time to wait 'till her mouth can
Enrich that smile her eyes began?

3. *The Kingdom of God*. "The streets of the city shall be full of boys and girls *playing in the streets*" (Zech. 8:5). The promise of the kingdom, as Lewis Smedes observes, is of restored playfulness. The year of jubilee was another foretaste, with its economic justice, joyful liberty, and peace. The Old Testament concept of *shalom* is at work here, and the psalmist's confidence:

Thou dost show me the path of life:
in Thy presence there is fullness of joy,
in Thy right hand are pleasures for evermore. (Ps. 16:11)

The Heidelberg Catechism (Day XIX) accordingly teaches that "God will take me to himself into heavenly *joy* and *glory*."

Play and its relatives find meaning and purpose, then, in a place reserved for them in God's Kingdom. There is time to laugh, time to dance, time to embrace (Eccles. 3:1-8). Like Tevye in *Fiddler on the Roof*, we can play and sing even in a strange land. Scripture begins with a garden in the cool of the day and ends with a city at play; so play—art and celebration and fun and games, and a playful spirit—is part of our calling, part of the creation mandate. It is not the play of self-indulgence, nor of shed responsibility, but of gladness and celebration in responsible relationship to God. Play requires a free spirit, rather than "free time," a spirit freed from thinking and acting as if life itself depends altogether on me. The Christian can afford to play.

So play is first an attitude of mind, and only secondly is it various kinds of activity. It is first an attitude that carries over into all of life, an attitude possible ultimately in a relationship to God that finds joyful expression in whatever we do, productive or not.

IV. A Play Ethic?

A Christian ethic must now take this theological understanding of the meaning and purpose of play, and ask how we can exercise its meaning and achieve its purpose with justice and with love. As a result of sin, work has become toil, workers are exploited, and economic life is perverted. As a result of sin also, leisure has become laziness and play self-indulgence; players are exploited, and the playful life is perverted. We live in responsible relationship to God, or we fail to do so, in work and in play. Sin and grace extend into both these mandates of creation.

Thomas Aquinas therefore expressed three cautions which we would do well to observe. First, do not take pleasure in indecent or injurious play. Second, do not lose your mental or emotional balance and self-control. Third, do not play in ways ill-fitting either the hour or the man.[10] Stated positively, play should have positive moral and other consequences, it should be properly controlled, and it should be both timely and worthily human.

One way to develop a Christian play ethic is to explore what playing in responsible relationship to God should mean for playing in the other relationships of life. In relationship to nature and its resources, questions of stewardship and respect for God's creation necessarily arise. We can play responsibly in God's world or we can play destructively and profligately, spending our natural resources on riotous living. I question the use of scarce energy resources in auto racing. I question the stewardship in roaring around a placid lake in a gas-guzzling motor boat that exhales noxious fumes. I question not only bullfighting and cockfighting, but also hunting animals for "sport alone," not for food or other responsible purposes. I question play that heedlessly defaces nature's beauty or upsets its eco-balance. Such "games" disregard the stewardly purposes and consequent limitations of man's "dominion" over nature.

In relationship to other persons, "playing in relationship to God" will forbid games (and jokes) that tend to dehumanize people created in the image of God. Aquinas's words about indecent and injurious play are well-taken. The early church rightly objected to the Roman circus, and Christians since have protested violent sports, dueling, and sadistic games; a movie like *Rollerball* is a sad commentary on our times. Christians protest pornography, and they have censured the theater and entertainment world, for not everything can be justified in the name of art, any more than in the name of other kinds of play. Play that makes sex objects out of people, play that shatters self-respect, play that stifles growth, play that is unloving, unjust, unfair, or needlessly violent must be challenged. I object to boxing as a sport, and I have some moral reservations about football (as well as both economic and educational reservations about the overly large place it sometimes takes in college and high school). We need to reinforce in sport as well as in art and celebration the kinds of values society should have. We need to ask what Christian servanthood means in competition. "The family that plays together stays together," we quip; the point in this is that play can relax hard feelings and recreate togetherness, the sense of a shared existence we so greatly need.

In relationship to oneself, it is customary to talk of the psychological, physical, and re-creational values of play, and so we ought. But it also has aesthetic and intellectual potential, and leisure incubates ideas in art and science and society. Play can socialize us. It can discipline. It can develop precision and grace with aesthetic delight. It can produce transferable qualities of cooperation, persistence, and self-denial. But it can also produce sadistic, self-indulgent, self-exalting, self-abusive, even masochistic people utterly drained of other interests. Plato says that too much physical exercise without other things can make man a beast, and too little makes him effeminate.[11] No kind of play by itself can build character: how could a Christian claim that it does? But in can provide an arena of possibilities, both good and bad, for personal development.

Yet that is not enough. Play should indeed contribute to health and well-being and work, but like everything else in life it has a religious significance that is more basic than all of these. If Christian play is enjoyment of God, if play reminds us that we rest in his provision, if it expresses the *shalom* of his Kingdom, then I can no longer take myself with utmost seriousness, not even my theories about play. Play reminds me of this. It puts me in my place, win or lose. And so it gives perspective on life, on my life in relation to God. Winning is not the only thing; it isn't even the main thing. The playful attitude of the believer is the more important thing.

Notes

1. Sebastian De Grazia, *Of Time, Work, and Leisure* (New York: Twentieth Century Fund, 1962), pp. 11-14, 426.

2. Cf. "Artistically Man Acts," Nicholas Wolterstorff's phrase in *Art in Action* (Grand Rapids, Mich.: Eerdmans, 1980), Part 1.

3. Joseph Pieper, *Leisure, the Basis of Culture* (New York: Mentor Omega, 1952). For De Grazia see above, n. 1.

4. *Play, Dreams, and Imitation in Childhood* (New York: W.W. Norton, 1962), Part 2. Cited in David LeRoy Miller, *Gods and Games* (New York: Harper & Row, 1973), pp. 122 *et passim.*

5. This is the thesis of *The Feast of Fools* (Cambridge, Mass.: Harvard University Press, 1969).

6. Bruce Haley, *The Healthy Body and Victorian Culture* (Cambridge, Mass.: Harvard University Press, 1978), p. 258.

7. Quoted by Robert Lee, *Religion and Leisure in America* (New York: Abingdon, 1964), p. 25.

8. Sam Keen, *Apology for Wonder* (New York: Harper & Row, 1969).

9. I am indebted in this section to ideas and stimuli from Miller and Keen, cited above; also to Hugh Rahner, *Man at Play* (New York: Herder & Herder, 1972); Jürgen Moltmann, *Theology of Play* (New York: Harper & Row, 1972); and Lewis Smedes, "Theology of the Playful Life," in *God and the Good*, ed. C. Orlebeke and L. Smedes (Grand Rapids, Mich.: Eerdmans, 1975); unpublished papers by Ren Broekhuizen and Robert Johnston, and comments by Nicholas Wolterstorff. Like most human efforts, this article combines something old and something borrowed with relatively little that is new.

10. *Summa Theologica* II-II, Q. 168, Art. 2.

11. *Republic* III 410c.

Sports and the Christian Life:
Reflections on Pope John Paul II's Theology of Sports

Michael P. Kerrigan

The Second Vatican Council reminded Catholic Christians that the "Church exists in the modern world." We are not oblivious and unaffected by the recent sports explosion. In fact, this "social sports phenomenon" has demonstrated the increasing need for theological reflection in order to provide a Christian understanding and vision for sports. Do the Christian ideals and the values proclaimed by sports compete with one another? Or can they complete and enhance each other? Can one reconcile secular sports values with the Gospel message?

We currently have a "sports-conscious pope" who had a swimming pool installed at the papal residence and frequently uses skiing trips as a form of personal relaxation from the demands of his job. He has attempted to provide some leadership and direction regarding the Church and sports. During his pontificate, John Paul II has given many significant addresses pertaining to sports. The following summarizes the major points of his reflections on this topic.

The Importance of Physical Recreation for Personal Development

As John Paul II reminded the Italian Olympics Committee:

> The Church has always been interested in the problem of sport because she prizes everything that contributes constructively to the harmonious and complete development of the person, body and soul. She encourages, therefore, what aims at educating, developing, and strengthening the human body in order that it may offer a better service for the attainment of personal maturation.[1]

Clearly, the Church has a positive and favorable view toward sports. Sports are seen as a form of physical recreation which develops and strengthens the human body. Since the human body is part of God's creation, it is inherently good. As Catholic Christians, we are continually reminded of our need to be "stewards of creation." Taking care of one's physical body is an example of good stewardship. As John Paul recently remarked:

> Sport is making good use of the body, an effort to reach optimum physical condition which brings marked consequences of psychological well being.[2]

This view reflects the Aristotelian notion of "a healthy body producing a healthy mind which develops a balanced person."

Physical recreation also serves as a means for relaxation.

Sports Promotes Self-Awareness and Self-Discipline

Clearly, physical recreation which encourages personal human development is a value. Moreover, as John Paul II has stated repeatedly, sports can and do promote desirable and good values both for individuals and group participants. Once again, John Paul demonstrates his high esteem for physical recreation as a means to personal human development by remarking:

> Athletic competition draws out of the human person some of one's noblest qualities and talents. The athlete must learn the secrets of one's own body, its strength and weaknesses, its stamina and its breaking point. One must develop through long hours of exercise and effort the power of concentration and the habit of discipline, learning how to hold one's strength in reserve and to conserve energy for that final moment when the victory depends on a great burst of speed or one last surge of strength.[3]

This passage embodies three important implications.

a) sports enable individuals to realize their own strengths and weaknesses
b) sports encourage the habit of self-discipline
c) sports promote the desire to practice and to improve continually according to our ability.

Through sports, an individual can realize and appreciate his/her talents, strengths and weaknesses, possibilities and limitations. In a sense, athletics and physical recreation facilitate the process of truly "knowing oneself."

Sports Foster Community

Besides promoting individual and personal values, sports can highlight other benefits for group participants, especially as an opportunity for getting to know others.

Specifically, John Paul II espouses a list of characteristics that any coach would find desirable. He upholds loyalty, fair play, generosity, friendship, solidarity, respect, and a spirit of cooperation. Clearly, John Paul II sees an affinity between sports and Christian faith when he asks the question:

> Are not these athletic values the deepest aspirations and requirements of the Gospel message?[4]

Team sports can provide occasions for both personal and group fulfillment. Teamwork offers excellent opportunities for individuals to develop the values of loyalty (supporting each other, win or lose), fair play (learning to play by the rules of the game), generosity (putting the needs of the team ahead of individual interests), friendship (a way to meet new people) and a spirit of cooperation (learning how to work with others in order to accomplish a specific goal).

Further, John Paul II draws attention to the unique characteristic which exists among athletes:

> There is present among athletes a kind of universal brotherhood, a sincere respect for each person and a lively appreciation of one another's abilities and gifts. Athletes engage in stiff competition; they like to be challenged and enjoy the excitement of a great contest. But rather than leading to rivalry and dissension such competition, when carried out in a climate of friendship, leads to a still greater mutual respect and fraternal esteem.[5]

Competition Is Beneficial

This sporting respect for others sheds a new light on competition. As the pope emphasizes:

> The necessary competition, far from being a motive of division, is seen on the contrary to be a positive factor of *dynamic emulation* possible only in a framework of mutual relations accepted, measured, and promoted.[6]

Competition should not be divisive and spark animosity. Rather, competition should encourage one to excel, to try harder, to give one's best effort, to give one's all. Engaging in competitive athletics challenges one to improve upon one's skills and to strive for realistic goals. Competition encourages a desire for continual self-improvement so that one is not satisfied with the *status quo*. There is always some new standard of athletic excellence to be attained.

Sports Are a "Training Ground" for Life in the World

John Paul II maintains that athletics offer a beneficial way for personal development and group interaction. Relaxation in the various forms of physical recreation can serve as a training ground and a way to prepare one for living in the world. For example, using one's talents, self-discipline, dealing with adversity, learning to work with others, and mutually respecting each other's abilities (all values promoted by sports) can assist an individual to become a better person, an exemplary citizen, and a good Christian. What we learn from athletic participation should permeate the other areas of our life—such as our spiritual and social development. John Paul II sees sports as having valuable goals outside the realm of athletic competition:

> Sport, because of the wholesome elements it gives value to and exalts, may become more and more a vital instrument for the moral and spiritual elevation of the human person and therefore contribute to the construction of an orderly, peaceful, and hard-working society.[7]

He also notes:

> The Church approves and encourages sports seeing in it a form of gymnastics of the body and of the spirit, a training for social relations based on respect for others and for one's own person and an element of social cohesion which also fosters friendly relations on the international level.[8]

Sports Promote World Peace

Obviously, the pope values sports not only for the physical development of the body but also for its possibilities for moral and social education both on the national and international levels. Sports as an important and necessary part of human culture can serve to unite peoples of the world and even encourage world peace. As John Paul II notes, sports can enable us in a unique way:

> . . . to become citizens who love social order and peace; it will teach us to see in sports competition, not struggles between rivals, not factors of division but peaceful sporting events in which a sense of respect for the competitor must never be lacking even in the rightful effort to achieve victory.[9]

Likewise, we are reminded that when a sport is conducted on the international level:

> It becomes a propitious element to overcome multiple barriers in such a way to reveal and strengthen the unity of the human family beyond all differences of race, culture, politics, or religion.[10]

Indeed, John Paul II's theological reflections show us that sports and physical recreation offer more than initially meets the eye. The rightful practice of sports can benefit individuals, society, nations, and even the world.

The Papal Tradition Continues

The popes of the 20th century have repeatedly promoted and encouraged athletic endeavors. The present pontiff bases his reflections on the example of his predecessors. As he indicates, Pius X supported Baron Pierre de Coubertin's attempts to reinstitute the Olympic Games. The potential benefits of athletic recreation and physical development were topics for several of Pius XII's addresses. When the 1960 Summer Olympic Games were held in Rome, John XXIII held a special papal audience for athletes from 83 nations as well as the International Olympic Committee. In 1966, Paul VI reminded the members of the International Olympic Committee:

> The practice of sport at the international level has turned out to be a remarkable factor in the progress of brotherhood between people and the spread of the ideal of peace among nations. They learn to confront each other in the peaceful struggles of the stadium and the court and no longer in the fratricidal struggles of the battlefields.[11]

It is evident that John Paul II is not doing something new. He continues in the long-standing Church tradition which sees the value of sports.

A Christian Vision for Today

John Paul II extols the benefits of sports on three distinct levels:

1. they assist the individual in terms of bodily health and personal growth
2. they contribute to the development of society and human culture
3. they provide a means to overcome such barriers as race, culture, and language on the international level.

Overall, sports are a positive good that should be cultivated by individuals, societies, and nations. Yet, Pope John Paul is not naive regarding the negative and detrimental aspects which sports and athletic competition can provoke:

> When sporting competitions are swept away by violence, when there is injustice, fraud, eagerness for gain, economic and political pressures or discrimination, then sport is reduced to the level of a tool of power and money.[12]

In terms of our American situation, we are challenged both as participants and spectators to ask ourselves: as participants, do we value self-discipline, loyalty, fair play, respect, and a spirit of cooperation? What are the underlying reasons for strengthening our physical bodies? How do physical recreation and athletic competition influence our personal, social, and spiritual development? As spectators, do we see sports as an art and form of relaxation? Do we value fair play and respect opponents' abilities? Or do we become self-centered and advocate winning at any cost, cheating, physical violence, animosity, and a type of athletic competition which is counterproductive to improving the human condition?

John Paul II's reflections on sports articulate a positive and optimistic understanding. As a "church which exists in the modern world," we need to deal with the athletic explosion. Sports and the Gospel message do not compete with each other. In a sense, they enhance and complete one another in a unique way which encourages personal fulfillment, the development of society and human culture, and offer a path to world peace. Indeed, athletics can transform the world. As Christians we are continually challenged to seek ways to promote the value of sports in light of Christian ideals for today's world. John Paul II's insights give us some clear directions and goals for which to strive. May we, like St. Paul, continue "to fight the good fight, finish the race, and keep the faith!"

Notes

1. John Paul II, "Address to members of the Council of the National Olympic committee, the presidents of the Italian Sports Federation about sport as training ground for virtue" on 20 Dec. 1979, *L'Osservatore Romano* (English edition; no. 2 [615] 14 Jan. 1980), pp. 15-16.

2. John Paul II, "Homily at Mass for participants in the International Jubilee for Athletes" on 12 April 1984, *L'Osservatore Romano* (English edition; no. 17 [831] 24 April 1984), p. 3.

3. John Paul II, "Message to members of the International Athletic Group about athletic competition" on 20 March 1982, *L'Osservatore Romano* (English edition; no. 14-15 [729] 5-12 April 1982), p. 8.

4. John Paul II, "Message to participants in the Twelfth Youth Games held in Rome, urges them to integrate physical gifts with spiritual ones" on 2 Oct. 1980, *L'Osservatore Romano* (English edition; no. 44 [656] 3 Nov. 1980), p. 10.

5. Ibid, See note 3, p. 8.

6. John Paul II, "Address to participants in the 33rd water skiing competition of Europe, Africa, and the Mediterranean about the virtues of sports" on 31 Aug. 1979, *L'Osservatore Romano* (English edition; no. 38 [599] 17 Sept. 1979), p. 5.

7. Ibid. See note 1, p. 16.

8. John Paul II, "Address to directors and athletes of the Milan football team about the values of sports" on 12 May 1979, *L'Osservatore Romano* (English edition; no. 22 [583] 28 May 1979), p. 4.

9. John Paul II, "Address to young people taking part in the 13th Youth Games in Rome urging them to let the practice of sports always promote peace" on

11 Oct. 1981, *L'Osservatore Romano* (English edition; no. 42 [706] 19 Oct. 1981), p. 7.

10. Ibid. See note 6, p. 5.

11. Paul VI, *Insegnamenti de Paolo VI* (1966), p. 207.

12. John Paul II, "Address to the International Olympic Committee about the value of sports" on 27 May 1982, *L'Osservatore Romano* (English edition; no 40 [753] 4 Oct. 1982), p. 10.

Real Men, Short Hair

Tony Simpson

It is time that American coaches stopped allowing themselves to be personally represented by male athletic teams and individuals who look like females. It is time that American coaches realized that a male's hair is not just an American tradition but an issue involving biblical principles; time that coaches stopped rationalizing and compromising their common sense; time to show the American athlete that his most valuable characteristic is not physical ability but respect for authority. It is also time that American coaches or any real American anywhere realized that the authority issue is at stake as never before in the history of the United States. It's time that real men stand up for what they know to be right even if it means their job, loss of pseudofriends or anything else.

Short hair on the male is not just an American tradition; it's a matter of biblical principles. As translated from the Greek, the original language of the New Testament, 1 Corinthians 11:14 says, "Doesn't even common sense dictate to you that long hair on a man is a disgrace unto him?"

Apparently, most Texas coaches agree with this passage even if they did not previously know it existed. At the 1972 Texas High School Coaches Clinic in Houston, which was attended by more than 5,000 coaches, you would be hard-pressed to find one whose personal grooming habits did not show him to be a real man. However, it's a different story when you look at many of their athletic teams.

Why do many coaches rationalize and compromise their norms and standards of good grooming habits and allow themselves to be personally represented by males that look like females? If a coach has good grooming habits and looks like a male, only rationalization and compromise would permit him to be represented by anything resembling sloppiness and abnormality. Only in the animal world is the male designed to be the most attractive or the prettiest—for example, the male lion has the mane, the peacock the feathers. This is normal in the animal world only. Therefore, it should be obvious to anyone with an ounce of sense that imitating animals in this respect is ABNORMAL.

However, a male with long hair IS cute, he IS pretty, and he IS sweet. And that is just exactly what females, young and old, who are not real women in their souls like, isn't it? It is apparently what some of the so-called male coaches in this country like also. But since when are athletes' grooming standards set by females with warped norms and standards? It should be pointed out here that the only reason males are free to look like females and that their coaches are free to permit this is because we have had real men, who were not cute, not sweet and not pretty, with courage and sense enough to kill our enemies on battlefields all over the globe. What will our present-day cute, sweet and pretty boys do when it comes their turn to fight in battle as every generation of Americans has had to do? Maybe they will die the sin unto death like King Saul for failure to kill the enemy. If the coaches of America would grow long hair like their athletes, we might be able to scare the Russian and Chinese Communists to death with our lack of masculinity.

Let's stop compromising and rationalizing our commonsense standards that can be backed up with doctrine. If common sense dictates that long hair on a man is a disgrace, let's stop compromising our common sense by allowing it. The coaching profession is one of the few large professions with any common sense left.

A male with long hair is a sign of rejection of authority—his own authority over himself as well as the authority of the laws of establishment. Under the laws of establishment, God designed the male to dominate the woman and to initiate the woman (1 Cor. 11:3), just as He designed Christ to dominate man: "But I would have you know that the head of every man is Christ; and the head of the woman is the man; and the head of Christ is God [the Father]." A man's short hair is a sign of authority over the woman and means he recognizes his authority. A woman's long hair is a sign of submission to her man and means she recognizes the authority of her right man over her: "Doesn't even common sense dictate to you that long hair on a man is a disgrace unto him? But if a woman have long hair it is a glory to her; for her hair is given for a covering" (1 Cor. 11:14-15).

Before a man can have authority over his right woman, he must first have authority over himself. We have a generation of kids who have no authority over themselves. This means no self-discipline, which is the worst thing that can happen to an individual not only in athletics but with regard to life in general. With no self-discipline there is no recognition of authority, and this makes the athlete uncoachable, always trying to do his own garbage. Without self-discipline and respect for authority you have the current uncontrollable problem among the young with drug abuse, crime and sexual perversion.

It is not normal for a male to be in submission to a female and like it. But young American males, and many not so young, wear their hair long simply because they know the females will like it. These so-called males are in submission to the warped standards of females who like to set the dress and grooming standards for their mousy husbands, their pantywaist boyfriends or their feminine sons. A woman who wants a feminine-appearing mate is not a real woman in her soul. Apparently today's mousy males enjoy their submission and actually are fooled into believing they look better with long hair. Bible doctrine says this is ABNORMAL, a complete reversal of God's plan for the human race and a characteristic of national disintegration. A good hair code will get the abnormals out of athletics before they become coaches and bring their "loser" standards into the coaching profession.

The only visible person of the Trinity, Christ, had short hair, and his hair was white: "His head and His hairs were white like wool, as white as snow; and His eyes were as a flame of fire" (Revelation 1:14).

The word "hairs" in Revelation 1:14, as written in Greek, is *hae triches* and means "short hair." Now, if Christ had short hair, and His hair was white, and the Bible is the mind of Christ, then for Christ to have had long hair He had to be inconsistent with His own mind, which is impossible. Therefore, any drawing or image of Christ showing Him to be a skinny, weak, long-haired hippie is totally wrong, anti-biblical, anti-Christian and therefore stupid. This includes any drawings in any Bible that depict Christ in this manner. This is important to know because of those Bible "scholars" who say, "Christ had long hair, so it must be all right." Christ did not have long hair, and long hair on a male is *not* all right.

Many people have suggested that the story of Samson proves me wrong or contradicts the Bible, but actually it strengthens my point. Samson was a Nazarite who took a threefold Nazarite vow: 1) no razor or haircut; 2) no alcoholic beverages; 3) no women. The purpose of the vow was to test the man's complete *submission* to an abnormal way of life. The key word here is "submission," because this vow is an analogy to a woman voluntarily submitting to the authority of her right man in marriage. Since Samson was to be submissive he had *long hair*, which on a woman is a sign of submission. The vow was a bona fide Christian vow at that time in history only, and only for certain Nazarites. The reason Samson lost his strength when Delilah shaved his head was that he had broken all three vows and the Lord took his strength as discipline. Samson's strength was directly from the Lord, not directly from his hair. In Judges 16:22, Samson's hair had begun to grow out again, but he still had to call on the Lord to renew his strength in Judges 16:28. Too bad the long-haired males of today refuse to take all of Samson's vow.

Long hair on a male is abnormal and means:

a. He has rejected authority over himself and over his own woman.

b. He has the soul of a woman as indicated by:

    1. His free will dictating to him that he must look like a woman.

    2. The fact that long hair is a sign of submission. (Women's souls were not designed to lead or to fight but to submit to their right man. 1 Cor. 11:3 and 7-9.)

c. A nation of males with long hair is a nation of men with women's souls looking for someone or something to submit to. Therefore, every time you look at a male with long hair you're looking at a potential slave.

d. Long hair on a male is not just a fad that will pass but a sign of rejection of authority. Rejection of authority destroys individuals, teams and nations. One generation of authority- rejecting males makes a nation ripe for destruction and slavery. As written in Hosea 4:1 and 5-6:

> Hear the word of the Lord ye children of Israel; for the Lord hath a controversy with the inhabitants of the land, because there is no truth, nor mercy, nor knowledge of God in the land. . . .
>
> Therefore shalt thou fall in the day, and the prophets [false teachers] also shall fall with thee in the night, and I will destroy thy mother.
>
> My people are destroyed for lack of knowledge: because thou hast rejected knowledge I will also reject thee, that thou shalt be no priest to me: seeing thou has forgotten the law of thy God, I will also forget thy children.

The fact that males are wearing their hair long does not mean that the United States is going to be destroyed. But it does indicate that the condition of the soul is not only abnormal but *reversed*, and this is characteristic of national disintegration.

Whatever the reason for allowing long-haired male athletes to compete, it is never bona fide in any way. A coach should see each individual, and the team as a unit, as a personal representative of his own standards. They pick up your standards as a leader, and that's why your standards must be right. Now, when you make your decision between being personally represented by walking disgraces or males that look like males, at least you'll know the true issue: your free will to coach according to the absolute standards of doctrine, or your free will to go down with the rest of the women.

Death in the Ring:
A Pastoral Dilemma

Carmen and Dorothy Leone

The priest and the young prizefighter sit side by side before the television cameras on "Good Morning, America." The fighter, just weeks before, had struck a death-blow to the head of his opponent in a nationally televised title fight, rekindling the moral controversy over boxing. The priest? Of course, he is there to wage verbal battle with the fighter.

But wait. The priest is not on the attack. The boxer is not on the defense. They actually like each other. When it is the priest's turn to speak out, there is no admonishment. The promised battle never develops.

The story of Ray "Boom Boom" Mancini is now a familiar one: Young man sets out to win the World Lightweight Championship that his father was cheated out of many years earlier by the poor timing of World War II. He works his way up through the Golden Gloves, into professional fighting, into the contender ranks, fights gamely against the experienced, highly skilled World Boxing Council (W.B.C.) lightweight champion, Alexis Arguello, just after his father has undergone open heart surgery, and—here the fairy tale scenario goes awry—he loses. But the setback is short-lived: Almost as suddenly he gets a second chance—a fight for the World Boxing Association (W.B.A.) World Lightweight Championship, and in a spectacular first-round knockout wins the title for his ailing father and then proudly defends it before a hometown crowd.

Sounds a little like a "Rocky" script, but that is not the end. The script goes on to take a downbeat turn: In a spectacular fight, the young champion knocks out his opponent—almost a mirror image of himself in fighting style—and within hours that opponent lies brain-dead from the thrashing he took in the match. The stunned young champion reevaluates his role as a fighter, then announces his decision to continue in the ring, as critics come from all directions challenging the morality of boxing, calling for its banning and even pointing the finger of guilt at the young champion. A press agent, explaining the difficulty he has in lining up lucrative testimonials for the now nationally known young man, explains: "It's tough to market a guy that's just killed somebody."

Interestingly, standing beside Ray Mancini during all the furor—pictured in the *New York Post* giving him communion, saying Mass in a Las Vegas ballroom in close proximity to the ring where Korean challenger Duk Koo Kim suffered the death blow, appearing with him on "Good Morning, America"—is a boyish Irish priest, the Rev. Timothy O'Neill, aged 43, Ray's high school teacher, spiritual adviser and friend. "Father O'Neill is the man I admire most in my life other than my father," Ray has said, "and the man I would most like to be like."

It is a strange role for Father O'Neill. He has become a target for those who condemn boxing. As a priest and as the young man's spiritual adviser, is it not his function to instruct Ray on the "sinfulness" of boxing? Furthermore, is not his very conspicuous presence with the fighter an embarrassment to the church? On the other hand, if as priest he is expected to instruct in the faith, as friend is he not expected to stand by and offer support?

To understand the nature of Father O'Neill's dilemma fully, we have to know the man, for here is not the stereotypical priest. Father O'Neill looks and talks as if he might have been a boxer himself. Short, but trim and muscular, with streetwise speech speckled with color, but not off-color, almost doing the Brando imitation of the fighter. Is this part of some performance? But it all turns out to be real. This is the man. This is the way he talks. And it's part of his charm.

Tim O'Neill might have been, as far as appearance goes, a brother to Ray Mancini, but the red hair shouts out the Irish in him. Irish or not, there is something that is akin to his friend. Like Mancini, he too grew up in Youngstown, the former steel center in northeastern Ohio, a city which is staggering like a game but weary boxer itself from the hard blows of the economic depression.

The priest met Raymond Mancini when the boy was a ninth grader at Youngstown's Cardinal Mooney High School, where Father O'Neill still teaches religion classes. He started following his student's career during the Golden Gloves matches and soon became a friend of the family. He was there for the early ring triumphs, and he was there when tragedy struck the family: Ray's older brother, Lenny, was killed in a shooting accident. Through all the early triumph and the early tragedy, Ray never lost his boyish charm and his spirituality. "I'm awed by this kid," says Father O'Neill. "The more I'm with this kid, the more I'm impressed by him."

Ray's spirituality was evident in his response to the Kim tragedy: "I pray for him," Ray said in a public statement. "I also pray for his family. I'm very saddened, very sorry it had to happen. It hurts bad to know you're a part of it."

"Being a Christian," Mancini went on, "I rely on my faith in God that all things happen for a reason. I just have to rely on my faith to get through this." Then the bruised, swollen fighter added, "I just hope people will understand that in this profession it's one of the risks we take. I didn't intend to hurt him."

Herein lies the problem. Can a boxer sincerely say, "I didn't intend to hurt him?" Although death is rare enough and certainly not intended, one of the biggest problems theologians have with professional boxing is that it is the one "sport" in which the intention appears to be to hurt.

Even before the Kim death, many of Father O'Neill's colleagues in the Youngstown diocese had spoken out against boxing. In an article in the *Exponent*, the Youngstown diocesan newspaper, Pete Sheehan quotes Msgr. Robert Fannon: "Any sport which has the main object of inflicting physical injury should be called into question." The Rev. Joseph Martin stated, "Boxing is a totally unacceptable form of Christian behavior. I don't think it's a sport; it's an exercise in violence and brutality."

Since the Kim fight the voices of protest among the clergy have increased. The Rev. Bernard Bonnot, Youngstown diocesan director of communications, who is a personal friend of Father O'Neill, in a radio commentary equated the Mancini situation with the nuclear arms race: "To my way of thinking, both Boom Boom bang-banging Duk Koo Kim and the U.S. and the U.S.S.R. preparing to bang-bang, nuke-nuke each other are manifestations of sin. Not personal sin, but original sin, and both prizefighting and the arms race, as they are, ought to be abolished." Father Bonnot goes on to characterize the dilemma of Ray Mancini: "By common consent Boom Boom is a fine young man, a decent human being, a loving son, a dedicated professional, a Christian. He really didn't mean to kill Kim. But he did. For all his goodness and all his noble motivation, his life has entangled him in a brutal and brutalizing sport in which someone can get hurt."

Criticism of boxing has not been confined to Ray Mancini's home diocese. Richard A. McCormick, S.J., professor of Christian ethics at Georgetown University, said he stood by his opinions expressed over 20 years ago in *Sports Illustrated*, where he labeled professional boxing immoral. This conclusion has been echoed by virtually all theologians who have expressed themselves on the subject.

The facts substantiate the criticism. Kim is the sixth fighter to lose his life in the past year. *Ring* magazine's records show that since 1945, 345 boxers have died from ring injuries. The American Medical Association, responding to this most recent ring death and citing the fact that a significant percentage of professional fighters suffer permanent brain damage, has called for keeping life support systems at ringside and giving a designated physician the power to stop any bout at any time, presently a right reserved for the referee.

As might be expected, Father O'Neill himself has come under fire for his conspicuous, approving support of the lightweight champion. The priest recounts how, about a week after the fight, while he was breakfasting back home in Youngstown, he received a call from Ray. "Father," the young man's voice said in distress, "I'm in bad shape. Can I come up and talk to you?" In the conversation that ensued Father O'Neill recalls, "I said to him, 'Raymond, I think I'm a special person and I think you're a special person. If I were to leave the priesthood today, I would be denying people a gift I have. And if you were to leave the ring today you'd be denying people your gift.' Somehow, that sort of helped him."

About a week later Ray got a call from "Good Morning, America" asking him to appear on the show with Father O'Neill. The priest had misgivings about this, so he approached his bishop, the Most Rev. James Malone, about the advisability of the appearance. "Tim," the Bishop responded, "any time we have an opportunity to witness to the faith publicly, I think it's fine. Go ahead."

So Father O'Neill did his homework. Through Father Bonnot, he contacted theologians. He reached Msgr. Richard Malone, the executive director of the Bishops' Committee for Pastoral Research and Practices in Washington, D.C. Besides being supplied with valuable material, he was also put in touch with John R. Connery, S.J., professor of moral theology at Loyola University of Chicago and an expert on the boxing question. Father Connery pointed out that while the church has never made an official statement on boxing, practically all of its theologians say it is immoral. It is not so much a matter of the fighter putting himself in a position where he might kill or be killed that Father Connery saw as the moral dilemma, but rather, the overall physical, mental and possibly psychological damage done to the boxer himself over a period of years.

With his research well done, Father O'Neill found himself reexamining his own position on boxing. "I more and more am having trouble with the morality of boxing," he says. At the same time, he had the predicament of Ray to consider.

Thus, when Father O'Neill accompanied Ray to New York for the "Good Morning, America" interview, he went with much altered feelings on what his role concerning Ray was to be. Unfortunately, in the scant time allotted him to express this role, he was barely able to begin stating the church's position or his own on the matter. Frustrated, he returned home with the champion.

Today, Father O'Neill welcomes any opportunity to defend Ray. "The kid is taken up with the sport," he says. "He sees no moral issue at all. It wasn't until lately that my sensitivity about it had been aroused. So you can see why a 21-year-old kid would have some difficulty with the moral questions."

"After all," the priest continues, "he was driven into this game for laudable reasons: the tremendous love he has for his father, the need to right a wrong done a long time ago. He reached his goal and in the process was thrown into the limelight. He's a hero. This whole city that hasn't had any good news for a long time idolizes him. The Pride of Youngstown, they call him. And it's not only this city. Everybody loves this kid. He's recognized wherever he goes. Even in Italy, everybody knows about Boom Boom."

But what of Ray's negative reaction to the safety controls that the W.B.C. has recently put on boxing, for example, changing to 12-round title fights? And why is he against longer rests between rounds and mandatory safety helmets? If he is so sensitive, why does he scoff at these efforts to make boxing safer? "You have to remember Ray's a young kid. In a lot of ways he's an innocent child in a very tough world," Father O'Neill responds. "He doesn't want to hear anything. Boxing is boxing. The best man wins. After all, you have to understand, Ray idolizes his father. He's an old-time boxer. He slugs away. He's for the old style for the same reason the National League doesn't want the designated hitter."

In spite of the statistics the opponents are throwing around, Father O'Neill points out in defense of Ray's attitude that the fatality rate in boxing is one of the lowest in sports. College football is more dangerous. Jockeys have 10 times more chance of being killed.

"Ray is in favor of closer examinations before and after fights," Father O'Neill adds. Then quickly, lest one get the impression that he is defending boxing instead of his friend, Father O'Neill comes back to the point. "It's the long-range damage that prizefighting does that's the real problem, and it's difficult to get someone in Raymond's position to accept that."

"But he's getting there," Father O'Neill adds. "When I went to his hotel room after the Kim fight to break the news to him about how serious Kim was, he was just coming out of the shower. He was standing there with a towel wrapped around him. His body was bruised and swollen. Before I had the chance to break the news about Kim he said, 'Look at this, Father,' he said. 'Nothing's worth this much. Championship. Million dollars. Nothing.'"

"When I told him about Kim he in no way could comprehend the tragedy. The very natural defense mechanism of denial of reality unconsciously took over. Not until hours later did the nightmare strike."

So we have the dilemma: The priest has humbly come to accept the position of the theologians: "I'm just a religion teacher for sophomores and juniors in high school. Who am I to go against 99 percent of the moral theologians?" The young boxer, on the other hand, cannot or will not consider the theological arguments. Boxing, besides throwing him into international prominence and making him a millionaire, has made it possible to complete the dream his father had to give up. What is and what should be the priest's role under the circumstances?

The experience of Father O'Neill clearly illustrates the fact that the priest who serves his people well will sometimes find himself in the paradoxical position where his official status calls for one response while his human friendship calls for another.

"I'd like to say I support and love Ray without supporting the sport he's involved in," Father O'Neill says. "I feel like some father in Youngstown whose daughter wants to go to New York to become a dancer. He doesn't like the idea and has misgivings about the business, but he supports her in her decision."

"I have my reservations about boxing," Father O'Neill concludes, "but Ray is a good person, a friend whom I love. And I am going to support him."

Competition and God's Law*

Herbert W. Armstrong

Right now the world has its mind focused on the Olympic Games. Suppose we take an overview of Olympic history, down to its present nationalism, as seen from higher up—from the vantage point of the Almighty Creator—and understand what God thinks of this spectacular pageant, and of sports in general.

Let's view the whole thing from the higher-up "camera-setting."

Bear in mind, first, that the government of God had once been administered earthwide. The first human, Adam, had the opportunity to accept for himself, and to administer, that divine government worldwide. But he rebelled and rejected the principle of outflowing love, turning, instead, to the principle of "get" instead of the outgoing "give" principle.

Few know Adam accepted the philosophic way of Satan—self-centeredness, exemplified by vanity, lust and greed, jealousy and envy, competition, rebellion and destruction.

Few know that God then barred mankind, until Christ, from his Holy Spirit—which is the attitude of God-centeredness, of "give," serve, cooperate, share. This world has been based ever since on the "get" or competitive philosophy.

Few know that in barring humanity from God's Spirit, the Creator of all said, in effect, "Go form your own governments, develop your own way of life, based on your competitive principle."

So nations are competitive. Society is competitive. Sports are competitive.

As God Almighty looks down upon this world, he sees the governments of man and society's sports following the self- centered competitive principle. See this Olympic situation *as God sees it*!

All Sports Not Wrong

Competition, not cooperation, is the attitude with which Satan inoculates human minds. But that does not mean all sports are wrong or to be banned.

The law of God is the way of righteousness. Sin is the transgression of the law. The law of God is given us in the broadest principle and also magnified into the Ten Commandments, and even into many further specific points that are magnifications of the principles of the Ten Commandments. God expects us to apply these principles of his law to specific actions.

The basic law is love, outflowing toward God above all else, and secondarily, "Thou shalt love thy neighbor as thyself."

To harm the other fellow and to gain by so doing for self is a kind of competition that is wrong. Hostility toward the other is sin. To get the best of another in a deal for one's own benefit is wrong.

At golf the one who wins is not the one who gets the most by taking it away from the other. In golf the player does not prevent the other from doing his or her best. The architect who designs and lays out the plans for building a golf course is not breaking God's law when he designs sand traps, small lakes or pools or leaves certain trees to help the player to increase his skill. These hazards hurt no one, but are an incentive and help to develop skill.

Two men or women—or several—in a race are not harming the other runners if they run according to the rules.

So, golf is not a wrong competition—nor is any race at any distance, or hurdle race, or long jump, high jump, pole vault or other field competition in a track-and-field meet. At Ambassador College, with campuses in Pasadena, California, and Big Sandy, Texas, we have not included the hammer throw because it might endanger others—but not because it is unfair competition.

Now take basketball. Guarding on defense is, *if* within the rules, the same in principle as the sand trap, clump of trees or pond on a golf course. The rules make it a foul if a defensive player prevents a shot by actual bodily contact or holding. If basketball is played according to the rules—in a right attitude—it can be a very invigorating, enjoyable game, *not violating* God's law. All depends on the attitude of the players.

In interschool or intercollegiate competition, or the pro game, the attitude too often is bad. When it is—when there is a spirit of hostility toward the other side—then it does break God's law. Therefore, at Ambassador College intercollegiate competition is prohibited.

But intramural games between our own classes occur.

Boxing at Ambassador College is definitely banned. God did not design and create the human brain and head to be pummeled and knocked senseless by an antagonist.

Wherever a game in sports involves antagonists—in hostile attitude to harm the other and/or to "get" from the other—to get the best of the other—then a harmful, satanic and evil attitude enters in, and the sport is evil, not good.

Sometimes there is a fine line between what is within and what is outside God's law.

Football (American football) is a violent body-contact sport. It too often is played in an attitude of hostility and is dangerous and fraught with physical injury. Therefore it is not played, but we do play American flag football at Ambassador.

Soccer does not embody the same evils. Baseball, softball, volleyball, while competitive, do not necessarily involve hostility, harm to others or trying to prevent the opponent from doing his best. When played in God's attitude toward others these are acceptable and not prohibited.

This is sufficient to illustrate the application of the principle of God's law to sports. That sport participated in with an attitude of hostility toward the opponent is evil. *That which harms mentally or physically an opponent is evil.*

Satan is the author of competition based on hostility, harm to the opponent, getting by taking from an opponent—to his harm or loss.

God's way is love toward neighbor equal to love of self.

Competition in business that takes from or harms the competitor is evil competition. Competition that helps the opponent by stimulating him to do his best or to do better, but does not harm—rather benefits—the opponent, is healthy competition. So competition can be evil, or good, depending primarily on the attitude in which it is participated.

The very name *Satan* means "adversary." Satan is an evil adversary, who desires to harm—who has a spirit of hostility. *If it has God's spirit of "give"—help, encourage, cooperate, stimulate for good, based on an attitude of love—it is right, not wrong.*

Nimrod, Nephilim, and the *Athletae Dei*

Shirl J. Hoffman

In his wildly radical little book on theology, *To a Dancing God*, Sam Keen (1970) makes the very good point that the idealistic/Gnostic notion of the human being as a mind to which a body has been accidentally and incidentally attached—"a spirit sadly encased in matter"—has been all but universally rejected in the 20th century (p. 46). However, Keen notes, when it comes to practice we continue to embrace the working presupposition of a heady Gnostic dualism. Oddly enough, I found Keen's comments reassuring, if only because he described my general orientation to my body and to others' bodies rather succinctly, and it was comforting to know that the problem of linking theory to practice in this complicated area is not one I must endure in solitude. It is easy to speak of a phenomenological unity; it is quite another matter to live as one or to treat others as one.

I say this by way of assuring you at the outset that in analyzing the mind/body/ flesh/spirit problems that confront a particular group of athletes, I am in no way suggesting that I have finally attained some marvelous accord between my theory of the body and how I approach it or other bodies in everyday existence. In my speech (even my talk about my own body), in my behaviors, in my leisure, and in my work, I am uncomfortably aware of latent gnosticism decorating the halls of my being. (I'm lucky that nobody else has noticed.) Besides, I prefer to talk about other bodies and the problems other people have dealing with their bodies. I can be so much more objective and accurate in my perceptions.

The particular group of athletes in question were first dubbed "athletae Dei" in an article I wrote 15 years ago (Hoffman, 1976). These athletes, who by no means constitute a fringe element in modern professional sport (they are numbered among the superstars), attempt to make sense out of their athletic experiences in the context of their cosmology, more specifically, those doctrines of religion that circle in fairly tight orbits around what may be called orthodox Christianity. Increasingly, athletic performances are depicted by the athletae Dei as religious experiences, opportunities for worship in which an omniscient and understanding God recognizes the spirit in which they train and perform and appreciates it in some not altogether explicable way, as reflecting glory on his divinity.

Previously, I have described the athletae Dei as athletes in conflict, torn between the doctrinal pulls of their religion and the ethical pulls of organized sport (Hoffman, 1985). For example, there is an unconscious realization that sport may be best justified on religious/expressive grounds, that it, like art or music or dance, can be a way of glorifying God, but this is coupled with a deep suspicion that sport (unlike art or music) lacks intrinsic worth as a symbolic spiritual offering. This conflict is manifested in an obsession with the *acesis* of athletic training and performance, not only by romanticizing pain and suffering but by stressing the ethical importance of playing to the fullest extent of one's abilities, popularly called "Total Release Performance" (Neal, 1975). There is in this ingenious attempt to purge sport of its frivolity and increase its worth as a spiritual offering, the strong scent of 19th century Kantian thought, the Protestant-based notion that the intrinsic importance of an act is directly related to the level of effort required to perform it.

The other conflict that has been portrayed concerns the clash between the psychological and dispositional correlates of competition and the idealized Christian temperament of love, compassion, and subordination of self to others. Christian athletes speak openly of their struggle to achieve a balance, to temper competitive enthusiasm with just the right amount of spiritual grace, while team owners and sports reporters publicly worry that athletes who take their religion so seriously as to dampen what is known in the trade as "killer instinct" represent threats to the team and the organization.

I now turn my attention to another source of conflict, the conflict between the athletae Dei's explicit doctrinal conception of their bodies as *imago Dei*, the supreme divine creation, and the implicit appropriation by the athletic community of athletes' bodies as instruments of destruction, expendable machinery designed and developed to test the limits of expendability of the bodies of those with whom they compete. I contend that the force of these conceptions, one from the religious side and one from the athletic side, drive the athletae Dei toward opposite poles, yielding tension that can be diminished only by either relinquishing the high view of the body taught by the Christian tradition or radically revising one's approach to modern sports.

The Original Athletae Dei

The term *athletae Dei* has been applied by contemporary biographers to fourth-century hermits of the deserts of northern Egypt, who referred to their lives as *pietatis plaestrae*, "wrestling rings" in which they were the "athletes of God" (Workman, 1927, p. 45). The flight to the desert was motivated by several factors. To some extent it was an escape from a corrupt and wayward church. But mostly it was a search for a solitary life that would nurture personal and individual religious experiences, a way of discovering one's baseline religious personality, undistracted and undistorted by the tensions and pressures of community living. The soul who was judged nearest God was the soul for whom the highest ideal had become knowledge of his own self (Workman, 1927, p. 28). The austerities and special attention to the body (which is often misread as inattention) were, as Helen Waddell (1960) notes in *The Desert Fathers*, generally regarded as one of the rudiments of holy living, not as ends in themselves. Because historians have reserved most of their attention for Gnostic Eastern extremists, heretical proponents of an anthropological as well as metaphysical dualism, the conception of the body by early Christian ascetics in the West has been widely misunderstood.

In a provocative book, *Fullness of Life*, Harvard divinity professor Margaret Miles (1981) reveals, contrary to much of what has been written, that the writings of these ancients demonstrate an overwhelming and sometimes extravagant *affirmation* of the body. They reminded themselves that the "soul should not exhaust itself in caring for the body's needs, but it must care first for the body and then proceed to orient the entire human being toward the source of life itself" (p. 135). Notes Miles, "By the fourth century the doctrines of creation, incarnation, and resurrection of the body forced Christians to recognize that the classical anthropology of a stratified human being with irrational soul stacked on top of body, and a further rational soul stacked on top of that, did not fit comfortably with the strong affirmation of the body implicit in the earliest Christian doctrines" (p. 20). Although there is evidence that the early Christian writers shared some of our ambivalence about the connections between an obviously mortal and finite body and a vibrant and animated soul, Miles makes it clear that the athletae Dei of the Egyptian desert were not raving lunatics bent on self-destruction.

The goal of the Western ascetics, first and foremost, was self-understanding, which was regarded as an integral part of the process of participating in the kingdom of God. As Palladius (Robinson, 1907, p. 78) noted, "they wished to lay hold upon their souls." Their intentions were an attempt to purge old superficial, transient, self-constructed selves in order to permit the "gradual emergence of the true, secret self in which the Believer and Christ were 'one Spirit'" (Merton, 1970, p. 8). They came into the desert to please God and, noted modern monk Thomas Merton, simply "to be themselves, their *ordinary* selves, and to forget a world that divided them from themselves" (p. 23). They sought "the sanity and poise of a being that no longer has to look at itself because it is carried away by the perfection of freedom that is in it" (p. 8).

The theory of Christian asceticism presupposed a permanent connectedness of body and soul. What was good for the soul was deemed good for the body. Evagrius Ponticus, a theologian of the fourth-century desert movement, expressed it this way: "For those who have attained to purity of heart by means of the body and who in some measure have applied themselves to the contemplation of created things know the grace of the Creator in giving them a body" (Miles, 1981, p. 139). Tertullian wrote that "the flesh is the pivot of salvation since by it the soul becomes linked with God" (Miles, 1981, p. 13). Miles concludes that "far from implying a pejorative view of the body, [the teachings of the ancients reflect a belief that] its best interests are served in practices which enhance the soul's energy" (1981, p. 13). Thus, there was an acute awareness that "bodily practices intimately affect the psyche and can be used as a method for exploring one's characteristically well-defended psychic agenda, for understanding those unconscious but powerful insecurities, anxieties and angers which strip the psyche of energy and undermine its conscious attempts at joyous and loving being" (Miles, 1981, p. 141). Although some, upon discovering the raw power of ascetic practices for focusing and intensifying the energy of the soul, became carried away and abused their bodies, Miles notes that by and large the disciplines were moderate and temporary. Moveover, they were "designed to address the exact nature of the spiritual distraction and not applied to the body as if to control an enemy" (Miles, 1981, p. 139).

Thus, there was at the foundation of this branch of Christian asceticism not so much an attempt at salvation by works but a desire to seek an environment and a form of bodily existence—free of distractions and superficialities—that would cultivate a spirit of resignation and receptivity. The end result was to reveal their authentic religious persona and, upon taking stock of that revelation, to strive to move that persona closer to the *imago Dei*, the image of God. Self-knowledge was possible only by merging body and spirit, which, when realized, yielded revelation and restoration. There was in this an implicit understanding that the trials and tribulations that they joyfully undertook were, on the basis of the motivations that gave rise to them, accepted by God as a spiritual offering.

The task that they set for themselves was most difficult, which is why those who succeeded were given the title "the great athlete" or "the athlete of God." The term was a natural appellation since ascesis (from which we derive asceticism) was originally a term referring to the discipline of athletic training. Insofar as this connoted rigorously imposed self-denial and constraints on the body in order to attain a higher goal, the term may have been deserved, although there were many—St. Ambrose, Bishop of Milan, for one—that believed that asceticism was not a process of a soul imposing itself on a disobedient body but rather a process of cultivating a gift from God in such a way that attention was never directed to the ascetic activity but to the giver.

The Modern Athletae Dei

Several rough parallels can be drawn between the modern athletae Dei and their forefathers in the desert. For example, the belief is widespread among the athletae Dei that disciplining the body in athletic training can have spiritual payoffs. Like the hermits of the desert, the athletae Dei recognize the spiritual importance of bodily acts done with a certain amount of skill and competence and earnestness. There also is some evidence in the testimony of modern athletae Dei that their spiritual approach to athletics yields an attitude of resignation, a willingness to accept the trials of the sporting life as coming from the hand of God, an attitude that does not sit all that well with unsympathetic teammates and coaches. Finally, the modern athletae Dei share the belief held by the athletes of the desert that bodily performances are spiritually insignificant unless fueled by righteous motivations.

But the differences are as striking as the similarities. For example, the wellspring of Christian asceticism was renunciation for the sake of improving one's relation to

God. Yet no matter how much the modern athletae Dei attempt to clarify their spiritual missions in postgame interviews, it is clear that their ascesis is directly intended to improve athletic performance. Authentic Christian asceticism, notes Ziesler, "is quite distinct from self denial for reasons of charity, health, athletic powers or a dualistic view of the universe" (1973, p. 6). Higgs, drawing on Sisk (1973), put it more succinctly: "To the Fathers, the killing of the body meant the liberation for the spirit for holy living and holy dying; to the Greek athlete, it meant a triumphant return home and possibly a celebration by Pindar; to the Green Bay Packers, Vince Lombardi's ascetics, it meant two Super Bowls" (1983, p. 64).

As a religious experience, the spiritual ascesis of athletic training is at most a by-product of its more immediate purpose of improving athletic performance. Less obvious, but no less important, is the disparity between the status accorded the body in modern athletic enterprise—the desert, so to speak, of the modern athletae Dei—and the role of the body in religious experience. And it is to this point that I wish to direct the remainder of my remarks.

In a modest but penetrating work entitled *Body as Spirit: the Nature of Religious Feeling*, Charles Davis (1976) has developed in a remarkable way the thesis that for the Christian, religious feelings (properly understood) lie at the heart of all religious experience. This, I contend, is the germ from which all religious expression grows, and given the intent of the athletae Dei to use athletic performances as modes of religious expression, feelings (as defined by Davis) become fundamental to their religious exercises. Feelings, say Davis, consist of a "spontaneous, connatural response to religious reality, the vibration of our total being when we relate to the transcendent in and through religious activities and passivities" (1976, p. 25). Davis argues that in engendering religious feelings "the body patterns the spirit" so that "our personal being—our intelligent and bodily, spiritual and material selves—is aroused in . . . a direct relation to transcendent reality" (1976, p. 25). According to Davis, the religious impulse is human beings responding to "the pressure of an unknown reality," to what lies "beyond the whole world of apprehended objects." In fact, it is this "inability to make God properly an object of human thought" that elevates the importance of feelings in religion. In Davis's scheme, these feelings are more than emotion or a purely physical response to a perceived or imagined stimulus. They are not a materialistic physicalism but "an intelligent, insightful relationship with what is felt," an affectivity that is as rational and spiritual as it is bodily, a feeling that, in his words, is "both intelligent and visceral" (1976, p. 6).

Davis uses the term sensuousness to refer to the participation in the spontaneous rhythms and responses of the body with a receptiveness that opens to the joys and pains and stresses of bodily experience. Religious experience flows from sensuousness, a sacramental and mystical view of the world in which matter is endowed with meaning and grace, and from a "sanctification of the material environment and conditions of the human state" (Bottomley, 1979, p. 174), a context in which "the body and physical nature are mediatory of the spirit" (Bottomley, 1979, p. 172). Davis contrasts sensuousness with sensuality, which is described as a "submission of the body to the driving, straining consciousness of a mind alienated from its bodiliness'' (1976, p. 172), a condition that destroys the mediatory, symbolic character of the body and reduces it to pure physicality.

As few modern Christian writers have done, Davis underscores the importance of the body in religious experience. Because bodiliness ''mediates the movement of a self open to the mysterious transcendent'' (1976, p. 52), it becomes the foundation of authentic religious experience. ''Those who strive for a pure immateriality of response to God are not seeking him from the center of their being, but from the neurotic circle of an ego alienated from its bodiliness and, consequently, from the world and other people.'' Davis issues a call not only to encourage, train, and refine the bodily component to improve its capacities for affectivity as a medium of spiritual meaning but to ''prevent the misuse of the body by the mind in sensuality, power-seeking and money making'' and as ''machines for egocentric purposes'' (1976, pp. 56-57).

The Body and Modern Athletics

The athletae Dei's essential Christian theology provides a substantial base for approaching the body as a sacred entity, which has some obvious applications to sports. But Davis steers us to a point of more pragmatic importance, namely that the apprehension of God or the apprehension of relationship with him, the core of the religious experience, is accessed through feelings that are inextricably body and spirit. Thus, as a starting point in their quest for a religious experience through sport, it is essential that the athletae Dei recognize the sacramental character of the body and its mediatory role in all human acts, including its fundamental importance in endowing athletic performances with religious significance.

However, if Davis is correct in his formulation, it would seem that the athletae Dei are confronted with yet another obstacle in converting their athletic performances to religious experience. Unlike the solitaries of the ancient Egyptian desert, the athletae Dei attempt to work out their religious experiences in a very public (uncontrolled) context, a context which encourages severing body from spirit, subordinating it to a manipulated mind, and co-opting it for its own destructive purposes. This makes it unlikely that the athletae Dei can experience, within the context of modern big-time sports, a genuine confrontation with the Almighty.

At least two forces at work within the athletic enterprise can be identified as limiting the athlete's potential for participating fully in a realization of religious feeling that Davis has located at the heart of religious experience. These I have labeled the cults of Nimrod and Nephilim, after medical ethicist Ken Vaux's analysis of modes of body degradation apparent in broad sectors of modern society (Vaux, 1985).

The Cult of Nimrod

Nimrod was a Babylonian war deity, the Semitic precursor to Neptune and Mercury, warrior gods of the sea and sky. Nimrod's warriors, says Vaux, ''through sheer exercise of power . . . bend or break another's body to feed, fuel, or gratify oneself, one's clan or nation. He is the god of violence and terrorism, the god of unwarranted aggression on another'' (Vaux, 1985, p. 25). The cult of Nimrod thrives in modern athletics, especially in what we euphemistically refer to as ''contact sports.'' Boxing, football, and hockey are obvious examples of sports whose purpose and organization demands a Nimrodian mentality of all those who would be successful. These are sports that blur the distinction between war and recreation. Arguments that the goal of such sports is not to harm the bodies of opponents are uniformly unimpressive. When games are designed to yield a strategic advantage to players who can instigate and survive uninhibited violent interpersonal collisions that, not coincidentally, render opponents at least momentarily dysfunctional, there is little point in debating whether the player ''intended'' to injure his opponent or ''it was an accident.'' People who jump from two-story buildings usually get injured, as do the people they land on, regardless of their intentions. Likewise, it may be rationally deduced that when humans of great mass run directly and unflinchingly toward each other at breakneck speeds, somebody's neck will probably break, and when it does, it is a perversion of language and logic to call the incident an accident. When violence and bodily aggression, limited only by protective gear and the vulnerable psychological inhibitions of the players, are inextricably tied to the goal of a game, destruction of the opponent's body, rather than its glorification as a ''mediator of the spirit,'' is the logical goal.

In such sports, the evocation of feelings, which Davis claims awaken us ''as subjects to the objects that come before us and act on us'' (1976, p. 9), can make attainment of athletic success difficult or even impossible. Harboring sympathetic and empathetic feelings about opponents—opening oneself up to the reality of the other—dulls enthusiasm for disadvantaging them, a danger long recognized by the athletic fraternity as a good reason for separating teams before games and posting inanities about opponents on locker room bulletin boards. Theologian Harvey Cox probably was correct in noting that our culture has become unable to feel deeply about anything (Cox, 1977, p. 101), and, as an agent of institutionalized affectlessness, sport seems light-years ahead of the rest of society.

But more is required of devotees of Nimrod than a numbing of the fundamental human urge for relationship. Because mentally stable humans aren't naturally inclined to jump off two-story buildings or participate in violent collisions, an alternate reality must be concocted that renders the senseless sensical, the barbaric civil, the pathological exemplary. And the reality must extend beyond the temporal enclave prescribed by the game. Somehow a meaning must be discovered in the thousands of torn cartilages, the paralyzed bodies, the lifelong aches and pains. In a stimulating but disturbing book, *The Body in Pain: The Making and Unmaking of the World*, Elaine Scarry (1985) tells how destruction of the body in torture and war can be redescribed by those who inflict it to substantiate fictional issues. I can think of no better example than the Nimrodian mentality in sports where occasions of physical and mental brutality are described as convincing evidence of a team's inherent superiority (or the institution it represents) and the essential righteousness of its cause.

The Cult of Nephilim

This approach to the body borrows its name from the Nephilim mentioned in the sixth chapter of Genesis, who are described as gods or giants in the earth and who also appear in other cosmologies. Vaux claims that Nephilim aim for biomechanical perfectibility as exemplified in the encouragement offered by heart surgeon William DeVries to his famous artificial heart transplant patient Bill Schroeder, "Don't worry Bill, we'll make you better than you are" (1985, p. 26). The Nephilim cult of bodily perfection is humans seeking to be gods by exploiting science and technology. Says Vaux, "The body magnificent becomes the body tremulous, the body vulnerable, the body fixable, with interchangeable parts from the body shop of modern medicine" (1985, p. 26).

Nothing underscores quite so vividly the spread of the cult of Nephilim than its popularity in the athletic establishment. More and more, the athletic tradition is coming to embrace an exercise science that reduces marvelously human endeavors to discrete impersonal formulae. $\dot{V}O_2max$, reaction times, movement times, and percent body fat become more than anthropomorphic descriptors, they are "anthropofacts," symbols of bodies wrenched from human spirits. Frank Bottomley has observed correctly that when bodies are reduced to physical facts "then the sense experiences become mere physical objects and events, split off from the consciousness of the observer and deprived of any meaning other than their relationships to other, separate, physical objects. Such a world is of course no longer sacramental but utterly and fundamentally mechanical" (1979, p. 172).

For worshippers of Nephilim, physical attributes become separated from their essential (whole) natures. Sport broadcasters fawn over mesomorphic physiques as if they were admiring the latest version of the BMW. I do not mean by this that the importance of the physical and material are overemphasized. In point of fact, their real importance is ignored. Matter is subordinated to mind in a way that makes impossible any real appreciation for its rhythms and growth and sacramental nature (Bottomley, 1979, p. 171). Bodies become little more than mind-operated machines, and naturally enough, the scope of concern is narrowed to efficiency, productivity, and, inevitably, the vulnerable morphology of bones, ligaments, and muscles. Not surprisingly, athletic training assumes an exaggerated importance to worshippers of Nephilim. Training rooms become temples; whirlpools, baptismal fonts; and sports medicine is heralded as the new theology. Bodies unable to meet the athlete's demands are objectified, their loyalty questioned, the intrinsicality of their parts thrown open to doubt. Thirty years ago, psychiatrist Stephen Ward was struck by how easily athletes were able to dissociate themselves from injured body parts following contests in which their team lost.

> [The athlete] is unable to accept the fact that his body has failed in its requirements, but he will choose one small area of his body and single it out for attention and disapproval. . . . He displaces dissatisfaction from the whole to the part. . . . An athlete frequently refers to an injured member as "the leg," "the hand," "the foot," etc. This attitude reflects a detachment of the injured part from the remaining uninjured portion. (Ward, 1959, p. 60)

Thus, whereas the cult of Nimrod dulls feelings for each other, Nephilim dampens feelings of athletes toward their own bodies. They speak dispassionately of their injuries. San Francisco running back Roger Craig, who pays therapists $300 each week to help him recover from Sunday's beatings on the football field, seems unimpressed with the toll exacted by the game. Says Craig,

> After a game, I look like I've been locked in a cage with a tiger. . . . I can sense there's internal bleeding from all the blows and bruises, because for several hours my body temperature is very warm. I'll ice myself if I'm seriously injured. But regardless of the severity, I can't eat that night, and I have difficulty sleeping. (Lieber, 1988, p. 82)

In a splendid illustration of the subtle way language helps athletes gain effective distance between a debilitated body and "the true self," Texas Ranger catcher Jim Sundberg, who announced his retirement in the fall of 1989, told reporters: "I have a sore left shoulder, a bad right knee. If I played any longer I would need surgery. I also have a bad thumb on my catching hand. My body was giving me indicators" ("Jim Sundberg," 1989, p. B5).

The Dilemma of the Athetae Dei

This then is the dilemma of the modern athletae Dei. Theirs are futile attempts to seek an authentic encounter with the source of all being in a context that logically and inevitably denies the body as the source of feelings and, hence, hinders access to the reality that lies at the heart of religious experience. A body broken in the cause of proving physical superiority, or reduced to a machine, and separated from its spirit-spouse not only lacks potential for "mediating the spirit" but distracts and divorces and makes a religious response of the total being impossible. This is because contemplation of the religious range of reality demands a total and personal participation. As philosopher Douglas Steere described it,

> Sense- and intellect-bearing man, overlaid as he is with a filament of feeling, and charged with a pulsing current of will, can, if he wishes, yield all of himself, be swept and transformed by the presence of the compassionate religious reality that he confronts. And when this happens he is said to respond appropriately to the religious range of reality. (1957, p. 30)

There is nothing inherent in the germ of sport that neutralizes its value as a source of religious feeling and an avenue of religious expression. I believe that sport, as much as painting, sculpture, or poetry can be an "artpath" to God, a purveyor of what C.S. Lewis (1967) called "the sub-Christian values." As I have said elsewhere (Hoffman, 1985), if it was fitting for David to "dance before the Lord with all of his might" when the ark of the covenant was brought to Jerusalem, it would seem to be just as fitting for him to have thrown a javelin or run 1,500 meters to express the same sentiment. (In fact, given the stiff social agenda that confronts modern

Christians, the acts of charity and kindness yet to be done and the ephemerality of existence, they can scarcely argue a case for spending time, energy, and money on sport, save for apprehending in it some expressive and intrinsically religious quality.) But regardless of the expressive potential of sport qua sport, it always is embedded in a context—a context of rules, game objectives, and staging—and it is this context that so frequently seems to preclude a response of the total being to what Davis called the "pressure of the unknown reality." If there are compelling rationales for the athletae Dei to adopt an expressive approach to sport, one surely must be that in playing games they imitate the play of the Creator who, in fashioning them as body-spirits, cast them in the mold of the *imago Dei*. Play—which I contend is the germ of sport— is a way of regaining "a different and more finely tuned relation between body and soul than what we now possess." Our task, says theologian Hugo Rahner (1972) is to regain this "free, unfettered, eager harmony between body and soul" through human activity that "engages of necessity both soul and body" and in which the "spirit plays itself into the body of which it is a part." As play, sport can be "the expression of an inward spiritual skill, successfully realized with the aid of physically visible gesture, audible sound and tangible matter" but only when the body is accorded sacramental status (Rahner, 1972, p. 6, 7).

The early hermits of the desert—the original athletes of God—knew something about the power of the body to clarify and refine the inner dialogue as a path toward self-understanding and spiritual enlightenment. More importantly, they knew something about the power of their surroundings, the realities of their physical environment to limit or expand the reaches of their souls. It would appear that the potential of context to close rather than open one to the "pressure of the other reality" has been grossly underestimated by the athletae Dei. They seek fulfillment, not in the desert, but in the distractions of an environment resembling the Roman amphitheatre, which are not and cannot ever be sympathetic to their quest. Sport as religious experience, if it can be religious experience, is sport in the desert so to speak, sport on the playground and in the backyards, where the environment encourages the soul to play itself into the body rather than forcing it to maintain a healthy distance. Sport for religious experience is side-by-side noncontact sport, not face-to-face contact sport, because it must, if it is to be successful, afford the body the same dignity and protection it affords the soul.

Having said this, I would credit these modern athletes with understanding the potential for integrating sport and the contemplative experience, for appreciating (in ways that stodgy theologians cannot) that humanity can be simultaneously *homo ludens* and *homo contemplativus*. In their insistence on solitude and isolation, the ancient athletae Dei underestimated the power of religious contemplation to "draw the widest range of human activity within its hallowing orbit" (Steere, 1957), the ability of one to gather unto himself solitude at the center of furious physical activity. The modern athletae Dei, unlike their spiritual forefathers, seem intuitively to have recognized the possibility of this "rest most busy," the untapped potential of sport as a contemplative experience. But they would do well to recognize that when contemplation is joined with an activity, it rarely leaves the activity as it was. As Steere says, "it tests it, sorts it out, alters it, frames it, and in turn the frame bears up or carries that which it has consented to and approved" (1957, p. 34). My hope is that athletae Dei allow such contemplative moments as they might manage to sort out and alter their perception of the role and importance of their bodies and the environments in which they seek religious experience.

References

Bottomley, F. (1979). *Attitudes to the body in western Christendom*. London: Lepus Books.

Cox, H. (1977). *Turning east*. New York: Simon and Schuster.

Davis, C. (1976). *Body as spirit: The nature of religious feeling*. New York: Seabury Press.

Higgs, R.J. (1983, Fall). Muscular christianity, holy play and spiritual exercises: Confusion about Christ in sports and religion. *Arete*, **1**(1), 59-85.

Hoffman, S.J. (1976, September). The athletae Dei: Missing the meaning of sport. *Journal of the Philosophy of Sport*, **III**, 42-51.

Hoffman, S.J. (1985, Spring). Evangelicalism and the revitalization of religious ritual in sport. *Arete*, **2**, 63-87.

Jim Sundberg calls it quits (1989, September 12). *Greensboro News & Record*, p. B5.

Keen, S. (1970). *To a dancing god*. New York: Harper & Row.

Lewis, C.S. (1967). Christianity and culture. In W. Hooper (Ed.), *Christian reflections* (pp. 12-36). Grand Rapids, MI: William B. Eerdmans.

Lieber, J. (1988, November 28). The no-pain, no-gain kid. *Sports Illustrated*, pp. 82-88.

Merton, T. (1970). *The wisdom of the desert*. New York: New Directions.

Miles, M.R. (1981). Fullness of life: Historical foundations for a new asceticism. Philadelphia: Westminster Press.

Neal, W. (1975). *The handbook of athletic perfection*. Prescott, AZ: Institute for Athletic Perfection.

Rahner, H. (1972). *Man at play*. New York: Herder and Herder.

Robinson, J.A. (Ed.) (1907). *The paradise of the holy fathers: The Lausiac history of Palladius*. London: Chatto & Winder.

Scarry, E. (1985). *The body in pain: The making and unmaking of the world*. New York: Oxford University Press.

Sisk, J.P. (1973, March 2). Hot sporting blood. *The Commonweal*, pp. 495-498.

Steere, D. (1957). *Work and contemplation*. New York: Harper.

Vaux, K. (1985, September 20). How do I love me? *Christianity Today*, pp. 23-26.

Waddell, H. (1960). *The desert fathers*. New York: Barnes & Noble.

Ward, S. (1959). Some observations on athletes, Psychiatric Communications, January. Quoted in R. Boyle, *Sport: Mirror of American life* (p. 60). Boston: Little, Brown.

Workman, H.B. (1927). *The evolution of the monastic ideal*. London: Epworth.

Ziesler, J.A. (1973). *Christian asceticism*. Grand Rapids: Eerdmans.

Credits and Contributors

The following list indicates the source of each article appearing in this book. All articles were reprinted or adapted by permission.

Part I   Sport as Religion

"The Super Bowl as Religious Festival" by J.L. Price, February 22, 1984, *The Christian Century*, pp. 190-191. Copyright 1984 by Christian Century Foundation. Reprinted by permission from the February 22, 1984 issue of the *Christian Century*. Joseph Price is professor of religious studies at Whittier College, Whittier, CA.

"From Civil Religion to Folk Religion: The Case of American Sport" by J.A. Mathisen. This essay appears here in print for the first time after its original presentation in an expanded form at the annual meeting of the Society for the Scientific Study of Religion, Washington, DC, November, 1986. James Mathisen is associate professor of sociology at Wheaton College, Wheaton, IL.

"The Natural Religion" in *The Joy of Sports* (pp. 18-34) by M. Novak, 1988, Lanham, MA: University Press of America. Copyright 1988 by Michael Novak. Adapted by permission. Michael Novak, author and theologian, holds the George Frederick Jewett Chair in Religion and Public Policy at the American Enterprise Institute, Washington, DC.

"'Heavenly Father, Divine Goalie': Sport and Religion" by C.S. Prebish, 1984, *Antioch Review*, 42(3), pp. 306-318. Copyright © 1984 by the Antioch Review, Inc. First appeared in the *Antioch Review*, Vol. 42, No. 3 (Summer, 1984). Reprinted by permission of the editors. Charles Prebish is associate professor of religious studies at Pennsylvania State University.

"Sport Is Not a Religion" by J.M. Chandler. Adapted from a paper presented to the annual conference of the North American Society for the Sociology of Sport, Boston, 1985. The author acknowledges helpful comments on earlier drafts from Lois Pojman. Joan Chandler is professor of historical studies in the School of Arts and Humanities at University of Texas at Dallas.

Part II   Sport as Religious Experience

"Is Running a Religious Experience?" by H. Higdon, May 1978, *Runner's World*, pp. 76-79. Reprinted by permission from *Runner's World*, © 1978 by Hal

Higdon Communications, Inc. Hal Higdon is senior writer for *Runner's World* and author of *Run Fast*.

"Playing" from *Running and Being: The Total Experience* (pp. 71-83) by G.A. Sheehan, 1978, New York: Warner Books. Copyright © 1978 by George A. Sheehan, MD. Reprinted by permission of Simon & Schuster, Inc. George Sheehan is a cardiologist, writer, and running enthusiast.

"Muscular Christianity, Holy Play, and Spiritual Exercises: Confusion About Christ in Sports and Religion" by R.J. Higgs, Fall 1983, *Arete: The Journal of Sport Literature*, 1, pp. 59-85. Copyright 1983 by Sports Literature Association. Adapted by permission. Robert Higgs is professor of English at East Tennessee State University.

"Big-Time Spectator Sports: A Feminist Christian Perspective" by D.L. Carmody, July/August 1986, *New Catholic World*, pp. 173-177. Copyright 1986 by D.L. Carmody. Adapted by permission. Denise Lardner Carmody is university professor and chair of the Faculty of Religion, University of Tulsa, Tulsa, Oklahoma.

"Evangelicalism and the Revitalization of Religious Ritual in Sport" by S.J. Hoffman, Spring 1985, *Arete: Journal of Sport Literature*, pp. 63-87. Copyright 1985 by Sports Literature Association. Adapted by permission. An earlier version ("God, Guts and Glory: Evangelicalism in American Sport") was presented to the Sports Sociology Academy in Houston, April 23, 1982.

Part III   Religion in Sport

"From Ritual to Record" in *From Ritual to Record: The Nature of Modern Sports* (pp. 16-26, 165-167) by A. Guttmann, 1978, New York: Columbia University Press. Copyright © 1978 Columbia University Press, New York. Used by permission. Allen Guttmann is professor of English and American studies at Amherst College, Amherst, MA.

An earlier version of "Recovering a Sense of the Sacred in Sport" by S.J. Hoffman appeared in *The Nebraska Humanist*, 8(2), Fall 1985, pp. 16-24. Copyright 1985 by Nebraska Committee for the Humanities. Adapted by permission.

"The Spirit of Winning: Sports and the Total Man" from *Redemptorama: Culture, Politics, and the New Evangelicalism* (pp. 91-113, 283-285) by Carol Flake, 1984, Garden City, NY: Doubleday. Copyright © 1984 by Carol Flake. Used by permission of Doubleday, a division of Bantam Doubleday Dell Publishing Group, Inc. Carol Flake is a poet, scholar, and journalist.

"Pray Ball" by L. Rotenberk, August 22, 1988, *Chicago Sun-Times*. Copyright © with permission of the Chicago Sun-Times, Inc., 1988. Lori Rotenberk is a reporter for the *Chicago Sun-Times*.

"Are You Blocking for Me, Jesus?" by J.T. Baker, November 5, 1975, *The Christian Century*, pp. 997-1001. Copyright 1975 by Christian Century Foundation. Reprinted by permission from the November 5, 1975 issue of *The Christian Century*. James Baker is a professor of history at Western Kentucky University.

"Why Athletes Need Ritual: A Study of Magic Among Professional Athletes" by M. Womack. In *Sport and the Humanities: A Collection of Original Essays* (pp. 27-38) by W.J. Morgan (Ed.), 1979, Knoxville: University of Tennessee

Part IV   Sport, Religion, and Ethics